UNIX Systems Programming
for SVR4

UNIX Systems Programming
for SVR4

David A. Curry

O'Reilly & Associates, Inc.

Bonn · *Cambridge* · *Paris* · *Sebastopol* · *Tokyo*

UNIX Systems Programming for SVR4
by David A. Curry

Published by O'Reilly & Associates, Inc., 101 Morris Street, Sebastopol, CA 95472.

Editor: Mike Loukides

Production Editor: Nancy Crumpton

Printing History:

　　　　July 1996:　　　　First Edition

ISBN: 1-56592-163-1　　　　　　　　　　　　　　　　　　　　　　　　　　　[11/96]

Table of Contents

Preface

About This Book

When I wrote *Using C on the UNIX System* in 1988, people used UNIX primarily on large timesharing systems. It was administered and programmed by centralized staffs, and the everyday users of the system had little if any need to perform systems programming tasks. However, because there was not a great deal of third-party software available for UNIX, it was often necessary to "roll your own." This meant that you needed to know all about the system calls and library routines provided by the UNIX operating system. That's what *Using C* taught you.

Today, things are different. The large UNIX timesharing system is a dinosaur of the past, replaced by desktop workstations. Centralized staffs of administrators and programmers have diminished or vanished altogether, leaving the users of these workstations to fend for themselves. Fortunately, because UNIX has become so widespread, so has the amount of software available for it—it's quite likely that as a user of a UNIX workstation you may never need to write a program yourself. Someone has already written just what you need, and you can either purchase it or obtain it for free from the Internet or USENET. However, you still need to know all about the system calls and library routines provided by the UNIX operating system, because many of these packages must be ported from one version of UNIX to another.

Back in 1988, describing the UNIX programming environment required making distinctions between three principal versions of UNIX: Version 7 (Seventh Edition), System V, and the Berkeley Software Distribution (BSD). There were no UNIX standards at the time, and each system operated in a slightly different way. Even within each major version things were different—4.2BSD did things differently from 4.1BSD, System V Release 3 did things differently from System V Release 2, and so forth. This made for a rather messy and confusing book.

Again, things are different today. Although there are more versions of UNIX than ever, they all share, thanks to standards such as POSIX, ANSI C, and X/Open, a fairly common programming interface. Unfortunately, as someone once said, "the nice thing about standards is that there are so many to choose from." Although most modern versions of UNIX are very similar, each vendor has added its own little twists, reintroducing the difficulties the standards were supposed to eliminate. The trick now, rather than describing how to do something on each version of UNIX, is to describe how to do it on a "standard" version of UNIX and then describe how to port code written on other versions to this standard version. That's what this book does.

The principal focus of this book, our "standard" version of UNIX, is System V Release 4, henceforth abbreviated as SVR4. Released in late 1989, SVR4 was intended to merge the best features from Berkeley-based systems, such as SunOS, with the best of System V, provide compatibility with Microsoft's XENIX system, and conform to the IEEE POSIX standards. Although practically nobody uses "pure" SVR4 as it was originally released by UNIX System Laboratories, three of the four largest UNIX workstation vendors (Sun, Hewlett-Packard, and Silicon Graphics) have chosen it as the base for their most recent operating system releases. Together, these three companies' products account for over 60% of the UNIX workstation market.

In the following chapters, this book describes nearly every SVR4 system call and library routine related to systems programming (libraries for other purposes, such as the math library, are not discussed). This book provides examples using small code fragments, numerous short demonstration programs, and several "real world" applications that demonstrate a large number of functions working together.

One of the major features of the book, though, is the advice it offers on porting code between other versions of UNIX and SVR4-based systems. SVR4 is a completely new operating system. The amount of software currently running under these vendors' earlier, BSD-based systems that needs to be ported to SVR4 is simply staggering. There are millions of lines of code in the freely available software packages most people take for granted, such as *GNU Emacs*, the *X Window System*, and so forth. There are probably millions more lines of code in the locally developed applications in use at each site. To help with the porting process, most of the chapters in this book contain special sections targeted specifically at porting code. These sections describe how a task is performed on different versions of UNIX, and then explain how to change the code for these versions to perform the same task under SVR4. The porting sections also discuss differences in function names and parameters between other versions of UNIX and SVR4.

Scope of This Book

The book is organized in a "bottom up" fashion, first presenting the simple functions and concepts that form the building blocks for the more complex material at the end of the book.

Chapter 1, *Introduction to SVR4*, provides a brief history of the development of the UNIX operating system, culminating in the release of SVR4. It then presents the standards with which SVR4 complies, followed by some short notes on compiler usage and the *BSD Source Compatibility Package*.

Chapter 2, *Utility Routines*, introduces most of the utility routines provided for manipulating character strings, byte strings, and character classes; dynamically allocating memory; manipulating temporary files; and parsing command-line arguments. Much of the material in this chapter will be familiar to many readers, but it provides a common base from which to start.

Chapter 3, *Low-Level I/O Routines*, describes the low-level UNIX input/output (I/O) paradigm, in which buffering and other mundane tasks must be performed by the programmer.

Chapter 4, *The Standard I/O Library*, describes the high-level UNIX I/O paradigm, in which buffering and other mundane tasks are performed by a library of functions.

Chapter 5, *Files and Directories*, introduces the UNIX filesystem. This includes an overview of how the filesystem works, how to examine and change file attributes, how to create and delete files and directories, and how to traverse directory trees.

Chapter 6, *Special-Purpose File Operations*, describes special-purpose operations on files such as processing multiple input streams, file and record locking, and memory-mapped files.

Chapter 7, *Time of Day Operations*, describes how to examine the system's time of day clock and the wide variety of functions for reading and printing time and date strings.

Chapter 8, *Users and Groups*, explains the formats of the password, shadow password, and group files, and how to obtain information from them. It also describes how to determine who is logged in, when a user last logged in or out, and how to change a program's effective user ID or group ID. This chapter includes a special section on writing set user ID programs.

Chapter 9, *System Configuration and Resource Limits*, describes how to examine and change various system and user limits such as the hostname, maximum number of characters in a filename, maximum size of a file in bytes, maximum number of open files per process, or the maximum amount of CPU time a process can consume.

Chapter 10, *Signals*, explains the concept of signals, including how to send them, ignore them, and catch them.

Chapter 11, *Processes*, describes how to create new processes, how to execute other programs, how to redirect input and output from one process to another, how to use the job control facilities, and how to time process execution.

Chapter 12, *Terminals*, explains how to examine and change serial line characteristics such as baud rate, character echo, input buffering, and special characters.

Chapter 13, *Interprocess Communication*, describes the mechanisms that allow processes on the same host to communicate: pipes, FIFOs, UNIX-domain sockets, message queues, semaphores, and shared memory.

Chapter 14, *Networking with Sockets*, describes the most common UNIX network programming interface: Berkeley sockets.

Chapter 15, *Networking with TLI*, describes the *Transport Layer Interface* (TLI), which is a less popular, but more flexible interface to network programming.

Chapter 16, *Miscellaneous Routines*, describes all the "leftover" functions that are generally useful but don't fit into any of the preceding chapters. These include routines for exiting, printing and logging error messages, searching, table lookup, pattern matching, passwords, database management, modem management, environment variables, random numbers, and regular expressions.

The appendixes provide information on topics that are of less general use than those in the main part of the book, but are nevertheless important.

Appendix A, *Significant Changes in ANSI C*, provides a brief summary of the significant differences between ANSI C and the version of the language described by Kernighan and Ritchie.

Appendix B, *Accessing Filesystem Data Structures*, describes how to read raw filesystem data directly from the disk, as is done by programs such as *df, fsck,* and *ufsdump*.

Appendix C, *The /proc Filesystem*, explains how to read information directly from process memory, as is done by programs such as *ps*.

Appendix D, *Pseudo-Terminals*, describes how to allocate and use pseudo terminal devices for a variety of purposes. This appendix describes both the SVR4 interface and the more common BSD interface.

Appendix E, *Accessing the Network at the Link Level*, describes the *Data Link Provider Interface* (DLPI), which is used for sending and receiving raw network packets. Programs such as *snoop* and *in.rarpd* use DLPI. Conversion of programs using the SunOS 4.*x* *Network Interface Tap* (NIT) to DLPI is also described.

Audience

This book is intended to serve the following three groups of people:

- UNIX systems programmers who are familiar with some version of UNIX other than SVR4, particularly SunOS 4.*x* or BSD, and who are now faced with the daunting task of porting every program they ever wrote to the new system.

- People who aren't systems programmers and don't want to be, but nevertheless must port some piece of software from some other version of UNIX to SVR4.

- C programmers who wish to move into the area of UNIX systems programming, either for fun or profit.

Assumptions

This book does not teach the C programming language—although fluency in the language is not required, it is assumed that you can at least read a C program and figure out what it does.

All of the examples in this book are written in ANSI C. While there are some differences between ANSI C and K&R C, you shouldn't have any trouble following along even if you've never seen ANSI C before. However, if you are new to ANSI C, you may wish to skip ahead and read Appendix A first.

This book also assumes that you are a reasonably savvy UNIX user. You should be familiar with terms such as file, directory, user ID, environment variable, process ID, and so forth. You should also be familiar with your system's C compiler, debugger, and the *make* utility. If you haven't learned these things yet, or would like to refresh your memory, you may find the following books, also published by O'Reilly & Associates, helpful:

- *Learning the UNIX Operating System* by Grace Todino, John Strang, and Jerry Peek

- *UNIX in a Nutshell: System V Edition* by Daniel Gilly and the staff of O'Reilly & Associates

- *Managing Projects With Make* by Andrew Oram and Steve Talbott
- *Practical C Programming* by Steve Oualline

See the pages at the end of this book for information on how to order these and other O'Reilly & Associates titles.

Font Conventions

The following conventions are used in this book:

Italic
> is used for directories and to emphasize new terms and concepts when they are introduced. Italic is also used to highlight comments in examples.

Bold
> is used for C keywords.

`Constant Width`
> is used for programs and the elements of a program and in examples to show the contents of files or the output from commands. A reference in text to a word or item used in an example or code fragment is also shown in constant width font.

`Constant Bold`
> is used in examples to show commands or other text that should be typed literally by the user. (For example, **`rm foo`** means to type "rm foo" exactly as it appears in the text or the example.)

`Constant Italic`
> is used in examples to show variables for which a context-specific substitution should be made. (The variable *`filename`*, for example, would be replaced by some actual filename.)

Quotation marks
> are used to identify system messages or code fragments in explanatory text.

%   is the UNIX C shell prompt.

$ is the UNIX Bourne shell or Korn shell prompt.

is the UNIX superuser prompt (either Bourne or C shell). We usually use this for examples that should be executed only by root.

[ ]   surround optional values in a description of program syntax. (The brackets themselves should never be typed.)

. . .

> stands for text (usually computer output) that's been omitted for clarity or to save space.

The notation CTRL-X or ^X indicates use of *control* characters. It means hold down the "control" key while typing the character "x". We denote other keys similarly (e.g., RETURN indicates a carriage return).

All examples of command lines are followed by a RETURN unless otherwise indicated.

Example Programs

You can obtain the source code for the programs presented in this book from O'Reilly & Associates through their Internet server.

The example programs in this book are available electronically in a number of ways: by FTP, Ftpmail, BITFTP, and UUCP. The cheapest, fastest, and easiest ways are listed first. If you read from the top down, the first one that works for you is probably the best. Use FTP if you are directly on the Internet. Use Ftpmail if you are not on the Internet, but can send and receive electronic mail to Internet sites (this includes CompuServe users). Use BITFTP if you send electronic mail via BIT-NET. Use UUCP if none of the above works.

FTP

To use FTP, you need a machine with direct access to the Internet. A sample session is shown, with what you should type in **boldface**.

```
% ftp ftp.uu.net
Connected to ftp.uu.net.
220 FTP server (Version 6.21 Tue Mar 10 22:09:55 EST 1992) ready.
Name (ftp.uu.net:joe): anonymous
331 Guest login ok, send domain style e-mail address as password.
Password: yourname@domain.name (use your user name and host here)
230 Guest login ok, access restrictions apply.
ftp> cd /published/oreilly/nutshell/sys.prog
250 CWD command successful.
ftp> binary (Very important! You must specify binary transfer for compressed files.)
200 Type set to I.
ftp> get examples.tar.gz
200 PORT command successful.
150 Opening BINARY mode data connection for examples.tar.gz.
226 Transfer complete.
ftp> quit
221 Goodbye.
%
```

The file is a compressed tar archive; extract the files from the archive by typing:

```
% gzcat examples.tar.gz | tar xvf -
```

System V systems require the following tar command instead:

```
% gzcat examples.tar.gz | tar xof -
```

If *gzcat* is not available on your system, use separate *gunzip* and *tar* or *shar* commands.

```
% gunzip examples.tar.gz
% tar xvf examples.tar
```

Ftpmail

Ftpmail is a mail server available to anyone who can send electronic mail to and receive it from Internet sites. This includes any company or service provider that allows email connections to the Internet. Here's how you do it.

You send mail to *ftpmail@online.ora.com*. In the message body, give the FTP commands you want to run. The server will run anonymous FTP for you and mail the files back to you. To get a complete help file, send a message with no subject and the single word "help" in the body.

The following is a sample mail session that should get you the examples. This command sends you a listing of the files in the selected directory and the requested example files. The listing is useful if there's a later version of the examples you're interested in.

```
% mail ftpmail@online.ora.com
Subject:
reply-to username@domain.name      (Where you want files mailed)
open
cd /published/oreilly/nutshell/sys.prog
mode binary
uuencode
get examples.tar.gz
quit
.
```

A signature at the end of the message is acceptable as long as it appears after "quit."

BITFTP

BITFTP is a mail server for BITNET users. You send it electronic mail messages requesting files, and it sends you back the files by electronic mail. BITFTP currently serves only users who send it mail from nodes that are directly on BITNET, EARN, or NetNorth. BITFTP is a public service of Princeton University. Here's how it works.

To use BITFTP, send mail containing your ftp commands to *BITFTP@PUCC*. For a complete help file, send HELP as the message body.

The following is the message body you send to BITFTP:

```
FTP   ftp.uu.net   NETDATA
USER   anonymous
PASS   myname@podunk.edu   Put your Internet email address here (not your BITNET address)
CD /published/oreilly/nutshell/sys.prog
DIR
BINARY
GET   examples.tar.gz
QUIT
```

Once you've got the desired file, follow the directions under FTP to extract the files from the archive. Since you are probably not on a UNIX system, you may need to get versions of uudecode, uncompress, atob, and tar for your system. VMS, DOS, and Mac versions are available.

UUCP

UUCP is standard on virtually all UNIX systems and is available for IBM-compatible PCs and Apple Macintoshes. The examples are available by UUCP via modem from UUNET; UUNET's connect-time charges apply.

You can get the examples from UUNET whether you have an account there or not. If you or your company has an account with UUNET, you have a system some where with a direct UUCP connection to UUNET. Find that system, and type:

```
uucp uunet\!~/published/oreilly/nutshell/sys.prog/examples.tar.gz
yourhost\!~/yourname/
```

The backslashes can be omitted if you use the Bourne shell (sh) instead of csh. The file should appear some time later (up to a day or more) in the directory */usr/spool/uucppublic/yourname*. If you don't have an account, but would like one so that you can get electronic mail, contact UUNET at 703-204-8000.

It's a good idea to get the file */published/oreilly/ls-lR.Z* as a short test file containing the filenames and sizes of all the files available.

Once you've got the desired file, follow the directions under FTP to extract the files from the archive.

Once you've obtained, uncompressed, and extracted the examples distribution, you will have a directory called *examples* that contains directories for each chapter of the book. Each chapter's directory contains four directories. The *common* directory contains example programs that work identically across all versions of the operating system discussed in this book, while the *hpux*, *IRIX*, and *solaris* directories contain the example programs that differ slightly between the various operating system versions.

To compile the examples, first change to the *examples* directory. Then examine or edit one of the *Makedefs* files as appropriate for your operating system. These files define the name of the compiler to use and the flags to give to it when compiling the examples. When you are finished, simply issue the command *./build-examples*.

The examples in this book have been compiled and tested on the platforms shown below:

Hardware	Operating System	Compiler
Sun SPARCstation LX	Solaris 2.3	GNU C 2.6.3
Sun SPARCstation 5/70	Solaris 2.3	SPARCompiler C 3.0.1
Sun SPARCstation 20/HS12	Solaris 2.4	SPARCompiler C 3.0.1
Sun SPARCstation 5/85	Solaris 2.5	GNU C 2.7.2
Sun SPARCstation 5/85	Solaris 2.5	SPARCompiler C 4.0
HP 9000/819	HP-UX B.10.0	cc
Silicon Graphics IRIS	IRIX 5.3	cc

Comments and Questions

Please address comments and questions concerning this book to the publisher:

O'Reilly & Associates, Inc.
101 Morris Street
Sebastopol, CA 95472
1-800-998-9938 (in the U.S. or Canada)
1-707-829-0515 (international or local)
1-707-829-0104 (FAX)

Acknowledgments

First and foremost, I am grateful to my wife, Cathy, without whose love and support this book would not have been possible. I am also grateful to our sons, Trevor and Sean, who tried their best not to bother Daddy while he was writing. Thanks, guys.

At O'Reilly & Associates, I would like to thank my editor, Mike Loukides, who provided good advice and useful comments, as well as patience and understanding, throughout the writing process. I would also like to thank Tim O'Reilly, who, as before, was a pleasure to work for. And, I would like to thank all the people who helped to turn the manuscript into a real book: Dianna Vosburg and Toby Boyd, who copyedited the manuscript, Nancy Crumpton who, with Michael Deutsch, painstakingly made all the changes and checked everything twice; Seth Maislin, who wrote the index; and Clairemarie Fisher O'Leary, who, as project manager, kept it all together.

I used the Standard Generalized Markup Language (SGML) as the formatting markup for this book, rather than using *troff* or *TeX* as most UNIX books use. SGML is specified by the International Standards Organization (ISO) as International Standard ISO 8879, with the DocBook Document Type Definition (DTD) developed by the Davenport Group. As I was one of the first O'Reilly authors to attempt this, several people at O'Reilly & Associates provided special assistance. I would like to thank Lenny Muellner, Norm Walsh, and Lar Kaufman for all their work on the new formatting tools, which they developed as I was writing the book. They worked awfully hard to keep their tools current with what I was doing at the time, and almost always succeeded. I would also like to thank Terry Allen, who put up with my questions, complaints, and frustrations as I discovered problems and needed clarifications with the DocBook DTD.

I would like to thank James Clark, the author of the *sgmls* validating SGML parser, and Lennart Staflin, the author of the *psgml* SGML major mode for *GNU Emacs*. Both of these tools were invaluable in the preparation of the manuscript, and both of them were freely available because of their authors' generosity.

I would like to thank Larry Dunkel, at Hewlett-Packard, who arranged my access to a HP-UX 10.0 system and answered numerous questions.

At Purdue University, I would like to thank Debi Foster, who worked out all the bureaucratic mumbo-jumbo so that I could use parts of *Using C on the UNIX System* in this book.

Finally, I would like to thank my reviewers, Casper Dik, Gerry Singleton, and Dave Pfennighaus, for their patience and attention to detail. The book is better because of their efforts.

1

Introduction to SVR4

Between 1969 and 1970, Ken Thompson, Dennis Ritchie, and other members of the Computer Research Group at Bell Laboratories designed and built the original UNIX operating system on the now-famous "little-used PDP-7 sitting in the corner." In 1970, UNIX was ported from the PDP-7 to a PDP-11/20, along with a text editor and a program called *roff*, a predecessor to *troff*. This UNIX system, running with no memory protection and 500 Kbytes of disk space, supported three concurrent users editing and formatting, and also the original group of people doing further UNIX development. The documentation for this system, dated November 1971, was labeled "First Edition."

Between 1971 and 1979, a number of UNIX variants were created inside Bell Laboratories. The main version, developed by Thompson and his coworkers, evolved through Version 4 (the first version written in C), Version 6 (the first version to be licensed outside Bell Labs), and finally Version 7. Most people would not recognize any of these versions, except perhaps Version 7, as looking much like the UNIX of today. During this same time, a number of other lesser-known versions were developed by various groups inside Bell Labs, including PWB/UNIX, MERT, RT, and CB UNIX. UNIX by this time had been ported to several varieties of PDP-11, the Interdata 8/32, the IBM VM/370 environment, and even the IBM Series 1. Shortly after its release, Version 7 was ported to the VAX and called UNIX 32V.

Outside the Labs, UNIX development took place at several universities. The most notable was the University of California at Berkeley. The first Berkeley Software Distribution (BSD), based on UNIX Version 6 for the PDP-11, was released in 1977. Other notable releases from Berkeley included 4.0BSD for the VAX in 1980, 4.1BSD in 1981, 4.2BSD in 1983, and 4.3BSD in 1984. Development continued on the

PDP-11 as well, with 2.8BSD in 1982, 2.9BSD in 1983, and 2.10BSD in 1987. These releases essentially ported most of the new software from the 4.x BSD releases to the aging PDP-11. In 1993, the Computer Science Research Group at Berkeley made its last release of UNIX, 4.4BSD, and disbanded.

Meanwhile, back at Bell Laboratories, the UNIX System Development Laboratory had been created. Between 1977 and 1982, this group took several internal variants of UNIX, predominantly PWB/UNIX, CB UNIX, and UNIX 32V, and merged them into a single commercial system known as System III. This was the last version of UNIX licensed by AT&T through Western Electric before divestiture (caused by an antitrust suit brought by the U.S. government) broke AT&T into several pieces. As part of divestiture, UNIX was given to AT&T Information Systems, which in early 1983 announced UNIX System V. System V Release 2 (SVR2) was released in 1984, and System V Release 3 (SVR3) in 1986. Both of these releases became very popular.

In the late 1980s, AT&T and Sun Microsystems entered into a cooperative venture to develop a new version of UNIX. This version would merge the "best of the best" features from AT&T's SVR3, Berkeley's 4.3BSD, Sun's SunOS, and Microsoft's XENIX. In November 1989, UNIX System V Release 4 (SVR4), the result of this venture, was released. However, it would take two more years for a major computer vendor to release an SVR4-based operating system. Sun released Solaris 2.0 in 1991, followed by Silicon Graphics' IRIX 5.0 in 1994, and Hewlett-Packard's HP-UX 10.0 in 1995.

Standards Compliance

One of the principal features of SVR4 is standards compliance. Solaris 2.*x*, HP-UX 10.*x*, and IRIX 5.*x* comply with the following standards:

- *ANSI X3.159-1989 (ANSI C).* The ANSI C standard defines the syntax and semantics of the C programming language. It also specifies many of the library routines and header files used in C programs, and it specifies the interaction of a C program with the execution environment. The ANSI C standard was developed by the X3J11 Technical Committee on the C Programming Language under project 381-D of the American National Standards Committee on Computers and Information Processing (X3).

- *IEEE Std 1003.1-1990 Portable Operating System Interface Part 1 (POSIX.1).* An outgrowth of the 1984 */usr/group Standard,* POSIX.1 defines application interfaces to basic system services such as input/output, the filesystem, and process management using the C programming language. It is a set of library routines, system calls, and header files. POSIX.1 has been adopted as International Standard ISO/IEC 9945-1:1990 by the International Organization for Standardization (ISO) and the International Electrotechnical Commission (IEC).

- *IEEE Std 1003.2 Portable Operating System Interface Part 2 (POSIX.2).* Another part of the series of POSIX standards, POSIX.2 defines a set of standard shells and utility programs, and their interfaces (such as command-line arguments and exit codes).

- *X/Open Portability Guide, Issue 3 (XPG3).* X/Open is an international consortium of system vendors, ISVs, and users. Its purpose is to adopt existing standards and adapt them into a single, consistent Common Applications Environment (CAE). By awarding the X/Open brand trademark to products that comply with the CAE, X/Open hopes to ensure portability and connectivity of applications. The XPG3 includes IEEE Std 1003.1-1988, and has seven volumes covering system interface commands, utilities, system interfaces and headers, supplementary definitions, programming languages, data management, window management, and networking services. The current versions of Solaris 2.*x*, HP-UX 10.*x*, and IRIX 5.*x* also comply with XPG4, an updated version of the standard.

- *System V Interface Definition, Third Edition (SVID3).* First published by AT&T in 1985, the SVID specifies an operating system environment that allows users to create software that is independent of any particular computer hardware. It defines the components of the operating system and their functionality, but not their implementation. It specifies both the source-code interface and the run-time behavior of each component. An application using only SVID components is compatible with and portable to any other computer that supports the SVID. SVR4 is compliant with the Base System component of SVID3 and all its extensions.

- *System V Release 4 Application Binary Interface (ABI).* An ABI defines a standard format for application programs that are compiled and packaged for different hardware architectures. It includes a *generic* part that specifies the machine-independent parts of the format, and a *processor-specific* part that specifies the machine-dependent parts. A binary program produced in compliance with the ABI runs on any ABI-conformant operating system that supports the same ABI. For example, a program compiled on a SPARC system running Solaris 2.*x* should work without modification on a SPARC system running plain SVR4 from AT&T.

- *ANSI/IEEE 754-1985 Standard for Binary Floating-Point Arithmetic.* This standard defines the format of floating-point data types, the arithmetic that can be performed on them (and how it is performed), and the exception handling used when performing the arithmetic.

- *Federal Information Processing Standard Publication 158: The User Interface Components of the Applications Portability Profile (FIPS PUBS 158)*. A U.S. Government standard, FIPS 158 defines a standard set of tools for developing user interfaces for the Federal government. The standard is based on the *X Window System*, Version 11 Release 3.

- *International Standard: Information Processing—8-bit single-byte coded graphic character sets—Part 1: Latin alphabet No. 1 (ISO 8859-1)*. This standard specifies a set of 191 graphic characters, identified as Latin alphabet No. 1. The standard specifies the coding of each of these characters as a single 8-bit byte. The ASCII character set is a subset of ISO 8859-1.

- *International Standard: Information Processing—Volume and File Structure of CD-ROM for Information Interchange (ISO 9660-88)*. This standard specifies the filesystem structures for CD-ROM drives. The *Rock Ridge Interchange Protocol*, which defines support for the UNIX filesystem format on CD-ROMs, is also supported.

Notes on Compilers

Depending on what you're used to, compiling programs in an SVR4 environment may require you to read the compiler documentation again. Because SVR4 provides ANSI C compliance in its include files, it is generally desirable to use the C compiler in an ANSI C mode. Furthermore, since the main goal of SVR4 is to promote interoperability through standards compliance, it is desirable to enable standards-compliance whenever you're developing a new program.

This section briefly discusses the compilers available for each of the operating systems described in this book. The examples in the book have been compiled and tested using all of these compilers.

The HP-UX 10.x Compiler

HP-UX 10.*x* uses an unbundled ANSI C compliant compiler called *cc*. The compiler accepts a plethora of options, most of which are not of interest to us here. However, there is one option that is important. The compiler allows you to select the degree of conformance to the ANSI C standard by using the *-Ax* option, where *x* is one of the following options:

a   Pure ANSI C

c   K&R C

e   ANSI C with POSIX and UNIX extensions

The examples in this book have been compiled and tested using the *-Ae* option to the compiler.

The IRIX 5.x Compiler

IRIX 5.*x* ships with an ANSI C compliant compiler called *cc*. The compiler accepts a number of options, most of which are not of interest in this book. However, the option that controls the language features supported by the compiler is important, and is described as follows:

-ansi

> Pure ANSI C

-ansiposix

> ANSI C plus the definition of the `_POSIX_SOURCE` constant; this enables the inclusion of function prototypes for POSIX-defined functions

-cckr

> K&R C, with some ANSI C extensions such as function prototypes and the `void` type

-xansi

> ANSI C with POSIX and UNIX extensions. This is the default mode of the compiler

The examples in this book have been compiled and tested using the *-xansi* mode of the compiler.

The Solaris 2.x Compiler

Solaris 2.*x* does not ship with a compiler; you must purchase it as a separate, unbundled product called *SPARCompiler C*, a commercial C compiler offered by SunSoft, a subsidiary of Sun Microsystems. *SPARCompiler C* is available either by itself or as part of a package called *SPARCworks* that includes a source-code debugger and other software. *SPARCompiler C* is fully compliant with the ANSI C standard; it also accepts programs written in the older dialect of the language described by Kernighan and Ritchie.

SPARCompiler C offers a plethora of command-line options, almost all of which are beyond the scope of this book. However, there is one option that is important.

SPARCompiler C allows you to select the degree of conformance to the ANSI C standard by using the *-Ax* option, where *x* is one of the following options:

a   ANSI C with "Sun C" compatibility extensions and semantic changes required by ANSI C. In this mode, the compiler accepts both K&R C and ANSI C constructs. When it encounters a construct that has different semantics under K&R and ANSI C, it issues a warning and then interprets the construct in accordance with the ANSI C definition.

c   Fully conformant ANSI C, without "Sun C" compatibility extensions. In this mode, the compiler rejects constructs that are not ANSI C. Header files do not declare certain functions, or define certain macros, that are not required by the ANSI C standard.

s   "Sun C." In this mode, the compiler functions essentially as a K&R C compiler. However, it issues warnings about all constructs it encounters that have differing behavior between ANSI C and K&R C.

t   ANSI C with "Sun C" compatibility extensions, but not semantic changes required by ANSI C. In this mode, the compiler accepts both K&R C and ANSI C constructs. When it encounters a construct that has different semantics under K&R and ANSI C, it issues a warning and then interprets the construct in accordance with the K&R C definition.

The examples in this book have been compiled and tested using the *-Xa* option of *SPARCompiler C.*

The GNU C Compiler

The *GNU C Compiler* is distributed by the Free Software Foundation, and is available without charge, in source or binary form, to anyone who wants it. You can obtain it using anonymous FTP from numerous hosts on the Internet, from a tape from the Free Software Foundation, or from companies such as Cygnus Support. *GNU C* is available for all three of the operating systems described in this book; it is particularly popular on Solaris 2.*x*, because that system does not ship with a C compiler of its own.

GNU C is fully compliant with the ANSI C standard, and also accepts programs written in the older K&R dialect of the language.

GNU C accepts a profuse number of options, most of which are beyond the scope of this book. However, the options that let you select the degree of ANSI C conformance are important, and are described as follows:

-ansi

> Enables support for all ANSI C programs. This turns off features of *GNU C* that are incompatible with ANSI C, and turns off predefined symbols such as sun and unix that allow you to identify the type of system that you are using. The *-ansi* option also predefines the macro __STRICT_ANSI__; some header files recognize this macro and do not declare certain functions or define certain macros that are not part of the ANSI C standard. This option does not cause rejection of valid non-ANSI programs, however; for that, the *-pedantic* option is also required.

-ansi -pedantic

> Enables support for all ANSI C programs, and disables support for anything not specified in the ANSI C standard. Under this option, all warnings required by the ANSI C standard are issued, and any program that uses a forbidden extension is rejected. Valid ANSI C programs will compile with or without this option, however. Note that this option is not intended to verify a program as ANSI-compliant. It finds some non-ANSI constructs, but only those for which the ANSI standard *requires* a diagnostic.

-traditional

> Attempts to support most of the aspects of K&R C. Although this isn't really a K&R mode of the compiler, you can compile most K&R C programs without changes by specifying this option. The option enables several old, undocumented preprocessor features that were never an official part of the language, but nevertheless came to be relied upon by many people. It also enables some features of K&R C that are not part of the ANSI C standard.

The examples in this book have been compiled and tested using the *GNU C* compiler without specifying any of the previous options.

NOTE

> Because the authors of the *GNU C Compiler* do not agree with the authors of SVR4 in the interpretation of the ANSI C standard's definition of the __STDC__ macro, you cannot use the *GNU C Compiler* with the normal SVR4 include files.

> *GNU C* protects itself from this problem by generating its own version of the system include files with the *fixincludes* command. The *GNU C* installation procedure runs this command automatically. However, when upgrading to a new version of the operating system, you must be sure to re-run *fixincludes* on the new system's include files, or compilation problems occur.

The BSD Source Compatibility Package

One of the transition tools provided by Solaris 2.*x* is the *BSD Source Compatibility Package* (SCP). The SCP provides many of the SunOS 4.*x* and BSD interfaces otherwise not included, or that differ in functionality between SunOS 4.*x* and Solaris 2.*x*. It is a collection of commands, libraries, and header files that, while they may also be present in the default Solaris 2.*x* environment, have different behavior between the two versions. Generally, you should be able to take a program that compiles on SunOS 4.*x* and compile it under the SCP with no changes to obtain a working program.

The SCP is installed in several directories:

- The */usr/ucb* directory contains source compatibility package commands that existed in the */usr/ucb*, */usr/bin*, and */usr/etc* directories under SunOS 4.*x*.

- The */usr/ucblib* directory contains the source compatibility package libraries and class="osname">SunOS 4.*x*/BSD system calls that are implemented as library routines in the SCP. These interfaces existed in */usr/lib* under SunOS 4.*x*.

- The */usr/ucbinclude* directory contains the source compatibility package header files, which existed in */usr/include* under SunOS 4.*x*.

By setting your search path to include the */usr/ucb* directory, or by using the */usr/ucb/cc* command, you can use the SCP C compiler when you compile C programs. (The */usr/ucb/cc* command is not a compiler in itself; you must still install an unbundled compiler. Rather, it is a wrapper around the C compiler that causes it to use the SCP header files and libraries.) The SCP C compiler sets its default paths to pick up the following directories, in the following order:

- User-specified include directories and libraries

- The compatibility include directories and libraries

- The base Solaris 2.*x* include directories and libraries, if unresolved symbols remain

Use of the *BSD Source Compatibility Package*, while it can help you get a program up and running in a short amount of time, is not recommended, for the following reasons:

- Programs running under the SCP suffer a performance penalty. SunOS 4.*x*/BSD system calls and library routines that are unavailable or have different functionality in Solaris 2.*x* are emulated in library routines. Although in many cases the cost of emulation is minimal, for some often-used functions the cost can be significant.

- The SCP is intended as a transition tool only, to help you port your programs from SunOS 4.*x* to Solaris 2.*x*. As Solaris 2.*x* matures and SunOS 4.*x* becomes less widespread in the UNIX community, it is likely that the SCP will be removed from future versions of Solaris 2.*x*.

- Many of the programming interfaces offered by Solaris 2.*x* are more standard than their SunOS 4.*x*/BSD counterparts. By changing your program to make use of these standard interfaces, the program is more portable between different versions of UNIX.

- Programs compiled with the SCP can encounter incompatibilities between the SCP and non-SCP versions of some libraries, resulting in combinations that do not produce a working program.

HP-UX 10.*x* and IRIX 5.*x* do not provide the SCP.

None of the examples in this book depend on the SCP to compile. Because the focus of this book is to help you develop new programs in the SVR4 environment and to help you port your existing programs to SVR4, this book will not discuss the SCP further.

2

Utility Routines

This chapter examines most of the commonly used utility routines offered by the SVR4 C library, and gives brief examples of their use. The UNIX C library provides a large number of routines for performing common programming tasks such as comparing and copying strings, allocating memory, manipulating temporary files, and so forth. You are probably already familiar with many of these routines, but if you've been doing most of your programming in a BSD environment, several of them may be new to you. Many of these routines were first added to the C library in early versions of System V, and were later mandated by the ANSI C and POSIX standards. Since most commonly used versions of BSD UNIX predate these standards, these routines are often missing from those versions' C libraries.

Manipulating Character Strings

Probably the most often used utility routines are those that manipulate character strings. Because the C language does not provide any character string primitive operators, you must perform all operations with library routines.

All of the routines described in this section operate on *character strings*, which are arrays of one or more non-zero bytes terminated by a null (zero) byte. Passing so-called binary data to these routines, in which null bytes are legal values rather than terminators, does not produce the desired results.

All of the examples in this chapter assume the existence of two functions that are not part of the standard C library:

```
void outputLine(char *line);

char *inputLine(void);
```

outputLine prints the contents of the character array line on the standard output (the screen). inputLine reads one line of characters from the standard input (the keyboard) and returns a pointer to a character array containing the line. These two functions exist so that we can do input and output without explaining the use of the UNIX I/O functions, which the following two chapters describe.

Computing the Length of a String

The simplest function for computing the length of a string is strlen:

```
#include <string.h>

size_t strlen(const char *s);
```

The single argument s is the null-terminated string whose length is to be computed; the length of the string in bytes, not including the null character, is returned.

Two other functions, strspn and strcspn, are provided to compute the length of substrings:

```
#include <string.h>

size_t strspn(const char *s1, const char *s2);

size_t strcspn(const char *s1, const char *s2);
```

strspn returns the length of the initial segment of s1 that consists entirely of characters from the set contained in s2. In some sense, strcspn does the opposite, returning the length of the initial segment of s1 that consists entirely of characters *not* in the set contained in s2.

To demonstrate the use of strlen, Example 2-1 shows a program that implements a bubble sort. Bubble sort is a simple (but not very efficient) sorting algorithm that works by making several passes through the objects to be sorted, comparing items in adjacent locations and interchanging them if they are out of order. If no items are interchanged on any pass through the data, the data is completely sorted and the algorithm can stop.

Example 2-1: bsort-length

```c
#include <string.h>

#define NSTRINGS    16          /* max. number of strings      */
#define MAXLENGTH   1024        /* max. length of one string   */

void    bubbleSort(char **, int);
void    outputLine(char *);
char    *inputLine(void);

int
main(int argc, char **argv)
{
    int n, nstrings;
    char *p, *q, *line;
    char *strptrs[NSTRINGS];
    char strings[NSTRINGS][MAXLENGTH];

    /*
     * Read in NSTRINGS strings from the standard input.
     */
    for (nstrings = 0; nstrings < NSTRINGS; nstrings++) {
        /*
         * Get a line from the input.
         */
        if ((line = inputLine()) == NULL)
            break;

        /*
         * Copy the line.
         */
        for (p = line, q = strings[nstrings]; *p != '\0'; p++, q++)
            *q = *p;
        *q = '\0';

        /*
         * Save a pointer to the line.
         */
        strptrs[nstrings] = strings[nstrings];
    }

    /*
     * Sort the strings.
     */
    bubbleSort(strptrs, nstrings);

    /*
     * Print the strings.
     */
    for (n = 0; n < nstrings; n++)
        outputLine(strptrs[n]);

    exit(0);
```

Example 2-1: bsort-length (continued)

```
}

/*
 * bubbleSort - implementation of the basic bubble sort algorithm.
 */
void
bubbleSort(char **strings, int nstrings)
{
    int i, j;
    char *tmp;
    int notdone;

    j = nstrings;
    notdone = 1;

    while (notdone) {
        notdone = 0;
        j = j - 1;

        for (i = 0; i < j; i++) {
            /*
             * Use strlen() to compare the strings
             * by length.
             */
            if (strlen(strings[i]) > strlen(strings[i+1])) {
                tmp = strings[i+1];
                strings[i+1] = strings[i];
                strings[i] = tmp;
                notdone = 1;
            }
        }
    }
}


% cat input
xxxxxx
xxxxx
xxxxxxx
xx
x
xxxxxxxxx
xxxx
xxxxxxxx
xxx
xxxxxxxxxx
% bsort-length < input
x
xx
xxx
xxxx
xxxxx
```

```
xxxxxx
xxxxxxx
xxxxxxxxx
xxxxxxxxxx
xxxxxxxxxx
```

bsort-length begins by using `inputLine` to read in up to `NSTRINGS` lines of data and storing them in the `strings` array. The `strptrs` array points to the strings, so that by rearranging the pointers, you can achieve the sort. After reading in the strings, the `bubbleSort` function is called. `bubbleSort` makes several passes through the strings, comparing the lengths of adjacent strings with `strlen`. When the first string is longer than the second, the pointers to those two strings are exchanged. Finally, when the sort finishes, the strings are printed with `output-Line`.

Comparing Character Strings

To compare two character strings, use the `strcmp` and `strncmp` functions:

```
#include <string.h>

int strcmp(const char *s1, const char *s2);

int strncmp(const char *s1, const char *s2, size_t n);
```

`strcmp` compares `s1` and `s2` and returns an integer less than, equal to, or greater than zero, based on whether `s1` is lexicographically less than, equal to, or greater than `s2`. `strncmp` makes the same comparison, but looks at only the first `n` characters of each string. Characters following the null terminator of either string are not compared.

On systems that use the ASCII character set, "lexicographically less than" and "lexicographically greater than" correspond to "alphabetically before" and "alphabetically after." However, on systems that use character sets that do not preserve alphabetical order (such as EBCDIC), this relationship does not hold.

Example 2-2 shows another version of the bubble sort program; this one sorts the strings into alphabetical order.

Example 2–2: bsort-alpha

```
#include <string.h>

#define NSTRINGS    16      /* max. number of strings    */
#define MAXLENGTH   1024    /* max. length of one string */

void    bubbleSort(char **, int);
void    outputLine(char *);
char    *inputLine(void);
```

Example 2–2: bsort-alpha (continued)

```c
int
main(int argc, char **argv)
{
    int n, nstrings;
    char *p, *q, *line;
    char *strptrs[NSTRINGS];
    char strings[NSTRINGS][MAXLENGTH];

    /*
     * Read in NSTRINGS strings from the standard input.
     */
    for (nstrings = 0; nstrings < NSTRINGS; nstrings++) {
        /*
         * Get a line from the input.
         */
        if ((line = inputLine()) == NULL)
            break;

        /*
         * Copy the line.
         */
        for (p = line, q = strings[nstrings]; *p != '\0'; p++, q++)
            *q = *p;
        *q = '\0';

        /*
         * Save a pointer to the line.
         */
        strptrs[nstrings] = strings[nstrings];
    }

    /*
     * Sort the strings.
     */
    bubbleSort(strptrs, nstrings);

    /*
     * Print the strings.
     */
    for (n = 0; n < nstrings; n++)
        outputLine(strptrs[n]);

    exit(0);
}

/*
 * bubbleSort - implementation of the basic bubble sort algorithm.
 */
void
bubbleSort(char **strings, int nstrings)
{
    int i, j;
```

Example 2-2: bsort-alpha (continued)

```
    char *tmp;
    int notdone;

    j = nstrings;
    notdone = 1;

    while (notdone) {
        notdone = 0;
        j = j - 1;

        for (i = 0; i < j; i++) {
            /*
             * Use strcmp() to compare the strings
             * alphabetically.
             */
            if (strcmp(strings[i], strings[i+1]) > 0) {
                tmp = strings[i+1];
                strings[i+1] = strings[i];
                strings[i] = tmp;
                notdone = 1;
            }
        }
    }
}
```

```
% cat input
one
two
three
four
five
six
seven
eight
nine
ten
% bsort-alpha < input
eight
five
four
nine
one
seven
six
ten
three
two
```

This program is identical to *bsort-length*, except that the `strlen` comparison is replaced with a call to `strcmp`.

Solaris 2.*x*, HP-UX 10.*x*, and IRIX 5.*x* provide two additional functions for comparing strings, `strcasecmp` and `strncasecmp`:

```
#include <string.h>

int strcasecmp(const char *s1, const char *s2);

int strncasecmp(const char *s1, const char *s2, int n);
```

These functions are similar to `strcmp` and `strncmp`, except that they ignore the case of letters in the strings. Unfortunately, these two functions are not very portable—systems that use the Domain Name System (DNS) probably have them, because they are used for comparing host names (in which case is not significant), but systems that do not use the DNS probably do not.

Copying Character Strings

To copy one character string to another, the `strcpy` and `strncpy` functions are used:

```
#include <string.h>

char *strcpy(char *dst, const char *src);

char *strncpy(char *dst, const char *src, size_t n);
```

In both cases, the string pointed to by `src` is copied into the array pointed to by `dst`, and `dst` is returned. The first function, `strcpy`, copies characters until it encounters the null byte terminating `src`. The second function, `strncpy`, copies characters until it either encounters the null byte in `src` or until n characters are copied, whichever comes first.

The string returned by `strcpy` is always null terminated. However, the string returned by `strncpy` is not. If the number of characters in `src` is less than n, a null byte is appended to `dst`. However, if there are n or more than n characters in `src`, then `dst` is *not* null terminated. For this reason, it is customary to always explicitly place a null byte at the end of `dst` immediately following a call to `strncpy`, as shown below:

```
char dst[SIZE];

strncpy(dst, src, SIZE-1);
dst[SIZE-1] = '\0';
```

To append one string to another, the **strcat** and **strncat** functions are used:

```
#include <string.h>

char *strcat(char *dst, const char *src);

char *strncat(char *dst, const char *src, size_t n);
```

Both of these functions traverse **dst** until a null byte is found, copy **src** onto the end, and then return **dst**. **strcat** copies characters until it encounters a null byte in **src**, while **strncat** copies characters until it either encounters a null byte in **src** or until n characters have been copied, whichever comes first. Both **strcat** and **strncat** always null-terminate **dst**.

Example 2-3 shows a program that uses **strcpy** and **strcat** to make lists of strings.

Example 2-3: make-a-list

```
#include <string.h>

void    outputLine(char *);
char    *inputLine(void);

int
main(int argc, char **argv)
{
    int len;
    char *line;
    char list[1024];

    len = sizeof(list) - 2;
    list[0] = '\0';

    /*
     * For each line in the input...
     */
    while ((line = inputLine()) != NULL) {
        /*
         * Compute its length, plus room for a comma and a space.
         */
        len += strlen(line) + 2;

        /*
         * If we don't have room in the buffer, output
         * the buffer and start a new one.  Otherwise,
         * add a comma and this line.
         */
        if (len >= sizeof(list)) {
            if (list[0] != '\0')
                outputLine(list);

            strcpy(list, line);
```

Example 2-3: make-a-list (continued)

```
            len = strlen(line);
        }
        else {
            strcat(list, ", ");
            strcat(list, line);
        }
    }

    /*
     * Output the last part of the list.
     */
    if (list[0] != '\0')
        outputLine(list);

    exit(0);
}
```

```
% cat input
one
two
three
four
five
six
seven
eight
nine
ten
% make-a-list < input
one, two, three, four, five, six, seven, eight, nine, ten
```

The program reads lines until it encounters the end-of-file marker. It computes the length of each line using strlen, and then determines whether the current input fits into the array holding the current list or not. If not, it outputs the current list, and then uses strcpy to begin a new list. If the line will fit in the current list, strcat is used to append a comma and a space to the list, and then to append the current line as well.

All four of the functions described in this section assume that dst is large enough to hold the results of their work; no bounds checking is performed. If dst is not large enough, a memory access violation is likely to occur, resulting in abnormal program termination and a core dump.

Searching Character Strings

A number of routines are provided to search a character string for either a single character or a substring. The two simplest functions are strchr and strrchr:

```
#include <string.h>

char *strchr(const char *s, int c);

char *strrchr(const char *s, int c);
```

Both functions traverse the string s and return a pointer to the first occurrence of the character c, or the predefined constant NULL if the character is not found. strchr starts at the beginning of the string and searches toward the end, while strrchr starts at the end of the string and searches toward the beginning. Example 2-4 shows a program that reads lines from its standard input and searches each line for the character given as the program's first argument.

Example 2–4: search-char

```
#include <string.h>

void    markLine(char *, char *, char *);
void    outputLine(char *);
char    *inputLine(void);

int
main(int argc, char **argv)
{
    char c;
    char *p, *line;

    if (argc != 2) {
        outputLine("Usage: search-char character");
        exit(1);
    }

    c = argv[1][0];

    while ((line = inputLine()) != NULL) {
        if ((p = strchr(line, c)) != NULL) {
            outputLine(line);
            markLine(line, p, p);
            outputLine(line);
        }
    }

    exit(0);
}
```

```
% cat input
one
two
three
four
five
six
seven
eight
nine
ten
% search-char e < input
one
  ^

three
    ^

five
   ^


seven
    ^

eight
   ^

nine
    ^

ten
   ^
```

In the example shown, the program searches for the letter *e* on each line. When it
finds one, the program prints the line, and then uses the markLine function to
mark the position in which the letter was found. The markLine function is
defined as follows:

```c
#include <stdio.h>

void
markLine(char *line, char *start, char *stop)
{
    char *p;

    for (p = line; p < start; p++)
        *p = ' ';

    for (p = start; p <= stop; p++)
        *p = '^';

    for (p = stop+1; *p != '\0'; p++)
        *p = ' ';
}
```

If instead of a single character you need to search a string for the first occurrence of any of several characters, you can use strpbrk:

```
#include <string.h>

char *strpbrk(const char *s1, const char *s2);
```

strpbrk searches the string s1, starting at the beginning, for the first occurrence of any character in the string s2. It returns a pointer to the character, or the predefined constant NULL if none of the characters are found. Example 2-5 shows another version of our searching program using strpbrk.

Example 2-5: search-charset

```
#include <string.h>

void    markLine(char *, char *, char *);
void    outputLine(char *);
char    *inputLine(void);

int
main(int argc, char **argv)
{
    char *p, *line, *charset;

    if (argc != 2) {
        outputLine("Usage: search-charset character-set");
        exit(1);
    }

    charset = argv[1];

    while ((line = inputLine()) != NULL) {
        if ((p = strpbrk(line, charset)) != NULL) {
            outputLine(line);
            markLine(line, p, p);
            outputLine(line);
        }
    }

    exit(0);
}


    % cat input
    one
    two
    three
    four
    five
    six
    seven
    eight
```

```
nine
ten
% search-charset onx < input
one
^

two
  ^

four
   ^

six
  ^

seven
    ^

nine
   ^

ten
   ^
```

To locate the first occurrence of a substring instead of a single character, use the `strstr` function:

```
#include <string.h>

char *strstr(const char *s1, const char *s2);
```

`strstr` traverses the string `s1` from the beginning, and returns a pointer to the start of the first occurrence of the substring `s2`, or the predefined constant `NULL` if no substring is found. Example 2-6 shows a third version of our searching program; this one uses `strstr` to find the substring given as the program's first argument.

Example 2-6: search-string

```
#include <string.h>

void    markLine(char *, char *, char *);
void    outputLine(char *);
char    *inputLine(void);

int
main(int argc, char **argv)
{
    char *p, *line, *string;

    if (argc != 2) {
        outputLine("Usage: search-string string");
        exit(1);
    }

    string = argv[1];

    while ((line = inputLine()) != NULL) {
```

Example 2–6: search-string (continued)

```
        if ((p = strstr(line, string)) != NULL) {
            outputLine(line);
            markLine(line, p, p + strlen(string) - 1);
            outputLine(line);
        }
    }

    exit(0);
}
```

```
% cat input
john smith
sally jones
bob johnson
bill davis
mary upjohn
% search-string john < input
john smith
^^^^

bob johnson
    ^^^^

mary upjohn
        ^^^^
```

This example also shows another use of the `strlen` function, to compute the end of the matched sequence as an argument to the `markLine` function.

Our last string-searching function is really intended for breaking a string into *tokens*, each separated from the others by some set of field-separator tokens such as spaces, tabs, colons, or periods. The function is called `strtok`:

```
#include <string.h>

char *strtok(char *s1, const char *s2);
```

The string `s1` is considered to be a sequence of zero or more text tokens separated by spans of one or more characters from the set contained in `s2`. The first call to `strtok` places a null character into `s1` immediately following the first token, and returns a pointer to the token.

`strtok` keeps track of its position in `s1`, and subsequent calls, made with the predefined constant NULL as the first argument (to tell `strtok` to continue using the same input string), work through `s1`, extracting each token in turn. When no more tokens remain, `strtok` returns NULL. Example 2-7 gives a sample usage of `strtok`.

Example 2-7: search-token

```c
#include <string.h>

void    markLine(char *, char *, char *);
void    outputLine(char *);
char    *inputLine(void);

int
main(int argc, char **argv)
{
    char copyline[1024];
    char *p, *line, *token, *fieldsep;

    if (argc != 3) {
        outputLine("Usage: search-token token fieldsep");
        exit(1);
    }

    token = argv[1];
    fieldsep = argv[2];

    /*
     * For each line in the input...
     */
    while ((line = inputLine()) != NULL) {
        /*
         * Save a copy of the line.
         */
        strcpy(copyline, line);

        /*
         * Find the first token.
         */
        if ((p = strtok(line, fieldsep)) == NULL)
            continue;

        /*
         * Search through all the tokens.
         */
        do {
            if (strcmp(p, token) == 0) {
                outputLine(copyline);
                markLine(copyline, copyline + (p - line),
                        copyline + (p - line) + strlen(token) - 1);
                outputLine(copyline);
                p = NULL;
            }
            else {
                p = strtok(NULL, fieldsep);
            }
        } while (p != NULL);
    }
```

Example 2-7: search-token (continued)

```
    exit(0);
}
```

```
% cat input
one,two:three,four:five,six
ten:eight:six:four:two
two,four:six,eight,ten
one,two,three,four:five
% search-token two , < input
two,four:six,eight,ten
^^^

one,two,three,four:five
    ^^^

% search-token two : < input
ten:eight:six:four:two
              ^^^

% search-token two ,: < input
one,two:three,four:five,six
    ^^^

ten:eight:six:four:two
              ^^^

two,four:six,eight,ten
^^^

one,two,three,four:five
    ^^^
```

This example shows the different results obtained on the same input file when you use different field separator characters. Note that when you use both characters together, `search-token` makes another match that was not possible when using each character individually. Although not shown in this example, you can change the contents of the s2 string in between calls to `strtok`; for example, to extract a specific field from a line and then extract a subfield from the field.

This example also shows the use of the `strcpy` function discussed earlier. Because `strtok` destroys the string contained in s1 (by placing nulls into it), `search-token` makes a copy of the string before searching it, so that it can print it out later. `search-token` also uses the `strcmp` function to match the tokens, and the `strlen` function to tell `markLine` how to highlight the match.

Non-Standard Character String Functions

All of the functions described up until this point (except `strcasecmp` and `strn-casecmp`) are specified in the ANSI C standard, and should be present on most modern UNIX systems. However, SVR4 provides a number of additional functions for manipulating character strings that are not part of the ANSI C or POSIX standards. Do not use these functions if portability is an issue, but they may be useful to you otherwise.

You can include all of the functions described in this section in your program by linking with the *-lgen* library on Solaris 2.*x* and IRIX 5.*x*. Hewlett-Packard elected not to include most of these functions in their version of the system.

Searching character strings

The `strfind` function is similar to `strstr`, described earlier:

```
#include <libgen.h>

int strfind(const char *s1, const char *s2);
```

As with `strstr`, `strfind` searches the string s1 for the first occurrence of the string s2. However, instead of returning a pointer to the substring, `strfind` returns the integer offset of the beginning of the substring from the beginning of s1. If it cannot find the substring, `strfind` returns −1.

The `strfind` function is only available in Solaris 2.*x*.

The `strrspn` function is sort of the opposite of `strpbrk`:

```
#include <libgen.h>

char *strrspn(const char *s1, const char *s2);
```

`strrspn` traverses the string s1, and returns a pointer to the first character *not* in the set contained in s2. If s1 contains only characters from s2, `strrspn` returns the predefined constant NULL. This function can be useful for trimming unwanted "junk" characters (such as whitespace) from the end of a string.

The `strrspn` function is only available in Solaris 2.*x*.

Processing character escape sequences

There are four functions provided to assist with expanding and compressing C-language escape codes such as \n, \t, \001, and so forth:

```
#include <libgen.h>

char *strccpy(char *dst, const char *src);

char *strcadd(char *dst, const char *src);

char *strecpy(char *dst, const char *src, const char *except);

char *streadd(char *dst, const char *src, const char *except);
```

The first two functions, `strccpy` and `strcadd`, copy the source string, `src`, to the destination string, `dst`. As they encounter multi-character C-language escapes, the functions compress the escapes to the single character they represent. Thus, the two characters \ and `n` are replaced with a newline character, the four characters \, 0, 1, and 0 are replaced with a backspace character (\010 is the octal representation for the ASCII CTRL-H), and so on.

The second two functions, `strecpy` and `streadd`, do the reverse. They also copy the source string `src` to the destination string `dst`, but as they encounter special characters, they replace them with their multi-character C-language escapes. For example, a tab character is replaced by the two-character sequence \t, and a CTRL-G is replaced by the four-character sequence \007. The third argument to these functions, `except`, specifies characters that should not be expanded into their escape sequences. For example, if you do not want to have tabs expanded, you place a tab character into `except`.

`strccpy` and `strecpy` both return a pointer to the destination string, `dst`. `strcadd` and `streadd` on the other hand, return a pointer to the null byte terminating `dst`. This allows repeated calls to `strcadd` or `streadd` to be used to append to `dst`. Because these functions generate outputs of different sizes than their inputs, it is important that the `dst` string be sized appropriately. For `strccpy` and `strcadd`, `dst` should be at least as large as `src`, because if no translations are performed, the output is the same size (otherwise it is smaller). For `strecpy` and `streadd`, `dst` should be four times as large as `src`, since potentially each input character could be expanded to a four-character escape sequence (a backslash and three octal digits) on output.

The `strccpy`, `strcadd`, `strecpy`, and `streadd` functions are not available in HP-UX 10.*x*.

Breaking up delimited strings

To break up a string into individual words delimited by tabs or newlines, as is often necessary when parsing lines from configuration files, use the `bufsplit` function:

```
#include <libgen.h>

size_t bufsplit(char *buf, size_t n, char **a);
```

`bufsplit` moves through the string contained in `buf` and replaces the delimiter characters (tab and newline) with null bytes. `a` is an array of `n` pointers that are set to point at the start of each word in `buf`. `bufsplit` returns the number of words broken out (if there are more than `n` words in `buf`, then the last "word" is the rest of the string).

To change the delimiter characters used by bufsplit to something other than tab and newline, you can pass the new set of characters in as buf, with n and a set to zero. For example, to change the delimiters to period, comma, and colon, you use a call such as the following:

```
bufsplit(".,:", 0, (char **) 0);
```

The bufsplit function is not available in HP-UX 10.*x.*

Two other functions, useful when working with file and directory names, are basename and dirname:

```
#include <libgen.h>

char *basename(char *path);

char *dirname(char *path);
```

Given that path contains a filesystem pathname, basename returns a pointer to the last element of path (the part after the last /), with any trailing slashes removed. dirname, on the other hand, returns all but the last element of path. Thus, dirname returns the name of the parent directory, and basename returns the name of the file in that directory. Unfortunately, dirname works by placing a null byte into path at the slash that separates the directory and filenames, so if you need the full pathname later in the program, make a copy before calling this function.

Translating characters

The last function, strtrns, is used to replace one set of characters in a string with another set:

```
#include <libgen.h>

char *strtrns(const char *s1, const char *old, const char *new, char *s2);
```

strtrns copies characters from s1 to s2, replacing any character contained in old with the character in the corresponding position in new. A pointer to s2 is returned. Example 2-8 shows a sample usage of strtrns.

Example 2–8: translate

```
#include <string.h>
#include <libgen.h>

void    outputLine(char *);
char    *inputLine(void);

int
main(int argc, char **argv)
```

Example 2-8: translate (continued)

```
{
    char newline[1024];
    char *p, *old, *new, *line;

    if (argc != 3) {
        outputLine("Usage: translate old new");
        exit(1);
    }

    old = argv[1];
    new = argv[2];

    if (strlen(old) != strlen(new)) {
        outputLine("old and new strings must be same length.");
        exit(1);
    }

    while ((line = inputLine()) != NULL) {
        p = strtrns(line, old, new, newline);
        outputLine(p);
    }

    exit(0);
}
```

```
% cat input
one
two
three
four
five
six
seven
eight
nine
ten
% translate onetwhrfuivsxg ONETWHRFUIVSXG < input
ONE
TWO
THREE
FOUR
FIVE
SIX
SEVEN
EIGHT
NINE
TEN
```

The strtrns function is not available in HP-UX 10.*x*.

Porting Notes

The functions described in this section, except those in the *-lgen* library, `strcasecmp`, and `strncasecmp`, exist on most modern UNIX systems. However, when porting code from one system to another, bear the following notes in mind:

- On "pure" BSD systems, do not expect to find any of the routines described in this section except `strlen`, `strcpy`, `strncpy`, `strcat`, `strncat`, `strcmp`, and `strncmp`. Most BSD-based vendor systems should have the other functions, though.

- On BSD-based systems, the include file for these functions is called *strings.h*, rather than *string.h*. In fact, you can usually use the presence or absence of the *string.h* file to determine whether or not all of the functions described in this section are present. Some systems, such as SunOS 4.*x*, provide both files, but their contents are not the same.

- On BSD-based systems, the `strchr` and `strrchr` functions are called `index` and `rindex`, respectively. The arguments and return values are the same however, and it usually sufficient to add the following lines to your program when porting it from a BSD environment to SVR4:

```
#define index(s,c)  strchr(s,c)
#define rindex(s,c) strrchr(s,c)
```

Manipulating Byte Strings

The functions described in the previous section all operate on character strings, which are arrays of non-zero bytes terminated by a zero (null) byte. However, there are also times when you need to perform similar operations on strings in which the null byte is not a terminator, but a legal value. Because every byte value is legal, these strings, called *byte strings*, do not have a terminator character. Instead, they are always paired with an integer value indicating how many bytes are in the string.

The routines described in this section, for manipulating byte strings, closely resemble the character string routines described in the previous section. However, you can use these functions not only with strings of characters (which are a subset of byte strings), but also with any other arbitrary "chunk" of memory, such as a two-dimensional array, an array of pointers, an integer, an array of floating-point numbers, a structure, or an array of structures (although some of the routines don't really make sense on all these data types).

Comparing Byte Strings

To compare two byte strings (areas of memory), use the `memcmp` function:

```
#include <string.h>

int memcmp(const void *s1, const void *s2, size_t n);
```

`memcmp` compares the first n bytes of the areas of memory pointed to by `s1` and `s2`. Just like `strcmp`, `memcmp` returns an integer less than, equal to, or greater than zero depending upon whether `s1` is lexicographically less than, equal to, or greater than `s2`. Usually, this distinction is not meaningful for arbitrary "binary" data (what is the meaning of an array of floating-point numbers being lexicographically greater than another array of floating-point numbers?), and thus `memcmp` is usually just used to test for equivalence.

Copying Byte Strings

To copy one array of bytes to another, use the `memcpy` function:

```
#include <string.h>

void *memcpy(void *dst, const void *src, size_t n);
```

`memcpy` copies exactly n bytes from `src` into `dst`, and returns a pointer to `dst`.

`memcpy` is the preferred function for copying byte strings, but there is one case in which it does not work properly. If the areas pointed to by `src` and `dst` overlap, the algorithm used by `memcpy` fails. For this purpose, the `memmove` function is provided:

```
#include <string.h>

void *memmove(void *dst, const void *src, size_t n);
```

This function performs the same task as `memcpy`, but correctly handles the case where `src` and `dst` overlap. (There are two separate functions because the implementation of `memcpy` is more efficient than `memmove` on some architectures, and so you can use the faster implementation when overlap is not a concern.)

A third function for copying one byte string to another is called `memccpy`:

```
#include <string.h>

void *memccpy(void *dst, const void *src, int c, size_t n);
```

`memccpy` copies bytes from `src` to `dst`, stopping after a byte with the value c copied, or after n bytes are copied, whichever comes first. It returns a pointer to the next byte in `src` to copy (the one after the byte with value c), or a null pointer if no bytes with value c are found. Unlike the rest of the functions described in this section, `memccpy` is not specified by the ANSI C standard.

Searching Byte Strings

To search an array of bytes for the first occurrence of a specific value, use the `memchr` function:

```
#include <string.h>

void *memchr(const void *s, int c, size_t n);
```

`memchr` searches the first n bytes of s, starting from the beginning, until a byte with value c (interpreted as an `unsigned char`) is found. It returns a pointer to the byte, or the predefined constant NULL, if the byte is not found.

When using integers as bit fields, where each bit is interpreted as a Boolean true/false value, it is convenient to find the first bit in the integer that is "set" (non-zero). To do this, use the `ffs` function:

```
#include <string.h>

int ffs(int i);
```

`ffs` finds the first bit set in the argument it is passed and returns the index of that bit. Bits are numbered starting with 1 (one) from the low order bit. A return value of zero indicates that no bits are set (i.e., the value passed was equal to zero). This function is not specified by the ANSI C standard.

Initializing Byte Strings

When working with arrays of data, it is frequently necessary to initialize the entire array to a known value (often zero or null). To do this, use the `memset` function:

```
#include <string.h>

void *memset(void *s, int c, size_t n);
```

`memset` fills the area pointed to by s with n bytes of value c and returns a pointer to s. The value in c is interpreted as an unsigned character, so only values between 0 and 255 can be used.

Porting Notes

The functions described in this section were first introduced in System V UNIX, and therefore exist on any System V-based system. Because they are a part of the ANSI C standard, they exist on most modern versions of UNIX as well, regardless of whether or not they are System V-based. However, when porting code from BSD-based systems, there are a number of things you need to consider:

- On BSD-based systems, the include file for these functions is called *strings.h*, rather than *string.h*. In fact, you can usually use the presence or absence of the *string.h* file to determine whether or not all of the functions described in this section are present. Some systems, such as SunOS 4.*x*, provide both files but their contents are not the same.

- The BSD equivalent of the `memcmp` function is called `bcmp`:

  ```
  #include <strings.h>

  int bcmp(const char *s1, const char *s2, int n);
  ```

  `bcmp` returns 0 if the two strings are equal, and 1 if they are not.

- The BSD version of the `memcpy` and `memmove` functions is called `bcopy`:

  ```
  #include <strings.h>

  void bcopy(const char *src, char *dst, int n);
  ```

  Note that the `src` and `dst` arguments are in the opposite order from that used by `memcpy` and `memmove`. `bcopy` is more properly replaced by `memmove`, because it does properly handle the case in which the source and destination strings overlap.

- The BSD version of the `memset` function is called `bzero`:

  ```
  #include <strings.h>

  void bzero(char *s, int n);
  ```

  `bzero` initializes the array pointed to by `s` to zero; there is no choice of value as there is with `memset`.

- There are no BSD equivalents for `memchr` or `memccpy`.

- When porting from a BSD environment to SVR4, it is usually sufficient to add the following lines to your program:

  ```
  #define bcmp(b1, b2, n)      memcmp(b1, b2, n)
  #define bcopy(src, dst, n)   memmove(dst, src, n)
  #define bzero(b, n)          memset(b, '0', n)
  ```

Manipulating Character Classes

Particularly when parsing strings, it is often necessary to test characters for membership in particular sets, or *character classes*. The functions described in this section are provided for this purpose.

Testing Character Class Membership

The three functions `isalpha`, `isupper`, and `islower` test for three classes of letters:

```
#include <ctype.h>

int isalpha(int c);

int isupper(int c);

int islower(int c);
```

`isupper` tests for any character that is an uppercase letter and returns non-zero if it is, or zero if it is not. `islower` tests for any character that is a lowercase letter and returns non-zero if it is, or zero if it is not. `isalpha` returns non-zero for any character for which either `isupper` or `islower` is true, and zero otherwise.

The two functions `isdigit` and `isxdigit` test for two classes of numbers:

```
#include <ctype.h>

int isdigit(int c);

int isxdigit(int c);
```

`isdigit` returns non-zero for any character that is a decimal digit (0 through 9). `isxdigit` returns non-zero for any character that is a hexadecimal digit, (0 through 9, A through F, and a through f).

The `isalnum` function tests for letters or digits:

```
#include <ctype.h>

int isalnum(int c);
```

It returns non-zero for any character that satisfies either `isalpha` or `isdigit`.

The functions `isspace`, `ispunct`, and `iscntrl` test for non-alphanumeric characters:

```
#include <ctype.h>

int isspace(int c);
```

```
int ispunct(int c);

int iscntrl(int c);
```

isspace returns non-zero for any space, tab, carriage return, newline, vertical tab, or form feed, and zero for anything else. ispunct returns non-zero for any printable character for which neither isspace nor isalnum are true. This generally equates to the set of punctuation and other special symbols. iscntrl tests for any control character, as defined by the character set. For ASCII, these are the characters with decimal values 0 through 31, inclusive.

The last three functions test for membership in broader character classes:

```
#include <ctype.h>

int isprint(int c);

int isgraph(int c);

int isascii(int c);
```

isprint returns non-zero for any printable character (generally, this means any non-control character) *including* space. isgraph returns non-zero for any printable character *not including* space. isascii returns non-zero for any ASCII character; these are the characters with decimal values 0 through 127, inclusive.

Changing Character Class Membership

Three functions move characters from one character class to another:

```
#include <ctype.h>

int toupper(int c);

int tolower(int c);

int toascii(int c);
```

toupper, when given a lowercase letter as an argument, returns the corresponding uppercase letter. If the argument is not a lowercase letter, it is returned unchanged. tolower, when given an uppercase letter as an argument, returns the corresponding lowercase letter. If the argument is not a lowercase letter, it is returned unchanged. toascii strips the eighth bit off any character it is passed, thus coercing the character into the ASCII character set. Example 2-9 shows a program that uses toupper and tolower to invert the case of all the letters it is given.

Example 2-9: caseconv

```c
#include <ctype.h>

void    outputChar(char);
int     inputChar(void);

int
main(int argc, char **argv)
{
    int c;

    while ((c = inputChar()) >= 0) {
        if (isupper(c))
            outputChar(tolower(c));
        else if (islower(c))
            outputChar(toupper(c));
        else
            outputChar(c);
    }

    exit(0);
}
```

```
% cat input
One
Two
Three
Four
Five
Six
Seven
Eight
Nine
Ten
% caseconv < input
oNE
tWO
tHREE
fOUR
fIVE
sIX
sEVEN
eIGHT
nINE
tEN
```

Porting Notes

All of the functions described in this section, except for isascii and toascii, are specified by the ANSI C standard. They exist in all versions of UNIX, even those that predate ANSI C.

On newer systems such as SVR4 that understand international character sets, isalpha, isupper, and islower return the proper values even for non-ASCII values such as letters with umlauts and other diacritical marks. isspace and ispunct also work properly for non-ASCII values such as the British pound symbol. On older UNIX systems, these functions work properly only on the ASCII character set.

On older versions of UNIX, toupper and tolower do not check their inputs before attempting to convert them to upper- or lowercase; this is the responsibility of the programmer. The ANSI C standard rectified this by prescribing that toupper and tolower should simply return their inputs if the conversion makes no sense. However, for portability, it is a good idea to always check the input yourself:

```
if (isupper(c))
    c = tolower(c);

if (islower(c))
    c = toupper(c);
```

On some older versions of UNIX, the isprint function returns false for the space character.

Dynamic Memory Allocation

Dynamic memory allocation allows a program to allocate memory for data storage as needed. By using dynamic memory allocation instead of pre-allocated arrays, programs can be more flexible in the amount of data they can handle and more efficient by using only the memory they need.

The basic dynamic memory functions provided by all versions of UNIX are malloc and free:

```
#include <stdlib.h>

void *malloc(size_t size);

void free(void *ptr);
```

`malloc` attempts to allocate `size` bytes of memory and returns a pointer to the allocated block, or a null pointer if the request could not be satisfied. The memory is aligned for any use, meaning that any data type can be stored in it (many hardware architectures are picky about certain data types, especially floating-point numbers, beginning at addresses that are multiples of some power of two, usually four).

`free` releases memory that was previously allocated by `malloc` or one of the other memory allocation functions described later in this section. The memory is not actually released by the process (removed from its address space), but it is marked as available for reuse by future calls to the allocation functions.

After calling `free`, the memory pointed to by `ptr` is no longer guaranteed to be valid, and the results of accessing this memory are undefined. Nevertheless, you will often see code fragments such as this used to free dynamically allocated linked lists:

```
while (ptr != NULL) {
    free(ptr);
    ptr = ptr->next;
}
```

In most implementations of `malloc` and `free`, this works acceptably, because `free` just performs bookkeeping tasks and doesn't actually do anything to the freed memory. However, the previous example is technically incorrect, and does not work in certain implementations. Here is a more portable (and correct) way to do the same thing:

```
while (ptr != NULL) {
    nextptr = ptr->next;
    free(ptr);
    ptr = nextptr;
}
```

When allocating an array of items, you can use the `calloc` function instead of `malloc`:

```
#include <stdlib.h>

void *calloc(size_t nelem, size_t elsize);
```

`calloc` allocates `nelem` contiguous elements of memory, each of size `elsize` and returns a pointer to the first element, or a null pointer if the request could not be satisfied. This is identical to calling `malloc` as follows:

```
ptr = malloc(nelem * elsize);
```

Using `calloc` would be pointless, except that `calloc` initializes the memory it allocates to zero, a service not performed by `malloc`. (Initialize to zero means all the bits are set to zero; this is not necessarily the same thing as 0 or 0.0 as far as the variable's data type is concerned.)

To increase the size of a previously allocated memory segment, use the `realloc` function:

```
#include <stdlib.h>

void *realloc(void *ptr, size_t size);
```

`ptr` is a pointer to a segment of memory returned by a previous call to `malloc`, `calloc`, or `realloc`, and `size` is the desired new size, in bytes. `realloc` returns a pointer to the new memory segment, or a null pointer if the request cannot be satisfied. Note that in order to satisfy a request, `realloc` may have to copy the existing block pointed to by `ptr` to a new (larger) area in memory. This means that after a call to `realloc`, any variables pointing into the old block may be invalid.

For the specific purpose of saving a string in dynamically allocated memory, most modern UNIX systems provide a function called `strdup`:

```
#include <string.h>

char *strdup(const char *s);
```

`strdup` allocates a block of memory large enough to hold `s`, copies `s` into it, and returns a pointer to the saved string, or a null pointer if no memory could be allocated. This is particularly useful for saving strings of arbitrary length (such as those entered in response to prompts from the program) without having to preallocate many arrays of the largest possible size. If you are writing a program that has to be portable to older UNIX systems, you can include the following implementation of `strdup` for portability:

```
#include <string.h>

char *
strdup(char *s)
{
    char *p;

    if ((p = (char *) malloc(strlen(s) + 1)) != NULL)
        strcpy(p, s);

    return(p);
}
```

Look at Example 2-1 and Example 2-2 for a moment, and notice that they both work on only a predefined number of lines (the `NSTRINGS` constant). This is fine for the examples in this chapter, which used fairly small files. But, if you were to use these programs on larger files, they would only sort the first NSTRINGS lines of the file, and not even read in the rest of the file. Up to a point, you can simply increase the value of NSTRINGS to handle larger files, but after a while this becomes too cumbersome. It would be extremely inefficient to allocate enough memory to handle a 1,000,000-line file every time, even when you are normally sorting files that are much smaller.

Example 2-10 shows a reworked version of Example 2-2 that uses dynamic memory allocation to allow the program to work on files of any arbitrary size (up to the maximum amount of memory available to a single program on your machine).

Example 2-10: bsort-malloc

```c
#include <stdlib.h>
#include <string.h>

void    bubbleSort(char **, int);
void    outputLine(char *);
char    *inputLine(void);

int
main(int argc, char **argv)
{
    char *line;
    char **strptrs = NULL;
    int n, nstrings, nstrptrs;

    nstrings = 0;
    nstrptrs = 0;

    /*
     * For each line in the input...
     */
    while ((line = inputLine()) != NULL) {
        /*
         * If we're full up, allocate some more pointers.
         */
        if (nstrings == nstrptrs) {
            if (nstrptrs == 0) {
                nstrptrs = 8;
                strptrs = malloc(nstrptrs * sizeof(char *));
            }
            else {
                nstrptrs += 8;
                strptrs = realloc(strptrs, nstrptrs * sizeof(char *));
            }

            if (strptrs == NULL) {
                outputLine("out of memory.");
                exit(1);
            }
```

Example 2–10: bsort-malloc (continued)

```
        }

        /*
         * Save a pointer to the line, stored in dynamically
         * allocated memory.
         */
        strptrs[nstrings++] = strdup(line);
    }

    /*
     * Sort the strings.
     */
    bubbleSort(strptrs, nstrings);

    /*
     * Print the strings and free the memory.
     */
    for (n = 0; n < nstrings; n++) {
        outputLine(strptrs[n]);
        free(strptrs[n]);
    }

    free(strptrs);
    exit(0);
}

/*
 * bubbleSort - implementation of the standard bubble sort algorithm.
 */
void
bubbleSort(char **strings, int nstrings)
{
    int i, j;
    char *tmp;
    int notdone;

    j = nstrings;
    notdone = 1;

    while (notdone) {
        notdone = 0;
        j = j - 1;

        for (i = 0; i < j; i++) {
            /*
             * Use strcmp() to compare the strings
             * alphabetically.
             */
            if (strcmp(strings[i], strings[i+1]) > 0) {
                tmp = strings[i+1];
                strings[i+1] = strings[i];
                strings[i] = tmp;
```

Example 2–10: bsort-malloc (continued)

```
                notdone = 1;
        }
    }
  }
}
```

As each line is read in, it is saved in dynamically allocated memory with a call to `strdup`. The return values from `strdup` are saved in dynamically allocated memory, too. Initially, an array of eight pointers is allocated with `malloc`, and then as more pointers are needed, they are allocated eight more at a time with `realloc`. After sorting the lines, the strings allocated by `strdup` are freed as they are printed out, and then the array of pointers is freed. (It is not necessary to free memory before exiting, because the operating system does it automatically, but it is aesthetically pleasing from a programming style viewpoint to do so.)

Porting Notes

Before ANSI C, most versions of `malloc`, `calloc`, and `realloc` were declared to return pointers of type `char *` instead of type `void *`. This can cause portability problems if you declare the functions yourself; it is always better to use the appropriate include file instead and then typecast as appropriate. Unfortunately, before the ANSI C standard specified that these functions are declared in *stdlib.h*, various vendors used different include files to declare them. Often a *malloc.h* exists, but if it doesn't, you may have to search for the proper file.

Another memory allocation function, `alloca`, deserves special mention here:

```
    void *alloca(size_t size);
```

Like `malloc`, `alloca` returns a pointer to `size` bytes of memory, or a null pointer if the memory is unavailable. However, unlike `malloc`, which allocates the memory from the program's data segment, `alloca` allocates it from the program's stack segment. Thus, when the current function returns, the memory is automatically freed by being popped off the stack. This simplifies bookkeeping for programs that allocate large amounts of memory in numerous places. Unfortunately, it is also a portability nightmare. The implementation of `alloca` is very machine-, compiler-, and, most of all, system-dependent. Some hardware architectures cannot implement it all. For this reason, `alloca` should *never* be used by a program that must be portable to many different systems.

Manipulating Temporary Files

When a program needs to create a temporary file, it is usually desirable to use a filename that is not likely to be used by another program or by another invocation of the current program. For example, if the C compiler always used the temporary file */tmp/c-compile*, then only one program could be compiled on the system at a time. If two people tried to compile programs simultaneously, they would both be writing to the same temporary file, and neither would get anything useful out of the experience. For this reason, UNIX offers several functions for creating temporary files with unique names.

The most often-used function is `mktemp`. Although it is not specified by the ANSI C standard, it is nevertheless available on almost all modern UNIX platforms:

```
#include <stdlib.h>

char *mktemp(char *template);
```

(In HP-UX 10.*x*, `mktemp` is declared in *unistd.h* instead of *stdlib.h*.)

The `template` parameter points to a character string that contains a prototype temporary filename; this prototype must include six trailing X characters, which are replaced with a unique identifier (usually based on the process ID number). Because `mktemp` modifies the string pointed to by `template` in place, you cannot use constant strings as defined in ANSI C. In other words, do not use code like this:

```
#include <stdlib.h>

    ⋮

    char *tempf;

    tempf = mktemp("/tmp/mytempXXXXXX");

    ⋮
```

Instead, use code like this:

```
#include <stdlib.h>

    ⋮

    char *tempf;
    char *template[32];

    strcpy(template, "/tmp/mytempXXXXXX");
    tempf = mktemp(template);

    ⋮
```

If `mktemp` cannot construct a unique filename, it assigns the empty string to `template`.

The ANSI C standard specifies two different functions, `tmpnam` and `tempnam`, for creating temporary files:

```
#include <stdio.h>

char *tmpnam(char *s);

char *tempnam(const char *dir, constr char *pfx);
```

These functions also exist in most versions of System V UNIX, but are not usually present in BSD versions. `tmpnam` places its result in the character array pointed to by `s`; if `s` is null then the result is left in an internal area that is overwritten with each call. If `s` is not null, then it must point to an array of at least `L_tmpnam` (defined in *stdio.h*) bytes. The temporary filename generated by `tmpnam` always has the path prefix defined as `P_tmpdir` in *stdio.h*; on SVR4 systems it is defined as `/tmp/`.

`tempnam` allows you to control the directory in which you create the temporary file by passing it in as `dir`. If `dir` is null, the path defined as `P_tmpdir` in *stdio.h* is used. The `pfx` string allows you to choose a prefix for the filenames generated by `tempnam`; if it is null, no prefix is used. If the environment variable `TMPDIR` is set, its value overrides any value specified by `dir`.

A fourth function for creating a temporary file, also specified by the ANSI C standard, is called `tmpfile`:

```
#include <stdio.h>

FILE *tmpfile(void);
```

This function uses `tmpnam` to create a temporary filename and then opens the file for reading and writing. It returns a *Standard I/O Library* file pointer (see Chapter 4, *The Standard I/O Library*) for the file.

Porting Notes

The most portable of these functions is probably `mktemp`. Although it is not specified by the ANSI C standard, it has existed in UNIX for the longest time, and is likely to be present on almost any system.

BSD UNIX provides one other function, called `mkstemp`:

```
int mkstemp(char *template);
```

Use the `template` parameter as described for `mktemp`, previously. After the temporary filename is obtained, `mkstemp` opens the file for reading and writing and returns a low-level I/O file descriptor (see Chapter 3, *Low-Level I/O Routines*) for the file. When porting programs that use this function to SVR4 systems, use the following compatibility routine:

```
#include <sys/types.h>
#include <stdlib.h>
#include <fcntl.h>

int
mkstemp(char *template)
{
    char *tempf;

    tempf = mktemp(template);

    if (strlen(template) == 0)
        return(-1);

    return(open(tempf, O_RDWR | O_CREAT | O_TRUNC, 0666));
}
```

Parsing Command-Line Arguments

Almost every UNIX command has arguments, and most commands follow a generally accepted set of rules for how these arguments are formatted:

1. Command names must be between two and nine characters long.

2. Command names must include only lowercase letters and digits.

3. Option names must be one character long.

4. You must precede all options with a dash (–).

5. You can group options with no arguments after a single dash (–). This means that you can use either *-a -b -c* or *-abc*.

6. You must precede the first option argument following an option with a tab or space character. This means that you must use *-a arg*; *-aarg* is illegal.

7. Option arguments cannot be optional. This means that you cannot allow both *-a* and *-a arg*.

8. You must separate groups of option arguments following an option by commas or by space or tab characters and quotes. This means that you must use either *-a xxx,yyy,zzz* or *-a "xxx yyy zzz"*.

9. All options must precede operands on the command line. This means that *command -a -b -c filename* is legal, while *command -a filename -b -c* is not.

10. You can use a double dash (--) to indicate the end of the options. This allows operands that begin with a dash.

11. The order of the options relative to one another should not matter.

12. The relative order of the operands can affect their significance in ways determined by the command with which they are used. This means that a command is allowed to assign meaning to the order of its operands; for example, the *cp* command takes its first operand as the input file and its second operand as its output file. Reversing the order of these operands produces different results.

13. A dash (-) preceded and followed by a space character should only be used to mean standard input. This tells a program that generally reads from files, such as *troff*, to read from the standard input. It allows files to be read before processing the standard input.

Depending on how long you've been using UNIX and how many versions you've used, most of these rules, except perhaps number 8, should look familiar. Early versions of System V provided a library routine, `getopt`, that enforced most of these rules and allowed a program to easily parse command lines that followed the rules. Later versions provided a shell command, *getopt*, which enabled shell scripts to use these rules as well.

In SVR4, the *getopt* command is available, as well as a newer command that is built in to the shell, called *getopts*. Two library routines are provided as well: `getopt`, which enforces the rules described previously and parses command lines that follow these rules, and `getsubopt`, which enforces rule number 8 and parses option arguments that follow that rule. These functions are called as follows:

```
#include <stdlib.h>

int getopt(int argc, char * const *argv, const char *optstring);

extern char *optarg;
extern int optind, opterr, optopt;

int getsubopt(char **optionp, const char * const *tokens, char **valuep);
```

`optstring` contains a list of characters that are legal options for the command. If the option letter is to be followed by an option argument, then the letter should be followed by a colon (`:`) in `optstring`.

When `getopt` is called, it returns the next option letter in `argv` that matches one of the letters in `optstring`. If the option letter has an argument associated with it (as indicated by a colon character in `optstring`), `getopt` sets the external variable `optarg` to point to the option argument.

The external variable `optind` contains the index into `argv` of the next argument to process; it is initialized to 1 before the first call to `getopt`. When all options are processed, `getopt` returns -1. The special option two dashes (`--`) can be used to delimit the end of the options; when it is encountered, `getopt` skips over it and returns -1. This is used to stop option processing before encountering non-option arguments that begin with a dash.

When `getopt` encounters an option letter not included in `optstring` or cannot find an argument after an option that should have one, it prints an error message and returns a question mark (`?`). The character that caused the error is placed in the external variable `optopt`. To disable `getopt`'s printing of the error message, the external variable `opterr` should be set to zero.

`getsubopt` is used to parse the suboptions in an option argument initially parsed by `getopt`. These suboptions are separated by commas (unlike rule 8 above, `getsubopt` does not allow them to be separated by spaces), and consist either of a single token or a token-value pair, separated by an equal sign (`=`). Since commas delimit suboptions in the option string, they are not allowed to be part of the suboption or the value of a suboption.

When calling `getsubopt`, `optionp` is the address of a pointer to the suboption string, `tokens` is a pointer to an array of strings representing the possible token values the option string can contain, and `valuep` is the address of a character pointer that can be used to return any value following an equal sign.

`getsubopt` returns the index of the token (in the `tokens` array) that matched the suboption in the option string, or -1 if there was no match. If the suboption has a value associated with it, `getsubopt` updates `valuep` to point at the first character of the value; otherwise, it sets `valuep` to null. If `optionp` contains only one suboption, `optionp` is updated to point to the null character at the end of the string. Otherwise, the suboption is isolated by replacing the comma character with a null character, and `optionp` is updated to point to the next suboption.

Although this sounds relatively complicated, Example 2-11 should make this clear. Example 2-11 shows a program that uses `getopt` and `getsubopt` to parse its command line.

Example 2-11: parse-cmdline

```c
#include <stdlib.h>
#include <string.h>

/*
 * Sub-options.
 */
char    *subopts[] = {
#define COLOR   0
    "color",
#define SOLID   1
    "solid",
    NULL
};

int
main(int argc, char **argv)
{
    int c;
    char buf[1024];
    extern int optind;
    extern char *optarg;
    char *options, *value;

    /*
     * Process the arguments.
     */
    while ((c = getopt(argc, argv, "cf:o:st")) != -1) {
        switch (c) {
        case 'c':
            outputLine("circle");
            break;
        case 'f':
            strcpy(buf, "filename: ");
            strcat(buf, optarg);
            outputLine(buf);
            break;
        case 's':
            outputLine("square");
            break;
        case 't':
            outputLine("triangle");
            break;
        case '?':
            outputLine("command line error");
            break;
        case 'o':
            options = optarg;

            /*
             * Process the sub-options.
             */
            while (*options != '\0') {
```

Example 2-11: parse-cmdline (continued)

```c
                switch (getsubopt(&options, subopts, &value)) {
                case COLOR:
                    if (value != NULL) {
                        strcpy(buf, "color: ");
                        strcat(buf, value);
                    }
                    else {
                        strcpy(buf, "missing color");
                    }

                    outputLine(buf);
                    break;
                case SOLID:
                    outputLine("solid");
                    break;
                default:
                    strcpy(buf, "unknown option: ");
                    strcat(buf, value);
                    outputLine(buf);
                    break;
                }
            }

        break;
        }
    }

    /*
     * Process extra arguments.
     */
    for (; optind < argc; optind++) {
        strcpy(buf, "extra argument: ");
        strcat(buf, argv[optind]);
        outputLine(buf);
    }

    exit(0);
}


% parse-cmdline -c -f picture.out -o solid
circle
filename: picture.out
solid
% parse-cmdline -o color=red,solid -t
color: red
solid
triangle
% parse-cmdline -s -z
square
parse-cmdline: illegal option -- z
command-line error
```

This program represents the argument-parsing section for a hypothetical graphics program that draws a circle, square, or triangle, as specified by the *-c*, *-s*, or *-t* arguments. The *-f* argument allows you to specify an output file; otherwise, the program writes to the standard output. The *-o* argument allows you to specify two options: *solid*, which indicates that the figure should be filled in instead of hollow, and *color*, which allows you to specify a color for the figure.

As shown in the third command invocation in the example, an illegal option (*-z*) produces an error message. As mentioned earlier, you can disable this message by setting the external variable `opterr` to zero. Note that the program also parses additional operands on the command line (for example, the command might require two additional arguments, the height and width of the figure); this is done by the last few lines of code.

Porting Notes

The use of `getopt` has never really caught on. Some people use it, other people don't. One of the primary arguments against it is that the arguments to many commands simply don't fit into the set of rules that it enforces. Indeed, in SVR4, the modification of a number of commands to use `getopt` resulted in noticeable changes to the command lines with which most users are familiar.

Most versions of System V have some version of `getopt`, but `getsubopt` is new to SVR4 and is not very portable. Older BSD systems usually do not have either function, although a number of vendors have added one or both of them to their System V compatibility libraries. However, there are several public domain implementations of `getopt` available; if you really want to use it, consider obtaining one of these and distributing it with your program.

Miscellaneous Functions

There are many more functions provided by the C library on most UNIX systems, especially on SVR4. This section describes a few of the more generally useful ones. For a complete list of all the functions provided by your system, read Chapter 3 of the *UNIX Programmer's Manual*, which describes the C library.

String to Number Conversion

There are several functions provided to convert character strings to numbers:

```
#include <stdlib.h>

int atoi(const char *str);

long atol(const char *str);
```

```
double atof(const char *str);

long strtol(const char *str, char **ptr, int base);

unsigned long strtoul(const char *str, char **ptr, int base);

double strtod(const char *str, char **ptr);
```

Both `strtol` and `strtoul` scan `str` up to the first character inconsistent with a number in the given `base`. Leading white space is ignored while a leading minus sign produces a negative number. If `ptr` is non-null, then a pointer to the character in `str` that terminated the scan is placed into it. Legal inputs to `strtol` and `strtoul` are determined by the value of `base`. If `base` is 10, decimal numbers are assumed; if `base` is 16, hexadecimal numbers are assumed, and so forth. Following an optional minus sign, leading zeros are ignored and, if `base` is 16, a leading 0X or 0x is ignored, too. If `base` is zero, the string itself determines the base. Following an optional sign, a leading zero indicates octal (base 8), a leading 0X or 0x indicates hexadecimal, and anything else indicates decimal.

`strtod` scans `str` up to the first character inconsistent with a floating-point number. If `ptr` is non-null, then a pointer to the character in `str` that terminated the scan is placed into it. After ignoring leading white space, `strtod` accepts an optional sign, a string of digits optionally containing a decimal point, and then an optional exponent part including an `E` or `e`, followed by an optional sign, followed by an integer. Thus, the string 123.456 represents the number 123.456, while the string 987.654e-2 represents the number 9.87654. The decimal point character defaults to a period (.), but can vary with international custom (for example, many European countries use a comma).

The other three functions have been around much longer, and are generally provided only for backward compatibility. You can write all three of them in terms of the newer functions:

```
#include <stdlib.h>

int
atoi(char *str)
{
    return((int) strtol(str, (char **) 0, 10));
}

long
atol(char *str)
{
    return(strtol(str, (char **) 0, 10));
}

double
atof(char *str)
```

```
{
    return(strtod(str, (char **) 0));
}
```

Printing Error Messages

Every UNIX system call, and many of the library routines, returns an error code when something goes wrong. This error code is stored as a small integer in the external variable errno. The values that can be placed in errno are defined in the include file *errno.h*, and the manual page for each system call describes the errors that it can return.

The errors defined in *errno.h* can vary between different versions of UNIX, although most versions have at least a subset of them in common. However, because the errors do vary, it is unwise for a program to interpret the numerical values of errno directly. Instead, only the constant names defined in *errno.h* should be used. Additionally, to provide some consistency between applications, programs should use a standard set of error messages to describe these errors. To do this, use the perror function:

```
#include <stdio.h>

void perror(const char *s);
```

perror prints the contents of the string s, followed by a colon, followed by a string describing the error in errno, followed by a newline character to the standard error output. For example, the following code prints out the string myprogram: systemcall:, followed by a specific error message describing the way in which systemcall failed:

```
if (systemcall(...arguments...) < 0) {
    perror("myprogram: systemcall");
    exit(1);
}
```

ANSI C defines another function, strerror:

```
#include <string.h>

char *strerror(int errnum);
```

This function takes the error number as an argument (simply pass in the value of errno) and returns a pointer to a character string that describes the error. This is often more flexible than perror, since the program has more control over what happens to the error message.

Porting Notes

`perror` is available on all UNIX systems, and you should use it whenever appropriate. `strerror`, unfortunately, is not as widely available. On many older systems, an external character array called `sys_errlist` is defined; you can use `errno` as an index into this array to achieve the same result:

```
char *
strerror(int errnum)
{
    extern int sys_nerr;
    extern char *sys_errlist[];

    if (errnum < 0 || errnum >= sys_nerr)
        return(NULL);

    return(sys_errlist[errnum]);
}
```

Pausing a Program

Sometimes a program needs to wait for something to happen by "sitting there" for a few seconds. To do this, use the `sleep` routine:

```
#include <unistd.h>

unsigned int sleep(unsigned int seconds);
```

When called, `sleep` causes the program to pause for **seconds** seconds; when the time expires, `sleep` returns.

Exiting a Program

To exit a program, use the `exit` function:

```
#include <stdlib.h>

void exit(int status);
```

The lower eight bits of the `status` argument are passed to the parent process when the program terminates; the parent can use this value to determine whether the program terminated normally or abnormally.

UNIX convention dictates that a zero exit status represents normal termination, while a non-zero status indicates abnormal termination. Some programs assign special meanings to their exit status values; for example, *grep* exits with status 0 if matches are found, status 1 if no matches are found, and status 2 if the command line contained syntax errors or one of the files it was told to search could not be opened. However, most programs exit with status 0 if everything went fine and status 1 if there was a problem.

Chapter Summary

This chapter discussed a number of utility routines offered by the C library on most UNIX systems. The examples throughout the rest of this book use the routines described in this chapter, so you should try to familiarize yourself with most of them. However, the primary purpose of this chapter is to serve as a reference, so if you encounter a function in a later example that is not described in the surrounding text, check back here if you don't remember what it does.

3

Low-Level I/O Routines

The C language, unlike PASCAL or FORTRAN, does not provide any built-in operators for performing input and output (I/O). Rather, all I/O services are offered to the programmer directly by the operating system, in the form of system calls and library routines.

This chapter examines the I/O interface provided by all versions of UNIX, including SVR4. All of the functions described in this chapter, except for `readv` and `writev`, are specified by the POSIX 1003.1 standard.

The routines described in this chapter are usually referred to as the *low-level* I/O interface, because they are a direct interface to the operating system and, to some extent, the hardware itself. The next chapter discusses a *high-level* interface, the *Standard I/O Library*.

File Descriptors

All of the functions described in this chapter use a *file descriptor* to reference an open file. A file descriptor is simply a small integer that identifies the open file to the operating system. There are three file descriptors that are predefined when each program is invoked. The standard input, usually the keyboard, is identified by file descriptor 0. The standard output, usually the screen, is identified by file descriptor 1. The standard error output, also usually the screen, is identified by file descriptor 2.

File descriptors are allocated from a table maintained for each process by the operating system, and each file descriptor is simply an index into that table. Most older versions of UNIX limit the maximum number of files a process can have open at once to approximately 20. Newer versions have larger limits such as 32 or 64, and SVR4 allows up to 256. One of the features of this table-based implementation is that opening a file always returns the lowest-numbered available file descriptor. Thus, because a process starts out with three open files (0, 1, and 2), the first file it opens is attached to file descriptor 3. If the program later closes its standard input (file descriptor 0), then the next file it opens is attached to file descriptor 0, not file descriptor 4. This behavior is found in all versions of UNIX, and is also specified by the POSIX standard.

Opening and Closing Files

Before any data can be read from or written to a file, that file must be opened for reading or writing (or both). Opening a file causes the operating system to locate (or create) the file on the disk, allocate an entry in the process' open file table, and set up assorted internal structures for moving data between the file and your program. The function used to open a file is called **open**:

```
#include <sys/types.h>
#include <sys/stat.h>
#include <fcntl.h>

int open(const char *path, int oflag, /* mode_t mode */);
```

The **path** argument is a character string containing the pathname of the file to be opened, and **oflag** is a set of flags that control how the file is to be opened. **oflag** is constructed by or-ing together flags from the following list (the first three flags are mutually exclusive):

O_RDONLY
>   Open the file for reading only.

O_WRONLY
>   Open the file for writing only.

O_RDWR
>   Open the file for both reading and writing.

O_APPEND
>   If set, the read/write offset for the file (the point at which the next read or write is performed) is set to the end of the file prior to each write, causing all data written to be appended to the file.

O_CREAT

> If the file exists, this option does nothing (except when O_EXCL is set; see the next option). If the file does not exist, this option tells the operating system to create it. The file is created with the permission bits provided in the third argument, mode, as modified by the process' *umask* value (see Chapter 6, *Special-Purpose File Operations*).

O_EXCL

> If O_CREAT is also set, this option checks to see if the file already exists. If the file does not exist, it is created. However, if the file does exist, the call to open fails. This allows cooperating processes to make use of the same file, because only one process can create the file at any given instant.

> If O_EXCL and O_CREAT are both set, and the last path component of the filename to be opened is a symbolic link, open does not follow the link.

O_NDELAY or O_NONBLOCK

> These constants affect the behavior of future reads and writes to a file. If the file is a regular disk file, a read or write returns -1 immediately if no data can be read or written, and errno is set to EAGAIN. This is true regardless of which flag (O_NDELAY or O_NONBLOCK) is used.

> If the file is a terminal device or a FIFO (see Chapter 13, *Interprocess Communication*), a read or write still returns immediately if no data can be read or written. If the O_NONBLOCK flag is used, the read or write returns -1 and sets errno to EAGAIN. If the O_NDELAY flag is used, however, the read or write returns 0 (which is not considered an error).

O_NOCTTY

> If the file being opened is a terminal device, do not allocate that terminal as this process' controlling terminal. The controlling terminal is discussed in Chapter 11, *Processes*, and Chapter 12, *Terminals*.

O_DSYNC

> Normally, write operations complete once the data to be transferred has been successfully copied to an operating system buffer; the transfer from the buffer to the physical storage media takes place without the process' knowledge. However, if this option is set, write operations on the descriptor do not complete until the data has been successfully transferred to the physical storage medium. This makes the process run much more slowly but allows it to be absolutely sure that the data is stored on the disk.

> This flag is not available in IRIX 5.*x*.

O_RSYNC

Normally, a read request is satisifed with whatever data is stored on the disk at the time the request is processed. If another process is writing to the file at the same time, it is indeterminate whether the read will retrieve the old data or the new data (this is subject to the order in which the operating system processes the requests). However, if this option is set, the read request does not complete until any pending write operations affecting the data have been processed.

This flag is not available in IRIX 5.*x*.

O_SYNC

This option is similar to O_DSYNC, except that while O_DSYNC allows a write to complete once the data is successfully updated, O_SYNC forces the write to wait until both the data and the file's attributes (such as modification time) are updated.

This flag is not available in IRIX 5.*x*.

O_TRUNC

If the file exists and is being opened for writing, this option truncates its length to zero, deleting any existing data in the file.

If the file is opened successfully, **open** returns a file descriptor for the file. If the file cannot be opened, -1 is returned and an error code describing the reason for failure is placed into the external variable **errno**, where it can be examined or printed out with the **perror** function (see Chapter 2, *Utility Routines*).

On older UNIX systems such as Version 7 and pre-4.2 versions of BSD UNIX, **open** only accepted three values for **oflag**: 0 to open the file for reading, 1 to open it for writing, and 2 to open it for reading and writing. (For backward compatibility, the constants O_RDONLY, O_WRONLY, and O_RDWR are defined as 0, 1, and 2 respectively.) All of the other options described above were not available, and furthermore, **open** only opened existing files—to create a file, a separate system call, **creat**, was provided:

```
#include <sys/types.h>
#include <sys/stat.h>
#include <fcntl.h>

int creat(const char *path, mode_t mode);
```

If the file named in **path** does not exist, **creat** creates it, with the permission bits set to those in **mode**, as modified by the process' *umask* value (see Chapter 6). If the file named in **path** already exists, and is writable, it is truncated to zero length. If the file can be created successfully, **creat** returns a file descriptor (open for writing only) for the file. If the file cannot be created, `creat` returns -1 and places an error code describing the reason for failure into the external variable `errno`.

Once a program is finished using a file, it should close the file. This flushes any data written to the file but not yet placed on the disk by the operating system and frees up the resources (buffers, file table entry, etc.) used by that file. The function to close a file is called `close`:

```
#include <unistd.h>

int close(int fd);
```

If the file is closed successfully, `close` returns 0. If an error occurs during closing, `close` returns -1 and stores an error code in the external variable `errno`.

Porting Notes

As mentioned previously, older versions of UNIX do not support all the various flags to the `open` system call. The O_NOCTTY and O_NONBLOCK options are new to POSIX implementations; the O_DSYNC, O_RSYNC, and O_SYNC options are new to SVR4 implementations. These options are not supported by BSD or pre-SVR4 systems.

On BSD systems, the meaning of O_NDELAY applies only to the `open` call and does not affect future reads and writes.

The POSIX standard says that if O_EXCL is set when O_CREAT is *not* set, the result is implementation-defined. On some systems, it means that the file is opened for exclusive use (only one process may open the file at a time). However, on SVR4 systems, it simply has no effect.

Finally, on BSD systems, the O_ constants are defined in the include file *sys/file.h* instead of *fcntl.h*.

Input and Output

To move data between a file and your program, use the `read` and `write` functions:

```
#include <unistd.h>

ssize_t read(int fd, void *buf, size_t nbytes);

ssize_t write(int fd, const void *buf, size_t nbytes);
```

The `read` function transfers up to `nbytes` bytes from the file referenced by `fd` and stores them in the area of memory pointed to by `buf`. The number of bytes actually read is returned. If 0 is returned, this indicates that end-of-file is reached and there is no data left to read. The `write` function transfers up to `nbytes` bytes of data from the area of memory pointed to by `buf` to the file referenced by `fd`. The number of bytes actually written is returned. Both routines return -1 if an error occurs and store an error code in the external variable `errno`.

Unlike languages in which the I/O instructions are built into the language, `read` and `write` do not perform any formatting or data conversion. Although you can pass a pointer to any C data type to both functions, you are working with the actual contents of memory, not the human-readable form of those contents. For example, the following program writes 12 bytes (4 bytes for each integer) to the standard output:

```
main()
{
    int n;

    for (n = 1; n <= 3; n++)
        write(1, &n, sizeof(int));
}
```

Here is the standard output:

```
00000000 00000000 00000000 00000001
00000000 00000000 00000000 00000010
00000000 00000000 00000000 00000011
```

Contrast this with the PASCAL program:

```
program x;
    var n : integer;
begin
    for n := 1 to 3 do begin
        writeln(n);
    end
end.
```

or the FORTRAN program:

```
    integer n

    do 10 n = 1,3
        print *, n
10  continue
    stop
    end
```

Both the PASCAL and FORTRAN programs print out the ASCII representations of the number n:

```
1
2
3
```

To accomplish the same thing with **write**, you need to convert the integer n to a character string and then write it out:

```
int n;
char buf[32];

intToString(n, buf);
write(1, buf, strlen(buf));
```

Similarly, if you use the **read** function to read in a number, you must enter four bytes containing the appropriate binary bits to give you a number of the appropriate value:

```
int n;

read(0, &n, sizeof(int));
```

Instead, if what you want is for the user to enter a number (say, 123) and have that value stored in n, you need code like this:

```
int i, n;
char buf[32];

i = read(0, buf, sizeof(buf));
buf[i] = '\0';
n = atoi(buf);
```

Note that because **read** does not automatically null-terminate the data it reads in, the program must do this explicitly.

Example 3-1 shows a program that takes two filenames as arguments. It opens the first file for reading and the second file for writing and then appends the contents of the first file to the second file.

Example 3-1: append

```
#include <sys/types.h>
#include <sys/stat.h>
#include <unistd.h>
#include <fcntl.h>

int
main(int argc, char **argv)
{
    int n, in, out;
    char buf[1024];
```

Example 3-1: append (continued)

```c
    if (argc != 3) {
        write(2, "Usage: append file1 file2\n", 26);
        exit(1);
    }

    /*
     * Open the first file for reading.
     */
    if ((in = open(argv[1], O_RDONLY)) < 0) {
        perror(argv[1]);
        exit(1);
    }

    /*
     * Open the second file for writing.
     */
    if ((out = open(argv[2], O_WRONLY | O_APPEND)) < 0) {
        perror(argv[2]);
        exit(1);
    }

    /*
     * Copy data from the first file to the second.
     */
    while ((n = read(in, buf, sizeof(buf))) > 0)
        write(out, buf, n);

    close(out);
    close(in);
    exit(0);
}
```

```
% cat a
file a line one
file a line two
file a line three
% cat b
file b line one
file b line two
file b line three
% append a b
% cat b
file b line one
file b line two
file b line three
file a line one
file a line two
file a line three
```

Note the calls to `read` and `write`: when calling `read`, we pass the size of the buffer `buf`, but when calling `write`, we pass the number of bytes read, `n`. If we were to pass the size of the buffer instead, then we would end up writing out some number of correct bytes (the ones we read) and a large number of "garbage" bytes.

Two other functions for reading and writing, `readv` and `writev`, were introduced in BSD UNIX and are also present in SVR4. These functions allow a program to perform "scatter-gather" I/O, by passing in the addresses of several buffers in one call. Because these functions are rarely used and are not very portable anyway, this book will not discuss them further.

Repositioning the Read/Write Offset

One of the values the operating system associates with each file is the *read/write offset*, also called the *file offset*. The read/write offset specifies the "distance," measured in bytes from the beginning of the file, at which the next read or write takes place. When a file is first opened or created, the file offset is zero. The first read or write starts at the beginning of the file. As reads and writes are performed, the offset is incremented by the number of bytes read or written each time. There is only one read/write offset for each file, so a read of 10 bytes followed by a write of 20 bytes leaves the read/write offset at 30.

To examine and change the value of the read/write offset, use the `lseek` function:

```
#include <sys/types.h>
#include <unistd.h>

off_t lseek(int fd, off_t offset, int whence);
```

`lseek` sets the read/write offset to `offset` bytes from the position in the file specified by `whence`, which can have one of the following values:

SEEK_SET
> Set the read/write offset to `offset` bytes from the beginning of the file.

SEEK_CUR
> Set the read/write offset to `offset` bytes from the current offset.

SEEK_END
> Set the read/write offset to `offset` bytes from the end of the file.

On success, `lseek` returns the new read/write offset. On failure, it returns -1 and stores an error code in the external variable `errno`. Note that the `offset` parameter is a signed value, so negative seeks are permitted.

To move to the beginning of a file, use the following call:

```
lseek(fd, 0, SEEK_SET);
```

To move to the end of a file, use the following call:

```
lseek(fd, 0, SEEK_END);
```

To obtain the value of the current offset without changing it, use the following call:

```
off_t offset;

offset = lseek(fd, 0, SEEK_CUR);
```

The concept of the end of a file is somewhat fluid—it is perfectly legal to seek past the end of the file and then write data. This creates a "hole" in the file that does not take up any storage space on the disk. However, when reading a file with holes in it, the holes are read as zero-valued bytes. This means that once a file with holes is created, it is impossible to copy it precisely, because all the holes are filled in when the copy takes place. (There are ways around this, but they involve reading the raw disk blocks rather than simply opening the file and reading it directly.)

Example 3-2 shows a program that writes five strings to a file and then prompts for a number between 1 and 5. It seeks to the proper location for the string of that number, reads it from the file, and prints it. Note the use of the `mktemp` function to create a temporary filename (see Chapter 2 for a description of `mktemp`).

Example 3-2: seeker

```
#include <sys/types.h>
#include <sys/stat.h>
#include <unistd.h>
#include <stdlib.h>
#include <fcntl.h>

#define NSTRINGS    5
#define STRSIZE     3

char *strings[] = {
    "aaa", "bbb", "ccc", "ddd", "eee"
};

int
main(int argc, char **argv)
{
    int n, fd;
    char *fname;
    char buf[STRSIZE], answer[8], template[32];

    /*
```

Example 3-2: seeker (continued)

```
 * Create a temporary file name.
 */
strcpy(template, "/tmp/seekerXXXXXX");
fname = mktemp(template);

/*
 * Create the file.
 */
if ((fd = open(fname, O_RDWR | O_CREAT | O_TRUNC, 0666)) < 0) {
    perror(fname);
    exit(1);
}

/*
 * Write strings to the file.
 */
for (n = 0; n < NSTRINGS; n++)
    write(fd, strings[n], STRSIZE);

/*
 * Until the user quits, prompt for a string and retrieve
 * it from the file.
 */
for (;;) {
    /*
     * Prompt for the string number.
     */
    write(1, "Which string (0 to quit)? ", 26);
    n = read(0, answer, sizeof(answer));
    answer[n-1] = '\0';
    n = atoi(answer);

    if (n == 0) {
        close(fd);
        exit(0);
    }

    if (n < 0 || n > NSTRINGS) {
        write(2, "Out of range.\n", 14);
        continue;
    }

    /*
     * Find the string and read it.
     */
    lseek(fd, (n-1) * STRSIZE, SEEK_SET);
    read(fd, buf, STRSIZE);

    /*
     * Print it out.
     */
    write(1, "String ", 7);
```

Example 3-2: seeker (continued)

```
        write(1, answer, strlen(answer));
        write(1, " = ", 3);
        write(1, buf, STRSIZE);
        write(1, "\n\n", 2);
    }
}
```

```
% seeker
Which string (0 to quit)? 1
String 1 = aaa

Which string (0 to quit)? 5
String 5 = eee

Which string (0 to quit)? 3
String 3 = ccc

Which string (0 to quit)? 4
String 4 = ddd

Which string (0 to quit)? 2
String 2 = bbb

Which string (0 to quit)? 0
```

Note the number of steps involved in printing the prompts in this program. This is one of the principal drawbacks to using low-level I/O; complex input and output formatting involves a lot of work. Contrast this example with the redesigned version shown in the next chapter.

Porting Notes

On most pre-POSIX systems, the constants used with lseek are called L_SET, L_INCR, and L_XTND. On even older UNIX systems, no constants are defined at all. The integers 0, 1, and 2 are used instead. In either case, you can replace them with the POSIX constants SEEK_SET, SEEK_CUR, and SEEK_END, respectively.

Duplicating File Descriptors

Sometimes you may want to have more than one file descriptor referring to the same file or a specific file descriptor refer to a file. This is most commonly needed when reassigning the standard input, standard output, and standard error output. The following two functions duplicate file descriptors:

```
#include <unistd.h>

int dup(int fd);

int dup2(int fd, int fd2);
```

dup returns a new file descriptor that references the same file as fd. The new descriptor has the same access mode (read, write, or read/write) and the same read/write offset as the original. The file descriptor returned is the lowest numbered one available. dup2 causes the file descriptor fd2 to refer to the same file as fd. If fd2 refers to an already-open file, that file is closed first.

These functions require advanced concepts to demonstrate, so I will defer their demonstration until Chapter 11.

Chapter Summary

This chapter examined the I/O interface offered by all versions of the UNIX operating system. This interface is frequently called a *low-level* interface, because it does not provide any formatting or data conversion facilities (refer to the *seeker* program in Example 3-2). The next chapter discusses the *Standard I/O Library*, which is a *high-level* interface comparable to the built-in I/O operators in languages such as PASCAL and FORTRAN.

4

The Standard I/O Library

The last chapter examined the low-level I/O interface provided by the UNIX operating system. Although, as you'll see later in the book, this interface is useful for a number of applications, it isn't very convenient to use for everyday programming.

To understand why, think about writing a program that computes your monthly budget. This program prompts you for budget items (strings) and monthly costs (numbers). It then performs some calculations and displays a nice table of values. The table contains the names of the budget items (strings) and several columns of numbers, nicely lined up at the decimal point. Sounds pretty simple, until you realize that you have to write not only the functions to compute your budget but also a function to read in a string up to a newline character, a function to convert strings of characters like `123.456` to numbers, a function to line up all the numbers in columns and print them out, and so forth. These functions aren't terribly difficult, but imagine having to write them for every program you develop—you'd be spending more time writing I/O formatting routines than you would actually writing your program!

Fortunately, the original developers of UNIX realized this too, and they developed a powerful set of functions called the *Standard I/O Library*. The primary purpose of the library is to separate the mechanics of coding I/O, so that you can spend your time writing "real" code instead of writing mundane things like string-to-integer conversion functions. Specifically, the library performs three major tasks for you:

- The library automatically buffers I/O. When reading or writing data, it is much more efficient to do so in large chunks, rather than one byte (or a few bytes) at a time. This is because each read or write request results in a call to the operating system and then usually initiates action on the part of some piece of hardware, such as a disk. Reading or writing one byte at a time to a disk drive is horrendously inefficient—for each byte, the operating system has to tell the disk to seek to some address, wait for the disk to do so, request the disk to transfer a byte to or from memory, wait for the disk to do so, and then return the result to your program. Imagine hundreds of programs doing this at the same time, each with thousands of bytes of data.

  By *buffering* reads and writes, the *Standard I/O Library* makes programs more efficient. When a program reads a single character, the library routine actually reads a large bufferful of characters (using `read`) and then returns the first character in the buffer to the program. The next several one-character reads are filled from the same buffer, without making any request to the operating system (or to a device such as a disk drive). When the program uses the entire buffer, the next one-character read causes the library to read another bufferful of characters, and so forth. Thus, assuming a buffer size of one Kbyte (1,024 characters), a program can read a ten-Kbyte file a character at a time with only ten calls to the operating system's `read` function, instead of 10,240 calls. Writes are handled in a similar fashion. Each time the program writes some data, the library routines transfer that data to a buffer. When the buffer fills up, it is written out using `write` and a new buffer is started. All of this happens invisibly to you, the programmer.

- The library performs I/O conversions. As you know, data is stored in binary form inside a computer. For example, the decimal integer 1234 is stored internally (on a 32-bit system) in the following binary form:

  ```
  00000000 00000000 00000100 11010010
  ```

  Floating-point numbers are even more unwieldy—the decimal number 1234.5678 is stored internally (on a system using the IEEE 754 floating-point format) in the following binary form:

  ```
  01000100 10011010 01010010 00101011
  ```

Because human beings don't think very well in binary, it is necessary to convert between the binary system used by the computer and the decimal system used by people. The *Standard I/O Library* provides a number of convenient ways to do this.

- The library can format I/O. Most programs that produce output intended to be read by humans make an effort to print their data in a format that is easy to read. For example, programs that produce large amounts of numerical data try to line that data up into columns, programs that produce lists try to make each line of the list line up somehow, and so forth. The *Standard I/O Library* makes it easy to perform these tasks.

The *Standard I/O Library* exists in pretty much the same form on all versions of UNIX, although some of the more obscure options vary from release to release. The version of the library discussed in this chapter is the one specified by the ANSI C standard.

Data Types and Constants

When using the *Standard I/O Library* functions, an open file with its associated buffers is called a *stream* and is referenced by a *file pointer*. A file pointer is a variable of type FILE *, as defined in the include file *stdio.h*. There are three predefined file pointers associated with the three open files given to each process when it is invoked: *stdin* refers to the standard input file (usually the keyboard), *stdout* refers to the standard output file (usually the screen), and *stderr* refers to the standard error file (also usually the screen).

The *Standard I/O Library* functions also make use of three constants defined in the include file *stdio.h*:

EOF
> Returned by most of the integer-valued functions upon encountering an end-of-file condition.

NULL
> Returned by most of the pointer-valued functions, signifying a null pointer.

BUFSIZ
> The size of buffers that should be used with most of the routines. Other buffer sizes may be used with some functions, but this constant serves as a useful value for declaring character arrays and other variables.

Opening and Closing Files

Before any data can be read from or written to a file, that file must be opened for reading or writing (or both). Opening a file causes the operating system to locate (or create) the file on the disk, allocate an entry in the process' open file table, and set up assorted internal structures for moving data between the file and your program. In the case of the *Standard I/O Library*, opening a file also allocates buffers internal to the library that are used to move data between your program and the file in an efficient manner. The *Standard I/O Library* function for opening a file is called `fopen`:

```
#include <stdio.h>

FILE *fopen(const char *filename, const char *type);
```

The character string `filename` contains the pathname of the file to be opened, and the `type` character string describes the type of stream that is to be created. `type` can have any of the following values:

r   Open the file for reading only. The file must already exist.

w   Open the file for writing only. If the file does not exist, it is created. If the file does exist, it is truncated to zero length (any data already in the file will be lost).

a   Open the file for writing (appending). If the file does not exist, it is created. If the file does exist, all writes to the file are appended to the end (any data already in the file will not be lost).

r+ Open the file for both reading and writing. The file must already exist.

w+ Open the file for both reading and writing. If the file does not exist, it is created. If the file does exist, it is truncated to zero length.

a+ Open the file for both reading and writing (appending). If the file does not exist, it is created. If the file does exist, all writes to the file are appended to the end.

All `type` strings can also have a b contained in them, as in `rb`, `w+b`, or `ab+`. The b informs the library routines that the file is a "binary" file (as opposed to a text file), which is necessary on some operating systems. Because UNIX does not distinguish between binary and text files, the b is simply ignored.

If the file can be opened successfully, a file pointer to the open stream is returned. If the file cannot be opened, the constant `NULL` is returned and an error code is placed in the external variable `errno`.

Once a program is finished with a file, it should close the file. This causes any buffered writes to be flushed to the disk, frees up memory in the library associated with the file's buffering, and frees up the operating system resources (such as buffers and file table entry) used by that file. The *Standard I/O Library* function to close a file is called `fclose`:

```
#include <stdio.h>

int fclose(FILE *stream);
```

If the file referenced by **stream** is closed successfully, `fclose` returns zero. If the close fails, the constant **EOF** is returned and an error code is placed in the external variable **errno**.

Porting Notes

As mentioned earlier, the *Standard I/O Library* has been around for a long time, and there aren't too many significant differences between versions. The **b** character in the **type** argument was first introduced in XENIX and may not be understood by older versions of the library. However, it is a part of the ANSI C standard, and so most newer versions should support it. To be safe, though, always place the + after the first type character, followed by the **b**.

Some very old versions of the library may not understand the + notation, but as this should not be of concern on any modern system, don't worry about portability when using it.

Character-Based Input and Output

The simplest way to perform I/O is to treat a file as an unformatted stream of bytes. The simplest way to process a stream of bytes is one byte at a time. The *Standard I/O Library* provides several functions to do this:

```
#include <stdio.h>

int fgetc(FILE *stream);

int getc(FILE *stream);

int getchar(void);

int fputc(int c, FILE *stream);

int putc(int c, FILE *stream);

int putchar(int c);
```

The `getc` function returns the next character (byte) from the file referenced by `stream`. If there are no more characters to read (end-of-file is reached) or if an error occurs, `getc` returns the constant `EOF`.

The `putc` function converts `c` to an `unsigned char` and places it on `stream`. If it succeeds, `putc` returns `c`, otherwise it returns the constant `EOF`.

The `getchar` and `putchar` functions are actually just macros, defined as:

```
#define getchar()     getc(stdin)
#define putchar(c)    putc(c, stdout)
```

These are often used as shorthand in programs that read from the standard input, write to the standard output, or both.

The `fgetc` and `fputc` functions behave exactly like `getc` and `putc`. The difference is that `getc` and `putc` are usually implemented as preprocessor macros, while `fgetc` and `fputc` are implemented as genuine C-language functions. This means that `fgetc` and `fputc` run more slowly than `getc` and `putc` (because of the overhead incurred when making a function call), but they take up less space in the executable code because they are not expanded in-line as macros are. Their other advantage is that because they are functions, they can be passed as arguments to other functions.

All of these functions use variables of type `int` to hold byte values, rather than type `char`. This is necessary to allow the functions to return the constant `EOF`, which is usually defined as -1. If the `char` type were used instead of `int`, then reading a character with decimal value 255 could erroneously cause a program to think end-of-file had been reached, because the `char` value -1 can get sign-extended to the `int` value -1 during comparisons. For this reason, it is important to *always* use variables of type `int` when working with these functions.

Example 4-1 shows another version of the *append* program introduced in Chapter 3, *Low-Level I/O Routines*. The program takes two filenames as arguments. It opens the first file for reading, the second file for writing, and then appends the contents of the first file to the second file.

Example 4–1: append-char

```
#include <stdio.h>

int
main(int argc, char **argv)
{
    int c;
    FILE *in, *out;

    if (argc != 3) {
        fprintf(stderr, "Usage: append-char file1 file2\n");
```

Example 4-1: append-char (continued)

```
        exit(1);
    }

    /*
     * Open the first file for reading.
     */
    if ((in = fopen(argv[1], "r")) == NULL) {
        perror(argv[1]);
        exit(1);
    }

    /*
     * Open the second file for writing.
     */
    if ((out = fopen(argv[2], "a")) == NULL) {
        perror(argv[2]);
        exit(1);
    }

    /*
     * Copy data from the first file to the second, a character
     * at a time.
     */
    while ((c = getc(in)) != EOF)
        putc(c, out);

    fclose(out);
    fclose(in);
    exit(0);
}



% cat a
file a line one
file a line two
file a line three
% cat b
file b line one
file b line two
file b line three
% append-char a b
% cat b
file b line one
file b line two
file b line three
file a line one
file a line two
file a line three
```

The internal buffering providing by the *Standard I/O Library* means that, even though this example reads and writes one character at a time, the data is actually transferred to disk in large chunks. This is very important—it allows a program to process files one byte at a time while preserving the efficiency of reading and writing large buffers of data. If the program in the example above were converted to use the low-level I/O routines described in the previous chapter, it would become too inefficient to use on all but the smallest input files.

The buffering features provided by the *Standard I/O Library* allow the library to provide another interesting function, ungetc:

```
#include <stdio.h>

int ungetc(int c, FILE *stream);
```

This function is quite literally the reverse of getc, causing the character c to be placed back onto the input stream referenced by stream. The next call to getc returns the character contained in c.

This function is often used in programs that read from a file until they encounter a special character. When a program reads the special character, the collection of input is stopped for the current token. The special character is placed back onto the input with ungetc so that another part of the program can deal with it later. For example, consider a program that reads lists of words separated by colon (:) characters:

```
while ((c = getc(fp)) != EOF) {
    if (c == ':') {
        word[nchars] = '\0';
        ungetc(c, fp);
        return;
    }

    word[nchars++] = c;
}
```

As each character is read, it is checked to see if it is the colon character. If it is not, it is appended to the current word. If the colon character is read, the word is terminated, the colon is placed back on the input stream, and the subroutine returns. The next character read from the input stream is the colon character again.

There is actually no requirement that the character passed to ungetc be the same character that was just read from the stream; in reality, any character can be placed onto the input. However, the library only guarantees that up to four characters can be pushed back on the input stream. It is not possible, for example, to "unread" an entire file.

Line-Based Input and Output

The *Standard I/O Library* also provides functions that you can use to process files a line at a time, where a line is defined as some sequence of bytes terminated by a newline character:

```
#include <stdio.h>

char *gets(char *s);

char *fgets(char *s, int n, FILE *stream);

int puts(const char *s);

int fputs(const char *s, FILE *stream);
```

The `gets` function reads characters from `stdin` and places them into `s` until either a newline character is read or end-of-file is encountered. The `fgets` function reads characters from `stream` and places them into `s` until either a newline character is encountered, n-1 characters have been read, or end-of-file is encountered. Both functions terminate `s` with a null character and return `s`, or return the constant `NULL` if end-of-file is encountered before any characters have been read. For historical reasons, `gets` discards the newline character, while `fgets` copies it into `s`.

NOTE

> There is a significant problem with `gets`: it has no way of knowing the size of the array pointed to by its argument, `s`. It will happily continue reading characters and copying them to memory, even after `s` is filled, until it encounters a newline character or end-of-file. This has the unfortunate side effect of destroying the contents of whatever variables follow `s` in memory, resulting in unexpected program behavior. This "feature" of `gets` was used with great success by the 1988 Internet worm to gain unauthorized access to systems. Because of this problem, the `gets` function should be considered "evil" and you should avoid using it at all costs.

The `puts` function writes the string pointed to by `s`, followed by a newline character, to the standard output. The `fputs` function writes the string pointed to by `s` to `stream` but does not append a newline character. On success, both functions return the number of characters written. If an error occurs, they return the constant `EOF`.

Example 4-2 shows another version of our file-appending program; this one uses `fgets` and `fputs` to process the file a line at a time.

Example 4-2: append-line

```c
#include <stdio.h>

int
main(int argc, char **argv)
{
    FILE *in, *out;
    char line[BUFSIZ];

    if (argc != 3) {
        fprintf(stderr, "Usage: append-line file1 file2\n");
        exit(1);
    }

    /*
     * Open the first file for reading.
     */
    if ((in = fopen(argv[1], "r")) == NULL) {
        perror(argv[1]);
        exit(1);
    }

    /*
     * Open the second file for writing.
     */
    if ((out = fopen(argv[2], "a")) == NULL) {
        perror(argv[2]);
        exit(1);
    }

    /*
     * Copy data from the first file to the second, one line
     * at a time.
     */
    while (fgets(line, sizeof(line), in) != NULL)
        fputs(line, out);

    fclose(out);
    fclose(in);
    exit(0);
}
```

```
    % cat a
    file a line one
    file a line two
    file a line three
    % cat b
    file b line one
    file b line two
    file b line three
    % append-line a b
    % cat b
```

```
file b line one
file b line two
file b line three
file a line one
file a line two
file a line three
```

Buffer-Based Input and Output

A third I/O paradigm offered by the *Standard I/O Library* is that of buffer-based I/O, in which buffers full of characters are read and written in large chunks. This method is almost identical to the paradigm offered by the low-level interface described in Chapter 3, except that the library still provides internal buffering services regardless of the size of the buffers used by the program.

There are two functions for performing buffer-based I/O, `fread` and `fwrite`:

```
#include <stdio.h>

size_t fread(void *ptr, size_t size, size_t nitems, FILE *stream);

size_t fwrite(const void *ptr, size_t size, size_t nitems, FILE *stream);
```

The `fread` function reads `nitems` of data, each of size `size`, from `stream`, and places them into the array pointed to by `ptr`. It returns the number of items (*not* the number of bytes) read, zero if no items were read, or the constant EOF if end-of-file is encountered before any data was read. The `fwrite` function copies `nitems` of data, each of size `size`, from the array pointed to by `ptr` to the output stream `stream`. It returns the number of items (*not* the number of bytes) written, or EOF if an error occurs.

Example 4-3 shows one last version of our file-appending program; this one uses `fread` and `fwrite`.

Example 4-3: append-buf

```
#include <stdio.h>

int
main(int argc, char **argv)
{
    int n;
    FILE *in, *out;
    char buf[BUFSIZ];

    if (argc != 3) {
        fprintf(stderr, "Usage: append-line file1 file2\n");
        exit(1);
    }
```

Example 4-3: append-buf (continued)

```
/*
 * Open the first file for reading.
 */
if ((in = fopen(argv[1], "r")) == NULL) {
    perror(argv[1]);
    exit(1);
}


/*
 * Open the second file for writing.
 */
if ((out = fopen(argv[2], "a")) == NULL) {
    perror(argv[2]);
    exit(1);
}


/*
 * Copy data from the first file to the second, a buffer
 * full at a time.
 */
while ((n = fread(buf, sizeof(char), BUFSIZ, in)) > 0)
    fwrite(buf, sizeof(char), n, out);

fclose(out);
fclose(in);
exit(0);
}


% cat a
file a line one
file a line two
file a line three
% cat b
file b line one
file b line two
file b line three
% append-buf a b
% cat b
file b line one
file b line two
file b line three
file a line one
file a line two
file a line three
```

Formatted Input and Output

Up to this point, this chapter discussed methods of performing unformatted I/O. The programs in Example 4-1 through Example 4-3 simply read and write bytes, without assigning any particular meaning to them. Although this type of I/O is performed all the time, it is also necessary to be able to read or write data that is formatted in a particular way, usually to make it easier for human beings to understand and work with. The *Standard I/O Library* provides two sets of functions to do this: the `printf` functions handle writing formatted output, and the `scanf` functions handle reading formatted input.

The printf Functions

The `printf` functions allow you to print data in a wide variety of formats:

```
#include <stdio.h>

int printf(const char *format, ...);

int fprintf(FILE *stream, const char *format, ...);

int sprintf(char *s, const char *format, ...);
```

All three functions convert, format, and print their arguments according to the instructions contained in the `format` string. The `printf` function writes to the standard output, the `fprintf` function writes to the referenced `stream`, and the `sprintf` function copies its output to the array of characters pointed to by `s`. The number of arguments passed to each of these functions can vary, because the contents of the `format` string specify unambiguously how many arguments there are. Each function returns the number of characters written or the constant `EOF` if an error occurs.

The `format` string can contain three types of characters:

- Plain characters that are simply copied to the output

- C-language escape sequences that represent non-graphic characters (such as \n and \t)

- Conversion specifications

A conversion specification, in its simplest form, is a percent sign (`%`) followed by a single character that indicates the type of conversion to perform. For each conversion specification, another argument is passed to the `printf` function following `format`. The arguments are passed in the same order in which their conversion specifications appear.

There are three basic data types that can be specified in a conversion specification: integers, floating-point numbers, and characters and character strings.

Integers

The conversion specifications for integers are as follows:

`%d` or `%i`

The argument, of type `int`, is converted to a signed decimal number. The `%i` specification is specific to ANSI C.

`%o` The argument, of type `int`, is converted to an unsigned octal number.

`%u` The argument, of type `int`, is converted to an unsigned decimal number.

`%X` or `%x`

The argument, of type `int`, is converted to an unsigned hexadecimal number. The `X` conversion uses the letters `ABCDEF;`, and the `x` conversion uses `abcdef`.

Example 4-4 shows some examples of how these conversion specifications are used.

Example 4–4: printf-int

```
#include <stdio.h>

#define N    4

int numbers[N] = { 0, -1, 3, 169 };

int
main(int argc, char **argv)
{
    int i;

    for (i = 0; i < N; i++) {
        printf("Signed decimal:       %d\n", numbers[i]);
        printf("Unsigned octal:       %o\n", numbers[i]);
        printf("Unsigned decimal:     %u\n", numbers[i]);
        printf("Unsigned hexadecimal: %x\n\n", numbers[i]);
    }

    exit(0);
}


    % printf-int
    Signed decimal:       0
    Unsigned octal:       0
    Unsigned decimal:     0
    Unsigned hexadecimal: 0
```

```
Signed decimal:       -1
Unsigned octal:        37777777777
Unsigned decimal:      4294967295
Unsigned hexadecimal: ffffffff

Signed decimal:        3
Unsigned octal:        3
Unsigned decimal:      3
Unsigned hexadecimal: 3

Signed decimal:        169
Unsigned octal:        251
Unsigned decimal:      169
Unsigned hexadecimal: a9
```

An optional h character can be used to indicate that the argument corresponding to one of the above conversions is a short int (such as %hd) or unsigned short int (such as %hu). Likewise, an optional l character can be used to indicate a long int or unsigned long int.

Floating-point numbers

The conversion specifications for floating-point numbers are as follows:

%f The argument, of type double, is converted to decimal notation in the style *[-]ddd.ddd*. By default, six decimal digits are output.

%E or %e
The argument, of type double, is converted to decimal notation in the style *[-]d.dddE±dd*, where there is always one digit before the decimal point. By default, there are six digits after the decimal point. The E conversion causes an E to be used in the output, and the e conversion causes an e to be used.

%G or %g
The argument, of type double, is converted to decimal notation in either of the above two styles, depending on the number of significant digits in the result.

Example 4-5 shows some examples of how these conversion specifications are used.

Example 4–5: printf-float

```
#include <stdio.h>

#define N    4

double numbers[N] = { 0, -1.234, 67.890, 1234567.98765 };

int
```

Example 4–5: printf-float (continued)

```
main(int argc, char **argv)
{
    int i;

    for (i = 0; i < N; i++) {
        printf("f notation: %f\n", numbers[i]);
        printf("e notation: %e\n", numbers[i]);
        printf("g notation: %g\n\n", numbers[i]);
    }

    exit(0);
}
```

```
% printf-float
f notation: 0.000000
e notation: 0.000000e+00
g notation: 0

f notation: -1.234000
e notation: -1.234000e+00
g notation: -1.234

f notation: 67.890000
e notation: 6.789000e+01
g notation: 67.89

f notation: 1234567.987650
e notation: 1.234568e+06
g notation: 1.23457e+06
```

An optional L character can be used to indicate that the argument corresponding to one of the above conversions is a `long double` (such as `%Lf`).

Characters and character strings

The conversion specifications for characters and character strings are as follows:

`%c` The argument, of type `int`, is converted to an `unsigned char` and printed.

`%s` The argument, a pointer to a character string, is copied to the output character-by-character up to (but not including) a terminating null character.

`%%` This specification allows a percent sign to be printed; no argument is converted.

Field width and precision

Example 4-6 shows a small program that prints out the cost of purchasing some number of items.

Example 4-6: cost

```c
#include <stdio.h>

#define COST_PER_ITEM    1.25

void    printCost(int);

int
main(int argc, char **argv)
{
    int i;

    for (i = 1; i < 1000; i *= 10)
        printCost(i);

    exit(0);
}

void
printCost(int n)
{
    printf("Cost of %d items at $%f each = $%f\n", n, COST_PER_ITEM,
            n * COST_PER_ITEM);
}
```

```
% cost
Cost of 1 items at $1.250000 each = $1.250000
Cost of 10 items at $1.250000 each = $12.500000
Cost of 100 items at $1.250000 each = $125.000000
```

There are a couple of problems with this example. First, because the numbers representing the quantity of items you want to purchase are of different sizes, the equal signs don't line up, making the total prices difficult to compare easily. Second, because you're dealing with dollars and cents, you really want only two decimal places on each of the dollar amounts.

You can solve the first of these problems by using a *field width*. A field width specifies how many character positions should be used by a specific output conversion. If you change the %d in the format string to %3d, then you are telling printf to print each integer in a field three characters wide:

```
Cost of   1 items at $1.250000 each = $1.250000
Cost of  10 items at $1.250000 each = $12.500000
Cost of 100 items at $1.250000 each = $125.000000
```

If you specify a positive number as a field width, the output is right justified in the field. If you use a negative number, as in %-3d, the output is left justified:

```
Cost of 1    items at $1.250000 each = $1.250000
Cost of 10   items at $1.250000 each = $12.500000
Cost of 100  items at $1.250000 each = $125.000000
```

If you specify a leading zero in the field width, as in %03d, the output is padded with zeros instead of spaces:

```
Cost of 001 items at $1.250000 each = $1.250000
Cost of 010 items at $1.250000 each = $12.500000
Cost of 100 items at $1.250000 each = $125.000000
```

To fix the second problem (the number of decimal places), you can use a *precision* specification. The precision is specified with a decimal point and then a number, and it indicates:

- For the d, i, o, u, x, and X conversions, the minimum number of digits to appear (the field is padded with leading zeros)

- For the e, E, and f conversions, the number of digits to appear after the decimal point

- For the g and G conversions, the number of significant digits

- For the s conversion, the maximum number of characters to be copied from the string

So, you can fix the printing of the cost per item by changing the %f to %.2f:

```
Cost of   1 items at $1.25 each = $1.250000
Cost of  10 items at $1.25 each = $12.500000
Cost of 100 items at $1.25 each = $125.000000
```

To fix the total cost, you need not only print just two decimal digits, but you also need to get the decimal points to line up. To do this, use a field width *and* a precision. Since the largest number occupies six character positions, you can change the %f to %6.2f. Example 4-7 shows the final result of all of these changes.

Example 4-7: cost-fmt

```c
#include <stdio.h>

#define COST_PER_ITEM   1.25

void    printCost(int);

int
main(int argc, char **argv)
{
    int i;
```

Example 4-7: cost-fmt (continued)

```
    for (i = 1; i < 1000; i *= 10)
        printCost(i);

    exit(0);
}

void
printCost(int n)
{
    printf("Cost of %3d items at $%.2f each = $%6.2f\n", n, COST_PER_ITEM,
            n * COST_PER_ITEM);
}


    % cost-fmt
    Cost of   1 items at $1.25 each = $  1.25
    Cost of  10 items at $1.25 each = $ 12.50
    Cost of 100 items at $1.25 each = $125.00
```

You can also specify both field widths and precisions with an asterisk character
(*) instead of a number. In this case, the field width or precision is read from the
next argument in the argument list. For example:

```
double n;
int fieldwidth, precision;

fieldwidth = 10;
precision = 4;

printf("%*.*f\n", fieldwidth, precision, n);
```

Note that the field width and precision *precede* the value to be printed in the argument list.

Variable argument lists

Most newer versions of the *Standard I/O Library* offer a set of `printf` functions
that accept varargs-style argument lists instead of explicit lists of arguments:

```
#include <stdarg.h>
#include <stdio.h>

int vprintf(const char *format, va_list ap);

int vfprintf(FILE *stream, const char *format, va_list ap);

int vsprintf(char *s, const char *format, va_list ap);
```

These functions make calling the functions from routines that accept a variable
number of arguments much easier. For example, to create a function `error` that

works just like `printf` except that it always prepends the name of the program to its output, you could use the following code:

```
#include <stdarg.h>
#include <stdio.h>

void
error(const char *format, ...)
{
    va_list ap;
    extern char *programName;

    va_start(ap, format);

    fprintf(stderr, "%s: ", programName);
    vfprintf(stderr, format, ap);

    va_end(ap);
}
```

The scanf Functions

The `scanf` functions allow data in almost any format to be read:

```
#include <stdio.h>

int scanf(const char *format, ...);

int fscanf(FILE *stream, const char *format, ...);

int sscanf(const char *s, const char *format, ...);
```

All three functions read characters, interpret them according to the instructions contained in the `format` string, and store the results in their arguments. The `scanf` function reads from the standard input, the `fscanf` function reads from the referenced `stream`, and the `sscanf` function copies its input from the array of characters pointed to by `s`. The number of arguments passed to each of these functions can vary, because the contents of the `format` string specify unambiguously how many arguments there are. Each function returns the number of input items successfully matched and assigned. This number can be zero if the input does not match the `format` string or if end-of-file is encountered prematurely. If end-of-file is encountered before the first matching failure or conversion is performed, the constant `EOF` is returned.

The `format` string can contain three types of characters:

• Whitespace characters (spaces, tabs, newlines, and form feeds) that, except in two cases described below, cause input to be read up to the next non-whitespace character

- An ordinary character (not %) that must match the next input character

- Conversion specifications

A conversion specification, in its simplest form, is a percent sign (%) followed by a single character that indicates the type of conversion to be performed. For each conversion specification, another argument is passed to the `scanf` function following `format`. The arguments are passed in the same order that their conversion specifications appear.

There are three basic data types that can be specified in a conversion specification: integers, floating-point numbers, and characters and character strings.

Integers

The conversion specifications for integers are as follows:

%d Matches an optionally signed decimal integer. The corresponding argument should be a pointer to a variable of type `int`.

%i Matches an optionally signed integer, whose format is interpreted in the same fashion as `strtol` with a `base` argument of 0 (`strtol` is described in Chapter 2, *Utility Routines*). That is, numbers starting with 0 are taken to be octal, numbers starting with 0x or 0X are taken to be hexadecimal, and all others are taken to be decimal. The corresponding argument should be a pointer to a variable of type `int`. The %i specification is specific to ANSI C.

%o Matches an optionally signed octal integer. The corresponding argument should be a pointer to a variable of type `unsigned int`.

%u Matches an optionally signed decimal integer. The corresponding argument should be a pointer to a variable of type `unsigned int`.

%x Matches an optionally signed hexadecimal integer. The corresponding argument should be a pointer to a variable of type `unsigned int`.

Example 4-8 shows an example of how to use the %d specification. It reads in lines telling how many quarters, dimes, and nickels you have and prints out the total amount of money.

Example 4–8: scanf-int

```
#include <stdio.h>

int
main(int argc, char **argv)
{
    double total;
    int n, quarters, dimes, nickels;

    for (;;) {
```

Example 4-8: scanf-int (continued)

```
        printf("Enter a line like:\n");
        printf("%%d quarters, %%d dimes, %%d nickels\n");
        printf("--> ");

        n = scanf("%d quarters, %d dimes, %d nickels", &quarters, &dimes,
                  &nickels);

        if (n != 3)
            exit(0);

        total = quarters * 0.25 + dimes * 0.10 + nickels * 0.05;

        printf("You have: $ %.2f\n\n", total);
    }
}
```

```
% scanf-int
Enter a line like:
%d quarters, %d dimes, %d nickels
--> 3 quarters, 2 dimes, 1 nickels
You have: $ 1.00

Enter a line like:
%d quarters, %d dimes, %d nickels
--> 6 quarters, 0 dimes, 2 nickels
You have: $ 1.60

Enter a line like:
%d quarters, %d dimes, %d nickels
--> 0 quarters, 2 dimes, 9 nickels
You have: $ 0.65

Enter a line like:
%d quarters, %d dimes, %d nickels
--> ^D
```

You can use an optional h to indicate that the argument corresponding to one of the above conversions is a pointer to a short int (such as %hd) or unsigned short int (such as %hu). Likewise, you can use an optional 1 character to indicate a long int or unsigned long int.

Floating-point numbers

The conversion specifications for floating-point numbers are as follows:

%e or %f or %g

> Matches an optionally signed floating-point number, in any of the formats produced by the corresponding `printf` output conversions. The corresponding argument should be a pointer to a variable of type `float`.

An optional `l` character may be used to indicate that the argument corresponding to the above conversions is a pointer to type `double` (e.g., `%lf`). Likewise, an optional `L` may be used to indicate a pointer to type `long double`.

This brings up an important difference between `printf` and `scanf`. Since all floating-point arguments to `printf` are passed by value, it doesn't matter whether they are of type `float` or type `double`—either way, C's argument-type promotion rules make them all `double`s inside `printf`. However, because `scanf`'s arguments are all passed by reference (that is, pointers are used), the type promotion rules do not apply. You must specifically tell `scanf` whether you're giving it a pointer to an argument of type `float` or an argument of type `double`. This is a common source of problems that you should be careful to avoid.

Characters and character strings

The conversion specifications for characters and character strings are as follows:

%c Matches a sequence of characters of the number specified by the field width (see below). If no field width is specified, matches one character. The corresponding argument should be a pointer of type `char *` that points to an array large enough to accept the sequence. No terminating null character is added. The normal skip over whitespace is suppressed during this conversion.

%s A character string is expected. The corresponding argument should be a pointer of type `char *` and should point to an array of characters large enough to hold the string and a terminating null character. The input field is terminated by a whitespace character.

%[*scanlist*]

> Matches a nonempty sequence of characters from a set of expected characters called the *scanset*. The corresponding argument should be a pointer of type `char *` and should point to an array of characters large enough to accept the sequence and a terminating null character. The characters between the brackets, called the *scanlist*, comprise the scanset unless the first character after the left bracket is a circumflex (^), in which case the scanset comprises all the characters that do *not* appear in the scanlist. A right bracket in the scanlist must immediately follow the left bracket or the circumflex. You can specify a range of characters by separating the first and last characters in the range with a hyphen; for example, `%[0-9]` matches a string of digits. A hyphen character in the scanlist should be either the first or last character in the list.

%% This specification allows a percent sign to be matched in the input; no argument assignment is performed.

Field widths

As with `printf`, you can use a *field width* to tell `scanf` how wide an expected field should be. This is particularly useful with the `%c` conversion, which can be told how many characters to read in.

Note, however, that field widths used with the `%s` conversion do not work quite as you might expect. Many programmers expect `%12s` to read in the first 12 characters of a string regardless of the string's length. However, this is not the case, because `%s` does not consider anything but whitespace as a field terminator. To obtain the desired behavior, use `%12c` instead. Don't forget that the `%c` does not add a terminating null character.

Instead of a field width, you can use an asterisk character (`*`). However, unlike the asterisk in `printf` (which indicates that the field width should be obtained from a parameter) this asterisk indicates that the field it is attached to should be skipped over in the input rather than assigned to a variable.

Porting Notes

The `printf` and `scanf` functions are generally pretty standard across all platforms, provided that you stick to the conversions described in this chapter. The only exception to this is the `%i` conversion, which is specific to ANSI C. There are a number of other conversion specifications and modifiers that are much less widespread; indeed, the ANSI C standard introduced a number of them itself. These are described in the manual pages for your specific version of UNIX and will not be used in this book. Although they are fine for local programs, those other conversions and modifiers should not be used if portability is an issue.

Repositioning the Read/Write Offset

One of the values the operating system associates with each file is the *read/write offset*, also called the *file offset*. The read/write offset specifies the "distance," measured in bytes from the beginning of the file, at which the next read or write takes place. When a file is first opened or created, the file offset is zero (unless it was opened for appending); the first read or write starts at the beginning of the file. As reads and writes are performed, the offset is incremented by the number of bytes read or written each time. There is only one read/write offset for each file, so a read of 10 bytes followed by a write of 20 bytes leaves the read/write offset at 30.

The *Standard I/O Library* provides three primary functions for manipulating the read/write offset:

```
#include <stdio.h>

int fseek(FILE *stream, long offset, int whence);

void rewind(FILE *stream);

long ftell(FILE *stream);
```

The `fseek` function sets the read/write offset to `offset` bytes from the position in the file specified by `whence`, which can have one of the following values:

SEEK_SET
Set the read/write offset to `offset` bytes from the beginning of the file.

SEEK_CUR
Set the read/write offset to `offset` bytes from the current offset.

SEEK_END
Set the read/write offset to `offset` bytes from the end of the file.

On success, `fseek` returns zero (this is different from `lseek`, described in Chapter 3, which returns the new read/write offset). On failure, the constant EOF is returned. Note that the `offset` is a signed value, so negative seeks are permitted.

To move to the beginning of a file, you can use the following call:

```
fseek(stream, 0, SEEK_SET);
```

You can also use this call:

```
rewind(stream);
```

This call has the side effect of clearing any error condition (described later) on the stream. To move to the end of a file, use this call:

```
fseek(stream, 0, SEEK_END);
```

To obtain the value of the current offset without changing it, use this call:

```
long offset;

offset = ftell(stream);
```

Note that, unlike `lseek`, you cannot use the following call for this purpose, because `fseek` does not return the current offset:

```
offset = fseek(stream, 0, SEEK_CUR);
```

The concept of the end of a file is somewhat fluid—it is perfectly legal to seek past the end of the file and then write data. This creates a "hole" in the file that does not take up any storage space on the disk. However, when reading a file with holes in it, the holes are read as zero-valued bytes. This means that once a file with holes is created, it is impossible to copy it precisely, because all the holes are filled in when the copy takes place. (There are ways around this, but they involve reading the raw disk blocks rather than simply opening the file and reading it directly.)

Example 4-9 shows the *Standard I/O Library* version of the *seeker* program introduced in Chapter 3. The program writes five strings to a file and then prompts for a number between 1 and 5. It seeks to the proper location for the string of that number, reads it from the file, and prints it out.

Example 4-9: seeker

```c
#include <stdlib.h>
#include <stdio.h>

#define NSTRINGS    5
#define STRSIZE     3

char *strings[] = {
    "aaa", "bbb", "ccc", "ddd", "eee"
};

int
main(int argc, char **argv)
{
    int n;
    FILE *fp;
    char *fname;
    char buf[STRSIZE], template[32];

    /*
     * Create a temporary file name.
     */
    strcpy(template, "/tmp/seekerXXXXXX");
    fname = mktemp(template);

    /*
     * Open the file.
     */
    if ((fp = fopen(fname, "w+")) == NULL) {
        perror(fname);
        exit(1);
```

Example 4-9: seeker (continued)

```
    }

    /*
     * Write strings to the file.
     */
    for (n = 0; n < NSTRINGS; n++)
        fwrite(strings[n], sizeof(char), STRSIZE, fp);

    /*
     * Until the user quits, prompt for a string and retrieve
     * it from the file.
     */
    for (;;) {
        /*
         * Prompt for a string number.
         */
        printf("Which string (0 to quit)? ");
        scanf("%d", &n);

        if (n == 0) {
            fclose(fp);
            exit(0);
        }

        if (n < 0 || n > NSTRINGS) {
            fprintf(stderr, "Out of range.\n");
            continue;
        }

        /*
         * Find the string and read it.
         */
        fseek(fp, (n-1) * STRSIZE, SEEK_SET);
        fread(buf, sizeof(char), STRSIZE, fp);

        /*
         * Print it out.
         */
        printf("String %d = %.*s\n\n", n, STRSIZE, buf);
    }
}
```

```
% seeker
Which string (0 to quit)? 1
String 1 = aaa

Which string (0 to quit)? 5
String 5 = eee

Which string (0 to quit)? 3
String 3 = ccc
```

```
Which string (0 to quit)? 4
String 4 = ddd

Which string (0 to quit)? 2
String 2 = bbb

Which string (0 to quit)? 0
```

Compare this version of *seeker* with the one in Chapter 3 and note how much less work this version has to do to print the prompts and results. This demonstrates one of the principal benefits of using the *Standard I/O Library*.

The ANSI C standard specifies two additional functions for manipulating the read/write offset:

```
#include <stdio.h>

int fsetpos(FILE *stream, const fpos_t *pos);

int fgetpos(FILE *stream, fpos_t *pos);
```

The `fgetpos` function stores the current read/write offset for `stream` into the object pointed to by `pos`. The `fsetpos` function sets the current read/write offset to the value of the object pointed to by `pos`, which should be a value returned by a call to `fgetpos` on the same stream. If successful, both functions return zero; otherwise, they return non-zero.

These two functions allow a program to save its place in a file so it can return to it later. However, they are new to ANSI C, and are therefore not portable to non-ANSI C environments. Fortunately, their behavior is easily duplicated using `ftell` and `fseek`.

Reassigning a File Pointer

Sometimes it is necessary to change the file that is associated with a specific file pointer. This is most often done with the pre-defined file pointers: `stdin`, `stdout`, and `stderr`. The function that does it is called `freopen`:

```
#include <stdio.h>

FILE *freopen(const char *filename, const char *type, FILE *stream);
```

The `filename` argument contains the path to the new file, and `type` indicates how the new file should be opened, as described earlier for `fopen`. The original file that `stream` referred to is closed. If `freopen` succeeds, it returns `stream`; if it fails, it returns the constant `NULL`.

Buffering

As mentioned previously, the *Standard I/O Library* buffers I/O internally. There are a number of quirks to the way things get buffered, which causes some inconsistencies. The quirks exist in an attempt to make the library "do the right thing" under all circumstances:

- Disk files, both for reading and writing, are buffered in large chunks (usually 1,024 bytes or more).

- The `stdout` stream is line-buffered if it refers to a terminal device; otherwise, it is buffered like a disk file. Therefore, when `stdout` refers to a terminal, the buffer is flushed each time a newline character is printed.

- The `stderr` stream is completely unbuffered (except on some BSD-based systems, where it is line-buffered). This causes writes to `stderr` to appear immediately. This is necessary to allow errors to show up even when a program fails and dumps core. If the writes were buffered, they would not be flushed before the program was terminated.

- If the `stdin` stream refers to a terminal device, the `stdout` stream is flushed automatically whenever a read from `stdin` is performed. This allows prompts (which typically do not contain newline characters) to appear.

- A call to `fseek` or `rewind` flushes any write buffers that contain outstanding data.

Usually, the library does what is expected (the "principle of least surprise"). However, there are situations in which the library's default behavior is not good enough. Thus, a number of routines are provided for overriding the library's buffering decisions:

```
#include <stdio.h>

int fflush(FILE *stream);

void setbuf(FILE *stream, char *buf);

void setvbuf(FILE *stream, char *buf, int type, size_t size);
```

If `stream` is open for writing, `fflush` causes any buffered data waiting to be written to the file. If `stream` is open for reading, `fflush` causes any unread data in the buffer to be discarded. If `stream` is `NULL`, `fflush` flushes data to disk for all streams that are open for writing.

Use the `setbuf` function after a stream is opened but before it is read or written. It causes the array pointed to by `buf` (which should be of size `BUFSIZ`) to be used instead of an automatically allocated buffer. If `buf` is `NULL`, the stream is completely unbuffered.

Use the `setvbuf` function after a stream is opened but before it is read or written. The `type` argument indicates how `stream` is buffered, using the following values:

`_IOFBF`
> Fully buffers I/O.

`_IOLBF`
> Line buffers output. The output is flushed when a newline is written, the buffer is full, or input is requested.

`_IONBF`
> Completely unbuffers I/O.

If `buf` is not `NULL`, the array it points to is used for buffering instead of an automatically allocated buffer. In this case, `size` specifies the size of `buf` in bytes.

Porting Notes

BSD UNIX provides two other buffering functions, `setbuffer` and `setlinebuf`. The `setbuffer` function is like `setbuf`, except that it also allows the size of the buffer to be specfied. You can replace it with the following call:

```
setvbuf(stream, buf, _IOFBF, sizeof(buf));
```

The `setlinebuf` function changes a stream to be line-buffered; it can be used any time the stream is active. You can replace it with the following call, which must be made before the stream is read or written:

```
setvbuf(stream, NULL, _IOLBF, 0);
```

Stream Status

The *Standard I/O Library* also provides functions for inquiring about and changing the status of a stream:

```
#include <stdio.h>

int ferror(FILE *stream);

int feof(FILE *stream);

void clearerr(FILE *stream);
```

The `ferror` function returns non-zero when an error occurred while reading from or writing to `stream`; otherwise, it returns zero. The `feof` function returns non-zero when the end-of-file condition was detected while reading from `stream`; otherwise, it returns zero. The `clearerr` function resets the error and end-of-file indicators on `stream`.

One of the most common errors made with the *Standard I/O Library* is to read from a terminal device (usually `stdin`) and allow the user to indicate an end-of-file with CTRL-D (programs such as *mail* do this). If the program attempts to read from the terminal again, the second read immediately fails, because the end-of-file condition was already detected on the stream. The proper way to implement this is to call `clearerr` on the stream immediately after detecting end-of-file.

This error is especially common when porting older programs to newer systems, because the library used to automatically clear the end-of-file condition on `stdin` if it referred to a terminal device. This behavior was changed several years ago to make things more consistent. Fortunately, it's easy to detect the problem—if the program goes into an infinite loop of reprinting the prompt after you type CTRL-D, you need to add a call to `clearerr`.

File Pointers and File Descriptors

There are two functions provided for "translating" between file pointers and file descriptors:

```
#include <stdio.h>

int fileno(FILE *stream);

FILE *fdopen(int fd, const char *type);
```

The `fileno` function returns the file descriptor associated with `stream`. This is useful for performing specialized I/O operations on files with which the *Standard I/O Library* is being used (these operations are described in later chapters).

The `fdopen` function allows a low-level file descriptor to be converted to a file pointer so that the library's buffering and formatting features can be used. The file descriptor is given in `fd`; `type` indicates how the stream should be opened. Note that `type` must match how the file descriptor was originally opened; for example, it won't work to specify a `type` of `w` if the file descriptor is only open for reading.

Chapter Summary

This chapter examined how to open, close, and create files using the *Standard I/O Library*. It also discussed how to perform both unformatted and formatted I/O on those files. We have seen how the library handles the tasks of I/O buffering, I/O conversion, and I/O formatting for us, saving us the trouble of doing these things ourselves. Input and output are the two most important things a program can do—without them, computers wouldn't be good for much more than heating up the room.

5

Files and Directories

Chapter 3, *Low-Level I/O Routines*, and Chapter 4, *The Standard I/O Library*, explained how to open and create files, and how to transfer data between a program and a file. For many types of application programs, this is all there is to it. But for systems programming, there are a number of other tasks that may be necessary, such as discovering the contents of directories, changing the ownership and permission bits of files, determining the last modification time of a file, figuring out whether a user has the permissions necessary to access a file, and so forth. These topics are the subject of this chapter.

Filesystem Concepts

A *filesystem* is the set of data types, data structures, and system calls used by an operating system to store data onto one or more disk drives. The simplest form of a filesystem, called a *flat filesystem*, is analogous to the "cardboard box" filing system used by some people to keep track of their bills for tax purposes. In the cardboard box method, each bill is simply tossed into a box, with more recent additions being placed on top of earlier ones. There is no sense of order within the box; mortgage bills, credit card bills, and utility bills are all intermixed in a random fashion. The only way to impose any type of order is to use multiple boxes: one for mortgage bills, one for credit card bills, and one for utility bills. A flat filesystem treats the disk like a cardboard box. Each file created in the filesystem is like a bill—it is simply created in an empty place on the disk, with no particular organization. Listing all the files is like dumping the cardboard box on the floor: system files, homework files, correspondence files, program files, and so forth are all mixed together. The only way to impose any type of order on a flat filesystem is to use multiple disks: one for system files, one for homework files, one for correspondence files, and so on.

A flat filesystem is easy to implement. It doesn't require very much computation to figure out where a file is located or where the next file should be stored. It doesn't require very much memory to keep track of the filesystem bookkeeping. In the early days of computers, both of these characteristics were very important: most systems were capable of processing tens of thousands of instructions per second, and usually had memory sizes measured in the tens or perhaps hundreds of Kbytes. Hard disks, which were very expensive, usually held a few Mbytes. Because the disks were not that large, it was not much of a problem to keep separate disks for each group of files, much like keeping separate cardboard boxes for each group of receipts.

Depending on your age, you will recognize the previous paragraph as a description of either the first personal computers of the early 1980s or the first minicomputers of the early 1970s. In either case, later systems had increased processing power, larger memories, and larger disks. This not only made more complex filesystems possible, but also necessary. As disks became larger, the number of files they could store also increased. A flat filesystem was fine for storing a few dozen (or even a hundred or so) files. But now that disks were capable of storing many thousands of files, flat filesystems became too difficult for humans to use.

The operating system designers of the day recognized this, and in response, developed a new tool called a *hierarchical filesystem*. A hierarchical filesystem is analogous to the "file cabinet" method of filing. In this method, each drawer of the file cabinet is used to hold a different category of files. For example, one drawer is used to store bills, another to store correspondence, and so on. Within each drawer are a number of hanging folders to futher subdivide the files: one for credit card bills, one for bank statements, one for utility bills, and so forth. Within each hanging folder, manila folders are used to further subdivide the bills; there is a folder for the gas company, a folder for the water company, and a folder for the telephone company. The hierarchical filesystem duplicates this structure by using *directories* to represent the file cabinet drawers and *subdirectories* to represent the hanging folders and manila folders. Each directory or subdirectory contains other files and subdirectories, allowing a user to organize his data to his heart's content.

The UNIX Filesystem

UNIX was not the first operating system to use a hierarchical filesystem, nor is it the last. Almost every modern operating system has some type of hierarchical filesystem.

When it was first developed, the UNIX filesystem was different from other filesystems of the day, however. Unlike most systems, in which hardware devices were accessed by using their own special abstractions, UNIX folded everything into the filesystem. Instead of using a special set of system calls to print a file on a printer or write data on a tape drive, the UNIX programmer could access these devices simply by opening a file and then writing data to it. The centrality of the filesystem is one of the things that has made UNIX one of the most popular operating systems in the world.

The remainder of this section discusses the different types of objects provided by the UNIX filesystem.

Basic File Types

There are three basic file types in the UNIX filesystem: *regular files*, *special files*, and *directories*.

Regular files

The simplest object in the filesystem is a regular file. This object can contain whatever data the user chooses to place there; the operating system does not interpret it in any way. Unlike some other operating systems, which have several different types of files such as sequential, random access, fixed-length records, and so on, UNIX does not impose any format on a regular file at all. Instead, the file is simply interpreted as a string of bytes, and these bytes may be read and written in any way the user chooses. Certain programs, of course, expect this string of bytes to have a specific format. For example, the assembler generates an object file that must be in a particular format (header, followed by executable code, followed by initialized data) to be understood by the linker. But these formats are imposed by user-level programs, not the operating system. As far as UNIX is concerned, there is no difference whatsoever between a program's source code, its object code, its input, and its output. They're all just regular files, each of which contains a string of bytes.

Special files

Special files, also called device files, are one of the most unusual aspects of the UNIX filesystem. Each I/O device connected to the computer system (disk drive, tape drive, serial port, printer, and so on) is associated with at least one such file. To access a device, a program opens the special file associated with the device and then reads data from or writes data to the device as if it were a regular file. The difference between special files and regular files is that when reads and writes are performed on special files, the devices connected to the computer system do things. For example, reading from the special file associated with a tape drive causes the tape to spin, the drive to transfer data from the tape and into the computer's memory, and so forth. Writing to the special file associated with a printer causes the print head to move, the hammers to strike the ribbon, and letters to appear on the page.

There are two types of special files: *character-special* files, also called "raw" devices, and *block-special* files. The character-special file is the most like a regular file, because it simply transfers data between a program and a device in whatever units the program cares to use. For example, if a program reads one character at a time from the character-special file associated with a tape drive, the tape drive literally transfers a character at a time to the computer. If the program writes in blocks of several sizes to the tape drive, then the tape contains an assortment of different block sizes. A block-special file, on the other hand, is buffered by the operating system. If a program reads one character at a time from the block-special file associated with a tape drive, the operating system tells the tape drive to transfer a block of data (usually some multiple of 512 bytes) to memory and then satisfies the program's read request from this buffer. After the program reads enough data to exhaust the buffer, another buffer is requested from the tape drive. Similarly, if a program writes in several different quantities to the tape drive, the operating system buffers that data, resulting in a tape with a uniform block size.

Directories

Directories provide the mapping between the names of files and the files themselves, thus imposing a structure on the filesystem as a whole. A directory contains some number of files, and it can also contain other directories. You can open and read a directory just like any other file; it is simply a stream of bytes with a meaningful format. However, a program cannot open a directory for writing, because all writes to a directory are handled by the operating system itself.

The operating system maintains one special directory for each filesystem, called the *root* directory. This directory serves as the root of the filesystem hierarchy.

Every other file or directory in the filesystem is subordinate to the root directory. Any file in the filesystem can be located by specifying a path through a chain of directories starting at the root.

Each file in the filesystem is identified by a *pathname*, which is a sequence of filenames separated by slash (/) characters, for example, */dir/subdir/file*. All names in a pathname, except for the one following the last slash character, must be directories. If the pathname begins with a slash character, it is called an *absolute pathname* and specifies the path to the file beginning from the root directory. If the pathname does not begin with a slash character, it is called a *relative pathname* and specifies the path to the file from the program's current working directory (see below). As limiting cases, the pathname / refers to the root directory, and a null filename (for example, */a/b/*) refers to the directory whose name precedes the last slash. Multiple slashes (///) are interpreted as a single slash.

A directory always has two entries, named . (dot) and .. (dotdot). The special name . in a directory refers to the directory itself; this enables a program to open its current working directory for reading, without knowing its pathname, by opening the . file. The special name .. refers to the parent directory of the directory in which it appears; that is, the directory one level up in the hierarchy. A program can move from its current directory, regardless of where it is located in the hierarchy, to the root directory by repeatedly changing to the directory .. until the root directory is reached. As a limiting case, in the root directory the .. name is a circular link.

Removable Filesystems

In its simplest case, the filesystem is a single directory hierarchy contained on a single storage device. There is a single root directory, and under that directory are files and directories. These directories in turn contain more files and directories, and so on. What happens, though, when the storage device runs out of room, and more storage space must be added to the system? Since a filesystem is a single directory hierarchy on a single device, does this mean that the existing disk must be replaced with a larger one, and that no filesystem can be larger than the largest capacity disk currently manufactured?

Fortunately, no. To explain this requires that you use the term *filesystem* to describe two different things. The first definition is that a filesystem is the directory hierarchy that exists on a single storage device, composed of a root directory, files, and subdirectories, as described in the previous paragraph. The second definition is a recursive one: a filesystem is a directory hierarchy composed of a root directory, files, subdirectories, and *other filesystems*. This second definition is achieved by telling the operating system that whenever a reference is made to a specific directory, the system should move its frame of reference from the directory hierarchy stored on the first disk to the hierarchy stored on some other disk.

This is best explained by an example. Suppose that you have a single disk on your system, and it contains the entirety of the UNIX filesystem: /, /etc, /usr, and so forth. Assume that users' home directories, in which they keep all their personal files, are stored in the directory /home, with names such as /home/joe, /home/mary, and so on. Now suppose that your disk is running out of space, and you just purchased a second disk. You would like to leave the system files on the first disk, but move all the user files to the new disk. There are four steps to this process:

1. You use the *newfs* command to create a filesystem on the new disk. This process involves initializing a number of new data structures on the disk and creating a root directory to serve as the base of the directory hierarchy. For a discussion of the data structures that are actually placed on the disk in this step, see Appendix B, *Accessing Filesystem Data Structures*.

2. You use the *mount* command to *mount* the new directory hierarchy into the filesystem, using the /mnt directory as a *mount point*. The mounting process tells the operating system that whenever a reference is made to a file whose pathname from the root includes the directory /mnt, the system should look in the directory hierarchy stored on the second disk. The process of mounting a filesystem hierarchy on /mnt causes any previous contents of /mnt to be hidden until the filesystem is again unmounted.

3. Using any of a variety of tools, you copy the contents of the /home directory (on the old disk) to the /mnt directory (on the new disk). Then you delete the contents of the /home directory, removing the data from the old disk.

4. Finally, you unmount the new disk's filesystem from /mnt and mount it on /home instead. Now, whenever a file whose absolute pathname contains the /home directory is referenced, the operating system knows to look for the file on the new disk, instead of the old one.

The filesystem hierarchy created on the second disk is called a *removable filesystem*. It can be mounted or unmounted, and the system will still operate correctly. However, the files in /home are accessible only when the hierarchy is mounted. Otherwise, /home is just an empty directory. It doesn't have to be empty, but it makes little sense to store things there, because they are inaccessible whenever the /home filesystem is mounted.

Filesystems can be mounted on directories at any level in the filesystem hierarchy. For example, you could have mounted the new disk on */home/mary*. In this case, Joe's home directory (*/home/joe*) is stored on the old disk, but Mary's home directory (*/home/mary*) is stored on the new disk. You can also nest mounts; for example, you could have one filesystem mounted on */home*, and another filesystem mounted on */home/mary*. To do this, you must mount the filesystems in a particular order: mounting the */home/mary* disk before the */home* disk does not produce the desired result.

Device Numbers

Each special file in the filesystem has two *device numbers* associated with it. The *major device number* tells the operating system which device driver to use when the device is referenced. For example, a disk drive might have major device number 23, and a tape drive might have major device number 47. Whenever a reference is made to a file on the disk, the operating system looks up number 23 in a table and then uses the disk device driver to access the requested data. The *minor device number* is passed to the device driver. This number tells the device driver which physical device to use in the case of a driver that handles multiple devices, or how to access a device, in the case of devices like tape drives that support multiple densities. Several devices (such as all of the disks connected to the system) can have the same major device number, since they are all accessed with the same device driver, but they each need a different minor device number.

I-numbers, the I-list, and I-nodes

As mentioned earlier, directories provide the mapping between the names of files and the files themselves. Each directory file contains a series of structures that perform this mapping. Each structure contains the name of a file and a pointer to the file itself. The pointer is in the form of an integer called an *i-number* (for index number). When a file is accessed, the i-number is used as an index into a system table (the *i-list*) where the entry for the file (the *i-node*) is stored. The i-node contains all the information about a file:

- The user ID and group ID of the file's owner
- The protection bits for the file, specifying who can access it and in what modes
- The physical disk addresses of the data blocks that contain the file's contents

- The size of the file, in bytes

- The last time the file was modified (written), and the last time the file was accessed (read)

- The last time the file's i-node was changed (for example, the last time the permission bits were changed)

- A tag indicating the file's type (regular file, directory, character special file, and so on)

One piece of information about a file is not stored in the i-node: the file's name. This information is stored in the directory file for the directory that contains the file, and nowhere else.

The operating system maintains a separate i-list for each mounted filesystem. I-numbers are unique within each removable filesystem, but when several filesystems are mounted, the i-number alone is not enough to distinguish a file uniquely.

Recall that each special file has two device numbers associated with it: a major device number and a minor device number. Because a filesystem is associated with a disk drive, it is also associated with a special file. Each disk drive is unique, so it must have a unique major and minor device number pair. Therefore, you can use three numbers (major device number, minor device number, i-number) to uniquely specify each file in the overall filesystem.

Other File Types

There are several other file types available in the UNIX filesystem besides the three basic types already presented.

Hard links

It is possible to have more than one name refer to the same file by making a *hard link* to that file. The link is created by making a new entry in a directory file with the new name and the i-number for the file. There can be any number of links to the same file; every link has a different name, but the same i-number. However, because a hard link only uses the i-number of the file, it is impossible to make a hard link across two filesystems. Hard links must all reside on the same filesystem. It is possible, though, for the links to reside in different directories on that filesystem.

Symbolic links

In 4.2BSD, a new type of file, called a *symbolic link*, was introduced to solve the problem of linking across filesystem boundaries. A symbolic link is a special file type that contains the pathname of the file to which the link points. The pathname can either be an absolute pathname, in which case the link's target is located from the root of the filesystem, or a relative pathname, in which case the link's target is located relative to the directory that contains the link's source. Because i-numbers are not involved in symbolic links, they can be used to make links across filesystem boundaries.

FIFOs

A *FIFO* (first-in, first-out), also called a named pipe, is a special type of file used for interprocess communication. A program creates a FIFO in the filesystem using a special library routine. After the FIFO is created, other processes can open it, read from it, and write to it just as if it were a regular file. However, whenever a read is performed, the data is transferred from the process owning the FIFO, not from the disk. Whenever a write is performed, the data are transferred to the process owning the FIFO, not to the disk. When the process that created the FIFO exits, the FIFO can no longer be opened or used. However, it remains as an entry in the filesystem until it is explicitly removed. FIFOs were introduced in System V UNIX and are often not available in BSD-derived systems.

UNIX-domain sockets

A *UNIX-domain socket* serves more or less the same function as a FIFO, in that it is created by a process and results in an entry in the filesystem. After the socket is created, other programs can communicate with the process that created the socket. However, unlike a FIFO, which preserves the open/read/write conventions of regular files, UNIX-domain sockets require a special set of system calls (the same set of system calls used for intermachine communication over Internet-domain sockets). UNIX-domain sockets were introduced in BSD UNIX and are often not available in System V-derived systems.

Obtaining File Attributes

Something that systems-level programs need to do quite often is obtain information about files. For example, it's important to make sure that files are owned by the right user, that they have the right permission bits, and so forth. This is discussed further in the section on writing set-user-id programs in Chapter 8, *Users and Groups*.

Getting Information from an I-node

As mentioned earlier, all of the information about a file, except its name, is contained in an on-disk structure called an *i-node*. You can use three system calls to obtain this information:

```
#include <sys/types.h>
#include <sys/stat.h>

int stat(const char *path, struct stat *st);

int lstat(const char *path, struct stat *st);

int fstat(int fd, struct stat *st);
```

The `stat` function is the most commonly used of the three. It obtains the information about the file whose name is given by `path` and places the data into the variable pointed to by `st`, which should be of type `struct stat`. The `lstat` function is identical to `stat`, *except* when the last component of the pathname is a symbolic link. In that case, `stat` returns information about the file to which the link points, while `lstat` returns information about the link itself. The `fstat` variant, rather than taking the name of a file, takes a file descriptor to an open file and returns information about that file.

In all cases, the file being asked about does not have to have any special permissions; that is, it is possible to obtain information about an unreadable file or an unwritable file. However, the file must be accessible to the calling program. All directories along the pathname contained in `path` must have the appropriate search permissions set. This is discussed in more detail later in this chapter. If `stat`, `lstat`, or `fstat` succeed, a value of zero is returned. If an error occurs, -1 is returned and an error code describing the reason for failure is placed in the external variable `errno`.

The `struct stat` data type is declared in the include file *sys/stat.h*. The file *sys/types.h* must also be included, to get the definitions of a number of basic operating system data types. The structure includes at least the following members:

```
struct stat {
    dev_t       st_dev;
    ino_t       st_ino;
    mode_t      st_mode;
    nlink_t     st_nlink;
    uid_t       st_uid;
    gid_t       st_gid;
    dev_t       st_rdev;
    off_t       st_size;
    time_t      st_atime;
    time_t      st_mtime;
    time_t      st_ctime;
```

```
        long        st_blksize;
        long        st_blocks;
};
```

The elements of the structure are interpreted as:

st_dev

> The major and minor device numbers of the device on which the i-node asso-
> ciated with this file (and therefore the file itself) is stored. You can extract the
> major and minor device numbers from this field by using the `major` and
> `minor` macros, which are defined in *sys/mkdev.h* in Solaris 2.*x* and IRIX 5.*x*,
> and in *sys/sysmacros.h* in HP-UX 10.*x*.

st_ino

> The i-node number of the file. The root directory of a filesystem always has i-
> node number 2, and the special directory *lost+found* in each filesystem always
> has i-node number 3. For historical reasons, i-node number 1 is never used.
> All other files in the filesystem have i-node numbers greater than 3; they are
> usually allocated in a lowest-available-number fashion.

st_mode

> A set of bits encoding the file's type and access permissions; see the explana-
> tion following this list for how to interpret this data.

st_nlink

> The number of links (filenames) associated with the file. A just-created file
> has the value 1 in this field, and the field is incremented by 1 for every hard
> link made to it. Symbolic links to the file are not counted here (nor anywhere
> else).

st_uid

> The user ID of the user owning the file.

st_gid

> The group ID of the group owning the file.

st_rdev

> If the file is a character-special or block-special device file, this field contains
> the major and minor device numbers of the file (as opposed to `st_dev`,
> which contains the major and minor device numbers of the device on which
> the file is stored). If the file is not a character-special or block-special device
> file, the contents of this field are meaningless.

st_size

> The size of the file, in bytes.

st_atime

> The last time the file was accessed for reading, or, in the case of an executable program, the last time the file was executed, stored in UNIX time format (see Chapter 7, *Time of Day Operations*).

st_mtime

> The last time the file was modified (written).

st_ctime

> The last time the i-node was changed. This time is updated whenever the file's owner, group, or permission bits are changed. It is also updated whenever the file's modification time is changed, but *not* when the file's access time is changed. Note that, contrary to popular belief (and contrary to many UNIX programming books), this field does *not* represent the time the file was created. File creation time is not recorded anywhere in the filesystem.

st_blksize

> A hint to programs about the best buffer size to use for I/O operations on this file. Generally speaking, it is most efficient to perform I/O with the same block size that is used by the filesystem itself (that way, the filesystem does not have to copy data between multiple buffers); this field allows programs that care to obtain this information. This field is undefined for character- and block-special device files.

st_blocks

> The total number of physical blocks, 512 bytes each, actually allocated on the disk for this file. Note that this number can be much smaller than (st_size / 512) if there are holes in the file.

The st_mode field mentioned previously is important, because it encodes both the file's type and its permission bits. These can be extracted using a number of constants defined in *sys/stat.h*:

S_IFMT

> This constant extracts the file type bits from the st_mode word; st_mode should be *and*ed with this and then compared against the following constants:
>
> S_IFREG
> > Regular file

S_IFDIR

    Directory

S_IFCHR

    Character-special device file

S_IFBLK

    Block-special device file

S_IFLNK

    Symbolic link

S_IFIFO

    FIFO file

S_IFSOCK

    UNIX-domain socket

Newer, POSIX-compliant systems also define a set of macros that you can use to determine file type:

S_ISREG(st_mode)

    If true, the file is a regular file.

S_ISDIR(st_mode)

    If true, the file is a directory.

S_ISCHR(st_mode)

    If true, the file is a character-special device file.

S_ISBLK(st_mode)

    If true, the file is a block-special device file.

S_ISLNK(st_mode)

    If true, the file is a symbolic link.

S_ISFIFO(st_mode)

    If true, the file is a FIFO file.

S_ISSOCK(st_mode)

    If true, the file is a UNIX-domain socket.

S_ISUID

    If the result of *and*ing this constant with st_mode is non-zero, the file has the set-user-id-on-execution bit set (see below).

S_ISGID

    If the result of *and*ing this constant with st_mode is non-zero, the file has the set-group-id-on-execution bit set (see below).

S_ISVTX

If the result of *and*ing this constant with `st_mode` is non-zero, the file has the "sticky bit" set (see below).

S_IREAD

By *and*ing this constant with `st_mode`, you can determine if the owner of the file has read permission. By right-shifting the constant three places (or left-shifting `st_mode` three places) and *and*ing the two, you can determine if the group owner of the file has read permission. And by right-shifting the constant six places (or left-shifting `st_mode` six places) and *and*ing, you can determine if the rest of the world has read permission. Newer, POSIX-compliant systems define three constants that you can use in place of shifting:

S_IRUSR

If the result of *and*ing this contant with `st_mode` is non-zero, the owner has read permission for the file.

S_IRGRP

If the result of *and*ing this constant with `st_mode` is non-zero, the group owner has read permission for the file.

S_IROTH

If the result of *and*ing this constant with `st_mode` is non-zero, the world (everyone except the owner and group owner) has read permission for the file.

S_IWRITE

By *and*ing this constant with `st_mode`, you can determine if the owner of the file has write permission. By right-shifting the constant three places (or left-shifting `st_mode` three places) and *and*ing the two, you can determine if the group owner of the file has write permission. By right-shifting the constant six places (or left-shifting `st_mode` six places) and *and*ing, you can determine if the rest of the world has write permission. Newer, POSIX-compliant systems define three constants that you can use in place of shifting:

S_IWUSR

If the result of *and*ing this contant with `st_mode` is non-zero, the owner has write permission for the file.

S_IWGRP

If the result of *and*ing this constant with `st_mode` is non-zero, the group owner has write permission for the file.

S_IWOTH

> If the result of *and*ing this constant with st_mode is non-zero, the world (everyone except the owner and group owner) has write permission for the file.

S_IEXEC

By *and*ing this constant with st_mode, you can determine if the owner of the file has execute permission. By right-shifting the constant three places (or left-shifting st_mode three places) and *and*ing the two, you can determine if the group owner of the file has execute permission. By right-shifting the constant six places (or left-shifting st_mode six places) and *and*ing, you can determine if the rest of the world has execute permission. Newer, POSIX-compliant systems define three constants that you can use in place of shifting:

S_IXUSR

> If the result of *and*ing this contant with st_mode is non-zero, the owner has execute permission for the file.

S_IXGRP

> If the result of *and*ing this constant with st_mode is non-zero, the group owner has execute permission for the file.

S_IXOTH

> If the result of *and*ing this constant with st_mode is non-zero, the world (everyone except the owner and group owner) has execute permission for the file.

Note that the concept of execute permission only makes sense for files. For directories, this bit implies permission to search the directory. You cannot access a file unless the search (execute) bit is set on the directory that contains it. Note also that read permission on a directory only lets you obtain the contents of the directory; it does not let you access them. A file can be accessible even though its parent directory is not readable; likewise, a file can be visible but inaccessible if its parent directory is not searchable.

All of these constants can seem pretty overwhelming, and by now you're probably a little confused about just what it is you're supposed to do with them. To clarify the material presented in this section, Example 5-1 shows a program that uses lstat to obtain and print information about each file named on the command line. This example shows the "old-fashioned way," rather than using the POSIX-defined constants described previously. The POSIX constants, while more convenient, are not portable to older systems, and any code that you are porting to SVR4 is not likely to use them.

Example 5–1: lstat

```
#include <sys/types.h>
#include <sys/stat.h>
#include <sys/mkdev.h>
#include <stdio.h>

char    *typeOfFile(mode_t);
char    *permOfFile(mode_t);
void     outputStatInfo(char *, struct stat *);

int
main(int argc, char **argv)
{
    char *filename;
    struct stat st;

    /*
     * For each file on the command line...
     */
    while (--argc) {
        filename = *++argv;

        /*
         * Find out about it.
         */
        if (lstat(filename, &st) < 0) {
            perror(filename);
            putchar('\n');
            continue;
        }

        /*
         * Print out the information.
         */
        outputStatInfo(filename, &st);
        putchar('\n');
    }

    exit(0);
}

/*
 * outputStatInfo - print out the contents of the stat structure.
 */
void
outputStatInfo(char *filename, struct stat *st)
{
    printf("File Name:          %s\n", filename);
    printf("File Type:          %s\n", typeOfFile(st->st_mode));

    /*
     * If the file is not a device, print its size and optimal
     * i/o unit; otherwise print its major and minor device
```

Example 5-1: lstat (continued)

```
     * numbers.
     */
    if (((st->st_mode & S_IFMT) != S_IFCHR) &&
        ((st->st_mode & S_IFMT) != S_IFBLK)) {
        printf("File Size:           %d bytes, %d blocks\n", st->st_size,
               st->st_blocks);
        printf("Optimum I/O Unit:    %d bytes\n", st->st_blksize);
    }
    else {
        printf("Device Numbers:      Major: %u   Minor: %u\n",
               major(st->st_rdev), minor(st->st_rdev));
    }

    /*
     * Print the permission bits in both "ls" format and
     * octal.
     */
    printf("Permission Bits:     %s (%04o)\n", permOfFile(st->st_mode),
           st->st_mode & 07777);

    printf("Inode Number:        %u\n", st->st_ino);
    printf("Owner User-Id:       %d\n", st->st_uid);
    printf("Owner Group-Id:      %d\n", st->st_gid);
    printf("Link Count:          %d\n", st->st_nlink);

    /*
     * Print the major and minor device numbers of the
     * file system that contains the file.
     */
    printf("File System Device: Major: %u   Minor: %u\n",
           major(st->st_dev), minor(st->st_dev));

    /*
     * Print the access, modification, and change times.
     * The ctime() function converts the time to a human-
     * readable format; it is described in Chapter 7,
     * "Time of Day Operations."
     */
    printf("Last Access:        %s", ctime(&st->st_atime));
    printf("Last Modification:  %s", ctime(&st->st_mtime));
    printf("Last I-Node Change: %s", ctime(&st->st_ctime));
}

/*
 * typeOfFile - return the letter indicating the file type.
 */
char *
typeOfFile(mode_t mode)
{
    switch (mode & S_IFMT) {
    case S_IFREG:
        return("regular file");
```

Example 5-1: lstat (continued)

```
    case S_IFDIR:
        return("directory");
    case S_IFCHR:
        return("character-special device");
    case S_IFBLK:
        return("block-special device");
    case S_IFLNK:
        return("symbolic link");
    case S_IFIFO:
        return("FIFO");
    case S_IFSOCK:
        return("UNIX-domain socket");
    }

    return("???");
}

/*
 * permOfFile - return the file permissions in an "ls"-like string.
 */
char *
permOfFile(mode_t mode)
{
    int i;
    char *p;
    static char perms[10];

    p = perms;
    strcpy(perms, "---------");

    /*
     * The permission bits are three sets of three
     * bits: user read/write/exec, group read/write/exec,
     * other read/write/exec.  We deal with each set
     * of three bits in one pass through the loop.
     */
    for (i=0; i < 3; i++) {
        if (mode & (S_IREAD >> i*3))
            *p = 'r';
        p++;

        if (mode & (S_IWRITE >> i*3))
            *p = 'w';
        p++;

        if (mode & (S_IEXEC >> i*3))
            *p = 'x';
        p++;
    }

    /*
     * Put special codes in for set-user-id, set-group-id,
```

Example 5-1: lstat (continued)

```
     * and the sticky bit.  (This part is incomplete; "ls"
     * uses some other letters as well for cases such as
     * set-user-id bit without execute bit, and so forth.)
     */
    if ((mode & S_ISUID) != 0)
        perms[2] = 's';

    if ((mode & S_ISGID) != 0)
        perms[5] = 's';

    if ((mode & S_ISVTX) != 0)
        perms[8] = 't';

    return(perms);
}
```

```
% lstat lstat.c
File Name:         lstat.c
File Type:         regular file
File Size:         3571 bytes, 8 blocks
Optimum I/O Unit:  8192 bytes
Permission Bits:   rw-r----- (0640)
Inode Number:      21558
Owner User-Id:     40
Owner Group-Id:    1
Link Count:        1
Filesystem Device: Major: 32    Minor: 31
Last Access:       Sun Feb 13 13:54:18 1994
Last Modification: Sun Feb 13 13:54:15 1994
Last I-Node Change: Sun Feb 13 13:54:15 1994
```

The results that you get from running *lstat* on your version of *lstat.c* can vary a little from the example; the i-node number, owner and group, filesystem device numbers, and of course the times can be different. You should experiment with running *lstat* on a number of different files on your system, to be sure you understand what it does.

Getting Information from a Symbolic Link

To find out what a symbolic link points to, use the `readlink` function:

```
#include <unistd.h>

int readlink(const char *path, void *buf, size_t bufsiz);
```

The contents of the symbolic link named by `path` are placed into the buffer `buf`, whose size is given by `bufsiz`. The contents are *not* null-terminated when they are returned. If `readlink` succeeds, the number of bytes placed in `buf` are returned; otherwise, -1 is returned and an error code is placed in the external variable `errno`.

Sometimes, it is desirable to convert a pathname that may contain symbolic links into one that is known not to contain any symbolic links. One good reason for wanting to do this is that because symbolic links can cross filesystems, the concept of the parent directory is a bit confusing. For example, on Solaris 2.*x* systems, */bin* is a symbolic link to */usr/bin*. Try executing the following commands:

```
% cd /bin
% cd ..
% pwd
```

The parent directory of */bin* is */*, so you would expect the output from *pwd* to be */*. However, because */bin* is actually a symbolic link to */usr/bin*, the parent directory is actually */usr*, which is what *pwd* tells you.

To obtain a path that contains no symbolic links from one that may or may not contain symbolic links, SVR4 provides a function called `realpath`:

```
#include <stdlib.h>

char *realpath(const char *filename, char *resolvedname);
```

If no error occurs while processing the pathname in `filename`, the "real" path is placed in `resolvedname` and a pointer to it is returned. If an error occurs, the constant `NULL` is returned, and `resolvedname` contains the name of the pathname component that produced the error.

The `realpath` function is not available in HP-UX 10.*x*.

Determining the Accessibility of a File

Determining the accessibilty of a file can be a tricky proposition. Certainly, the `stat` function can tell you the permission bits on a file, but that is not the same thing as telling you whether a file can actually be read (or written, or executed) by a user. For example, consider a world-readable file (mode 0444, or `r--r--r--`) that is in a directory that is searchable only by its owner (mode 0700, or `rwx------`). The owner can read the file, but another user cannot. Even though the file has read permission for her, the directory that contains the file does not have access permission for her, so she cannot reach the file to open it. Thus, to properly test whether or not a file is accessible, you must check the complete path to the file from the root of the filesystem, one directory at a time. This requires some non-trivial programming to handle all the special cases.

Fortunately, the designers of UNIX foresaw this problem, and they created a function called `access`:

```
#include <unistd.h>

int access(const char *path, int amode);
```

The `path` parameter contains the pathname of the file whose access is to be checked, and `amode` contains some combination of the following constants, *ored* together:

R_OK
> Test for read permission.

W_OK
> Test for write permission.

X_OK
> Test for execute (search) permission.

F_OK
> Test for existence of file.

If the user running the program has the access permissions in question, `access` returns zero. If the user does not have the proper access permissions, -1 is returned and `errno` is set to indicate the reason why. Note that `access` works properly even when called from a set-user-id or set-group-id program (see Chapter 8), because it uses the real user ID and group ID to make its checks, not the effective user ID and group ID.

Changing File Attributes

Most of a file's attributes can be changed, and this is something that systems programs do quite often. This section describes how to change each of the following attributes: permissions, owner, group, size, access time, and modification time. In the next section, you will learn how to change one other attribute, the number of links.

Changing a File's Permission Bits

Each file or directory has three sets of permissions associated with it; one set for the user who owns the file, one set for the users in the group with which the file is associated (the *group owner* of the file), and one set for all other users (the *world* permissions). Each set of permissions contains three identical permission bits that control the following:

read

> If set, the file or directory can be read. In the case of a directory, read permission allows a user to see the contents of the directory (the names of the files it contains), but not to access them.

write

> If set, the file or directory can be written (modified). In the case of a directory, write permission implies the ability to create, delete, and rename files. Note that the ability to delete a file is *not* controlled by the file's permission bits, but rather by the permission bits on the directory containing the file.

execute

> If set, the file or directory can be executed (searched). In the case of a file, execute permission implies the ability to run the program contained in that file. Executing compiled (binary) programs requires only execute permission on the file, while executing shell scripts requires both read and execute permission, because the shell must be able to read commands from the file. In the case of a directory, execute permission implies permission to search the directory; that is, permission to access the files contained therein. Note that access to files is *not* controlled by read permission on the directory (read permission controls whether the files are visible, not accessible).

In addition, there is a fourth set of three bits that indicate special features associated with the file:

set-user-id

> If set, this bit controls the set user ID status of a file. Set user ID status means that when a program is executed, it executes with the permissions of the user who owns the program, in addition to the permissions of the user running the program. For example, the *sendmail* command is usually set user ID root, because it has to be able to write in the mail spool directory, which ordinary users are not allowed to do. This bit is meaningless on non-executable files and on directories.

set-group-id

> If set on an executable file, this bit controls the set group ID status of a file. This behaves in exactly the same way as the set-user-id bit, except that the program operates with the permissions of the group associated with the file. On directories, it controls how the group associated with a file is determined. If set, the group associated with a newly created file is the same as the group associated with the directory. If not set, the group associated with a newly created file is the user's primary group ID. If this bit is set on a file and the group execute bit is *not* set on that file, then manadatory file and record locks are enabled on that file (see Chapter 6, *Special-Purpose File Operations*).

sticky

> If set, the sticky bit originally told the operating system to keep the text segment of an executable file on the swap disk, so that the program could start more quickly. This use has been mostly discarded now that UNIX is a paging system instead of a swapping system. Now, the sticky bit is used on directories. If a directory is writable and has the sticky bit set, files in that directory can be removed or renamed only if one or more of the following conditions are true:
>
> - The user owns the file he is trying to rename or remove.
>
> - The user owns the directory itself.
>
> - The file is writable by the user (this condition is not checked by all versions of UNIX).
>
> - The user is the superuser.
>
> SunOS 4.*x* and Solaris 2.*x* also use the sticky bit on files that are used for swapping, to disable some filesystem cache operations.

When specifying file permissions, octal numbers are usually used, because each octal digit corresponds to three bits. Table 5-1 shows the numbers that correspond to the various permissions.

Table 5-1: File Permission Bits

Permission	Owner	Group	Others	Permission	Value
read	0400	040	04	set-user-id	04000
write	0200	020	02	set-group-id	02000
execute	0100	010	01	sticky	01000
none	0000	000	00	none	00000

To determine the value to use for a specific set of permissions, you can just add these values together. For example, to create the value that grants the owner read, write, and execute permission; the group read and execute permission; and no permissions for all others, you use:

```
mode = 0400 + 0200 + 0100 + 040 + 010 + 0
mode = 0700 + 050 + 0
mode = 0750
```

The following two functions change the mode of a file:

```
#include <sys/types.h>
#include <sys/stat.h>
```

```
int chmod(const char *path, mode_t mode);

int fchmod(int fd, mode_t mode);
```

The chmod function changes the permission bits on the file named in path to the bits contained in mode; the fchmod function changes the permission bits on the file referred to by the open file descriptor fd. The values for mode are chosen as described previously. Note that although the *chmod* command accepts a number without a leading zero and interprets it as octal, the leading zero must always be used in C programs to tell the compiler that the number is octal and not decimal. Only the owner of a file or the superuser can change its permissions. Upon success, chmod and fchmod return 0. If an error occurs, they return -1 and place an error code in the external variable errno.

Changing a File's Ownership

Sometimes, it is necessary for a system program to change the ownership of a file. This is often the case when a program running as the superuser creates files; it must change the ownership of those files so that regular users can access them. There are three functions provided for changing the ownership of a file:

```
#include <sys/types.h>
#include <unistd.h>

int chown(const char *path, uid_t owner, gid_t group);

int lchown(const char *path, uid_t owner, gid_t group);

int fchown(int fd, uid_t owner, gid_t group);
```

The chown function changes the user ID of the file specified by path to the one contained in owner, and the group ID of the file to the one contained in group; the fchown function performs the same changes, but on the file referred to by the open file descriptor fd. The lchown function is exactly like chown, except when path refers to a symbolic link. In this case, lchown changes the user ID and group ID of the link itself, while chown changes the user ID and group ID of the file to which the link points. If either owner or group are given as -1, then the corresponding user ID or group ID is not changed. All three functions return 0 if the changes succeed; if the changes fail, -1 is returned and the reason for failure is stored in the external variable errno.

If chown, lchown, or fchown are invoked by a process that is not operating with superuser permissions, then the set-user-id and set-group-id bits on the file are cleared.

On POSIX systems such as SVR4, there are two different ways in which these functions can be used, based on a system configuration option called _POSIX_CHOWN_RESTRICTED. If this option is not in effect, then the process calling these functions must either have the same effective user ID as the owner of the file or be operating with superuser permissions, to be allowed to change the ownership of the file. It can change the owner and group of the file to any value. In effect, this allows a user to give away her files to any other user. Most System V systems behave in this way. If the _POSIX_CHOWN_RESTRICTED option is in effect, then only the superuser can change the owner of a file. A process that is not running with superuser permissions can only change the group of a file to one of the groups of which that process is a member. This is the way most BSD systems behave; the original reason for this restriction was to make disk quotas possible.

The methods used to obtain the values for **owner** and **group** are discussed in Chapter 8.

Changing a File's Size

Sometimes it is desirable to set a file's length to a specified size. There are two functions available to do this:

```
#include <unistd.h>

int truncate(const char *path, off_t length);

int ftruncate(int fd, off_t length);
```

The `truncate` function sets the size of the file named in `path` to `length` bytes, while `ftruncate` sets the size of the file referred to by the open file descriptor `fd`. If the file is longer than `length` bytes, the excess data is discarded. If the file is shorter than `length` bytes, it is padded on the end with zero bytes. The process must have write permission on the file (and `fd` must be open for writing) for these functions to succeed. If they succeed, 0 is returned; if an error occurs, -1 is returned and the reason for failure is stored in the external variable `errno`.

Changing a File's Access and Modification Times

It is also sometimes necessary to change the access and modification times for a file; for example, the *tar* program does this to preserve the original access and modification times on files extracted from the archive. There are two functions available to do this:

```
#include <sys/types.h>
#include <utime.h>
```

```
int utime(const char *path, const struct utimbuf *times);

#include <sys/types.h>
#include <sys/time.h>

int utimes(const char *path, const struct timeval *tvp);
```

The two functions are identical except in the format of their second argument. The `utime` function is derived from System V versions of UNIX, while `utimes` is derived from BSD UNIX. SVR4 provides both of them, but Hewlett-Packard has removed `utimes` from HP-UX 10.*x*.

Both functions change the access and modification times on the file named by `path` to the times contained in their second argument. The second argument to `utime` is a pointer to type `struct utimbuf`:

```
struct utimbuf {
    time_t      actime;
    time_t      modtime;
};
```

The `actime` element of the structure contains the desired new access time in UNIX time format, and `modtime` contains the desired new modification time. The second argument to `utimes` is a pointer to an array of two objects of type `struct timeval`:

```
struct timeval {
    long      tv_sec;
    long      tv_usec;
};
```

The `tv_sec` element of the structure contains the desired new time in UNIX time format (the `tv_usec` element is ignored); the first structure contains the access time, the second contains the modification time. UNIX time format is described in Chapter 7.

In order to change the times on a file, the process must either own the file or be executing with superuser permissions. If the change succeeds, 0 is returned. If it fails, -1 is returned and the reason for failure is stored in the external variable `errno`. Whenever the access and modification times of a file are changed, the file's inode change time is updated.

Creating and Deleting Files and Directories

Chapter 3 and Chapter 4 explained how to create files using the functions `creat`, `open`, and `fopen`. It is also important to be able to delete files, create links, create and delete directories, and change the names of files and directories.

Deleting Files

The function provided to delete a file is called `unlink`:

```
#include <unistd.h>

int unlink(const char *path);
```

This function removes the directory entry named by `path` and decrements the link count (`st_nlink` in the `struct stat` structure). When the link count reaches zero, and no processes have the file open, the space occupied by the file is deallocated and the file ceases to exist. If one or more processes has the file open when the last link is removed, the link is removed from its directory (making the file inaccessible), but the space is not freed until all references to the file are closed. The process must have write permission in the directory that contains the file in order for `unlink` to succeed. If it does succeed, `unlink` returns 0; if it fails, it returns -1 and the reason for failure is stored in the external variable `errno`. The `unlink` function is not used for deleting directories. Use the `rmdir` function (see the next section) for that purpose.

The ANSI C standard specifies another function, called `remove`:

```
#include <stdio.h>

int remove(const char *path);
```

The `remove` function is identical to `unlink` for files; for directories, it is identical to `rmdir` (see the next section). On success, `remove` returns 0; on failure, it returns -1 and sets the external variable `errno` to the reason for failure.

Creating and Deleting Directories

To create a directory, use the `mkdir` function:

```
#include <sys/types.h>
#include <sys/stat.h>

int mkdir(const char *path, mode_t mode);
```

The `mkdir` function creates a new directory with the name given in `path`. The directory is empty except for entries for itself (.) and its parent (..). The permission bits on the directory are set from `mode`, which is specified as described earlier in this chapter and modified by the process' *umask* value (see Chapter 6). Upon successful completion, `mkdir` returns 0; on failure it returns -1 and sets `errno` to the reason for failure.

To remove a directory, use the `rmdir` function:

```
#include <unistd.h>

int rmdir(const char *path);
```

The `rmdir` function removes the directory named by `path`. The directory must be empty except for entries for itself (.) and its parent (..). When the directory's link count becomes zero and no process has the directory open, the space used by the directory is freed, and the directory ceases to exist. If one or more processes have the directory open when the last link is removed, . and .. are removed and no new entries can be created in the directory, but the directory is not removed until all references to it are closed. The process must have write permission in the directory's parent directory in order for `rmdir` to succeed. On success, `rmdir` returns 0, on failure, it returns -1 and the reason for failure is placed into the external variable `errno`.

Creating Links

To create a hard link, use the `link` function:

```
#include <unistd.h>

int link(const char *existing, const char *new);
```

The `link` function creates a new link (directory entry) with the name specified in `new` to an existing file whose name is given in `existing`. To create hard links, both files must be on the same removable filesystem. Only the superuser can create hard links to directories. Upon successful completion, `link` returns 0; it returns -1 on failure and stores the error indication in the external variable `errno`.

To create a symbolic link, use the `symlink` function:

```
#include <unistd.h>

int symlink(const char *name1, const char *name2);
```

The `symlink` function creates a symbolic link with the name specified in `name2` that points to the file named in `name1`. Either name can be an arbitrary pathname, they do not have to reside on the same filesystem, and the file named by `name1` does not have to exist. If `symlink` is successful, it returns 0. If it fails, it returns -1 and stores the reason for failure in the external variable `errno`.

Renaming Files and Directories

To change the name of a file or directory, use the `rename` function:

```
#include <stdio.h>

int rename(const char *old, const char *new);
```

The `rename` function changes the name of the file or directory whose name is contained in `old` to the name contained in `new`. If the file named in `new` already exists, it is deleted first. Files and directories can only be renamed within the same filesystem using this call; to move a file or directory between two different filesystems, a copy operation must be performed. The `rename` function is implemented such that even if the system crashes in the middle of executing the function, at least one copy of the file or directory will always exist. If it succeeds, `rename` returns 0. If it fails, it returns -1 and stores the failure code in the external variable `errno`.

Working with Directories

Up to this point, this chapter discussed how to manipulate files and directories from one place in the filesystem, the current working directory. However, it is often necessary for systems programs to be able to work with the entire filesystem hierarchy, traversing up and down directory trees. This section describes the tools needed to do this.

Determining the Current Working Directory

Each running program has an attribute associated with it called the *current working directory*. This is the pathname of the directory in which the program exists. When the program specifies a relative pathname for a file, the name is taken relative to the current working directory. For example, if a program's current working directory is */one/two/three* and it creates a file called *foo*, the full pathname to the file is */one/two/three/foo*.

To determine a program's current working directory, use the `getcwd` function:

```
#include <unistd.h>

char *getcwd(char *buf, size_t size);
```

When called, `getcwd` determines the absolute pathname of the current working directory and places it into the character string pointed to by `buf`, whose size is given by `size`. If `buf` is the null pointer, `getcwd` allocates a string with `malloc` (see Chapter 2, *Utility Routines*), copies the pathname to it, and returns a pointer to the allocated string. If buf is not large enough or some other error occurs, getcwd returns the predefined constant NULL.

Porting notes

BSD variants provide a slightly different function, called getwd, instead of getcwd:

```
#include <sys/param.h>

char *getwd(char *path);
```

The pathname of the current directory is placed into path, which should be of length MAXPATHLEN. If an error occurs, an error message is placed in path and getwd returns a null pointer; otherwise, path is returned.

Changing the Current Working Directory

Two functions are provided for changing the current working directory:

```
#include <unistd.h>

int chdir(const char *path);

int fchdir(int fd);
```

The chdir function changes the current working directory to the directory named by path, which can be either an absolute or a relative pathname. The fchdir function changes the current working directory to the directory referred to by the open file descriptor fd. Both functions return 0 on success and -1 on failure, storing the reason for failure in the external variable errno.

Reading Directories

Many programs, even simple ones like *ls*, need to read directories to learn their contents. Very old UNIX systems required the programmer to read the directory "manually" a record at a time, but most newer versions provide a library of functions to do this:

```
#include <dirent.h>

DIR *opendir(const char *path);

struct dirent *readdir(DIR *dp);

long telldir(DIR *dp);

void seekdir(DIR *dp, long pos);
```

```
void rewinddir(DIR *dp);

int closedir(DIR *dp);
```

The opendir function opens the directory named in **path** for reading, and returns a directory stream pointer of type DIR *. If the directory cannot be opened, NULL is returned. The closedir function closes the directory stream referred to by dp.

The readdir function returns the next directory entry from the stream dp. The information is returned as a pointer to type **struct dirent**:

```
struct dirent {
    ino_t           d_ino;
    off_t           d_off;
    unsigned short  d_reclen;
    char            *d_name;
};
```

The d_ino field of the structure contains the i-node number of the entry, d_off contains the offset of the record in the directory file, d_reclen contains the length of the directory entry record, and d_name contains the name of the entry. When readdir encounters the end of the directory file, it returns the constant NULL.

The telldir function returns the current file offset in the directory file. The seekdir function sets the current offset to the value specified by **pos**. Both telldir and seekdir express the offset in bytes from the beginning of the directory file. The rewinddir function sets the current offset to zero.

Example 5-2 shows a program that behaves much like the *ls -l* command; it reads each directory named on the command line and displays one line for each file in the directory.

Example 5-2: listfiles

```
#include <sys/types.h>
#include <sys/stat.h>
#include <sys/mkdev.h>
#include <dirent.h>
#include <stdio.h>

char    typeOfFile(mode_t);
char    *permOfFile(mode_t);
void    outputStatInfo(char *, char *, struct stat *);

int
main(int argc, char **argv)
{
    DIR *dp;
    char *dirname;
```

Example 5-2: listfiles (continued)

```
    struct stat st;
    struct dirent *d;
    char filename[BUFSIZ+1];

    /*
     * For each directory on the command line...
     */
    while (--argc) {
        dirname = *++argv;

        /*
         * Open the directory.
         */
        if ((dp = opendir(dirname)) == NULL) {
            perror(dirname);
            continue;
        }

        printf("%s:\n", dirname);

        /*
         * For each file in the directory...
         */
        while ((d = readdir(dp)) != NULL) {
            /*
             * Create the full file name.
             */
            sprintf(filename, "%s/%s", dirname, d->d_name);

            /*
             * Find out about it.
             */
            if (lstat(filename, &st) < 0) {
                perror(filename);
                putchar('\n');
                continue;
            }

            /*
             * Print out the information.
             */
            outputStatInfo(filename, d->d_name, &st);
            putchar('\n');
        }

        putchar('\n');
        closedir(dp);
    }

    exit(0);
}
```

Example 5-2: listfiles (continued)

```
/*
 * outputStatInfo - print out the contents of the stat structure.
 */
void
outputStatInfo(char *pathname, char *filename, struct stat *st)
{
    int n;
    char slink[BUFSIZ+1];

    /*
     * Print the number of file system blocks, permission bits,
     * number of links, user-id, and group-id.
     */
    printf("%5d ", st->st_blocks);
    printf("%c%s ", typeOfFile(st->st_mode), permOfFile(st->st_mode));
    printf("%3d ", st->st_nlink);
    printf("%5d/%-5d ", st->st_uid, st->st_gid);

    /*
     * If the file is not a device, print its size; otherwise
     * print its major and minor device numbers.
     */
    if (((st->st_mode & S_IFMT) != S_IFCHR) &&
        ((st->st_mode & S_IFMT) != S_IFBLK))
        printf("%9d ", st->st_size);
    else
        printf("%4d,%4d ", major(st->st_rdev), minor(st->st_rdev));

    /*
     * Print the access time.  The ctime() function is
     * described in Chapter 7, "Time of Day Operations."
     */
    printf("%.12s ", ctime(&st->st_mtime) + 4);

    /*
     * Print the file name.  If it's a symblic link, also print
     * what it points to.
     */
    printf("%s", filename);

    if ((st->st_mode & S_IFMT) == S_IFLNK) {
        if ((n = readlink(pathname, slink, sizeof(slink))) < 0)
            printf(" -> ???");
        else
            printf(" -> %.*s", n, slink);
    }
}


/*
 * typeOfFile - return the letter indicating the file type.
 */
char
```

Example 5-2: listfiles (continued)

```
typeOfFile(mode_t mode)
{
    switch (mode & S_IFMT) {
    case S_IFREG:
        return('-');
    case S_IFDIR:
        return('d');
    case S_IFCHR:
        return('c');
    case S_IFBLK:
        return('b');
    case S_IFLNK:
        return('l');
    case S_IFIFO:
        return('p');
    case S_IFSOCK:
        return('s');
    }

    return('?');
}

/*
 * permOfFile - return the file permissions in an "ls"-like string.
 */
char *
permOfFile(mode_t mode)
{
    int i;
    char *p;
    static char perms[10];

    p = perms;
    strcpy(perms, "---------");

    /*
     * The permission bits are three sets of three
     * bits: user read/write/exec, group read/write/exec,
     * other read/write/exec.  We deal with each set
     * of three bits in one pass through the loop.
     */
    for (i=0; i < 3; i++) {
        if (mode & (S_IREAD >> i*3))
            *p = 'r';
        p++;

        if (mode & (S_IWRITE >> i*3))
            *p = 'w';
        p++;

        if (mode & (S_IEXEC >> i*3))
            *p = 'x';
```

Example 5-2: listfiles (continued)

```
      p++;
    }

    /*
     * Put special codes in for set-user-id, set-group-id,
     * and the sticky bit.  (This part is incomplete; "ls"
     * uses some other letters as well for cases such as
     * set-user-id bit without execute bit, and so forth.)
     */
    if ((mode & S_ISUID) != 0)
        perms[2] = 's';

    if ((mode & S_ISGID) != 0)
        perms[5] = 's';

    if ((mode & S_ISVTX) != 0)
        perms[8] = 't';

    return(perms);
}
```

```
% lsfiles /home/msw/a
/home/msw/a:
     2 drwxr-sr-x    7    0/1           512 Dec 21 22:20 .
     2 drwxr-xr-x    3    0/0           512 Dec 21 20:45 ..
    16 drwx------    2    0/0          8192 Apr 19 16:04 lost+found
     2 drwxr-sr-x   12   40/1          1024 Mar 12 10:16 davy
     2 drwxr-sr-x    2   43/1           512 Apr 19 17:57 sean
     2 drwxr-sr-x    3   42/1           512 Jan 12 19:59 trevor
     2 drwxr-sr-x    6   41/1           512 Feb 22 13:34 cathy
```

Porting notes

On BSD systems, the include file for the directory routines is called *sys/dir.h* instead of *dirent.h*, and the directory structure is of type `struct direct` instead of type `struct dirent`.

BSD systems provide two other functions as part of the directory library that didn't make it into the POSIX standard:

```
#include <sys/types.h>
#include <sys/dir.h>

int scandir(char *dirname, struct direct *(*namelist[]),
        int (*select)(), int (*compare)());

int alphasort(struct direct *d1, struct direct *d2);
```

The `scandir` function reads the entire contents of the directory `dirname` into a dynamically allocated array of structures pointed to by `namelist`. For each entry, it calls the user-defined `select` function with the name of the entry. `select` returns non-zero if the entry is of interest and zero if it is not. The entire `namelist` is sorted according to the comparison routine `compare`, which is passed pointers to two directory entries. It returns less than, equal to, or greater than zero depending on whether the first argument is considered less than, equal to, or greater than the second argument in the sort. You can use the `alphasort` function for this purpose if alphabetical order is desired.

There are public domain implementations of the directory library routines for use on very old UNIX systems that do not provide them. For portability reasons, these implementations are preferred over doing things "the hard way."

Chapter Summary

This chapter discussed how the UNIX filesystem is structured, the types of objects in the filesystem, and how file permission bits work. It also examined most of the general-purpose functions used for working in the filesystem. With just the tools described in this and the two preceding chapters, you can perform a dazzling number of tasks that you may never have thought about before. The next chapter covers even more things that you can do with files.

6

Special-Purpose File Operations

Previous chapters discussed the regular file operations: creating, opening, and closing files; reading and writing data; removing files; renaming files; setting file permissions; and so forth. They also discussed some common operations on file descriptors, such as setting the read/write offset and duplicating a file descriptor. However, there are also a number of less common, yet nevertheless important, operations that you can perform when circumstances warrant. These special-purpose file operations are the subject of this chapter.

File Descriptor Attributes

Each open file descriptor has associated with it several attributes that you can examine and change. This book has already discussed one of these attributes, the read/write offset, which is examined and changed with the `lseek` function (or the `fseek` function, in the case of the *Standard I/O Library*). To examine and change the other file descriptor attributes, you can use two other functions, `fcntl` and `ioctl`.

The `ioctl` function was originally intended primarily for performing device control operations (that is, telling a tape drive to rewind the tape). However, as the need for other similar control functions arose, more and more duties were added to `ioctl` until it became used not only for performing device control operations, but also for regular file operations, operations on file descriptors, and operations on network communications modules. Unfortunately, because it was only designed for device control, `ioctl` was not very well suited for some of the tasks it was asked to perform.

Fortunately, the designers of System V UNIX recognized this and began working to reverse the trend of piling everything onto `ioctl`. They created the `fcntl` function, and moved all of the operations on regular files and file descriptors out of `ioctl`'s area of responsibility. However, even the best laid plans don't go as well as they ought to. Because many vendors' operating systems were based on Berkeley UNIX, even though most of the vendors adopted `fcntl` (especially once it became a part of the POSIX standard), they still left some functionality under `ioctl`. Thus, most versions of UNIX, and SVR4 is no exception, use both `ioctl` and `fcntl` to perform operations on files and file descriptors, with some overlap for reasons of backward compatibility.

```
#include <unistd.h>
#include <sys/ioctl.h>

int ioctl(int fd, int cmd, /* arg */ ...);

#include <sys/types.h>
#include <fcntl.h>

int fcntl(int fd, int cmd, /* arg */ ...);
```

The `ioctl` function performs the request identified by `cmd` on the open file descriptor referenced by `fd`. The `arg` parameter is of varying type depending on the value of `cmd`, but it is usually either an integer or a pointer. The `ioctl` function returns a value greater than or equal to zero, depending on the value of `cmd`, on success. On failure, it returns -1 and stores the reason for failure in the external variable `errno`. In SVR4, the legal values for `cmd` are:

FIOCLEX

Set the close-on-exec flag for the file descriptor. This means that if the calling program executes another program with one of the **exec** system calls (see Chapter 11, *Processes*), the file descriptor is automatically closed before the new program is executed. The `arg` parameter is ignored by this command.

FIONCLEX

Clear the close-on-exec flag (see **FIOCLEX**) for the file descriptor. The `arg` parameter is ignored by this command.

FIONBIO

Set or clear non-blocking I/O on the file. The `arg` parameter is given as a pointer to an integer; if the integer's value is 1 then non-blocking I/O is enabled, if the integer's value is 0 then it is disabled. Non-blocking I/O means that reads and writes to the file return immediately if no data is available to be read, or no space (in the operating system buffers or on the disk) is available to store the data. If non-blocking I/O is not set, then reads and writes block, waiting for more data or space to become available. You can also set this attribute when the file is opened by using the O_NDELAY or O_NONBLOCK options.

FIOASYNC

Set or clear asynchronous I/O on the file. The `arg` parameter is given as a pointer to an integer; if the integer's value is 1 then asynchronous I/O is enabled, if the integer's value is 0, then it is disabled. Asynchronous I/O in this context means that when data becomes available for reading on the file descriptor, or when data can be written, the process is sent a SIGIO signal (see Chapter 10, *Signals*) notifying it of the change in the descriptor's status.

FIONREAD

Determine the number of characters available to be read. The `arg` parameter is given as a pointer to an integer in which the value is returned. While this is a valid way of determining whether there is input to be read, the `select` and `poll` functions described later in this chapter are more efficient.

FIOSETOWN

Set the process-group identifier (see Chapter 11) that subsequently receives SIGIO or SIGURG signals for the file descriptor. The `arg` parameter is a pointer to an integer containing the process-group identifier.

This command is not available in HP-UX 10.*x*.

FIOGETOWN

Get the process-group identifier that is receiving SIGIO or SIGURG signals for the file descriptor. The `arg` parameter is a pointer to an integer; after this call the integer contains the process-group identifier.

This command is not available in HP-UX 10.*x*.

There are numerous other commands as well, but their use is less common and beyond the scope of this chapter.

The `fcntl` function performs the request identified by `cmd` on the open file descriptor referenced by `fd`. The `arg` parameter is of varying type depending on the value of `cmd`, but it is usually either an integer or a pointer. In SVR4, the legal values for `cmd` are:

F_DUPFD

Return a new file descriptor with the following characteristics:

- Lowest numbered available file descriptor greater than or equal to the integer value given in `arg`

- Same open file (or pipe) as the original file

- Same read/write offset as the original file (that is, both file descriptors share the same read/write offset)

- Same access mode (read, write, read/write) as the original file

- Shares any locks associated with the original file descriptor

- Same file status flags (see below) as the original file (that is, both file descriptors share the same file status flags)

- Clears the close-on-exec flag associated with the new descriptor

F_GETFD

Get the close-on-exec flag associated with the file descriptor **fd**. If the low-order bit of the return value is 0, the file remains open across an **exec**. If the low-order bit is 1, the file closes on **exec**.

F_SETFD

Set the close-on-exec flag associated with the file descriptor **fd** to the low-order bit of the integer value given in **arg**, as described previously.

F_GETFL

Get the current status flags (see **F_SETFL**) for the file descriptor **fd**.

F_SETFL

Set the current status flags for the file descriptor **fd** to those contained in **arg**. Most of these flags can also be set when the file is opened with the **open** function described in Chapter 3, *Low-Level I/O Routines*; see the description there for more information on the meaning of each of these flags. The valid status flags are:

FD_CLOEXEC

Set the file descriptor's close-on-exec flag; this can also be set with **F_SETFD**, described previously

O_RDONLY

Open for reading only (this can only be set by the **open** function, but can be returned by the **F_GETFL** command)

O_WRONLY

Open for writing only (this can only be set by the **open** function, but can be returned by the **F_GETFL** command)

O_RDWR
> Open for reading and writing (this can only be set by the **open** function, but it can be returned by the **F_GETFL** command)

O_APPEND
> Append mode

O_NDELAY
> Non-blocking mode

O_NONBLOCK
> Non-blocking mode

O_DSYNC
> Synchronous write operations (data only)

O_RSYNC
> Synchronous read operations

O_SYNC
> Synchronous write operations (data and file attributes)

Both `ioctl` and `fcntl` have other uses besides those described in this section. You will encounter these functions in several chapters throughout the rest of the book.

Managing Multiple File Descriptors

Sometimes a single program must be able to manage several file descriptors, acting immediately on any input received from them, and yet also performing other computations when no input is received. For example, consider a multi-player Star Trek game. While none of the players are typing, the program must draw the ships, planets, and so forth, and move them about on each player's screen. But when a player types a command (such as *turn left*), the program must immediately receive that input and act on it.

Doing something like this is difficult with the functions you have learned about so far, primarily because the **read** function blocks until input is available. This means that when the program issues a **read** call, it becomes "stuck" until the player types something—it cannot perform its other duties, such as updating the screen. Fortunately, most modern versions of the UNIX operating system provide a way to handle this task.

The **select** and **poll** functions provide a mechanism for a program to check on a group of file descriptors and learn when any of those descriptors are ready to provide input, ready to receive output, or have an exceptional condition pending on them. The `select` function is usually provided on BSD-based systems, while `poll` is usually provided on System V-based systems. SVR4 provides both `select` as a library emulation routine and `poll` as a system call.

The select Function

Although emulated with a library routine in SVR4, `select` is more frequently used than `poll`. The `select` function is called as follows:

```
#include <sys/types.h>
#include <sys/time.h>

int select(int maxfd, fd_set *readfds, fd_set *writefds,
       fd_set *exceptfds, struct timeval *timeout);

void FD_SET(int fd, fd_set *fdset);

void FD_CLR(int fd, fd_set *fdset);

int FD_ISSET(int fd, fd_set *fdset);

void FD_ZERO(fd_set *fdset);
```

NOTE

In HP-UX 10.0, the ANSI C function prototype is misdeclared as taking parameters of type `int *` instead of type `fd_set *`. This is a typographical error only; `select` still uses the `fd_set` type.

When called, `select` examines the file descriptor sets pointed to by `readfds`, `writefds`, and `exceptfds` to see if any of their file descriptors are ready for reading, ready for writing, or have an exceptional condition pending on them. Out-of-band data (see Chapter 14, *Networking with Sockets*) is the only exceptional condition. When `select` returns, it replaces the file descriptor sets with subsets containing those file descriptors that are ready for the requested operation.

Each file descriptor set is a bit field in which a non-zero bit indicates that the file descriptor of that number should be checked. The `maxfd` parameter indicates the highest-numbered bit that should be checked; the file descriptors from 0 to `maxfd`-1 are examined in each file descriptor set. (Much of the documentation on `select` calls this parameter `nfds`, implying that it is the number of file descriptors to check.) If a particular condition is not of interest, any of `readfds`, `writefds`, and `exceptfds` can be given as null pointers.

The `FD_ZERO` macro clears all the bits in a file descriptor set; always call this before setting any bits. The `FD_SET` and `FD_CLR` macros set and clear individual bits corresponding to file descriptors in a file descriptor set. The `FD_ISSET` macro returns non-zero if the bit corresponding to the file descriptor `fd` is set, and zero otherwise.

If `timeout` is not a null pointer, it specifies a maximum interval to wait for the requested operations to become ready. If `timeout` is given as a null pointer, then `select` blocks indefinitely (you can use this to have the program "just sit there" until something happens). To effect a poll, in which the `select` call just checks all the file descriptors and returns their status, `timeout` should be a non-null pointer to a zero-valued `struct timeval` structure. (The `struct timeval` structure is discussed in Chapter 7, *Time of Day Operations*.)

When `select` returns, it usually returns a number greater than zero, indicating the number of ready file descriptors contained in the file descriptor sets. If the `timeout` expires with none of the file descriptors becoming ready, `select` returns 0. If an error occurs, `select` returns -1 and places an error code in the external variable `errno`.

Example 6-1 shows a program that reads from three terminal devices. Each time you type something on one of the terminals, the program reads it and prints it. If no one types anything on any of the devices within 10 seconds, the program prints a reminder to the user. When the string S-T-O-P is read from one of the terminals, the program exits.

Example 6-1: select

```c
#include <sys/types.h>
#include <sys/time.h>
#include <fcntl.h>
#include <stdio.h>

#define NTTYS        3          /* number of ttys to use     */
#define TIMEOUT      10         /* number of seconds to wait */

int      fds[NTTYS];            /* file descriptors          */
char     *fileNames[NTTYS];     /* file names                */

int      openFiles(char **);
void     readFiles(fd_set *);

int
main(int argc, char **argv)
{
    fd_set readfds;
    int i, n, maxfd;
    struct timeval tv;

    /*
     * Check that we have the right number of arguments.
     */
```

Example 6-1: select (continued)

```
    if (argc != (NTTYS+1)) {
        fprintf(stderr, "You must supply %d tty names.\n", NTTYS);
        exit(1);
    }

    /*
     * Open the files.  The highest numbered file descriptor
     * (plus one) is returned in maxfd.
     */
    maxfd = openFiles(++argv);

    /*
     * Forever...
     */
    for (;;) {
        /*
         * Zero the bitmask.
         */
        FD_ZERO(&readfds);

        /*
         * Set bits in the bitmask.
         */
        for (i=0; i < NTTYS; i++)
            FD_SET(fds[i], &readfds);

        /*
         * Set up the timeout.
         */
        tv.tv_sec = TIMEOUT;
        tv.tv_usec = 0;

        /*
         * Wait for some input.
         */
        n = select(maxfd, &readfds, (fd_set *) 0, (fd_set *) 0, &tv);

        /*
         * See what happened.
         */
        switch (n) {
        case -1:                /* error           */
            perror("select");
            exit(1);
        case 0:                 /* timeout         */
            printf("\nTimeout expired.  Type something!\n");
            break;
        default:                /* input available */
            readFiles(&readfds);
            break;
        }
    }
```

Example 6-1: select (continued)

```
}

/*
 * openFiles - open all the files, return the highest file descriptor.
 */
int
openFiles(char **files)
{
    int i, maxfd;

    maxfd = 0;

    /*
     * For each file...
     */
    for (i=0; i < NTTYS; i++) {
        /*
         * Open it.
         */
        if ((fds[i] = open(*files, O_RDONLY)) < 0) {
            perror(*files);
            exit(1);
        }

        /*
         * Make sure it's a tty.
         */
        if (!isatty(fds[i])) {
            fprintf(stderr, "All files must be tty devices.\n");
            exit(1);
        }

        /*
         * Save the name.
         */
        fileNames[i] = *files++;

        /*
         * Save the highest numbered fd.
         */
        if (fds[i] > maxfd)
            maxfd = fds[i];
    }

    return(maxfd + 1);
}

/*
 * readFiles - read input from any files that have some.
 */
void
readFiles(fd_set *readfds)
```

Example 6-1: select (continued)

```
{
    int i, n;
    char buf[BUFSIZ];

    /*
     * For each file...
     */
    for (i=0; i < NTTYS; i++) {
        /*
         * If it has some input available...
         */
        if (FD_ISSET(fds[i], readfds)) {
            /*
             * Read the data.
             */
            n = read(fds[i], buf, sizeof(buf));
            buf[n] = '\0';

            /*
             * Print it out.
             */
            printf("\nRead %d bytes from %s:\n", n, fileNames[i]);
            printf("\t%s\n", buf);

            /*
             * Is it telling us to stop?
             */
            if (strcmp(buf, "S-T-O-P\n") == 0)
                exit(0);
        }
    }
}
```

```
% select /dev/pts/3 /dev/pts/4 /dev/pts/5
```

Running this program for yourself requires a bit of work to see how it works. It's best if you start up a window system such as *X11* or *OpenWindows*, although you can also do it if you have access to several hard-wired terminals. To run the example, perform the following steps:

1. Start up four terminal windows, or log in on four separate terminals.

2. On each of the first three terminals, type *tty*. This command tells you the name of the terminal device file that you are using.

3.   On each of the first three terminals, type *sleep 1000000*. This allows the pro-
     gram to read from these terminals without competing for input with the shell
     process running on each terminal. When you finish with the demonstration,
     you can just interrupt this command.

4.   On the fourth terminal, type the *select* command followed by the device
     names of the other three terminals. Note that if you use the Korn shell, *select*
     is a special command to the shell, so use the command *./select* to invoke the
     example program.

5.   Type something on each of the first three terminals and watch what the pro-
     gram prints on the fourth terminal. Then don't type anything on the terminals
     for 10 seconds and watch the program print its timeout message. Finally, type
     the string S-T-O-P on any one of the terminals to make the program exit.

The poll Function

The `poll` function is similar to `select`, except that it uses a structure of type
`struct pollfd` for each file descriptor instead of file descriptor sets.

```
#include <stropts.h>
#include <poll.h>

int poll(struct pollfd *fds, unsigned long nfds, int timeout);
```

The `fds` parameter points to an array of `nfds` structures of type `struct`
`pollfd`, one for each file descriptor of interest. The structure contains three elements:

```
struct pollfd {
    int    fd;
    short events;
    short revents;
};
```

The `fd` element contains the file descriptor of interest. If `fd` is equal to -1, the
structure is ignored; this allows particular descriptors to be turned "on" and "off"
without rearranging the array. The `events` element contains a set of flags describing the events of interest for that file descriptor. The `revents` element contains a
subset of these flags, indicating the events that are actually set on that file descriptor. The flags in the `events` and `revents` elements are constructed by *or*ing
together the following values:

POLLIN
     Data other than high priority data can be read without blocking.

POLLRDNORM

Normal data (priority band 0) can be read without blocking.

POLLRDBAND

Data from a non-zero priority band can be read without blocking.

POLLPRI

High-priority data can be read without blocking.

POLLOUT

Normal data can be written without blocking.

POLLWRNORM

The same as POLLOUT.

POLLWRBAND

Priority data (non-zero priority band) can be written. This event only examines bands that have been written to at least once.

POLLERR

An error has occurred on the device or stream. This flag is only valid in the revents element of the structure.

POLLHUP

A hangup has occurred on the stream. This event and POLLOUT are mutually exclusive; a stream is never writable once a hangup has occurred. This flag is only valid in the revents element of the structure.

POLLNVAL

The specified fd value is not a valid file descriptor. This flag is only valid in the revents element of the structure.

If none of the defined events has occurred on any of the selected file descriptors when poll is called, it waits for at least timeout milliseconds before returning. If the value of timeout is INFTIM, then poll blocks until one of the selected events occurs. To effect a poll, specify timeout as zero.

When poll returns, it normally returns a number greater than zero, indicating the number of file descriptors for which the revents element of their struct pollfd structure is non-zero. If the timeout expires before any selected events have occurred, poll returns 0. If an error occurs, poll returns -1 and places an error code in the external variable errno. When poll returns, the fd and events elements of the descriptor array are not modified; this allows the array to be immediately reused without having to reinitialize it.

Example 6-2 shows another program that reads from three terminal devices. Each time someone types on one of the terminals, the program reads it and prints it. If no one types anything on any of the devices within 10 seconds, the program prints a reminder to the user. When the string S-T-O-P is read from one of the terminals, the program exits.

Example 6–2: poll

```
#include <stropts.h>
#include <fcntl.h>
#include <stdio.h>
#include <poll.h>

#define NTTYS       3            /* number of ttys to use    */
#define TIMEOUT     10           /* number of seconds to wait */

int     fds[NTTYS];              /* file descriptors          */
char    *fileNames[NTTYS];       /* file names                */

int     openFiles(char **);
void    readFiles(struct pollfd *);

int
main(int argc, char **argv)
{
    int i, n, maxfd;
    struct pollfd pfds[NTTYS];

    /*
     * Check that we have the right number of arguments.
     */
    if (argc != (NTTYS+1)) {
        fprintf(stderr, "You must supply %d tty names.\n", NTTYS);
        exit(1);
    }

    /*
     * Open the files.  The highest numbered file descriptor
     * (plus one) is returned in maxfd.
     */
    maxfd = openFiles(++argv);

    /*
     * We only need to initialize these once.
     */
    for (i=0; i < NTTYS; i++) {
        pfds[i].fd = fds[i];
        pfds[i].events = POLLIN;
    }

    /*
     * Forever...
     */
    for (;;) {
        /*
         * Wait for some input.
```

Example 6-2: poll (continued)

```c
     */
    n = poll(pfds, NTTYS, TIMEOUT * 1000);

    /*
     * See what happened.
     */
    switch (n) {
    case -1:              /* error          */
        perror("poll");
        exit(1);
    case 0:               /* timeout        */
        printf("\nTimeout expired.  Type something!\n");
        break;
    default:              /* input available */
        readFiles(pfds);
        break;
    }
    }
}


/*
 * openFiles - open all the files, return the highest file descriptor.
 */
int
openFiles(char **files)
{
    int i, maxfd;

    maxfd = 0;

    /*
     * For each file...
     */
    for (i=0; i < NTTYS; i++) {
        /*
         * Open it.
         */
        if ((fds[i] = open(*files, O_RDONLY)) < 0) {
            perror(*files);
            exit(1);
        }

        /*
         * Make sure it's a tty.
         */
        if (!isatty(fds[i])) {
            fprintf(stderr, "All files must be tty devices.\n");
            exit(1);
        }

        /*
         * Save the name.
```

Example 6-2: poll (continued)

```
             */
             fileNames[i] = *files++;

             /*
              * Save the highest numbered fd.
              */
             if (fds[i] > maxfd)
                 maxfd = fds[i];
     }

     return(maxfd + 1);
}

/*
 * readFiles - read input from any files that have some.
 */
void
readFiles(struct pollfd *pfds)
{
     int i, n;
     char buf[BUFSIZ];

     /*
      * For each file...
      */
     for (i=0; i < NTTYS; i++) {
         /*
          * If it has some input available...
          */
         if (pfds[i].revents & POLLIN) {
             /*
              * Read the data.
              */
             n = read(fds[i], buf, sizeof(buf));
             buf[n] = '\0';

             /*
              * Print it out.
              */
             printf("\nRead %d bytes from %s:\n", n, fileNames[i]);
             printf("\t%s\n", buf);

             /*
              * Is it telling us to stop?
              */
             if (strcmp(buf, "S-T-O-P\n") == 0)
                 exit(0);
         }
     }
}
```

```
% poll /dev/pts/3 /dev/pts/4 /dev/pts/5
```

To run this program, follow the instructions given for Example 6-1.

File and Record Locking

When more than one process is writing the same file, or when one process is writing the file while another is reading it, it is usually necessary for the processes to coordinate their actions to prevent havoc. Consider, for example, what happens when two processes start at about the same time and both open the same log file for writing. Each process seeks to the end of the file in order to append new log messages to the existing file. When the first process writes a log message, its read/write offset is advanced. However, the read/write offset of the second process is not advanced, and when this process writes a log message, it *overwrites* the message written by the first process.

One way to avoid this particular case is to open the file with the O_APPEND option (see Chapter 3), which guarantees that all writes to the file are appended to the end of the file. The kernel takes care of advancing the read/write offset before writing the data if the file has grown since the last write. However, this option does not solve other problems that can occur. For example, if two processes try to update a database at the same time, they will probably destroy each others' work, and they would certainly leave the database in an unknown state. In order to prevent these situations, most modern UNIX systems provide some form of *file locking*.

There are two types of file locking: *advisory* and *mandatory*. Advisory file locks, which are provided by most versions of UNIX, allow cooperating processes to block each other out during critical periods (such as when one of the processes is writing the file). In advisory file locking, each process is required to check for the existence of a lock on the file before going ahead with its work. If a lock is present, the process waits until the lock is removed and sets a lock of its own before proceeding. However, advisory file locking is only useful between processes that agree to follow the locking convention. Processes that do not care about file locks can still read or write the file, even if another process has a lock set.

Mandatory file locks are provided by some versions of UNIX, including SVR4. When a mandatory lock is present on a file, the kernel causes any calls to creat, open, read, and write issued by processes other than the one with the lock to fail, returning the EAGAIN error. This is more secure, in the sense that even processes that are not aware that the file must be accessed with a lock cannot access the file out of turn. However, mandatory file locks are also dangerous. If a process that holds a lock on some critical system file goes into an infinite loop or otherwise fails to remove the lock, it can cause the entire system to hang or even crash. For this reason, it is usually advisable to use advisory locks whenever possible. Mandatory locks are enabled on a per-file basis by setting the set-group-id bit and clearing the group execute bit in the file's permission modes (see Chapter 5, *Files and Directories*). This implies that it is not possible to set a mandatory file lock on a directory or an executable program.

There are two functions used for setting and removing file locks in SVR4. The fcntl function, introduced earlier in this chapter, provides the POSIX interface, and the lockf function provides the System V interface. The two interfaces are very similar; the principal reason for continuing to supply the lockf interface is to provide backward compatibility with earlier operating system versions.

Locking Files with fcntl

As discussed earlier, the fcntl function is called as follows:

```
#include <sys/types.h>
#include <fcntl.h>

int fcntl(int fd, int cmd, /* arg */ ...);
```

The fd argument is a file descriptor referring to the file to lock, the cmd argument indicates the operation to perform, and the arg parameter is a pointer to a structure of type flock_t that describes the type of lock to create.

Legal values for the cmd argument that apply to file locking are:

F_SETLK

> Set or clear a lock, according to the contents of the flock_t structure pointed to by arg (see below). If the lock cannot be created, fcntl immediately returns -1 and stores the reason for failure in the external variable errno.

F_SETLKW

> This command is identical to F_SETLK, except that if the lock cannot be created, the process is blocked until it can be created. This allows a process to request a lock and wait until it can be made, without having to test repeatedly to see if the file is unlocked.

F_GETLK

> If the type of lock requested by the flock_t structure pointed to by arg can be created, then the structure is passed back unchanged, except that the lock type is set to F_UNLCK, and the l_whence field is set to SEEK_SET.

If the lock cannot be created, then the structure is overwritten with a description of the first lock that is preventing its creation. The structure also contains the process ID and system ID of the process holding the lock.

This command never creates a lock; it only tests whether or not a particular lock could be created.

Two different types of locks can be created with `fcntl`. A read lock prevents any process from write locking the protected area. More than one read lock can exist for a given segment of a file at any given time. The file descriptor on which the read lock is placed must have been opened with read access. A write lock prevents any process from read locking or write locking the protected area. Only one write lock and no read locks can exist for a given segment of a file at any given time. The file descriptor on which the write lock is being placed must have been opened with write access.

The lock itself is described by a structure of type `flock_t` (declared in the include file *fcntl.h*) that contains at least the following members:

```
typedef struct flock {
    short      l_type;
    short      l_whence;
    off_t      l_start;
    off_t      l_len;
    long       l_sysid;
    pid_t      l_pid;
} flock_t;
```

The `l_type` field of the structure specifies the type of lock, and can be equal to one of the following:

F_RDLCK

   Establish a read lock.

F_WRLCK

   Establish a write lock.

F_UNLCK

   Remove a previously established lock.

The `l_start` field specifies the offset of the beginning of the region to be locked, and the `l_len` field specifies the length of the region to be locked. The `l_whence` field specifies the point in the file from which the starting offset is referenced, and can take on the same values as the third argument to the `lseek` function:

SEEK_SET
> The starting offset is relative to the beginning of the file.

SEEK_CUR
> The starting offset is relative to the current position in the file.

SEEK_END
> The starting offset is relative to the end of the file.

Locks can start and extend beyond the end of a file, but they cannot be negative relative to the beginning of the file. A lock can be set to extend to the end of the file by setting l_len to zero; if such a lock also has l_whence and l_start set to zero, the whole file is locked.

Unlocking a segment in the middle of a larger locked segment leaves two locked segments, one at each end. Locking a segment that is already locked by the same process results in removing the old lock and installing the new one.

Locks are removed from a file when the process removes them using F_UNLCK, when the process closes the file descriptor, or when the process terminates. Locks are not inherited by child processes.

Locking Files with lockf

The lockf function provides similar functionality to the file locking portion of fcntl, but it is called differently:

```
#include <unistd.h>

int lockf(int fd, int function, long size);
```

The fd argument is a file descriptor referencing the file to be locked; it must have been opened with either O_WRONLY or O_RDWR access permissions.

The function argument indicates the function to perform:

F_ULOCK
> Unlock a previously locked section.

F_LOCK
> Establish a lock on a section. If the section is already locked, the process blocks until the lock can be established.

F_TLOCK
> Test a section to see if it can be locked. If it can, establish the lock. If the section is already locked, this command causes lockf to return -1 and stores the reason for failure in errno.

`F_TEST`

> Test a section to see if it can be locked. If it can, `lockf` returns 0; otherwise, it returns -1 and stores the reason for the error in `errno`.

The `size` argument indicates the number of contiguous bytes to lock or unlock. The region extends forward from the current read/write offset for a positive value of `size`, and backward from the current read/write offset for a negative value of `size`. If `size` is zero, the region from the current read/write offset through the current or any future end of the file is indicated. An area does need to exist in the file to be locked; locks can extend past the end of the file.

It is possible to establish a lock on a section that overlaps with a previously locked section, although this results in the sections being combined so that a single, larger section is now locked (locks are a finite resource; this practice conserves them). If a section to be unlocked is part of a larger locked section, this results in two locked sections, one on either end of the unlocked area.

All locks held on a file by a process are released when the process closes the file or when the process terminates. Locks created by `lockf` are not inherited by children of the process creating the lock.

Porting Notes

BSD UNIX and vendor versions based on it offer another interface, called `flock`:

```
#include <sys/file.h>

int flock(int fd, int operation);
```

This function allows advisory locks to be created on the file referenced by the file descriptor `fd`. Only entire files can be locked; there is no facility to lock only a portion of a file. The `operation` argument indicates the function to perform:

`LOCK_SH`

> Establish a shared lock on the file. More than one process can have a shared lock on the same file at the same time. This is analogous to a read lock as used with `fcntl` and `lockf`.

`LOCK_EX`

> Establish an exclusive lock on the file. Only one exclusive lock can be placed on the file at a time, and no shared locks on the file can exist while the exclusive lock is in place. This is analogous to a write lock as used with `fcntl` and `lockf`.

LOCK_UN

Remove a previously established lock from the file.

LOCK_NB

This can be *or*ed with LOCK_SH or LOCK_EX to make the operation non-blocking; otherwise, these operations block until the lock can be created.

The flock function returns 0 on success. On failure, it returns -1 and places the reason for failure in the external variable errno.

Memory-Mapped Files

The concept of *memory-mapped files* was first introduced in UNIX by Berkeley in 4.2BSD (although Berkeley did not actually implement the concept until 4.4BSD). It has since been adopted by most vendor versions of the operating system, including SVR4. A memory-mapped file is basically what its name implies: a file (or portion of a file) that has been mapped into a process' address space.

Once a file is mapped into memory, a process can access the contents of that file using address space manipulations (that is, variables, pointers, array subscripts, and so on) instead of the read/write interface. The operating system takes care of transferring the file into memory (and, if the memory is modified, transferring it back to the file) through the virtual memory subsystem. In other words, as the process accesses the file, the operating system *pages* the file into and out of memory. This is usually (but not always) more efficient than reading the entire file into memory directly, especially when only small portions of the file's contents are actually used.

One of the most important uses for memory-mapped files is in the implementation of dynamically loadable shared libraries. In the old days, when a program was linked, all the executable code for the library routines it called (the code for the routines described in this book) was copied into the executable file. This consumed a lot of disk space and also took up a lot of memory, because there might be multiple copies of a routine (for example, printf) in memory at any given time. The introduction of dynamically loaded, shared libraries has solved both of these problems. Because the library is dynamically loaded, it does not have to be compiled into each program. Rather, when the program is executed, the system loads the library into memory and allows the program to transfer control to this area of memory. This conserves disk space by having only one copy of each library routine on the disk. Because the library is shared, each program that uses the library is using the same copy. Thus, there is only one copy of printf in memory at a time, and all programs that need it use the same copy.

Dynamically loadable shared libraries are implemented with memory-mapped files. When a program is linked, a *jump table* is created that contains an entry for each library routine. When the program is executed, the operating system maps the library into memory and then edits the jump table to fill in the address of each function. As the program calls library functions, the operating system pages those parts of the library into memory and lets the program use them. If part of the library is never used (for example, the part taken up by some obscure function), it is never loaded into memory.

Memory-mapped files are useful for other purposes, too. For example, a program that retrieves data from a very large database might use some type of index into the database. It searches for an item in the index, and when it finds the item, uses information stored in the index entry to retrieve the data. Indexes for large databases are usually very large themselves. If the program must retrieve only one or two items from the database, it is unlikely that it needs to examine each and every entry in the index (depending on its search algorithm). Thus, it would be a waste of both time and memory to read the entire index into memory. Instead, the program can map the index into memory, access it as if it were an array (or whatever), and the operating system only brings in those parts of the index the program actually needs. This both makes the program run faster and places less load on the system.

Mapping a File into Memory

A file is mapped into memory with the `mmap` function:

```
#include <sys/types.h>
#include <sys/mman.h>

caddr_t mmap(caddr_t addr, size_t len, int prot, int flags,
        int fd, off_t offset);
```

This function maps `len` bytes of the file referenced by `fd`, beginning at `offset`, into the process' address space. It returns a memory address that points to the start of the mapped segment on success, or `(caddr_t)` -1 on failure. If the call fails, `errno` contains the reason for failure.

The mapped segment can extend past the end of the file, but any reference to addresses beyond the current end of the file will result in the delivery of a `SIGBUS` signal (see Chapter 10). This means that `mmap` cannot be used to implicitly extend the length of a file.

NOTE

Mappings established for `fd` *are not* removed when the file descriptor is closed. The `munmap` function (see below) must be called to remove a mapping.

The `prot` parameter specifies the ways in which the mapped pages are accessed. These values are *or*ed together to produce the desired result:

PROT_READ
> The page can be read (that is, the contents of the page can be examined).

PROT_WRITE
> The page can be written (that is, the contents of the page can be changed).

PROT_EXEC
> The page can be executed (that is, the contents of the page can be executed as program code).

PROT_NONE
> The page cannot be accessed.

Most implementations of `mmap` do not actually support all combinations of the above values. They usually map some of the simpler modes into more complex ones (for example, the PROT_WRITE mode is usually implemented as PROT_READ | PROT_WRITE). However, no implementation allows a page to be written unless PROT_WRITE is specified.

The `flags` parameter provides additional information about how the mapped pages should be treated:

MAP_SHARED
> When changes are made to the mapped object, these changes are shared among other processes that also have the object mapped.

MAP_PRIVATE
> When changes are made to the mapped object, these changes cause the system to create a private copy of the affected pages, making the changes in the copy. Other processes that have the object mapped cannot see the changes.

MAP_FIXED
> Inform the system to map the file into memory exactly at address `addr` (see below). The use of this flag is discouraged because it can prevent the system from making the most efficient use of system resources.

MAP_NORESERVE

Normally, when MAP_PRIVATE mappings are created, the system reserves swap space equivalent to the size of the mapping. This space is used to store the private copies of any modified pages. When this flag is specified, the system does not preallocate space for the modified pages. This means that if swap space for a newly modified page is unavailable, the process receives a SIGBUS signal when it tries to modify that page.

This flag is not available in HP-UX 10.*x*.

The addr parameter specifies the suggested address at which the object is to be mapped. If addr is given as zero, the system is granted complete freedom to map the object wherever it wants for best efficiency. If addr is non-zero but MAP_FIXED is not specified, it is taken as a suggestion of an address near where the memory should be mapped. If addr is non-zero and MAP_FIXED is specified, it is taken as the exact address at which to map the object.

Removing a Mapping

A memory mapping is removed with the munmap function:

```
#include <sys/types.h>
#include <sys/mman.h>

int munmap(caddr_t addr, size_t len);
```

The mapping for the pages in the range addr to addr+len are removed. Further references to these pages result in the delivery of a SIGSEGV signal to the process (see Chapter 10). If the unmapping is successful, munmap returns 0; otherwise, it returns -1 and places the reason for failure in the external variable errno.

Example 6-3 shows a program that uses mmap to read files and print them on the standard output (much like the *cat* command).

Example 6–3: catmap

```
#include <sys/types.h>
#include <sys/stat.h>
#include <sys/mman.h>
#include <stdlib.h>
#include <fcntl.h>
#include <stdio.h>

int
main(int argc, char **argv)
{
    int fd;
    struct stat st;
    caddr_t base, ptr;
```

Example 6-3: catmap (continued)

```
    /*
     * For each file specified...
     */
    while (--argc) {
        /*
         * Open the file.
         */
        if ((fd = open(*++argv, O_RDONLY, 0)) < 0) {
            perror(*argv);
            continue;
        }

        /*
         * Find out how big the file is.
         */
        fstat(fd, &st);

        /*
         * Map the entire file into memory.
         */
        base = mmap(0, st.st_size, PROT_READ, MAP_SHARED, fd, 0);

        if (base == MAP_FAILED) {
            perror(*argv);
            close(fd);
            continue;
        }

        /*
         * We can close the file now; we can access it
         * through memory.
         */
        close(fd);

        /*
         * Now print the file.
         */
        for (ptr = base; ptr < &base[st.st_size]; ptr++)
            putchar(*ptr);

        /*
         * Now unmap the file.
         */
        munmap(base, st.st_size);
    }

    exit(0);
}
```

```
% catmap /etc/motd
Sun Microsystems Inc.  SunOS 5.3      Generic September 1993
```

Changing the Protection Mode of Mapped Segments

The mprotect function allows a process to change the protection modes of a previously mapped segment:

```
#include <sys/types.h>
#include <sys/mman.h>

int mprotect(caddr_t addr, size_t len, int prot);
```

The addr and len parameters specify the starting address and length of the segment whose permissions are to be changed. The prot parameter specifies the new protection mode to be set on the segment using the PROT_READ, PROT_WRITE, PROT_EXEC, and PROT_NONE flags as described earlier. Upon successful completion, mprotect returns 0; otherwise, it returns -1 and stores the reason for failure in errno.

Providing Advice to the System

Once a file is mapped into memory, the operating system's virtual memory subsystem is responsible for paging that file into memory. In order to make the mapping more efficient and consume fewer system resources, the madvise function allows a process to give "hints" to the system about how best to page the object into memory:

```
#include <sys/types.h>
#include <sys/mman.h>

int madvise(caddr_t addr, size_t len, int advice);
```

The addr and len parameters specify the starting address and length of the segment to which the advice applies. The advice parameter can contain one of the following:

MADV_NORMAL

This is the default mode. The kernel reads all the data from the object (or at least reads a reasonable amount) into pages that are used as a cache. System pages are a limited resource, and the kernel steals pages from other mappings if necessary. This can adversely affect system performance when large amounts of memory are accessed, but in general it is not a problem.

`MADV_RANDOM`

> The process jumps around in the object, and may access a tiny bit here and then a tiny bit there. This tells the kernel to read in a minimum amount of data from the mapped object on any particular access, rather than reading larger amounts in anticipation of other accesses within the same locality.

`MADV_SEQUENTIAL`

> The program is planning to access the object in order from lowest address to highest, and each address is likely to be accessed only once. The kernel frees the resources from the mapping as quickly as possible. (The *catmap* program could use this option to increase performance.)

`MADV_WILLNEED`

> Tells the system that a specific address range is definitely needed, so that it can start reading the specified range into memory. This can benefit programs that need to minimize the time needed to access memory the first time.

`MADV_DONTNEED`

> Tells the kernel that a specific address range is no longer needed, so that it can begin freeing the resources associated with that part of the mapping.

With the exception of `MADV_DONTNEED`, these constants are not supported in IRIX 5.*x*.

Synchronizing Memory with Physical Storage

When an object is mapped, the system maintains both an image of the object in memory and a copy of the image in *backing storage*. The backing storage copy is maintained so that the system can allow other processes to use the physical memory when it is their turn to run. The backing storage for a `MAP_SHARED` mapping is the file to which the mapping is attached; the backing storage for a `MAP_PRIVATE` mapping is its swap area. The `msync` function tells the system to synchronize the in-memory copy of the mapping with its backing storage (the system does this periodically on its own, but some programs need to have the object in a known state):

```
#include <sys/types.h>
#include <sys/mman.h>

int msync(caddr_t addr, size_t len, int flags);
```

The `addr` and `len` parameters specify the starting address and length of the segment to synchronize. The `flags` parameter consists of one or more of the following values *or*ed together:

MS_ASYNC

This causes all writes to be scheduled, after which msync returns. The writes are completed a short time afterward.

MS_SYNC

All write operations are performed before msync returns. This guarantees that the data is on the disk before the process proceeds, but it also causes the process to wait for a longer period of time.

MS_INVALIDATE

Invalidates any cached copies of the segment in memory, so that any subsequent references to the pages cause the system to bring them in from their backing storage locations.

If msync succeeds, it returns 0. Otherwise, it returns -1 and places the error indication in errno.

The /dev/fd Filesystem

The */dev/fd* filesystem allows each process to access its open file descriptors as names in the filesystem. If file descriptor n is open, the following two calls have the same effect:

```
fd = open("/dev/fd/n", mode);

fd = dup(n);
```

One of the most common uses for the */dev/fd* filesystem is to "trick" programs that insist on reading from or writing to a file to read from the standard input or write to the standard output. For example, consider the following program:

```
#include <stdio.h>
#include <ctype.h>
```

```
int
main(int argc, char **argv)
{
    int c;
    FILE *fp;

    if ((fp = fopen(*++argv, "r")) == NULL) {
        perror(*argv);
        exit(1);
    }

    while ((c = getc(fp)) != EOF) {
        if (islower(c))
            c = toupper(c);
        putc(c, stdout);
    }
```

```
        fclose(fp);
        exit(0);
}
```

This program opens the file named on its command line, reads the file, and prints it out in uppercase. Unfortunately, since this program insists on reading from a file, it cannot be used as part of a pipeline to convert the output from another command to uppercase.

The */dev/fd* filesystem remedies this by allowing the program's standard input to be specified as a filename. To use the above program in a pipeline then, we can do this:

```
% somecommand | toupper /dev/fd/0
```

The */dev/fd* filesystem was originally developed in Research UNIX. Shortly thereafter, public-domain implementations for BSD UNIX appeared, and it eventually appeared in SVR3. From there, it also became a part of SVR4. It is gradually appearing in other vendors' releases as well.

The */dev/fd* filesystem is not available in HP-UX 10.*x.*

Miscellaneous Functions

There are several other special-purpose functions that are occasionally useful as well. Some of these are described in this section.

Controlling File Creation Modes

When a file is created, its permission bits are specified in the call to **creat** or **open**. As indicated in Chapter 3, these bits are modified by the process' **umask** value. Quite simply, the **umask** value is a set of permission bits to turn back off in any file creation mode. When a file is created, the permission bits specified in the call to **creat** or **open** are *and*ed with the complement of the **umask** value to determine the actual bits that will be set:

```
actual_mode = create_mode & ~umask;
```

Convention dictates that whenever a file is created with **creat** or **open**, the permission bits should be specified as 0666 (read/write for owner, group, and world). Each user can then use the **umask** value to control the actual permissions with which the file is created. For example, if a file is created with mode 0666 and the user's **umask** is 022, you get:

```
actual_mode = create_mode & ~umask;
actual_mode = 0666 & ~022;
```

```
actual_mode = 0666 & 0755;
actual_mode = 0644;
```

The file is created readable and writable by the user and readable by everyone else. If the user's umask is 077 instead, you get:

```
actual_mode = create_mode & ~umask;
actual_mode = 0666 & ~077;
actual_mode = 0666 & 0700;
actual_mode = 0600;
```

The file is created readable and writable by the user and nobody else is able to access it.

A process' umask value is set with the umask function:

```
#include <sys/types.h>
#include <sys/stat.h>

mode_t umask(mode_t cmask);
```

The new value is specified by the cmask parameter, and the old value is returned. The umask is inherited by child processes, so all of the shells provide a built-in *umask* command to set the umask value of the shell (and therefore of all processes started by the shell).

The Root Directory

UNIX allows a process to change its notion of where the root of the filesystem is; that is, from where in the filesystem absolute pathnames begin. By default, each process uses / (the real root of the filesystem) as its root. However, in some instances, it is desirable to restrict a process to a specific area in the filesystem.

For example, many sites allow users from all over the world to connect to their hosts using the File Transfer Protocol (FTP) and log in as "anonymous" for the purpose of downloading files. However, these sites obviously don't want to give the entire world access to every file on the system; rather, these users should only be allowed to access files in a specific area. Even when one of these users specifies an absolute pathname (one that begins with a /), that pathname should be taken relative to this specific area.

To implement this, use the chroot function:

```
#include <unistd.h>

int chroot(const char *path);

int fchroot(int fd);
```

The `chroot` function changes the calling process' root directory to the directory named in `path`. The `fchroot` function changes the calling process' root directory to the directory referenced by the file descriptor `fd`. Once this call has succeeded, all absolute pathnames are taken relative to this directory. Note that on systems that do not offer `fchroot` (most of them), there is no way to undo this call— because there is no way to reference a directory outside of the one named in `path`, there is no way to go back up. With `fchroot`, however, the higher-level directory can be opened prior to calling `chroot` and then can be used later to reset the root directory. Use of these two functions is restricted to the superuser.

Synchronizing a File with the Disk

When a process issues a write, the operating system transfers that data to a disk buffer and returns control to the process. At some later time (within a few milliseconds), the data is actually written to disk. This makes the system run much more efficiently, by allowing processes to run without having to stop and wait on (relatively) slow devices, and also by allowing the system to optimize device accesses. However, there are times when a program needs to know that the data on the disk is an accurate representation of what is written; it can't wait those extra few milliseconds.

To do this, the program uses the `fsync` function:

```
#include <unistd.h>

int fsync(int fd);
```

This function moves all modified data and attributes of the file referenced by the file descriptor `fd` to a storage device. When `fsync` returns, the calling process can be certain that all disk buffers associated with the file are written to the physical storage medium.

NOTE

The `fsync` function is not simply an alternative form of the `sync` function. A call to `sync` causes all modified disk buffers (for all files, not just those belonging to the calling process) to be *scheduled* for writing to disk. However, the call returns as soon as scheduling is complete; it does *not* wait for all the writes to be performed. The `fsync` function, on the other hand, causes the calling process to block until the disk buffers associated with `fd` are actually written to the disk (or other device).

Chapter Summary

Although the title of this chapter might indicate that the functions just discussed are not used very often, this is only partially true. In particular, the `select` and `poll` functions are used frequently in programs that must manage multiple data streams; many network-based programs fall into this category. The `fcntl` function is also used fairly often, although only some of its options are used routinely. And finally, file and record locking is used with some regularity.

7

Time of Day Operations

The UNIX operating system keeps track of the current date and time by maintaining the number of seconds that have elapsed since Thursday, January 1, 1970 at 00:00:00 UTC (Coordinated Universal Time, also called Greenwich Mean Time or Zulu Time). This number is stored in a signed long integer, which means that, assuming a 32-bit system, UNIX timekeeping will break on Tuesday, January 19, 2038 at 03:14:08 UTC when the value overflows and becomes negative.

There are a number of systems programming applications that need to know how to convert the UNIX time format to something that can be understood by humans. You encountered one of these applications in Chapter 5, *Files and Directories*, to print out file access and modification times. This chapter examines the functions that are provided to convert between UNIX time format and human-readable date and time strings.

The Complexities of Time

Converting a quantity such as the number of seconds since some epoch time into a date and time string usable by humans is an extraordinarily difficult problem. If everyone used Coordinated Universal Time, it would be fairly simple. Divide the number of seconds since the epoch by 86,400 (the number of seconds in a day), and you have the number of days since the epoch and a remainder. Divide the remainder by 3,600 (the number of seconds in an hour) and you have the current hour. Divide the remainder of that by 60 and you have the current minute, and the remainder gives the current second. Divide the number of days by 365 and you have the current year (but don't forget leap years), and the remainder gives the current month and day, which can be separated just as easily.

Unfortunately, everyone doesn't use Coordinated Universal Time. Coordinated Universal Time is the time of day at the Prime Meridian, which passes through Greenwich, England (hence the name Greenwich Mean Time). Local time in other parts of the world is determined by taking an offset, either positive or negative, from Greenwich Mean Time. If the location is east of Greenwich, the offset is negative (meaning local time is earlier than UTC); if the location is west of Greenwich, the offset is positive (meaning local time is later than UTC). For example, local time in New York City is five hours earlier than UTC. So when it's 8:00 a.m. in New York, it's already 1:00 p.m. in Greenwich.

Each of these offsets is called a *time zone*. The purpose of time zones is to allow human beings to shift the clock such that it agrees with local day and night. For example, local noon should be the time at which the sun is at its highest point in the sky. But when it's local noon at Greenwich, England, it's still dark in Los Angeles, California. So Los Angeles shifts its local time by eight hours from UTC. In most parts of the world, the local time zone is offset by a whole number of hours from UTC. However, in some parts of the world, the local time zone is offset by some number of half hours from UTC; for example, in Adelaide, Australia, local time is 10.5 hours ahead of UTC.

To complicate things even further, humans have invented another artificial time adjustment called Daylight Savings Time (DST). This adjustment shifts clocks forward by (usually) one hour in the spring, and shifts them back again in the fall. The purpose of this shift is to seemingly make daylight last longer each day during the summer, so that farmers and other people who have to work outdoors can get more done. (Of course, the number of daylight hours doesn't actually change, DST just makes it seem like the days are longer by moving bedtime ahead one hour.)

In order to write a function that converts UNIX time format to a date and time string representing local time, you have to keep track of a number of different things. First, you have to know what time zone you are in and how that time zone is offset from UTC. This means that the conversion is different depending on whether you're in New York City, Los Angeles, or Moscow. Furthermore, you have to know the rules for DST in this time zone; this is even more complicated. DST is determined differently in different parts of the world; some areas observe it, and some don't. Consider the United States' rules for DST observance. Prior to 1967, observance of DST was by local option except during World War I and II, when it was mandatory. Since 1967, DST has been observed by nearly the entire country. But even this has exceptions; the state of Indiana, with the exception of the northwest and southeast corners, does not observe DST. To further complicate matters, prior to 1987, DST began on the last Sunday in April; since 1987 it has begun on the first Sunday in April. DST ends on the last Sunday in October. This seems fairly straightforward. But in 1974 and 1975, because of the energy crisis, DST began on January 6 and February 23, respectively. And in 1989, the U.S. House of Representatives passed a bill that would make DST in the Pacific time zone end on the first Sunday after November 7th in presidential election years and on the last Sunday in October otherwise (this bill was never signed into law).

Fortunately, this whole mess is taken care of for you by the UNIX library routines that manipulate time and date strings. However, I wanted to provide you with some idea of the complexity involved in making these conversions. Many older versions of UNIX had numerous problems with time zones. Some would only handle time zones that were whole hour offsets from UTC, some could not reliably convert between an offset and a time zone name, and so forth. More will be said about this below in the section on porting notes, but it's important to be aware that the routines described in the following sections, while they handle all time zone conversions known at the time they were released, may not handle conversions properly in the future. This is particularly true of the DST corrections, which are subject to the whims of our lawmakers.

Obtaining the Current Time

To obtain the current time of day in UNIX time format, all versions of UNIX provide the same function:

```
#include <sys/types.h>
#include <time.h>

time_t time(time_t *tloc);
```

The `time` function returns the number of seconds since January 1, 1970, 00:00:00 UTC. If `tloc` is non-null, `time` also stores this value in the memory location pointed to by `tloc`.

Porting Notes

In 4.2 BSD, another function was introduced to obtain the current time:

```
#include <sys/time.h>

int gettimeofday(struct timeval *tp, struct timezone *tz);
```

The `gettimeofday` function places the current time into the structure pointed to by `tp`, and the local time zone information into the structure pointed to by `tz`. The structures are defined in the include file *sys/time.h*:

```
struct timeval {
    long    tv_sec;
    long    tv_usec;
};

struct timezone {
    int     tz_minuteswest;
    int     tz_dsttime;
};
```

The `tv_sec` and `tv_usec` elements store the time in seconds and microseconds since January 1, 1970. The `tz_minuteswest` element stores the offset (positive or negative) from UTC in minutes, and the `tz_dsttime` element contains a flag indicating the type of DST correction (if any) to be applied.

IRIX 5.*x* and versions of Solaris prior to Solaris 2.5 provide a single-argument version of `gettimeofday` for backward compatibility; the `struct timezone` argument is ignored. HP-UX 10.*x* and versions of Solaris beginning with Solaris 2.5 provide a two-argument version.

Obtaining the Local Time Zone

Time zone determination has varied with almost every version of UNIX, owing mostly to the continual need to handle more and more special cases. In SVR4, the local time zone is stored in the `TZ` environment variable, which contains a string such as US/Eastern or Australia/West. In C programs, the program should first call the function `tzset`:

```
#include <time.h>


void tzset(void);
```

After calling `tzset`, four external variables are available for use:

```
extern time_t timezone, altzone;
extern char *tzname[2];
extern int daylight;
```

The `timezone` variable contains the difference, in seconds, between UTC and local standard time; the `altzone` variable contains the difference, in seconds, between UTC and the alternate time zone (DST). The `daylight` variable is non-zero if DST is in effect, zero otherwise. The `tzname` array contains the names (abbreviations) of the time zones for local standard time and DST; for example, in New York City `tzname[0]` contains EST and `tzname[1]` contains EDT. Prior to calling `tzset`, these four variables contain values that describe Coordinated Universal Time.

HP-UX 10.*x* does not provide the `altzone` variable.

Porting Notes

In SVR2, the `TZ` environment variable had to contain a three-letter time zone name, followed by a number indicating the difference between local time and UTC in hours, followed by an optional three-letter name for a daylight time zone. When DST was in effect, the standard United States rules were applied. This means that SVR2 could not handle time zones that were half-hour offsets from UTC, or daylight time rules that differed from the United States'. Otherwise, the interface is the same as described previously.

SunOS 4.*x* provides the same interface described previously, except that it also allows the time zone name to be obtained from the `struct tm` structure (described next). SunOS 4.*x* is the only operating system that allows the time zone name to be obtained in this manner.

BSD UNIX and Version 7 offered two other functions for working with time zones:

```
#include <sys/types.h>
#include <sys/timeb.h>

int ftime(struct timeb *tp);

char *timezone(int zone, int dst);
```

The `ftime` function placed the current time and time zone information into the structure of type `struct timeb` pointed to by `tp` and defined in *sys/timeb.h*:

```
struct timeb {
    time_t          time;
    unsigned short  millitim;
    short           timezone;
    short           dstflag;
};
```

The `time` element contains the time in UNIX time format, the `millitim` element contains up to 1,000 milliseconds of more precise information, the `timezone` element contains the local time zone measured in minutes west of Greenwich, and the `dstflag` element is non-zero when DST is in effect.

The `timezone` function returns the name associated with the time zone that is `zone` minutes west of Greenwich; if `dst` is zero, the standard time zone name is used, otherwise the daylight time zone name is used. This function has serious problems with returning the correct time zone name anywhere in the world, because there are multiple names for each zone depending on location.

Converting Between UNIX Time and Human Time

There are four functions provided to convert between UNIX time and human time:

```
#include <time.h>

struct tm *gmtime(const time_t *clock);

struct tm *localtime(const time_t *clock);

time_t mktime(struct tm *tp);

double difftime(time_t t1, time_t t0);
```

The `gmtime` function returns a structure of type `struct tm`. This structure contains the broken out components of the date and time represented by the value of the variable pointed to by `clock`, which should contain a value such as that returned by the `time` function. The time represented in the `struct tm` structure is in Coordinated Universal Time. The `localtime` function makes the same conversion, but if the program has called the `tzset` function first, the resulting time is corrected for the local time zone and daylight time. The `struct tm` structure is defined in the include file *time.h*:

```
struct tm {
    int    tm_sec;
    int    tm_min;
    int    tm_hour;
    int    tm_mday;
    int    tm_mon;
    int    tm_year;
    int    tm_wday;
    int    tm_yday;
    int    tm_isdst;
};
```

The `tm_sec` element contains the seconds after the minute (0–61; the 61 is for leap seconds), the `tm_min` element contains the minutes after the hour (0–59), the `tm_hour` element contains the hours since midnight (0–23), the `tm_mday` element contains the day of the month (1–31), the `tm_mon` element contains the month (0–11, 0=January), the `tm_year` element contains the year since 1900, the `tm_wday` element contains the day of the week (0–6, 0=Sunday), the `tm_yday` element contains the day of the year (0–365, 0=January 1st), and the `tm_isdst` element is non-zero if daylight time is in effect.

The `mktime` function performs the opposite conversion. It takes a `struct tm` structure as input and returns the number of seconds since January 1, 1970 00:00:00 UTC. The `mktime` function also normalizes the time in the structure, so that the values do not have to be within the limits described previously. For example, a `tm_hour` value of -1 indicates one hour before midnight. The conversions performed by `mktime` are corrected for the local time zone and daylight time; in general, you'll want to set the `tm_isdst` field to -1 to avoid surprises.

The `difftime` function computes the difference between two time values, `t1` and `t0`, and returns the result as a double precision value. This function is required by the ANSI C standard, because there are no arithmetic operations defined on the `time_t` data type (not all systems use a `long` for `time_t`).

One useful thing that `gmtime` (which should really be called `utctime`, but history prevails) can be used for is printing out the difference between two times in human-readable format. For example, if you have two times, a login time and a logout time, you can compute the duration of the login session as follows:

```
#include <time.h>
    ⋮
struct tm *tp;
time_t login, logout, session;
    ⋮
session = (time_t) difftime(logout, login);

tp = gmtime(&session);

printf("Session length: %d days, %d hours, %d minutes\n",
    tp->tm_yday, tp->tm_hour, tp->tm_min);
```

Porting Notes

The `difftime` function is specific to ANSI C environments, although it's easy to define for other environments.

The `mktime` function is a generalization of two other functions, `timelocal` and `timegm`, which have been introduced in a number of UNIX versions.

There is disagreement between various versions of UNIX as to whether the include file for these functions belongs in *time.h* or *sys/time.h*. Some versions have it in one place, others have it in the other. Newer versions have sidestepped the issue by making it available in both places.

Formatting Date Strings

Now that you can convert UNIX time to a `struct tm` structure and vice-versa, the next thing you need to do is convert the elements of this structure into something readable by human beings. There are five functions provided to do this:

```
#include <time.h>

char *ctime(const time_t *clock);

char *asctime(const struct tm *tm);

size_t *strftime(const char *s, size_t maxsize, const char *format,
    const struct tm *tm);

int cftime(char *s, const char *format, const time_t *clock);

int ascftime(char *s, const char *format, const struct tm *tm);
```

The `asctime` function converts the time contained in `tm` as returned by `localtime` or `gmtime` to a 26-character string and returns a pointer to that string. The string has the format:

```
DDD MMM dd hh:mm:ss yyyy\n\0
```

For example:

```
Thu Jan  1 00:00:00 1970\n\0
```

The `ctime` function is equivalent to calling:

```
asctime(localtime(&clock));
```

The `cftime`, `ascftime`, and `strftime` functions all do essentially the same thing, with `cftime` being to `ascftime` as `ctime` is to `asctime`. The `cftime` and `ascftime` functions are obsolete, and `strftime` should be used instead. HP-UX 10.*x* does not provide `cftime` or `ascftime`.

The `strftime` function copies characters into the array pointed to by `s`, which is of `maxsize` bytes in length. The contents of the string are controlled by the string contained in `format`. The `format` string is similar to a `printf` format string; all ordinary characters in the string (including the terminating null character) are copied into `s`, and characters in `format` that are preceded by a percent sign (%) represent formatting directives. The `strftime` function is internationalized, and uses values in formatting directives that are appropriate for the current locale.

The valid formatting directives are as follows. If the `format` string is null, the locale's default format is used:

%% A literal percent sign

%a The locale's abbreviated weekday name

%A The locale's full weekday name

%b The locale's abbreviated month name

%B The locale's full month name

%c The locale's appropriate date and time representation

%C The locale's date and time representation as produced by the *date* command

%d The day of the month (01–31)

%D The date as %m/%d/%y

%e The day of the month (1–31, single digits are preceded by a space)

%h The locale's abbreviated month name

%H The hour (00–23)

%I The hour (01–12)

%j The day of the year (001–366)

%k The hour (0–23, single digits are preceded by a space) (Solaris 2.*x* only)

%l The hour (1–12, single digits are preceded by a space) (Solaris 2.*x* only)

%m The month number (01–12)

%M The minute (00–59)

%n Same as \n

%p The locale's equivalent of A.M. or P.M.

%r The time as %I:%M:%S [AM|PM]

%R The time as %H:%M

%S The second (00–61); allows for leap seconds

%t Same as \t

%T The time as %H:%M:%S

%U The week number of the year (00–53); Sunday is the first day of week 01, days prior to the first Sunday in January are in week 00

%w The weekday number (0–6); Sunday is day 0

%W The week number of the year (00–53); Monday is the first day of week 01, days prior to the first Monday in January are in week 00

%x The locale's appropriate date representation

%X The locale's appropriate time representation

%y The year within the century (00–99)

%Y The year with the century (for example, 1962)

%Z The time zone name, or no characters if no time zone exists

Example 7-1 shows a small program that demonstrates the use of `strftime` and its output in several different locales (if your system does not have the internationalization options installed, all the output is in English). The `setlocale` function is used to set the locale; it is described in more detail in Chapter 16, *Miscellaneous Routines.*

Example 7-1: date

```c
#include <locale.h>
#include <stdio.h>
#include <time.h>

/*
 * Sample formats.
 */
char *formats[] = {
    "%A, %B %e, %Y, %H:%M:%S",
    "%I:%M %p, %d-%b-%y.",
    "%x %X",
    "%C",
    "%c",
    NULL
};

char *locales[] = {
    "C", "de", "fr", "it", "sv", NULL
};

char *localeNames[] = {
    "UNIX", "German", "French", "Italian", "Swedish", NULL
};

int
main(int argc, char **argv)
{
    int i, j;
    time_t clock;
    struct tm *tm;
    char buf[BUFSIZ];

    /*
     * Get current time.
     */
    time(&clock);
```

Example 7-1: date (continued)

```
tm = gmtime(&clock);

/*
 * For each locale...
 */
for (i=0; locales[i] != NULL; i++) {
    /*
     * Print the locale name and set it.
     */
    printf("%s:\n", localeNames[i]);
    setlocale(LC_TIME, locales[i]);

    /*
     * For each format string...
     */
    for (j=0; formats[j] != NULL; j++) {
        strftime(buf, sizeof(buf), formats[j], tm);
        printf("\t%-25s %s\n", formats[j], buf);
    }

    printf("\n");
}

exit(0);
}
```

```
% date
UNIX:
    %A, %B %e, %Y, %H:%M:%S    Sunday, March 20, 1994, 22:38:19
    %I:%M %p, %d-%b-%y         10:38 PM, 20-Mar-94
    %x %X                      03/20/94 22:38:19
    %C                         Sun Mar 20 22:38:19 GMT 1994
    %c                         Sun Mar 20 22:38:19 1994

German:
    %A, %B %e, %Y, %H:%M:%S    Sonntag, März 20, 1994, 22:38:19
    %I:%M %p, %d-%b-%y         10:38 PM, 20-Mär-94
    %x %X                      20.03.94 22:38:19
    %C                         Sonntag, 20. März 1994, 22:38:19 Uhr GMT
    %c                         So 20 Mär 94, 22:38:19 GMT

French:
    %A, %B %e, %Y, %H:%M:%S    dimanche, mars 20, 1994, 22:38:19
    %I:%M %p, %d-%b-%y         10:38 PM, 20-mar-94
    %x %X                      20.03.94 22:38:19
    %C                         dimanche, 20 mars 1994, 22:38:19 GMT
    %c                         dim 20 mar 94, 22:38:19 GMT

Italian:
    %A, %B %e, %Y, %H:%M:%S    domenica, marzo 20, 1994, 22:38:19
    %I:%M %p, %d-%b-%y         10:38 PM, 20-mar-94
```

```
%x %X                        20/03/94 22:38:19
%C                           domenica, 20 marzo 1994, 22:38:19 GMT
%c                           Dom 20 mar 94, 22:38:19 GMT

Swedish:
%A, %B %e, %Y, %H:%M:%S      söndag, mars 20, 1994, 22:38:19
%I:%M %p, %d-%b-%y           10:38 EM, 20-mar-94
%x %X                        94-03-20 22:38:19
%C                           söndag, 20 mars 1994 kl 22:38:19 GMT
%c                           sön 20 mar 94 kl 22:38:19 GMT
```

To perform conversions in the other direction, from a string to an internal time representation, use the `getdate` function:

```
#include <time.h>

struct tm *getdate(const char *string);
```

The `getdate` function converts user-defined date and time specifications pointed to by `string` into a `struct tm` structure. User-defined templates are used to parse and interpret the input string. The templates are text files created by the user and identified using the environment variable `DATEMSK`. Each line in the template file represents an acceptable date and/or time specification, using the same descriptors as described previously for `strftime`. The first template that matches the input specification is used. If successful, `getdate` returns a pointer to a `struct tm` structure; if it fails, it returns `NULL` and sets the external variable `getdate_err` to indicate the error.

The month and weekday names can contain any combination of upper- and lowercase letters. If only the weekday is given, today is assumed if the given day is equal to the current day, otherwise next week is assumed. If only the month is given, the current month is assumed if the given month is equal to the current month; otherwise, next year is assumed (unless a year is given). If no hour, minute, and second are given, the current hour, minute, and second are assumed. If no date is given, today is assumed if the given hour is later than the current hour, and tomorrow is assumed otherwise.

Example 7-2 shows an example use of the `getdate` function.

Example 7-2: getdate

```
#include <stdio.h>
#include <time.h>

extern int getdate_err;

int
main(int argc, char **argv)
{
```

Example 7-2: getdate (continued)

```
    struct tm *tm;
    char buf[BUFSIZ];

    for (;;) {
        /*
         * Prompt for a string.
         */
        printf("? ");

        /*
         * Read the string.
         */
        if (fgets(buf, sizeof(buf), stdin) == NULL) {
            putchar('\n');
            exit(0);
        }

        /*
         * Convert it.
         */
        if ((tm = getdate(buf)) != NULL)
            printf("%s\n", asctime(tm));
        else
            printf("Error (%d).\n", getdate_err);
    }
}
```

```
% cat getdate.template
%m
%A %B %d %Y, %H:%M:%S
%A
%B
%m/%d/%y %I %p
%d,%m,%Y %H:%M
at %A the %dst of %B in %Y
run job at %I %p,%B %dnd
%A den %d. %B %Y %H.%M Uhr
% setenv DATEMSK getdate.template
% getdate
? 10/1/87 4 PM
Thu Oct  1 16:00:00 1987

? Friday
Fri Mar 25 18:13:17 1994

? Friday September 18 1987, 10:30:30
Fri Sep 18 10:30:30 1987

? 24,9,1986 10:30
Wed Sep 24 10:30:00 1986
```

```
?   at monday the 1st of december in 1986
Mon Dec  1 18:13:23 1986

?   run job at 3 PM, december 2nd
Fri Dec  2 15:00:00 1994

?   ^D
```

Porting Notes

The `ctime` and `asctime` functions are common to all versions of UNIX; the other functions are less widespread.

The `getdate` function conflicts with a public domain function of the same name that is used in many programs. The public domain function attempts to produce a `time_t` given an arbitrary date string; it performs all the magic necessary to determine what format the string is in. The purpose of this function is to allow users to input dates and times in whatever format they're used to, without having to predetermine what format that is. Generally speaking, the public domain function is significantly more useful than the function provided by SVR4.

Chapter Summary

A number of systems programming applications need to be able to convert between the internal date and time format used by UNIX and the date and time strings that are used by humans. The library routines provided by the operating system encompass all the knowledge about complexities such as time zones and DST, so that the programmer does not have to worry about them. This book uses these functions in several of the examples in the remaining chapters.

8

Users and Groups

A UNIX system maintains several pieces of information about each user, including a login name, user ID, and one or more group IDs. The operating system uses this data to keep track of the privileges associated with each process (what files it may open, how many resources it may consume, etc.), who is currently logged in, when each user last logged in, and so on. In this chapter, we examine the information maintained by the operating system about users, and what it may be used for.

Login Names

When a user's account is created, the user is assigned a unique *login name*. The login name is used by user-level and system-level programs to identify individuals. The login name consists of from one to eight characters (some systems require a minimum of two; a few systems have been modified to allow more than eight). Usually, only lowercase letters and numbers are allowed in login names, although some systems will also allow some special characters such as a hyphen or underscore.

Most importantly, the login name is used when logging in to identify yourself to the system. When presented with a "`login:`" prompt, you enter your login name, followed by your password to gain access. Another important use for the login name is in addressing electronic mail. At some point, all electronic mail is identified by the login name of the person who sent it, and by the login name(s) of the intended recipient(s). Although it has recently become popular to allow mail to be addressed as "`Firstname.Lastname@host.domain`" (or something similar), this is almost universally handled by mapping the "`Firstname.Lastname`" strings (e.g., "`Robert M. Smith`," "`Robert Smith`," "`Bob Smith`") to the login name (e.g., "`bmsmith`") internally. Other uses for the login name include identifying output on the printer, granting or removing privileges in permissions files, and so forth.

An important part of the UNIX system that does *not* use the login name is the operating system kernel. The kernel instead uses your user ID number (described in the next section) to keep track of who you are and what you may do. The reason for this is quite simply that the underlying hardware makes it easier to deal with numbers than with character strings. Numbers may be tested for equality, copied from memory location to memory location, and so forth, with individual machine instructions. Character strings (login names) on the other hand, must be handled in subroutines. Since the kernel checks every request you make for permission to make such a request (e.g., if this file is readable only by the owner, you cannot open it for reading unless you own it), it is vital that these checks be as efficient as possible.

To obtain the login name of the user executing a program, all versions of UNIX provide the `getlogin` function:

```
#include <unistd.h>

char *getlogin(void);
```

This function searches the */var/adm/utmp* file (described later in this chapter) for the entry for the terminal line to which the program is attached, and returns the login name contained in that entry. This method is prone to error: if the user has logged off, or is running the program without a terminal (for example, with the *rsh* command), `getlogin` will return a null pointer, indicating that it could not find the information.

The creators of System V UNIX recognized this problem, and added the routine `cuserid` in an attempt to avoid it.

```
#include <stdio.h>

char *cuserid(char *buf);
```

Like `getlogin`, `cuserid` examines the */var/adm/utmp* file. However, if nothing is found, `cuserid` obtains the user ID number of the executing process, looks it up in the password file (how to do this is described later in this chapter), and returns the login name that way. If `buf` is a non-null pointer, the login name is copied into the array it points to. Otherwise, a pointer is returned to a static area that is overwritten with each call. If the login name cannot be found, a null pointer is returned.

Be aware that neither `getlogin` or `cuserid` should be trusted by programs that *must* know the name of the user executing a program. These include any program that uses this information to perform permissions or authorization checking. The problem with both of these functions is that they rely on the contents of the *utmp* file first: whatever is written there is assumed to be correct. Unfortunately, the *utmp* file is world-writable on many systems. This means that an unscrupulous user could change his entry in the file to the name of an authorized user, and then run your program, and you would be none the wiser. Programs that must know the true identity of the executing user should *only* use the user ID number to identify that user. If they also need to know the user's login name, this information can be obtained from the password file. The method for doing this is described later in this chapter.

The User ID Number

Each process executing on the system has associated with it two small integers called the *real user ID number* and the *effective user ID number*. The UNIX kernel uses these numbers to determine the process' access permissions, record accounting information, and so on. The real user ID always identifies the user executing the program, and is used for accounting purposes. Only the superuser may change his real user ID, thus becoming another user. The effective user ID is used to determine a process' access permissions. Normally, the effective user ID is equal to the real user ID. However, by changing its effective user ID, a process can gain the additional access permissions associated with the new user ID. It is possible for more than one login name to be associated with the same user ID, but as far as the operating system kernel is concerned, each user ID is unique and identifies one and only one person. Thus, the only purpose of multiple login names with the same user ID is to allow different people to access the same set of privileges with different passwords.

A program uses the `getuid` and `geteuid` functions to obtain its real and effective user IDs, respectively:

```
#include <sys/types.h>
#include <unistd.h>
```

```
uid_t getuid(void);

uid_t geteuid(void);
```

Both functions simply return the associated ID.

A process can change its real and/or effective user ID in two ways. The first, which changes only the effective user ID, is to execute a program that has the set-user-id permission bit set (see Chapter 5, *Files and Directories*). The other way is to use the `setuid` and `seteuid` functions:

```
#include <sys/types.h>
#include <unistd.h>

int setuid(uid_t uid);

int seteuid(uid_t euid);
```

The `setuid` function sets the real and effective user IDs of the calling process, plus a third value called the *saved user ID* (see below) to the value contained in `uid`. The `seteuid` function sets the effective user ID only of the calling process to the value contained in `euid`. Upon successful completion, both functions return 0. If an error occurs (usually the error is "permission denied"), -1 is returned and the reason for failure is stored in the external integer `errno`.

The `seteuid` function is not available in HP-UX 10.*x*.

At login time, the real, effective, and saved user-ids are set to the user-id of the user responsible for the creation of the login process. When a process executes a program however, the user ID associated with that new process can change. If the file containing the program has the set-user-id bit set in its permission bits, then the effective user ID and saved user ID of the process are set to the user ID of the owner of the program file (the real user ID is not changed). With that in mind, the following four rules govern the behavior of the `setuid` and `seteuid` functions:

1. If the effective user ID of the process calling `setuid` is that of the superuser, the real, effective, and saved user IDs are set to the value of `uid`.

2. If the effective user ID of the process calling `setuid` is not that of the super-user, but `uid` is equal to either the real user ID or the saved user ID of the calling process, the effective user ID is set to the value of `uid`.

3. If the effective user ID of the process calling `seteuid` is that of the superuser, the effective user ID is set to the value of `euid` (this allows the superuser to change only the effective user ID).

4. If the effective user ID of the process calling `seteuid` is not that of the superuser, but `euid` is equal to either the real user ID or the saved user ID of the calling process, the effective user ID is set to the value of `euid` (`setuid` and `seteuid` behave identically for non-privileged processes).

The saved user ID value allows a process to alternate its effective user ID between the value obtained by executing a set-user-id program and the value of the executing user's real user ID.

Porting Notes

Berkeley-based versions of UNIX do not use the saved user ID. Instead, they provide a function for changing the real and effective user IDs:

```
int setreuid(int uid, int euid);
```

The `setreuid` function differs from the saved user ID approach. It allows a process to *exchange* its real and effective user IDs. Although this provides the same functionality as the saved user ID feature (allowing a process to alternate between its real and effective user IDs), it is also prone to error. If a process calls `setreuid` to exchange its real and effective user IDs (so that its effective user ID is now its real user ID and vice-versa) and then executes a subprocess (for example, a shell), that process will run with its *real* user ID set to the original *effective* user ID. This can present a serious security problem if the programmer is not careful.

The Group ID Number

In addition to the real, effective, and saved user IDs, the operating system also associates with each process a *real group ID number*, an *effective group ID number*, and a *saved group ID number*. These values are also used to determine a process' access permissions, although they only affect the ability to access files (the user-id is also used to determine permissions to execute certain system calls, and for accounting purposes). An analogous set of functions lets you manipulate the group ID:

```
#include <sys/types.h>
#include <unistd.h>

gid_t getgid(void);

gid_t getegid(void);

int setgid(gid_t gid);

int setegid(gid_t egid);
```

All of these functions behave exactly like their user ID counterparts, including the rules for changing the real and effective group ID.

The `setegid` function is not available in HP-UX 10.*x.*

Porting Notes

Just as they do not use the saved user ID, Berkeley-based versions of UNIX do not use the saved group ID idea. Instead, they provide a different function for changing the real and effective group IDs:

```
int setregid(int gid, int egid);
```

This function has the same semantics, and the same problems, as the `setreuid` function described earlier.

Group Membership

In older versions of UNIX, such as Version 7 and pre-SVR4 versions of System V, a user could be a member of only one group at a time. To change groups, a user would use the command *newgrp*, which used `setgid` to change the process' real and effective group IDs.

In 4.2BSD, Berkeley introduced the concept of a *group set*. This allows a user to be in all her groups at once; processes execute with the combined permissions of all the groups, instead of a single group. This setup is much more convenient, and has been adopted by a number of vendors. SVR4 allows the system administrator to configure either behavior into the system; the default "out of the box" configuration uses the group set.

There are two system calls for manipulating the group set:

```
#include <unistd.h>

int getgroups(int gidsetsize, gid_t *grouplist);

int setgroups(int ngroups, const gid_t *grouplist);
```

The `getgroups` function gets the current group set and stores it in the array pointed to by `grouplist`, which has `gidsetsize` entries, and must be large enough to contain the entire list. The list can have a maximum of NGROUPS_MAX entries; this constant is defined in the include file. If `gidsetsize` is 0, `getgroups` returns the number of groups to which the calling process belongs without modifying the `grouplist` array. Upon successful completion, `getgroups` returns the number of groups placed into `grouplist`; -1 is returned if an error occurs and the reason for failure will be stored in `errno`.

The `setgroups` function sets the group set to the list of group IDs contained in the array pointed to by `grouplist`, which contains `ngroups` elements (`ngroups` may not exceed `NGROUPS_MAX`). This function may only be invoked by the superuser. If `setgroups` succeeds, it returns 0. Otherwise, it returns -1 and places an error code in the external integer `errno`.

The Password File

The password file, */etc/passwd*, stores most of the commonly maintained information about each user of the system, including login name, user ID number, full name, home directory, and preferred login shell. On older versions of UNIX, this file also stores each user's encrypted password. However, most newer versions of UNIX have taken the encrypted password out of this file, storing it in another file called a *shadow password file* that is readable only by the superuser. This is described in the following section.

Each line in the password file describes a single user, and is divided into several colon-separated fields. The include file *pwd.h* describes this format for programs with the `struct passwd` structure, which contains at least the following members:

```
struct passwd {
    char    *pw_name;
    char    *pw_passwd;
    uid_t    pw_uid;
    gid_t    pw_gid;
    char    *pw_age;
    char    *pw_comment;
    char    *pw_gecos;
    char    *pw_dir;
    char    *pw_shell;
};
```

The meanings of the fields are:

`pw_name`

 The user's login name.

`pw_passwd`

 The user's encrypted password; if the system uses a shadow password file, this field is meaningless.

`pw_uid`

> The user's user-id number.

`pw_gid`

> The user's login group ID number.

`pw_age`

> On many BSD-based systems, this field is an integer called `pw_quota`. The field is not used for anything, and does not appear in the password file line. (Some System V-based systems do make use of this field for password aging, but this has been superseded in SVR4 by the aging information stored in the shadow password file.)

`pw_comment`

> This field is also unused, and does not appear in the password file line. Although this field has been around since Version 7, it has never been used, and yet nobody has ever removed it from the structure.

`pw_gecos`

> This field contains the user's full name. It derives its name (pronounced "JEE-kohs") from its original use at Bell Laboratories to define an accounting identifier that was used to submit remote jobs to a General Electric mainframe computer. The operating system on the mainframe was called GECOS (General Electric Comprehensive Operating System). (When General Electric's computer division was bought out by Honeywell, GECOS was renamed GCOS, but the password file field retained its original name.)

> On many systems, the `pw_gecos` field is used to store more than just the user's full name. Its content varies with the local environment in which it is used. One method, used by most versions of BSD UNIX (although many vendors' BSD-based systems do not support it), subdivides the `pw_gecos` field into four comma-separated fields. The first field is the user's full name, the second is the user's office telephone number, the third is the user's office room number, and the last is the user's home telephone number. Any of the fields may be left blank, but commas must appear between fields. Trailing commas may be dropped.

`pw_dir`

> The absolute pathname to the user's home directory.

`pw_shell`

> The absolute pathname to the user's *login shell*, the program that will be started when he igr logs in. If this field is left blank, the Bourne shell (*/bin/sh*) is the default.

The following functions are provided for reading the password file:

```
#include <pwd.h>

struct passwd *getpwnam(const char *name);

struct passwd *getpwuid(uid_t uid);

struct passwd *getpwent(void);

void setpwent(void);

void endpwent(void);
```

The getpwnam function searches the password file for a line whose login name field is equal to name, and returns a pointer to a structure of type struct passwd containing the broken-out fields of the entry. The getpwuid function searches for a line whose user ID field is equal to uid. The getpwent function reads the password file sequentially; each successive call returns the next entry in the file. All three functions return pointers to static data that is overwritten on each call; if the calling program needs to retain the data across successive calls, it must copy it to other storage. If an entry cannot be found, or if the end of the file is reached, the routines return the constant NULL.

The setpwent function opens the password file if it is not already open, and resets the read/write offset to the beginning of the file. All three of the functions described above call setpwent internally. The endpwent function closes the password file.

System V-based versions of UNIX, including SVR4, provide a function to bypass the system password file, fgetpwent:

```
#include <stdio.h>
#include <pwd.h>

struct passwd *fgetpwent(FILE *fp);
```

This function reads a line from the file referenced by fp instead of the system password file, and returns a pointer to a structure of type struct passwd containing the broken-out fields. It returns the constant NULL when the end of the file is encountered.

BSD-based systems support a different method for reading alternate password files:

```
#include <pwd.h>

void setpwfile(const char *filename);
```

This changes the routine's notion of the name of the password file to the filename contained in `filename`. This has an advantage over the System V method, since it allows the program to continue to make use of the `getpwnam` and `getpwuid` functions.

Example 8-1, shown later in this chapter, demonstrates the use of these functions.

The Shadow Password File

As mentioned previously, each user's encrypted password used to be stored in the password file, */etc/passwd*. However, in recent years it has been recognized that this can be a security problem. Because the password file must be readable by everyone (programs such as *ls* and *finger* make use of it), it is possible for an unscrupulous user to write a program that attempts to guess each user's password by trying all possible combinations. Because the encrypted password is there in the file for all to see, the bad guy's program can simply encrypt each guess until it finds a matching string.

The solution to this problem is to recognize that the encrypted password is only needed by programs run with superuser permissions for the purposes of performing user authentication. The encrypted password string can be taken out of the password file, and stored in another file that is readable only by the superuser. This file is usually called a *shadow password file*. Most newer UNIX systems offer shadow password files, and a public domain set of functions is available for those systems that do not. The format of the shadow password file varies from vendor to vendor. The discussion in this section uses the format and functions provided by SVR4.

In SVR4, as in some other vendor's versions, the shadow password file also stores information for implementing *password aging*. The idea is to force each user to change his or her password periodically (say, every three months) so that even if an attacker gains access to the shadow password file, the knowledge will not be useful forever. Password aging has its pros and cons, and it is not our purpose to debate them here. Suffice it to say that, at least in SVR4, the use of password aging is optional.

Like the password file, the shadow password file, */etc/shadow*, contains lines of colon-separated fields, one line per user. The include file *shadow.h* describes these fields for programs with the `struct spwd` structure, which contains at least the following members:

```
struct spwd {
    char    *sp_namp;
    char    *sp_pwdp;
    long     sp_lstchg;
```

```
        long      sp_min;
        long      sp_max;
        long      sp_warn;
        long      sp_inact;
        long      sp_expire;
        unsigned long      sp_flag;
    };
```

The meanings of the fields are:

sp_namp

The user's login name.

sp_pwdp

A 13-character encrypted password for the user, a *lock string* (*LK*) indicating that the login is not accessible, or the empty string, indicating that the login may be accessed without providing a password.

sp_lstchg

The number of days between January 1, 1970 and the date that the password was last changed. This field is part of the password aging implementation, and may be blank if password aging is not in use.

sp_min

The minimum number of days required between password changes. This is provided to prevent a user from defeating the password aging system by changing her password to something new (the *passwd* program will not allow "changing" your password to the current password) and then immediately changing it back.

sp_max

The maximum number of days that the current password is valid.

sp_warn

The number of days before the current password expires that the user is warned of its expiration. This is an important part of password aging, because people typically cannot think up a good password without prior notice. Some password aging systems that do not warn users ahead of time that they will need to change their passwords have been plagued with easily-guessed passwords.

sp_inact

The number of days of inactivity allowed for this user. The idea here is to disable (lock) accounts that have been inactive for more than this number of days, so that an attacker cannot make use of the account (which nobody would notice, since the owner is not using it).

sp_expire

> An absolute date (in UNIX time format) after which the login may no longer be used.

sp_flag

> This field is not currently used.

The functions used to read the shadow password file are similar to those used for reading the regular password file, described above:

```
#include <shadow.h>

struct spwd *getspnam(const char *name);

struct spwd *fgetspent(FILE *fp);

struct spwd *getspent(void);

void setspent(void);

void endspent(void);
```

The getspnam function searches the shadow password file for an entry with a login name field that matches **name**. The getspent function returns the next shadow password file entry on each call; fgetspent reads an alternate shadow password file. All three of these functions return a pointer to a **struct spwd** structure with the fields of the entry broken out, or the constant **NULL** if the entry cannot be found or the end of the file is encountered.

The fgetspent function is not available in HP-UX 10.*x*.

The setspent and endspent functions are used, respectively, to open and rewind the shadow password file, or close the shadow password file.

Because the shadow password file is readable only by the superuser, all of these functions will fail if the calling program is not running with superuser permissions.

On other systems, the shadow password file is handled in different ways. One popular method is for the getpwent function and its counterparts to check the effective user ID of the calling program—if it is the superuser, the **pw_passwd** field in the **struct passwd** structure is filled in from the shadow file; otherwise it is left empty.

The Group File

The group file, */etc/group*, contains one entry for each group on the system. Each entry is contained on a single line, and consists of several colon-separated fields.

The last field is a comma-separated list of login names; these users are members of the group. The format of an entry is described for programs by the include file *grp.h*:

```
struct group {
    char    *gr_name;
    char    *gr_passwd;
    gid_t    gr_gid;
    char    **gr_mem;
};
```

The meanings of the fields are:

gr_name
> The name of the group.

gr_passwd
> This field is usually blank. If it is not blank, it contains a 13-character encrypted password (just like the password file). When the *newgrp* command is executed, if a password is present, the user must enter that password to gain access to the new group. With the advent of group membership lists, in which a user is in all of his groups at once, this field has become mostly obsolete.

gr_gid
> The group-id number of the group.

gr_mem
> An array of pointers to character strings; each string contains the login name of one of the members of the group. The list is terminated by a null pointer.

If you've been reading the previous sections, the functions for reading the group file should look very familiar:

```
#include <grp.h>

struct group *getgrnam(const char *name);

struct group *getgrgid(gid_t gid);

struct group *fgetgrent(FILE *fp);

struct group *getgrent(void);

void setgrent(void);

void endgrent(void);
```

The `getgrnam` function searches the group file for an entry with the group name contained in `name`. The `getgrgid` function searches for an entry with the group ID number equal to `gid`. To read the group file one entry at a time, `getgrent` is used; `fgetgrent` allows an alternate file to be read. All of these functions return a pointer to a structure of type `struct group`, or the constant `NULL` if an entry cannot be found or end-of-file is encountered.

The `setgrent` function opens the group file and sets the read/write offset to the beginning of the file, while `endgrent` closes the file.

In order to initialize a user's group membership list, the `initgroups` function is provided:

```
#include <sys/types.h>
#include <grp.h>

int initgroups(const char *name, gid_t basegid);
```

NOTE

The `initgroups` function prototype is declared in *unistd.h* on HP-UX 10.*x* systems.

The `name` parameter contains a login name, and `basegid` contains the login's primary group ID number from the password file. The `initgroups` function reads the group file, and for each group that lists `name` in its membership list, adds that group ID number to an array of group ID numbers. It then calls `setgroups` to initialize the group membership list. If the function is successful, 0 is returned. Otherwise, -1 is returned and the external integer `errno` is set to indicate the error.

Example 8-1 shows a modified version of the *listfiles* program from Chapter 5. This program, you'll recall, reads each directory named on its command line and displays a line for each file in the directory, much like the *ls -l* command. In the original program, we printed out the numeric user ID and group ID for each file; in Example 8-1, we have modified the program to print out the login name and group name.

Example 8-1: newlistfiles

```
#include <sys/types.h>
#include <sys/stat.h>
#include <sys/mkdev.h>
#include <dirent.h>
#include <stdio.h>
#include <pwd.h>
#include <grp.h>

char      typeOfFile(mode_t);
```

Example 8-1: newlistfiles (continued)

```c
char    *permOfFile(mode_t);
void     outputStatInfo(char *, char *, struct stat *);

int
main(int argc, char **argv)
{
    DIR *dp;
    char *dirname;
    struct stat st;
    struct dirent *d;
    char filename[BUFSIZ+1];

    /*
     * For each directory on the command line...
     */
    while (--argc) {
        dirname = *++argv;

        /*
         * Open the directory.
         */
        if ((dp = opendir(dirname)) == NULL) {
            perror(dirname);
            continue;
        }

        printf("%s:\n", dirname);

        /*
         * For each file in the directory...
         */
        while ((d = readdir(dp)) != NULL) {
            /*
             * Create the full file name.
             */
            sprintf(filename, "%s/%s", dirname, d->d_name);

            /*
             * Find out about it.
             */
            if (lstat(filename, &st) < 0) {
                perror(filename);
                putchar('\n');
                continue;
            }

            /*
             * Print out the information.
             */
            outputStatInfo(filename, d->d_name, &st);
            putchar('\n');
        }
```

Example 8-1: newlistfiles (continued)

```
            putchar('\n');
            closedir(dp);
    }

    exit(0);
}

/*
 * outputStatInfo - print out the contents of the stat structure.
 */
void
outputStatInfo(char *pathname, char *filename, struct stat *st)
{
    int n;
    struct group *gr;
    struct passwd *pw;
    char login[16], group[16], slink[BUFSIZ+1];

    /*
     * Print the number of file system blocks, permission bits,
     * and number of links.
     */
    printf("%5d ", st->st_blocks);
    printf("%c%s ", typeOfFile(st->st_mode), permOfFile(st->st_mode));
    printf("%3d ", st->st_nlink);

    /*
     * Look up the owner's login name.  Use the user-id if we
     * can't find it.
     */
    if ((pw = getpwuid(st->st_uid)) != NULL)
        strcpy(login, pw->pw_name);
    else
        sprintf(login, "%d", st->st_uid);

    /*
     * Look up the group's name.  Use the group-id if we
     * can't find it.
     */
    if ((gr = getgrgid(st->st_gid)) != NULL)
        strcpy(group, gr->gr_name);
    else
        sprintf(group, "%d", st->st_gid);

    /*
     * Print the owner and group.
     */
    printf("%-8s %-8s ", login, group);

    /*
     * If the file is not a device, print its size; otherwise
     * print its major and minor device numbers.
```

Example 8-1: newlistfiles (continued)

```
     */
    if (((st->st_mode & S_IFMT) != S_IFCHR) &&
        ((st->st_mode & S_IFMT) != S_IFBLK))
        printf("%9d ", st->st_size);
    else
        printf("%4d,%4d ", major(st->st_rdev), minor(st->st_rdev));

    /*
     * Print the access time.  The ctime() function is
     * described in Chapter 7, "Time and Timers".
     */
    printf("%.12s ", ctime(&st->st_mtime) + 4);

    /*
     * Print the file name.  If it's a symbolic link, also print
     * what it points to.
     */
    printf("%s", filename);

    if ((st->st_mode & S_IFMT) == S_IFLNK) {
        if ((n = readlink(pathname, slink, sizeof(slink))) < 0)
            printf(" -> ???");
        else
            printf(" -> %.*s", n, slink);
    }
}


/*
 * typeOfFile - return the english description of the file type.
 */
char
typeOfFile(mode_t mode)
{
    switch (mode & S_IFMT) {
    case S_IFREG:
        return('-');
    case S_IFDIR:
        return('d');
    case S_IFCHR:
        return('c');
    case S_IFBLK:
        return('b');
    case S_IFLNK:
        return('l');
    case S_IFIFO:
        return('p');
    case S_IFSOCK:
        return('s');
    }

    return('?');
}
```

Example 8-1: newlistfiles (continued)

```
/*
 * permOfFile - return the file permissions in an "ls"-like string.
 */
char *
permOfFile(mode_t mode)
{
    int i;
    char *p;
    static char perms[10];

    p = perms;
    strcpy(perms, "---------");

    /*
     * The permission bits are three sets of three
     * bits: user read/write/exec, group read/write/exec,
     * other read/write/exec.  We deal with each set
     * of three bits in one pass through the loop.
     */
    for (i=0; i < 3; i++) {
        if (mode & (S_IREAD >> i*3))
            *p = 'r';
        p++;

        if (mode & (S_IWRITE >> i*3))
            *p = 'w';
        p++;

        if (mode & (S_IEXEC >> i*3))
            *p = 'x';
        p++;
    }

    /*
     * Put special codes in for set-user-id, set-group-id,
     * and the sticky bit.  (This part is incomplete; "ls"
     * uses some other letters as well for cases such as
     * set-user-id bit without execute bit, and so forth.)
     */
    if ((mode & S_ISUID) != 0)
        perms[2] = 's';

    if ((mode & S_ISGID) != 0)
        perms[5] = 's';

    if ((mode & S_ISVTX) != 0)
        perms[8] = 't';

    return(perms);
}
```

```
% newlistfiles /home/msw/a
/home/msw/a:
      2 drwxr-sr-x   7 root      other       512 Dec 21 22:20 .
      2 drwxr-xr-x   3 root      root        512 Dec 21 20:45 ..
     16 drwx------   2 root      root       8192 Apr 19 16:04 lost+found
      2 drwxr-sr-x  12 davy      other      1024 May 29 10:19 davy
      2 drwxr-sr-x   2 sean      other       512 Apr 19 17:57 sean
      2 drwxr-sr-x   3 trevor    other       512 Jan 12 19:59 trevor
      2 drwxr-sr-x   6 cathy     other       512 Mar 19 11:33 cathy
```

Note that the method used in the example is awfully inefficient. In a directory with 100 files in it, all owned by the same user, the `getpwnam` function is called 100 times. A similar problem exists with group names. A more efficient method would be to store the information returned from these functions each time they are called, and to search the stored information first, calling the functions only when a user ID or group ID is encountered for the first time.

The utmp and wtmp Files

The files */var/adm/utmp* (*/etc/utmp* on older systems) and */var/adm/wtmp* (*/usr/adm/wtmp* or */etc/wtmp* on older systems) record user and accounting information for commands such as *who, finger*, and *login*. The format of these files on System V-based systems is substantially different than on all other versions of UNIX; the System V format is described here, and the more "traditional" format is described in the porting notes.

The *utmp* file contains records that describe the current state of the system. This includes one record for each logged-in user, and some additional records that will be described later. The *login* command writes a record to the *utmp* file each time a user logs in; the record is removed when the user logs out. The *wtmp* file contains historical data in the same format. Each time a user logs in, a record is written to the file. Each time a user logs out, the same record is written to the file again, except that the login name field (`ut_user` or `ut_name`) is empty, and the `ut_time` field contains the logout time instead of the login time. Programs such as *last* can read this file, match up the entries with login names and those without, and produce a summary of when each user logged in and out.

In System V versions of UNIX, the *utmp* file also records information about the execution of certain system processes such as a change in the system's run level or the programs that allow users to log in. This information is not transferred to the *wtmp* file. Two additional files, */var/adm/utmpx* and */var/adm/wtmpx*, are used to record additional information. These files have a slightly larger record than their counterparts; the primary difference is that the "x" files also contain the name of

the remote host for users who log in via the network. (It probably would have
made more sense to just add this information to the *utmp* and *wtmp* files, but this
would have broken older programs that read these files.)

The record format for the *utmp* and *wtmp* files is described in the include file
utmp.h:

```
struct utmp {
    char    ut_user[8];
    char    ut_id[4];
    char    ut_line[12];
    short   ut_pid;
    short   ut_type;
    struct exit_status    ut_exit;
    time_t  ut_time;
};

struct exit_status {
    short    e_termination;
    short    e_exit;
};
```

The fields of the structure have the following meanings:

ut_user

> The user's login name. Note that this field is not always null-terminated; an
> eight-character login name has no room in the string for a terminating null
> byte.

ut_id

> The id field from */etc/inittab* for a process spawned by the *init* program.

ut_line

> The name of the device on which the user is logged in; this string can be con-
> catenated with "*/dev/*" to obtain the pathname for the device.

ut_pid

> The process ID of the described process.

ut_type

> An indication of the type of data contained in this record. Legal values for this
> field are:

EMPTY

> The record is empty.

RUN_LVL

This record indicates a change in the system run-level. The new level can be determined from the ut_id field.

BOOT_TIME

A system boot. The time is recorded in the ut_time field.

OLD_TIME

A change in the system time with the *date* command. This record stores the time prior to the change.

NEW_TIME

A change in the system time with the *date* command. The record stores the time after the change.

INIT_PROCESS

A process spawned by *init*. The process' name is stored in ut_name, its process ID number is stored in ut_pid.

LOGIN_PROCESS

A process waiting for a user to log in; there is usually one of these for each terminal connected to the system.

USER_PROCESS

A user login session.

DEAD_PROCESS

A process that has exited. The exit status and return code are stored in ut_exit.

ACCOUNTING

An accounting record (not implemented).

ut_exit

The termination and exit status of a process recorded in a DEAD_PROCESS record.

ut_time

The time at which this record was last modified.

The record format for the *utmpx* file is described in the *utmpx.h* include file:

```
struct utmpx {
    char    ut_user[32];
    char    ut_id[4];
    char    ut_line[32];
    pid_t   ut_pid;
    short   ut_type;
    struct exit_status     ut_exit;
    struct timeval    ut_tv;
    long    ut_session;
    long    pad[5];
```

```
        short    ut_syslen;
        char     ut_host[257];
};
```

All of the common fields have the same meaning as those in the `struct utmp` structure. The new fields are:

ut_tv

The time this record was last modified (this is the same as `ut_time`, except a different format).

ut_session

The session ID number (see Chapter 11, *Processes*).

pad

Reserved for future use.

ut_syslen

The length, including the terminating null byte, of the hostname in the `ut_host` field.

ut_host

The name of the remote host, if a user is logged in via the network (e.g., with *rlogin* or *telnet*).

There are two essentially identical sets of functions provided for manipulating the *utmp* and *utmpx* files:

```
#include <utmp.h>

struct utmp *getutent(void);

struct utmp *getutid(const struct utmp *id);

struct utmp *getutline(const struct utmp *line);

struct utmp *pututline(const struct utmp *utmp);

void setutent(void);

void endutent(void);

int utmpname(const char *filename);

#include <utmpx.h>

struct utmpx *getutxent(void);

struct utmpx *getutxid(const struct utmpx *id);

struct utmpx *getutxline(const struct utmpx *line);
```

```
struct utmpx *pututxline(const struct utmpx *utmpx);

void setutxent(void);

void endutxent(void);

int utmpxname(const char *filename);
```

The getutent and getutxent functions read the next entry from a *utmp*-like or *utmpx*-like file. The getutid and getutxid functions search forward from the current location in the file for an entry whose ut_type field matches id->ut_type if the type is RUN_LVL, BOOT_TIME, OLD_TIME, or NEW_TIME. If the type is one of INIT_PROCESS, LOGIN_PROCESS, USER_PROCESS, or DEAD_PROCESS, then they search for an entry whose type is one of those four and whose ut_id field matches id->ut_id. The functions return the first entry found. The getutline and getutxline functions search forward from the current location in the file for an entry of type LOGIN_PROCESS or USER_PROCESS whose ut_line field matches line->ut_line and return the first entry found. All of these functions return the constant NULL if no entry is found or end-of-file is encountered.

The pututline and pututxline functions write out the supplied entry to the file. They first use getutid or getutxid to find the correct location in the file; if no slot for the entry exists, it is added to the end of the file.

The setutent and setutxent functions open the file and reset the read/write offset to the beginning of the file. The endutent and endutxent functions close the file. The utmpname and utmpxname functions allow the name of the file to be changed.

There are also functions provided for converting between the two record types:

```
#include <utmpx.h>

void getutmp(struct utmpx *utmpx, struct utmp *utmp);

void getutmpx(struct utmp *utmp, struct utmpx *utmpx);

void updwtmp(char *wfile, struct utmp *utmp);

void updwtmpx(char *wfilex, struct utmpx *utmpx);
```

The getutmp function copies the fields of the utmpx structure to the corresponding utmp structure. The getutmpx function does the reverse. The updwtmp and updwtmpx functions check the existence of the named file and its parallel file (named by adding or removing an "x") in the filename. If only one of them exists, the other file is created and the contents of the existing file are copied to it. Then the utmp or utmpx structure is written to the file, and the corresponding structure written to the parallel file.

Because the *utmpx* functions update the *utmp* file too, it is generally better to use them over their *utmp* counterparts.

Example 8-2 shows a program that reads the *utmpx* file and prints a list of currently logged-in users. For each user, the `getpwnam` function is used to obtain the user's real name. This program could just as easily use the *utmp* file, but then the remote host could not be printed.

Example 8-2: whom

```c
#include <sys/types.h>
#include <sys/time.h>
#include <utmpx.h>
#include <pwd.h>

int
main(void)
{
    char name[64];
    struct passwd *pwd;
    struct utmpx *utmpx;

    printf("Login     Name            Line      Time           Host\n");
    printf("------------------------------------------------------------\n");

    /*
     * Read each entry from the file.
     */
    while ((utmpx = getutxent()) != NULL) {
        /*
         * Skip records that aren't logins.
         */
        if (utmpx->ut_type != USER_PROCESS)
            continue;

        /*
         * Get the real name.
         */
        if ((pwd = getpwnam(utmpx->ut_user)) != NULL)
            strcpy(name, pwd->pw_gecos);
        else
            sprintf(name, "#%d", pwd->pw_uid);

        /*
         * Print stuff out.
         */
        printf("%-8s %-16.16s %-8.8s %.12s", utmpx->ut_user, name,
                utmpx->ut_line, ctime(&utmpx->ut_tv.tv_sec)+4);

        if (utmpx->ut_syslen > 0)
            printf(" %s", utmpx->ut_host);

        putchar('\n');
```

Example 8-2: whom (continued)

```
    }

    exit(0);
}


% whom
Login     Name            Line     Time            Host
---------------------------------------------------------
davy      David A. Curry  console  May 29 10:19
davy      David A. Curry  pts/1    May 29 10:19
davy      David A. Curry  pts/0    May 29 10:19
cathy     Cathy L. Curry  pts/2    May 29 15:30    big.school.edu
```

This example shows only the use of `USER_PROCESS` records. To see what the other types of records contain, the easiest thing to do is execute the *who -a* command.

NOTE

The *utmpx* functions are not provided in HP-UX 10.*x*, nor are the *utmpx* and *wtmpx* files. Instead, HP-UX 10.*x* provides an `unsigned long` ut_addr field in the `struct utmp` structure; this field contains the IP address of the remote host that a user has logged in from.

Example 8-3 shows a modified version of the *whom* program from the previous example; this one has been rewritten for HP-UX 10.*x* to use the *utmp* file and functions.

Example 8-3: whom

```
#include <sys/types.h>
#include <sys/socket.h>
#include <sys/time.h>
#include <netdb.h>
#include <utmp.h>
#include <pwd.h>

int
main(void)
{
    char name[64];
    struct utmp *utmp;
    struct passwd *pwd;
    struct hostent *hp;

    printf("Login      Name              Line     Time            Host\n");
    printf("---------------------------------------------------------------\n");
```

Example 8–3: whom (continued)

```
    /*
     * Read each entry from the file.
     */
    while ((utmp = getutent()) != NULL) {
        /*
         * Skip records that aren't logins.
         */
        if (utmp->ut_type != USER_PROCESS)
            continue;

        /*
         * Get the real name.
         */
        if ((pwd = getpwnam(utmp->ut_user)) != NULL)
            strcpy(name, pwd->pw_gecos);
        else
            sprintf(name, "#%d", pwd->pw_uid);

        /*
         * Print stuff out.
         */
        printf("%-8s %-16.16s %-8.8s %.12s", utmp->ut_user, name,
                utmp->ut_line,
                ctime(&utmp->ut_time)+4);

        /*
         * If there's a remote host, get its name and print it.  The
         * gethostbyaddr() function is described in Chapter 14,
         * Networking With Sockets.
         */
        if (utmp->ut_addr != 0) {
                hp = gethostbyaddr((char *) &utmp->ut_addr, sizeof(long),
                        AF_INET);

                if (hp != NULL)
                        printf(" %s", hp->h_name);
        }

        putchar('\n');
    }

    exit(0);
}
```

Porting Notes

As mentioned earlier, non-System V versions of UNIX do not use the rather elaborate *utmp* file described above. Instead, they use a simple record format, described in the include file *utmp.h*:

```
struct utmp {
    char    ut_line[8];
    char    ut_name[8];
    char    ut_host[16];
    long    ut_time;
};
```

The fields are:

ut_line

> The name of the device the user is logged in on, with the leading *"/dev/"* stripped off.

ut_name

> The user's login name. If this field is empty, the port is not in use.

ut_host

> The name of the remote host, if the user is logged in via the network. This field does not exist in all versions.

ut_time

> The time the user logged in.

There are no fancy functions provided for reading the *utmp* and *wtmp* files; instead, since each record is of fixed size, they can just be read with **read** or **fread**.

In order to insert a record into the *utmp* file, the **ttyslot** function is used:

```
#include <stdlib.h>

int ttyslot(void);
```

This function returns the index of the current user's entry in the *utmp* file. The function scans the files in */dev* for the device associated with the standard input, standard output, or standard error output, and returns the index of the **struct utmp** that contains that device's name in its **ut_line** field or -1 if an error occurs.

The Lastlog File

On Solaris 2.*x* systems, the */var/adm/lastlog* file is used to record the last login time of each user. This file is maintained by the *login* command. (Note that users who log in by using *rsh* to start a window system terminal emulator such as *xterm* do not pass through the *login* command, and hence do not appear in this file.) The file is indexed by user ID number, and contains one structure for each user.

On IRIX 5.*x* systems, there is an individual file for each user called */var/adm/lastlog/username* which contains a single structure for that user.

This functionality is not provided in HP-UX 10.*x*.

The `struct lastlog` structure is defined in the include file *lastlog.h*:

```
struct lastlog {
    time_t  ll_time;
    char    ll_line[8];
    char    ll_host[16];
};
```

The fields are:

`ll_time`

> The time the user last logged in.

`ll_line`

> The name of the terminal device the user last logged in on.

`ll_host`

> The name of the host the user logged in from, if she logged in via the network. This field is 257 bytes long in IRIX 5.*x*.

Example 8-4 shows a program that prints the last login time for each user named on its command line. This version is for Solaris 2.*x*.

Example 8–4: lastlog for Solaris

```
#include <sys/types.h>
#include <sys/time.h>
#include <lastlog.h>
#include <stdio.h>
#include <pwd.h>

int
main(int argc, char **argv)
{
    FILE *fp;
    struct lastlog ll;
    struct passwd *pwd;

    /*
     * Open the lastlog file.
     */
    if ((fp = fopen("/var/adm/lastlog", "r")) == NULL) {
        perror("/var/adm/lastlog");
        exit(1);
    }

    /*
     * For each user named on the command line...
```

Example 8-4: lastlog for Solaris (continued)

```
     */
    while (--argc) {
        /*
         * Look up the user's user-id number.
         */
        if ((pwd = getpwnam(*++argv)) == NULL) {
            fprintf(stderr, "unknown user: %s\n", *argv);
            continue;
        }

        /*
         * Read the right structure.
         */
        fseek(fp, pwd->pw_uid * sizeof(struct lastlog), 0);
        fread(&ll, sizeof(struct lastlog), 1, fp);

        /*
         * Print it out.
         */
        printf("%-8.8s %-8.8s %-16.16s %s", *argv, ll.ll_line, ll.ll_host,
                ctime(&ll.ll_time));
    }

    fclose(fp);
    exit(0);
}
```

```
% lastlog davy root cathy
davy       pts/3                       Sun May 29 15:28:18 1994
root       console                     Sun May 22 17:11:38 1994
cathy      pts/2     big.school.edu    Thu May  5 12:16:32 1994
```

Example 8-5 shows the same program as it would be written on an IRIX 5.*x* system.

Example 8-5: lastlog for IRIX

```
#include <sys/types.h>
#include <sys/time.h>
#include <lastlog.h>
#include <stdio.h>

int
main(int argc, char **argv)
{
    FILE *fp;
    struct lastlog ll;
    char lastlogfile[1024];

    /*
```

Example 8-5: lastlog for IRIX (continued)

```
    * For each user named on the command line...
    */
while (--argc) {
    /*
     * Open the lastlog file.
     */
    sprintf(lastlogfile, "/var/adm/lastlog/%s", *++argv);

    if ((fp = fopen(lastlogfile, "r")) == NULL) {
        perror(lastlogfile);
        continue;
    }

    /*
     * Read the structure.
     */
    fread(&ll, sizeof(struct lastlog), 1, fp);

    /*
     * Print it out.
     */
    printf("%-8.8s %-8.8s %-16.16s %s", *argv, ll.ll_line, ll.ll_host,
           ctime(&ll.ll_time));

    fclose(fp);
}

exit(0);
}


% lastlog davy root cathy
davy     pts/3                          Sun May 29 15:28:18 1994
root     console                        Sun May 22 17:11:38 1994
cathy    pts/2    big.school.edu        Thu May  5 12:16:32 1994
```

The Shells File

The */etc/shells* file exists so that a system administrator can list the valid shells on his system. This allows commands such as *ftp* to refuse access to users whose shells are not listed here. On systems that support the *chsh* command for changing a user's login shell, this file gives the legal values they may choose from.

The */etc/shells* file is simply a list of the pathnames of the legal shells. However, if it is not present, then the legal values are the normal system shells, usually */bin/sh*, */bin/csh*, */bin/ksh*, and sometimes */bin/rsh*. In order to allow programs to deal with this in a portable fashion, three functions are provided:

```
char *getusershell(void);

void setusershell(void);

void endusershell(void);
```

The `getusershell` function returns a pointer to a character string containing the name of the next shell listed in the file. If the file does not exist, it returns the name of the next shell listed in the list of standard shells. The `setusershell` and `endusershell` functions open and rewind, and close the file, respectively.

These functions are not available in IRIX 5.*x*.

Writing Set-User-Id and Set-Group-Id Programs

Set-user-id and set-group-id programs are extraordinarily useful tools (in fact, the set-user-id bit is the only part of the original UNIX operating system that was patented). These programs enhance security, by letting unprivileged users perform certain privileged tasks without "giving away the store" and letting everyone have the *root* password.

Before undertaking the writing of a set-user-id or set-group-id program, however, it is important to realize that there are several ways in which an unscrupulous user can attempt to trick these programs into granting him privileges that he should not have. This includes fooling the program into reading or writing files that the attacker does not have access to (e.g., the password file), getting the program to start an interactive shell with the wrong real or effective user ID, tricking the program into changing the permission bits on a file other than the one it thinks it's changing, making the program execute a command different from the one it thinks it's executing, and so forth.

The simplest rule to follow in writing set-user-id and set-group-id programs is, "if there's another way, don't." These programs should not be used indiscriminately. If there is a secure method with which you can accomplish what you want without using a set-user-id or set-group-id program, use that method instead. Don't create a set-user-id or set-group-id program just to save yourself the trouble of doing things right the first time.

And while we're speaking of doing things right, if you do decide to write a set-user-id program, always begin the program as follows:

```
int euid;

int
main(int argc, char **argv)
```

```
{
    /* variable declarations */

    euid = geteuid();
    seteuid(getuid());
    ⋮
```

This code causes the program to save its special privileges, but revert back to the calling user's "normal" privileges at once. In this way, if the program should encounter an error, it can only cause the damage that the user's privileges allow it to; it cannot cause extra damage because of its extra privileges. Then, when the program needs to do a privileged operation, the code for that can be bracketed as follows:

```
/* non-privileged code */

seteuid(euid);

/* privileged code */

seteuid(getuid());

/* non-privileged code */
```

In this way, the program only uses its special privileges when it absolutely has to, and the amount of code that has to be carefully examined for defects is much smaller. The same idea applies for set-group-id programs.

If you've read all the information above and still think you need to write a program, follow the list of rules below. This list has been adapted and expanded from a paper by Matt Bishop, entitled *How to Write a Setuid Program*, which appeared in the January/February 1987 issue of *;login:*, the newsletter of the USENIX Association. Some of these rules describe topics discussed later in the book; if you don't understand them now, don't worry. But be sure to come back and read this list if you ever need to write a set-user-id or set-group-id program.

1. The overall rule, upon which all the rest of these rules are based, is *even paranoids have enemies.* You cannot be too paranoid when writing these programs; one slip-up and the security of your system will be defeated. Don't trust anyone or anything, not even the operating system. Don't ever think "this can't happen." Sooner or later it will, and your program had better be prepared for it.

2. *Never, ever, write set-user-id or set-group-id interpreted scripts.* Some versions of UNIX allow command scripts, such as shell scripts, to be made set-user-id or set-group-id. Unfortunately, the power and complexity of the interpreters

make them easy to trick into performing functions that were not intended. This rule applies to Bourne shell scripts, C shell scripts, Korn shell scripts, Perl scripts, awk scripts, Tcl scripts, and indeed any other script that is processed by a command interpreter.

3. *Be as restrictive as possible in choosing the user ID and group ID.* Don't give a program more privilege than it needs. For example, if a game program is made set-user-id root so that it can write its score file, and an attacker can figure out how to get the game to start a subshell (as many can), the set-user-id bit will give the attacker a superuser shell. On the other hand, if the game programs were all made set-user-id to the "games" account, then the attacker would be able to do much less with his set-user-id subshell (he could change the game's high score, but not much else).

4. *Reset the effective user ID and group ID before calling* exec. This seems obvious, but is often overlooked. When it is, a user may find herself running a program with unexpected privileges. This is often a problem with programs that use the setreuid or setregid functions. It is important to remember that even if you don't call exec directly, some library routines such as popen and system call it for you. Whenever calling any function whose purpose is to execute another command as though that command were typed at the keyboard, the effective user ID and group ID should be reset as follows, unless there is a compelling reason not to:

```
setuid(getuid());
setgid(getgid());
```

5. *Close all unnecessary files before calling* exec. If your set-user-id or set-group-id program uses its privileges to open a file that would otherwise be inaccessible to the user, and then executes another process (such as a shell) without closing that file, the new process will also be able to read and/or write that file, because files stay open by default across calls to exec. The easiest way to prevent this is to set the file's close-on-exec flag, as described in Chapter 6, *Special-Purpose File Operations*, immediately after opening the file.

6. *Check ownership and access permissions on file descriptors, not filenames.* A favorite technique of attackers is to execute a set-user-id or set-group-id program that accesses one of their own files (programs that copy users' files into trusted areas such as spool directories are a prime example). The program uses stat or access to check the ownership or permissions on the file, and then opens the file and processes it. This creates a window between the time the program has checked things and the time it opens the file. The attacker can stop the program, replace the real file with a symbolic link to some other

file, and then continue the program. The program, already satisfied that it has made its checks, continues on as if nothing is wrong. To avoid this, always *open* the file first. Then use `fstat` on the file descriptor to check ownership and permissions. This technique insures that even if the attacker is trying to fool you with a symbolic link, you will be checking the information about the file you will actually be using, and not the file he substituted.

7. *Catch or ignore all signals.* As mentioned in the previous rule, an attacker can use some signals (stop and continue, in that case) to confuse your program. She can let your program check that everything is "right" before doing something, stop the program, change things around so they are no longer "right," and then let the program continue. Set-user-id and set-group-id programs should catch or ignore all signals possible. At the very minimum, the following signals should be caught or ignored: `SIGHUP`, `SIGINT`, `SIGQUIT`, `SIGILL`, `SIGTRAP`, `SIGABRT (SIGIOT)`, `SIGEMT`, `SIGFPE`, `SIGBUS`, `SIGSEGV`, `SIGSYS`, `SIGPIPE`, `SIGALRM`, `SIGTERM`, `SIGUSR1`, `SIGUSR2`, `SIGPOLL`, `SIGTSTP`, `SIGTTIN`, `SIGTTOU`, `SIGVTALRM`, `SIGPROF`, `SIGXCPU`, `SIGXFSZ`.

8. *Never trust your inherited environment.* Do not rely on the values of a user's environment variables, such as `PATH`, `USER`, `LOGNAME`, etc. When executing programs, always specify an absolute pathname to the program to be executed. If you rely on the user's search path, he can use this to trick you into executing something you don't expect. When checking identity, use only the real user ID and the password file. If you rely on the environment variables or the results of `getlogin` or `cuserid`, the user can lie to you. Always set your `umask` explicitly. If you don't, the user can trick you into creating world-writable files. (Don't create the file and then rely on using `chmod` to fix its mode; the user can stop your program and change the file's contents before you get to complete both steps.)

9. *Never pass on your inherited environment.* This relates to the item above, but is more insidious. Especially with shared libraries, it is possible for an attacker to put things in the environment that do not affect your program, but *do* affect programs executed by your program. Always provide programs you execute from a set-user-id or set-group-id program with a "clean" environment. If you must copy values from the inherited environment into the new one, check their contents for validity before passing them on.

10. *Never trust your input.* Never rely on the fact that your program's input is in the format you expect, or that it was created by whoever or whatever was supposed to have created it. If your program is given garbage as input, it should recognize this and discard it, rather than try to make sense of the

garbage. If your program reads input from somewhere, make sure that it is not possible to overflow your program's buffers. Never assume an array is big enough to hold the input; if you read data into an array, refuse to read more data than the array will hold. *Never, ever, use the* gets *function.*

11. *Never trust system calls or library routines.* Check the return values of everything, even those things that "can't happen." For example, it is often assumed that the close function cannot fail. But on an NFS filesystem, the only indication a process receives that a filesystem it tried to write to is full is delivered as a return code from close.

12. *Make only safe assumptions about error recovery.* If your program detects an error over which it has no control (such as no more file descriptors), the proper thing to do is *exit*. Do not, under any circumstances, attempt to handle unexpected or unknown situations; you may be operating under incorrect assumptions. For example, a long time ago, the *passwd* program assumed that if the password file could not be opened, something was seriously wrong with the system, and the user should be given a superuser shell to fix the problem. Not a good assumption.

Following these rules will help you keep your set-user-id or set-group-id program safe from attack. But no list of rules is perfect. Always approach the writing of these programs with the utmost care, and always verify that they do only what you want them to do. And remember, if you don't really, really need one, don't write one.

Chapter Summary

In this chapter, we examined the user ID and the group ID. The methods for "converting" these numbers to their text-based counterparts in the password and group files are used regularly by systems programs ranging from the *ls* command to the electronic mail system to the printer system. The methods for exchanging one user ID or group ID for another are frequently used by programs that must allow users to perform a privileged task. The last section of this chapter described many of the pitfalls the programmer may encounter when implementing these methods. Remember, almost everything the UNIX system does is tied, at some level, to the user ID and/or group ID; it is important to handle these quantities properly.

9

System Configuration and Resource Limits

To support a wide variety of applications, ranging from a single-user workstation system to a multi-user timesharing system, the UNIX operating system has always offered the system administrator a number of parameters that can be "tuned" to make the system perform better under specific types of load. Some of these parameters control the behavior of the operating system kernel proper: how many file table entries to allocate, how much memory to allocate for interprocess communication, how many process table slots to use, and so forth. Other parameters control individual processes, such as how many open files a process may have, how much memory it may use, and how large a file it may create, to prevent a single process from consuming the entire system's resources.

In early versions of the UNIX system, almost all of these parameters were defined using constants in system include files. This meant that after changing one of the parameters, every program that used the parameter had to be recompiled. Gradually, particularly as third-party vendors began selling software for the UNIX system, the values of more and more of these parameters could be determined, and sometimes changed, via system calls and library routines. This enabled software to be more portable: if a program could determine at runtime what its limits were, it did not have to be recompiled on each system where those limits were different. POSIX and other UNIX standardization efforts have improved this situation even more, by defining standard interfaces and standard resource names, enabling programs to portably determine almost any limit they may need to know.

In this chapter, we describe the system configuration parameters and the routines available for accessing and modifying them. We also examine the calls available for getting and setting per-process resource limits, and look at the routines available for determining how many system resources a process has used.

General System Information

Each system maintains a number of general information parameters, including the host name, operating system name, operating system release number, hardware serial number, and machine architecture. The system call to obtain this information is uname:

```
#include <sys/utsname.h>

int uname(struct utsname *name);
```

This function places system configuration information in the structure pointed to by name and returns a non-negative value on success. If a failure occurs, -1 is returned and the external integer errno is set to the error number.

The struct utsname structure has the following members:

```
struct utsname {
    char      sysname[SYS_NMLN];
    char      nodename[SYS_NMLN];
    char      release[SYS_NMLN];
    char      version[SYS_NMLN];
    char      machine[SYS_NMLN];
};
```

sysname
> A null-terminated string naming the current operating system

nodename
> A null-terminated string containing the name the system is known by on a communications network (its host name)

release
> A null-terminated string identifying the operating system release

version
> A null-terminated string identifying the operating system version

machine
> A null-terminated string identifying the type of hardware the operating system is running on (the machine architecture)

The uname call is specified by the POSIX standard, which adopted it from versions of System V UNIX. SVR4 also provides another call, sysinfo, that performs a similar function, but can provide some additional information:

```
#include <sys/systeminfo.h>

long sysinfo(int command, char *buf, long count);
```

The `sysinfo` function copies information about the operating system, as requested by `command`, into `buf`. The `count` parameter specifies the length of `buf`; it should be at least 257 bytes in size. Upon successful completion, `sysinfo` returns the number of bytes in `buf` required to hold the return value and the terminating null character. If this value is less than or equal to `count`, the whole value was copied, otherwise, `count-1` bytes plus a terminating null character were copied. If an error occurs, -1 is returned and the reason for failure is stored in `errno`.

The legal values for `command`, defined in *sys/systeminfo.h*, are:

SI_SYSNAME

Returns the operating system name. This is the same value returned by **uname** in the `sysname` field.

SI_HOSTNAME

Returns the name of the current host, as it is known on a communications network. This is the same value returned by **uname** in the `nodename` field.

SI_SET_HOSTNAME

Sets the system host name to the value contained in `buf`. This command is restricted to the superuser.

SI_RELEASE

Returns the operating system release. This is the same value returned by **uname** in the `release` field.

SI_VERSION

Returns the operating system version. This is the same value returned by **uname** in the `version` field.

SI_MACHINE

Returns the machine type. This is the same value returned by **uname** in the `machine` field.

SI_ARCHITECTURE

Returns the hardware instruction set architecture.

SI_HW_PROVIDER

Returns the name of the hardware manufacturer.

SI_HW_SERIAL

Returns the ASCII representation of the hardware-specific serial number of the physical machine. In common usage, this number is usually called the *hostid*, and does not necessarily represent the true serial number of the machine. However, it is assumed that when the two strings returned by

SI_HW_PROVIDER and SI_HW_SERIAL are combined, the result will be unique. This value may contain non-numeric characters. Note that on Sun systems, this value is usually represented as a hexadecimal number, but sysinfo returns it as a decimal number.

SI_SRPC_DOMAIN

Returns the Secure Remote Procedure Call domain name.

SI_SET_SRPC_DOMAIN

Sets the Secure Remote Procedure Call domain name to the value contained in buf.

The sysinfo function is not available in HP-UX 10.*x*.

Example 9-1 shows a program that prints out the information obtained by uname and sysinfo.

Example 9-1: systeminfo

```c
#include <sys/systeminfo.h>
#include <sys/utsname.h>
#include <stdio.h>

typedef struct {
    int     command;
    char    *string;
} Info;

Info info[] = {
    SI_SYSNAME,         "SI_SYSNAME",
    SI_HOSTNAME,        "SI_HOSTNAME",
    SI_RELEASE,         "SI_RELEASE",
    SI_VERSION,         "SI_VERSION",
    SI_MACHINE,         "SI_MACHINE",
    SI_ARCHITECTURE,    "SI_ARCHITECTURE",
    SI_HW_PROVIDER,     "SI_HW_PROVIDER",
    SI_HW_SERIAL,       "SI_HW_SERIAL",
    SI_SRPC_DOMAIN,     "SI_SRPC_DOMAIN",
    0,                  NULL
};

int
main(void)
{
    Info *ip;
    char buf[BUFSIZ];
    struct utsname name;

    /*
     * Request uname information.
     */
    if (uname(&name) < 0) {
        perror("uname");
```

Example 9–1: systeminfo (continued)

```
        exit(1);
    }

    /*
     * Print it out.
     */
    printf("Uname information:\n");
    printf("\t sysname: %s\n", name.sysname);
    printf("\tnodename: %s\n", name.nodename);
    printf("\t release: %s\n", name.release);
    printf("\t version: %s\n", name.version);
    printf("\t machine: %s\n", name.machine);

    /*
     * Request and print system information.
     */
    printf("\nSysinfo information:\n");

    for (ip = info; ip->string != NULL; ip++) {
        if (sysinfo(ip->command, buf, sizeof(buf)) < 0) {
            perror("sysinfo");
            exit(1);
        }

        printf("%16s: %s\n", ip->string, buf);
    }

    exit(0);
}


% systeminfo
Uname information:
          sysname: SunOS
         nodename: msw
          release: 5.3
          version: Generic
          machine: sun4m

Sysinfo information:
       SI_SYSNAME: SunOS
      SI_HOSTNAME: msw
       SI_RELEASE: 5.3
       SI_VERSION: Generic
       SI_MACHINE: sun4m
  SI_ARCHITECTURE: sparc
   SI_HW_PROVIDER: Sun_Microsystems
     SI_HW_SERIAL: 2147630684
   SI_SRPC_DOMAIN:
```

Porting Notes

Most systems based on a version of System V offer the `uname` system call, but not `sysinfo`. Versions based on BSD, however, offer two different calls that obtain only some parts of the information described above:

```
int gethostname(char *name, int len);

int sethostname(char *name, int len);

long gethostid(void);
```

The `gethostname` function copies the current name of the host, as it is known on a communications network, into the character array pointed to by `name`, which is `len` characters long. The `sethostname` function sets the current host name to the value contained in `name`. This call is restricted to the superuser. The `gethostid` function returns a 32-bit identifier for the system, which should be unique across all hosts. This value is equivalent to the one returned by the `SI_HW_SERIAL` command to the `sysinfo` function. (On early BSD systems such as the VAX, where the serial number was not available through software, this value was equal to the system's IP address.)

System Resource Limits

There are many limits imposed both by the operating system and by the native hardware architecture; these include such things as the maximum positive integer, the minimum decimal value of a floating-point number, the maximum number of characters in a terminal input buffer, the maximum length of a filename, and so forth. Prior to the adoption of the POSIX standard, these limits were defined in various include files and the programmer had to examine those to determine where items were defined.

The POSIX standard specifies that most of these limits should be described, using standard constant names, in the include file *limits.h*. The standard also specifies three functions that can be used to determine the values of the more "interesting" of these values at runtime:

```
#include <unistd.h>

long sysconf(int name);

long fpathconf(int fd, int name);

long pathconf(const char *path, int name);
```

The `sysconf` function returns the current value of a configurable system limit or option. If the call fails due to an error, it returns -1 and sets `errno` to indicate the error. If it fails due to an unknown value of name, it returns -1 but does not change the value of errno.

The legal values for name and their meanings are:

_SC_VERSION
The version of the POSIX.1 standard supported by this system.

_SC_XOPEN_VERSION
The version of the X/Open standard supported by this system.

_SC_JOB_CONTROL
A Boolean value indicating whether or not job control is supported.

_SC_SAVED_IDS
A Boolean value indicating whether or not saved IDs (used by setuid and setgid) are supported.

_SC_ASYNCHRONOUS_IO
A Boolean value indicating whether or not the system supports asynchronous input and output.

_SC_FSYNC
A Boolean value indicating whether or not the system supports file synchronization (the fsync system call).

_SC_MAPPED_FILES
A Boolean value indicating whether or not the system supports memory-mapped files.

_SC_MEMLOCK
A Boolean value indicating whether or not the system supports process memory locking.

_SC_MEMLOCK_RANGE
A Boolean value indicating whether or not the system supports process memory range locking.

_SC_MEMORY_PROTECTION
A Boolean value indicating whether or not the system supports memory protection.

_SC_MESSAGE_PASSING
A Boolean value indicating whether or not the system supports message passing.

_SC_PRIORITIZED_IO

A Boolean value indicating whether or not the system supports prioritized input and output.

_SC_PRIORITY_SCHEDULING

A Boolean value indicating whether or not the system supports process scheduling.

_SC_REALTIME_SIGNALS

A Boolean value indicating whether or not the system supports the POSIX real-time signals extension.

_SC_SEMAPHORES

A Boolean value indicating whether or not the system supports semaphores.

_SC_SHARED_MEMORY_OBJECTS

A Boolean value indicating whether or not the system supports shared memory objects.

_SC_SYNCHRONIZED_IO

A Boolean value indicating whether or not the system supports synchronized input and output.

_SC_TIMERS

A Boolean value indicating whether or not the system supports timers.

_SC_ARG_MAX

The maximum combined size, in bytes, of **argv** and **envp**.

_SC_CHILD_MAX

The maxmimum number of processes allowed to an individual user ID. This is often called NPROC on older systems.

_SC_CLK_TCK

The number of clicks per second of the system clock. This is often called HZ on older systems.

_SC_NGROUPS_MAX

The maximum number of simultaneous groups a process may belong to. This is often called NGROUPS_MAX on older systems.

_SC_OPEN_MAX

The maximum number of open files per process. This is often called NOFILE on older systems.

`_SC_STREAM_MAX`

The maximum number of open streams per process.

`_SC_TIMER_MAX`

The maximum number of timers per process.

`_SC_MQ_OPEN_MAX`

The maximum number of open message queue descriptors per process.

`_SC_SEM_NSEMS_MAX`

The maximum number of semaphores per process.

`_SC_SIGQUEUE_MAX`

The maximum number of queued signals that a process may send and have pending at the receiver(s) at any time.

`_SC_LOGNAME_MAX`

The maximum number of characters in a login name.

`_SC_PASS_MAX`

The maximum number of significant characters in a password.

`_SC_TZNAME_MAX`

The maximum length of a time zone name.

`_SC_NPROCESSORS_CONF`

The number of processors configured into the system.

`_SC_NPROCESSORS_ONLN`

The number of processors online.

`_SC_PAGESIZE`

The system memory page size. This is not necessarily the same as the hardware memory page size.

`_SC_PHYS_PAGES`

The total number of pages of physical memory in the system.

`_SC_AVPHYS_PAGES`

The number of pages of physical memory not currently in use by the system.

`_SC_AIO_LISTIO_MAX`

The maximum number of I/O operations in a single list I/O call supported by the system.

`_SC_AIO_MAX`

The maximum number of outstanding asynchronous I/O operations supported by the system.

_SC_AIO_PRIO_DELTA_MAX

    The maximum amount by which a process can decrease its asynchronous I/O priority level from its own scheduling priority.

_SC_DELAYTIMER_MAX

    The maximum number of timer expiration overruns.

_SC_MQ_PRIO_MAX

    The maximum number of message priorities supported by the system.

_SC_RTSIG_MAX

    The maximum number of real-time signals reserved for application use in this implementation.

_SC_SIGRT_MIN

    The lowest-numbered real-time signal available for application use.

_SC_SIGRT_MAX

    The highest-numbered real-time signal available for application use.

_SC_SEM_VALUE_MAX

    The maximum value for a sempahore.

The `pathconf` function returns the current value of a configurable limit or option associated with the file or directory named in `path`. The `fpathconf` function returns the same information, but about the file referenced by the open file descriptor `fd`. Both functions return -1 if an error occurs.

The legal values for `name` and their meanings are:

_PC_LINK_MAX

    The maximum number of links to a single file or directory. If `path` or `fd` refer to a directory, the value returned applies to the directory itself.

_PC_MAX_CANON

    The maximum number of bytes in a line of input from a terminal. If `path` or `fd` do not refer to a terminal device, the return value is meaningless.

_PC_MAX_INPUT

    The maximum number of bytes in a terminal input queue. If `path` or `fd` do not refer to a terminal device, the return value is meaningless.

_PC_NAME_MAX

    The maxmimum number of bytes in a filename. If `path` or `fd` do not refer to a directory, the return value is meaningless. Otherwise, the return value applies to the filenames within the directory.

_PC_PATH_MAX

The maximum number of characters in a pathname. If `path` or `fd` do not refer to a directory, the return value is meaningless. Otherwise, the value returned is the maximum length of a relative pathname when the specified directory is the working directory.

_PC_PIPE_BUF

The maximum number of bytes that are atomic in a write to a pipe or FIFO. If `path` or `fd` refer to a pipe or FIFO, the return value applies to the pipe or FIFO. If `path` or `fd` refer to a directory, the return value applies to any FIFOs that exist or can be created in that directory. If `path` or `fd` refer to any other type of file, the value returned is meaningless.

_PC_CHOWN_RESTRICTED

A Boolean value indicating whether or not unprivileged users may use the `chown` system call to change the ownership of their files. If `path` or `fd` refer to a directory, the returned value applies to any files, other than directories, that exist or can be created within that directory.

_PC_NO_TRUNC

A Boolean value indicating whether or not pathnames whose components are longer than _PC_NAME_MAX will generate an error. If `path` or `fd` do not refer to a directory, the return value is meaningless. Otherwise, the return value applies to the filenames within the directory.

_PC_VDISABLE

This value can be used to disable special terminal characters (see Chapter 12, *Terminals*) such as the interrupt character or the erase character. If `path` or `fd` do not refer to a terminal device, the return value is meaningless.

_PC_ASYNC_IO

A Boolean value indicating whether or not ansynchronous input and output may be performed on this file. If `path` or `fd` do not refer to a terminal device, the return value is meaningless.

_PC_PRIO_IO

A Boolean value indicating whether or not prioritized input and output may be performed on this file. If `path` or `fd` do not refer to a terminal device, the return value is meaningless.

_PC_SYNC_IO

Indicate whether or not synchronous input and output may be performed on this file. If `path` or `fd` refer to a directory, the return value applies to the directory itself.

Porting Notes

BSD systems, because they predate POSIX, do not offer the functions described in this section. Instead, most of their configuration parameters are stored in include files. However, two functions are available:

```
int getdtablesize(void);

int getpagesize(void);
```

The `getdtablesize` function returns the number of file descriptors available to the process; this is like the `_SC_OPEN_MAX` option to `sysconf`. The `getpage-size` function returns the system page size (not necessarily the same as the hardware page size); this is like the `_SC_PAGESIZE` option to `sysconf`.

Process Resource Limits

There are also several limits that are applied on a per-process basis. Many of these limits can be changed by the process, and are meant to aid in stopping "runaway" behavior.

All versions of UNIX provide the `ulimit` system call, although its behavior is slightly different in SVR4:

```
#include <ulimit.h>

long ulimit(int cmd, long newlimit);
```

The values of `cmd` are:

UL_GETFSIZE

Returns the maximum file size, in 512-byte block units, that the process may create. Any size file may be read, regardless of the value of this limit.

UL_SETFSIZE

Sets the maximum file size limit to the value in `newlimit`. Any process may decrease this value, but only a process with superuser permissions may increase it.

UL_GETMEMLIM

Returns the maximum amount of memory the process may use. This command is not available in HP-UX 10.*x*.

UL_GETMAXBRK

> Returns the maximum amount of memory the process may use. This command is only available in HP-UX 10.*x*.

UL_GETDESLIM

> Returns the maximum number of files the process may have open. This command is not available in HP-UX 10.*x*.

Upon successful completion, `ulimit` returns a non-negative value. If an error occurs, it returns -1 and sets the external integer `errno` to describe the error.

A more general interface to limits was first introduced by BSD UNIX, and later adopted by SVR4:

```
#include <sys/time.h>
#include <sys/resource.h>

int getrlimit(int resource, struct rlimit *rlp);

int setrlimit(int resource, const struct rlimit *rlp);
```

Each call to either `getrlimit` or `setrlimit` applies to a single resource, identified by `resource`. There are two limits to each resource, a current (soft) limit, and a maximum (hard) limit. Any process can change soft limits to any value less than or equal to the hard limit. Only a process with superuser permissions may raise the hard limit, but any process may (irreversibly) lower the hard limit. Limits may be specified as "infinity" by setting them to the constant `RLIM_INFINITY`; in this case, the operating system sets the maximum value.

The `rlp` parameter is a pointer to a structure of type `struct rlimit`:

```
struct rlimit {
    rlim_t    rlim_cur;
    rlim_t    rlim_max;
};
```

The possible resources are:

RLIMIT_CORE

> The maximum size of a *core* file, in bytes, that the process can create. A limit of 0 prevents the creation of a core file. The writing of a core file terminates when this size is reached, even if the file is incomplete.

RLIMIT_CPU

> The maximum amount of processor time, in seconds, that the process can use. This is a soft limit only; there is no hard limit. When the limit is exceeded, the system will send the process a `SIGXCPU` signal (see Chapter 10, *Signals*).

RLIMIT_DATA

> The maximum size of the process' data segment, in bytes. When this limit is reached, calls to `malloc` and other memory allocation routines will fail. This resource limit is not available in HP-UX 10.*x*.

RLIMIT_FSIZE

> The maximum size of a file, in bytes, that the process can create. A limit of 0 prevents file creation. When this limit is exceeded, the process will receive a `SIGXFSZ` signal.

RLIMIT_NOFILE

> The maximum number of file descriptors (and, hence, open files) that the process may create. When this limit is exceeded, further attempts to open files will fail.

RLIMIT_STACK

> The maximum size, in bytes, of the process' stack. The system will not automatically grow the stack beyond this limit. When this limit is reached, the process will receive a `SIGSEGV` signal. This resource limit is not available in HP-UX 10.*x*.

RLIMIT_VMEM

> The maximum size of the process' mapped address space, in bytes. When a process exceeds this limit, further calls to `malloc` and other memory allocation functions will fail, as will calls to `mmap`. Finally, the system will no longer automatically grow the process' stack. This resource limit is not available in HP-UX 10.*x*.

Upon successful completion, both calls return 0. Otherwise, -1 is returned and `errno` is set to indicate the error.

Porting Notes

On older versions of UNIX, the `ulimit` function can only be used to change the maximum file size. It takes a single parameter, the new value of the limit.

Resource Utilization Information

Most versions of UNIX provide the `times` system call, which can be used to find out how much processor time the current process and its children have used:

```
#include <sys/times.h>
#include <limits.h>

clock_t times(struct tms *buf);
```

The `struct tms` structure is defined as:

```
struct tms {
    clock_t tms_utime;
    clock_t tms_stime;
    clock_t tms_cutime;
    clock_t tms_cstime;
};
```

The information returned describes the calling process and all of its terminated child processes (see Chapter 11, *Processes*) for which it has executed a wait routine. The specific fields are:

`tms_utime`
> The amount of processor time used while executing instructions in the user space of the calling process

`tms_stime`
> The amount of processor time used by the system on behalf of the calling process (i.e., the amount of time performing system calls)

`tms_cutime`
> The sum of the `tms_utime` and `tms_cutime` values for the child process

`tms_cstime`
> The sum of the `tms_stime` and `tms_cstime` values for the child process

All times are reported in *clock ticks*; the number of clock ticks per second is defined as `CLK_TCK` in the *limits.h* include file, or may be obtained with `sysconf`.

Upon successful completion, `times` returns the elapsed real time, in clock ticks, from some time in the past (usually system boot time). This point does not change between calls, so two successive calls to `times` compute the elapsed time between calls. If the call fails, -1 is returned and an error code is placed in `errno`.

Porting Notes

On older systems, `times` reported time in seconds, rather than clock ticks.

BSD-based systems offer a much more comprehensive facility for obtaining process resource consumption information:

```
#include <sys/time.h>
#include <sys/resource.h>

int getrusage(int who, struct rusage *rusage);
```

The who parameter may be given as either RUSAGE_SELF or RUSAGE_CHILDREN; the struct rusage structure is defined as follows:

```
struct  rusage {
    struct timeval ru_utime;
    struct timeval ru_stime;
    long    ru_maxrss;
    long    ru_ixrss;
    long    ru_idrss;
    long    ru_isrss;
    long    ru_minflt;
    long    ru_majflt;
    long    ru_nswap;
    long    ru_inblock;
    long    ru_oublock;
    long    ru_msgsnd;
    long    ru_msgrcv;
    long    ru_nsignals;
    long    ru_nvcsw;
    long    ru_nivcsw;
};
```

The fields contain:

ru_utime

The total amount of time spent executing in user mode, in seconds and microseconds.

ru_stime

The total amount of time spent executing in system mode, in seconds and microseconds.

ru_maxrss

The maximum resident set size (amount of memory used), in pages.

ru_idrss

An "integral" value indicating the amount of memory in use by a process while the process is running. This is the sum of the resident set sizes of the process running when a clock tick occurs. The value is reported in pages times clock ticks.

ru_minflt

The number of minor page faults (faults that do not require physical I/O activity) serviced.

ru_majflt

The number of major page faults (faults that require physical I/O activity) serviced.

ru_nswap

The number of times the process was swapped out of main memory.

ru_inblock

The number of times the filesystem had to perform input when servicing a `read` request.

ru_outblock

The number of times the filesystem had to perform output when servicing a `write` request.

ru_msgsnd

The number of messages sent over sockets.

ru_msgrcv

The number of messages received over sockets.

ru_nsignals

The number of signals delivered to the process.

ru_nvcsw

The number of times a context switch resulted due to the process voluntarily giving up the processor before its time slice was completed (usually to wait on the availability of a resource).

ru_nivcsw

The number of times a context switch resulted due to a higher priority process becoming runnable or because the current process used up its time slice.

This information can be obtained in SVR4 through the */proc* filesystem, described in Appendix C, *The /proc Filesystem.*

Beginning with Solaris 2.5, `getrusage` has been restored as a system call in Solaris 2.*x.*

Chapter Summary

Before the standardization of POSIX, most of the configuration limits and other values discussed in this chapter were defined as constants in various system include files. This required the user to recompile programs on each system to which they were moved (in order to obtain the proper values for that system), and also to recompile any time one of these values changed. Now that these parameters are for the most part obtainable at run-time, you can write programs that are not only more portable, but also more efficient.

10

Signals

Signals are software interrupts. They provide asynchronous notification to a process that something has happened—either an unexpected problem has arisen, or a user (or another process) has requested that the process do something outside of its normal operational functions. Some signals, such as "illegal instruction" or "arithmetic exception," have a direct relationship to the computer hardware. Other signals, such as "window size change" or "CPU time limit exceeded," are purely software-oriented. Most of the signals provided by the UNIX operating system cause a process to exit when they are received, unless the process takes steps to handle that signal. Some of the signals also cause the process' memory image to be placed on disk in the file *core*, allowing debuggers to examine the image in order to determine what caused the problem.

UNIX signal handling used to be both simple to do and simple to explain—there was only one way to do things, and everyone followed it. However, as the need for more sophisticated signal handling increased, other ways of doing things evolved. As each new way was implemented, explaining things got harder—not only was there more to explain about how things worked, but it also became necessary to explain which methods were used for which situations. This problem has reached a peak in SVR4, which provides four different methods for handling signals: the original basic mechanism introduced in Version 7, the somewhat more robust mechanism introduced in SVR3, a compatibility library implementation of the Berkeley mechanism used by many vendors' operating systems, and, new to SVR4, the POSIX mechanism.

In this chapter, we will discuss all four of these signal handling mechanisms. Fortunately, the uses of the four mechanisms fairly closely parallel their complexity. That is, basic signal handling is easily performed using the easy-to-understand mechanisms; the more complicated mechanisms are only needed for more advanced functionality. Thus, we begin by introducing the basic concepts of signal handling that are common to all four mechanisms. We then examine basic signal handling as it was originally implemented in Version 7. Following this, we consider *reliable* signals, one of the most important additions to signal handling procedures. We next examine one of the more common uses for signals, implementing timeouts. After this, we move into the area of advanced signal handling, by looking at the sophisticated POSIX signal mechanism. We conclude with a detailed look at the Berkeley signal mechanism, upon which the POSIX mechanism is based. It is in this section that we present information on porting between the Berkeley mechanism and the others.

Signal Concepts

As mentioned earlier, a signal is a software interrupt—an asynchronous notification that something has happened. Signals are delivered to a process by the operating system. They may occur because of something the program did (e.g., an attempt to divide by 0), something a user did (e.g., press the interrupt key on the keyboard), or something another program did (processes may send signals to one another).

A process may indicate the *disposition* of each signal defined by the operating system. The four possible dispositions for a signal are given below:

- The signal may be *ignored*. This tells the operating system to immediately discard the signal, without delivering it to the process. The process is never told that a signal was even generated. Ignoring signals is useful when a process simply doesn't want to be bothered with them, or when it wants to continue performing its task regardless of what happens.

- The signal may be *blocked*, or *held*. When a signal is blocked, it will not be delivered to the process, much as if it were being ignored. However, rather than simply discarding the signal, the operating system will place it on a queue of pending signals to be delivered to the process. If the process ever unblocks or releases the signal, it will be delivered at that time. Blocking signals is useful in programs that contain "critical sections" that must not be interrupted, but that otherwise wish to process the signals.

- The signal may be *caught*, or *trapped*. The process may tell the operating system to call a user-defined function called a *signal handler* whenever the signal is delivered. When the signal is delivered, the operating system suspends the process' normal execution, and calls the signal handler function. When the handler function returns, the process' execution picks up where it left off. Catching signals is useful any time the programmer wants to deal with unexpected events in a special way. For example, text editors make sure to catch keyboard interrupt signals, so that an inadvertent keystroke doesn't terminate the editor without saving the file.

- Each signal has a *default* disposition. As mentioned earlier, most signals' default dispositions are to terminate the process, sometimes with an accompanying core dump. Default dispositions are useful when there's nothing special the process needs to do with that signal; they are also useful for resetting the disposition of a signal that was previously being caught or ignored.

Version 7 UNIX provided 15 different signals. As features such as job control, interprocess communication, and networking were added, however, the list grew. In SVR4, 35 different "regular" signals are provided, along with several special-purpose signals used for realtime programming. The signals are described below.

SIGHUP

> *Hangup.* This signal is sent to a process when its controlling terminal disconnects from the system (see Chapter 11, *Processes*). It is also commonly used to notify daemon processes to reread their configuration files; since daemon processes do not have controlling terminals, they would not normally receive this signal. The default disposition for this signal terminates the process.

SIGINT

> *Interrupt.* This signal is delivered to a process when the user presses the interrupt key (usually CTRL-C) on the keyboard. The default disposition for this signal terminates the process.

SIGQUIT

> *Quit.* This signal is delivered to a process when the user presses the quit key (usually CTRL-\) on the keyboard. The default disposition for this signal terminates the process and produces a core file.

SIGILL

> *Illegal instruction.* This signal is delivered to a process when it attempts to execute an illegal hardware instruction. The default disposition for this signal terminates the process and produces a core file.

SIGTRAP

> *Trace/breakpoint trap.* The name for this signal is derived from the PDP-11 "trap" instruction. This signal is delivered to a process when it is being traced by a debugger and encounters a breakpoint; this causes the process to stop and the parent process (the debugger) to be notified. If the process is not being traced, the default disposition for this signal terminates the process and produces a core file.

SIGABRT

> *Abort.* This signal is generated by the `abort` function (see Chapter 16, *Miscellaneous Routines*). The default disposition for this signal terminates the process and produces a core file.

SIGEMT

> *Emulator trap.* The name for this signal is derived from the PDP-11 "emulator trap" instruction. It is delivered to a process when an implementation-defined hardware fault is detected. The default disposition for this signal terminates the process and produces a core file.

SIGFPE

> *Arithmetic exception.* (FPE stands for Floating Point Exception, but this signal is used for non-floating-point arithmetic exceptions as well.) This signal is delivered to a process when it attempts an illegal arithmetic operation, such as division by 0, floating-point overflow, and so on. The default disposition for this signal terminates the process and produces a core file.

SIGKILL

> *Kill.* This signal is used to terminate a process "with extreme prejudice." It cannot be caught, blocked, or ignored. The default (only) disposition for this signal terminates the process.

SIGBUS

> *Bus error.* This signal is delivered to a process when an implementation-defined hardware fault is detected. It usually indicates an attempt to use an improperly aligned address or to reference a nonexistent physical memory address. The default disposition for this signal terminates the process and produces a core file.

SIGSEGV

> *Segmentation violation* (or *segmentation fault*). This signal is delivered to a process when it attempts to access an invalid virtual memory address, or attempts to access memory that it does not have permission to use. The default disposition for this signal terminates the process and produces a core file.

SIGSYS

> *Bad system call.* This signal is delivered to a process when it somehow executes an instruction that the kernel thought was a system call, but the parameter with the instruction does not indicate a valid system call. The default disposition for this signal terminates the process and produces a core file.

SIGPIPE

> *Broken pipe.* This signal is delivered to a process when it attempts to write on a pipe (see Chapter 13, *Interprocess Communication*) when there is no process on the other end to receive the data. The default disposition for this signal terminates the process.

SIGALRM

> *Alarm clock.* This signal is delivered to a process when an alarm it has scheduled with the **alarm** or **setitimer** system calls (see below) goes off. The default disposition for this signal terminates the process.

SIGTERM

> *Software termination.* This signal is used to tell a process to clean up whatever it's doing (close open files, etc.) and exit. It is the default signal sent by the *kill* command, and is also sent to all processes by the system shutdown procedure. The default disposition for this signal terminates the process.

SIGUSR1

> *User-defined signal one.* This signal may be used for any programmer-defined purpose. The default disposition for this signal terminates the process.

SIGUSR2

> *User-defined signal two.* This signal may be used for any programmer-defined purpose. The default disposition for this signal terminates the process.

SIGCHLD

> *Child status change.* This signal indicates a change in a child process' status (see Chapter 11). It was introduced in Berkeley UNIX, and is delivered to a process whenever one of its children exits or is stopped or continued due to job control. The parent process can then use one of the **wait** system calls to determine what happened. The default disposition for this signal is to discard it; it is only delivered to a process if the process is catching it.

> Versions of System V prior to SVR3 have a similar signal, **SIGCLD**. Unfortunately, this signal has very strange semantics, unlike those of any other signal:

> - The default disposition of this signal is to discard it; it is only delivered to a process if the process is catching it.

- If the process specifically sets the signal's disposition to *ignore*, then children of the calling process will not generate zombie processes (see Chapter 11). Instead, on termination, the exit status of these processes is just discarded. If the parent process issues a call to one of the `wait` functions, it will block until all its children have terminated, and then `wait` will return -1 and `errno` will be set to `ECHILD`.

- If the process requests that the signal be caught, the operating system immediately checks if there are any child processes to be `wait`ed for, and if so, calls the `SIGCLD` handler. Thus, the signal is in a sense *retroactive*—processes that exited before its disposition was changed to a signal handler can result in the calling of the signal handler!

In SVR4, `SIGCLD` and `SIGCHLD` refer to the same signal. In order to provide backward compatibility with previous versions of System V, if the signal's disposition is set with either `signal` or `sigset`, the `SIGCLD` behavior is used. If its disposition is set with `sigaction`, the `SIGCHLD` behavior is used. This is of particular importance when porting programs from Berkeley-based versions of UNIX to SVR4.

SIGPWR

Power fail/restart. On systems connected to uninterruptible power supplies or that have battery backup, this signal can be sent to the *init* process to start an orderly system shutdown when power is lost or the batteries are about to fail. The default disposition for this signal is to discard it; it is only delivered to a process if the process is catching it.

SIGWINCH

Window size change. This signal is delivered to a process when the number of rows or columns of its controlling terminal are changed, as when a user resizes a window on a workstation. The default disposition for this signal is to discard it; it is only delivered to a process if the process is catching it.

SIGURG

Urgent socket condition. This signal is used to tell a process that an urgent condition (out of band data) exists on a network communications channel (see Chapter 14, *Networking with Sockets*). The default disposition for this signal is to discard it; it is only delivered to a process if the process is catching it.

SIGPOLL

Pollable event. This signal is delivered to a process when an event occurs on a pollable device. It is used in conjunction with the `poll` system call. The default disposition for this signal terminates the process.

SIGSTOP

> *Stop.* This signal cannot be caught, blocked, or ignored. The default (only) disposition for this signal stops the process until a continue signal (SIGCONT) is received.

SIGTSTP

> *Stop.* This signal is delivered to a process when the user presses the suspend key (usually CTRL-Z) on the keyboard. The default disposition for this signal stops the process until a continue signal (SIGCONT) is received.

SIGCONT

> *Continue.* This signal can be caught, but it cannot be blocked or ignored. The default disposition for this signal starts the process if it was stopped, but it is otherwise discarded unless the process is catching it.

SIGTTIN

> *Stop for tty input.* This signal is delivered to a process if it tries to read from the terminal while it is in the background. The default disposition for this signal stops the process until a continue signal (SIGCONT) is received.

SIGTTOU

> *Stop for tty output.* This signal is delivered to a process if it tries to write to the terminal while it is in the background, and the terminal has the TOSTOP mode set (see Chapter 12, *Terminals*). The default disposition for this signal stops the process until a continue signal (SIGCONT) is received.

SIGVTALRM

> *Virtual timer expiration.* This signal is delivered to a process when a virtual timer alarm it has scheduled with the `setitimer` system call expires. The default disposition for this signal terminates the process.

SIGPROF

> *Profiling timer expiration.* This signal is delivered to a process when a profiling timer alarm it has scheduled with the `setitimer` system call expires. The default disposition for this signal terminates the process.

SIGXCPU

> *CPU time limit exceeded.* This signal is delivered to a process when it exceeds its CPU time limit (see Chapter 9, *System Configuration and Resource Limits*). The default disposition for this signal terminates the process and produces a core file.

`SIGXFSZ`

> *File size limit exceeded.* This signal is delivered to a process when it exceeds its maximum file size limit (see Chapter 9). The default disposition for this signal terminates the process and produces a core file.

All versions of UNIX provide the first 15 signals in the preceding list. Most modern versions of UNIX also provide the job control signals, and many provide the timer-related signals as well. The other signals are less common, and may or may not be present in other versions. Other versions may also offer signals that do not appear in the list.

Basic Signal Handling

In this section, we describe the basics of signal handling in terms of the oldest and simplest signal interface. The functions described in this section are available in all versions of UNIX, and are adequate for most uses.

Sending Signals

To send a signal to a process, use the `kill` function:

```
#include <sys/types.h>
#include <signal.h>

int kill(pid_t pid, int sig);
```

The `pid` parameter specifies the process or group of processes to send the signal to, and the `sig` parameter identifies the signal to be sent. If `sig` is 0, then error checking is performed, but no signal is delivered. Use this to check the validity of `pid`.

Unless the sending process has an effective user ID of superuser, the real or effective user ID of the sending process must match the real or saved user ID of the receiving process(es). The only exception to this rule is `SIGCONT`, which may be sent to any process with the same session ID as the sending process (see Chapter 11).

The `pid` parameter has a number of interpretations:

- If `pid` is greater than 0, `sig` will be sent to the process whose process ID is equal to `pid`.

- If `pid` is negative but not equal to -1, `sig` will be sent to all processes whose process group ID (see Chapter 11) is equal to the absolute value of `pid` and for which the process has permission to send a signal.

- If `pid` is equal to 0, `sig` will be sent to all processes whose process group ID is equal to that of the sender, except for special system processes (the scheduler, page daemon, filesystem flusher, and initialization process).

- If `pid` is equal to -1 and the effective user ID of the sending process is not superuser, `sig` will be sent to all processes (except special system processes) whose real user ID is equal to the effective user ID of the sender.

- If `pid` is equal to -1 and the effective user ID of the sending process is superuser, `sig` will be sent to all processes in the system except special system processes.

Upon successful delivery of the signal, `kill` returns 0. If an error occurs, -1 is returned and the reason for failure is placed in the external integer `errno`.

ANSI C defines another, not very useful, function for sending signals:

```
#include <signal.h>

int raise(int sig);
```

Because the ANSI C standard does not recognize multiple processes, `raise` does not accept a `pid` argument. When called, `raise` sends the signal specified in `sig` to the calling process.

Waiting for Signals

Sometimes, a process wants to stop processing until a signal is received. For example, it might want to wait until a specified amount of time has passed, or until data becomes available on a file descriptor. To do this, use the **pause** function:

```
#include <unistd.h>

int pause(void);
```

The **pause** function simply suspends the calling process until it receives a signal. The signal must be one that is not currently blocked or ignored by the calling process. If the signal causes termination of the calling process, **pause** does not return (because the process exits). If the signal is caught by the calling process and control is returned from the signal handling function, **pause** returns -1 and `errno` is set to `EINTR` (interrupted system call). Execution of the process then continues from the point of suspension.

Printing Signal Information

There are two functions for printing signal information, similar to `perror` and `strerror`:

```
#include <siginfo.h>

void psignal(int sig, const char *s);

#include <string.h>

char *strsignal(int sig);
```

The `psignal` function prints the message contained in `s`, followed by a colon, followed by a string identifying the signal whose number is contained in `sig`, on the standard error output. The `strsignal` function returns a character string describing the signal contained in `sig`; this string is the same one printed by `psignal`.

The `psignal` function is not available in HP-UX 10.*x*. An example of how to implement it is shown in the on-line example programs. The `strsignal` function is not available in HP-UX 10.*x* or IRIX 5.*x*.

Handling Signals

The basic function for changing a signal's disposition is called `signal`, and is declared as follows:

```
#include <signal.h>

void (*signal(int sig, void (*disp)(int)))(int);
```

This rather confusing prototype says that `signal` accepts two arguments, and returns a pointer to a function that returns nothing (`void`). The first argument, `sig`, is an integer, and represents the signal whose disposition is to be changed. The second argument, `disp`, is a pointer to a function that takes a single integer argument and returns nothing (`void`). This function is the signal handler for `sig`; whenever `sig` is received, the `disp` function will be called with `sig` as its argument (this allows a single handler function to handle multiple signals). The return value from `signal` is a pointer to the previous signal handler function.

In addition to the address of a function, the `disp` parameter can be given one of the following values:

SIG_IGN

Sets the signal's disposition to *ignore* all future occurrences of `sig` will be ignored.

SIG_DFL

> Sets the signal's disposition to the *default* disposition; any signal handler that was in place for this signal is discarded.

Example 10-1 shows a small program that catches the SIGUSR1 and SIGUSR2 signals, waits for them to arrive, and prints a message when they are received.

Example 10–1: signal1

```c
#include <signal.h>
#include <stdio.h>

void handler(int);

int
main(void)
{
    /*
     * Send SIGUSR1 and SIGUSR2 to the handler function.
     */
    if (signal(SIGUSR1, handler) == SIG_ERR) {
        fprintf(stderr, "cannot set handler for SIGUSR1\n");
        exit(1);
    }

    if (signal(SIGUSR2, handler) == SIG_ERR) {
        fprintf(stderr, "cannot set handler for SIGUSR2\n");
        exit(1);
    }

    /*
     * Now wait for signals to arrive.
     */
    for (;;)
        pause();
}

/*
 * handler - handle a signal.
 */
void
handler(int sig)
{
    /*
     * Print out what we received.
     */
    psignal(sig, "Received signal");
}
```

```
% signal1 &
[1] 12345
% kill -USR1 12345
```

```
Received signal: Signal User 1
% kill -USR2 12345
Received signal: Signal User 2
% kill 12345
[1] + Terminated      signal1
```

The last *kill* command sends SIGTERM to the process; since it does not catch this signal and the default disposition is to terminate the process, it exits.

Unreliable Signals

Signal handling in older versions of UNIX (Version 7, pre-SVR3 versions of System V, and pre-4.2BSD versions of Berkeley UNIX) was *unreliable*. Signals could get lost—a signal could occur and the process would never find out about it.

One of the most significant problems with these early implementations, though, is that they reset a caught signal's disposition to its default each time the signal was delivered. If the signal arrived a second time, the default disposition would be taken, instead of calling the signal handler. To see the problems that this can cause, start *signal1* again and send it two SIGUSR1 signals. The first one is caught as intended, but the second one causes the program to terminate! This is because the default disposition for SIGUSR1 terminates the process.

The usual method to avoid this situation is to modify the handler function to reset the signal's disposition each time it is called, as shown in Example 10-2.

Example 10-2: signal2

```
#include <signal.h>
#include <stdio.h>

void handler(int);

int
main(void)
{
    /*
     * Send SIGUSR1 and SIGUSR2 to the handler function.
     */
    if (signal(SIGUSR1, handler) == SIG_ERR) {
        fprintf(stderr, "cannot set handler for SIGUSR1\n");
        exit(1);
    }

    if (signal(SIGUSR2, handler) == SIG_ERR) {
        fprintf(stderr, "cannot set handler for SIGUSR2\n");
        exit(1);
    }

    /*
```

Example 10–2: signal2 (continued)

```
    * Now wait for signals to arrive.
    */
    for (;;)
        pause();
}

/*
 * handler - handle a signal.
 */
void
handler(int sig)
{
    /*
     * Reset the signal's disposition.
     */
    signal(sig, handler);

    /*
     * Print out what we received.
     */
    psignal(sig, "Received signal");
}
```

```
% signal2 &
[1] 12345
% kill -USR1 12345
Received signal: Signal User 1
% kill -USR2 12345
Received signal: Signal User 2
% kill -USR1 12345
Received signal: Signal User 1
% kill -USR2 12345
Received signal: Signal User 2
% kill 12345
[1] + Terminated     signal2
```

Unfortunately, this solution is imperfect. There is a window of vulnerability between the time that the signal handler is called and the time it resets the signal's disposition during which the default disposition is still in effect. On very busy systems, or when signals are being sent rapid-fire to the process, it is possible for the signal to be missed by the signal handler, resulting in unintended behavior.

NOTE

As mentioned previously, the SIGCHLD signal is different from all the others. Because SIGCHLDs "reappear" as soon as the signal handler is reset, using the above approach of resetting the handler as soon as it is entered will not work. Instead, the following model should be used:

```
void
handler(int sig)
{
    /* code */
    .
    .
    .
    signal(SIGCHLD, handler);
}
```

A second problem with the early implementations is that there was no way to turn a signal off when a process didn't want it to occur. The process could ignore the signal, but there was no way to say "don't deliver this signal right now, but save it for later when I'm ready." To see the problems this can cause, consider the following code fragment:

```
int flag = 0;
void handler(int);

int
main(void)
{
    ...
    signal(SIGALRM, handler);

    while (flag == 0)
        pause();
    ...
}

void
handler(sig)
{
    signal(SIGALRM, handler);
    flag = 1;
}
```

This program continually sits in **pause** until an alarm signal occurs, at which point **flag** will become 1 and it will exit the **while** loop. But, consider the case where the alarm signal arrives *after* the test of **flag**, but *before* the call to **pause**. The program will enter **pause** and never return (unless the signal is generated a second time). The signal has been lost.

Reliable Signals

Because of the problems alluded to in the previous section, 4.2BSD, and later SVR3, introduced *reliable* signals. The reliable signal mechanism makes two major changes: first, signal dispositions are no longer reset when a signal handler is called. The disposition remains the same until the program explicitly changes it. The second change is the introduction of the ability to *block* a signal for later delivery. The signal is not delivered to the process immediately, but it is not ignored. The system remembers that the signal occurred, and, if the process ever unblocks the signal, delivers it then.

Both Berkeley and System V implemented reliable signals by inventing (different) new system calls. Berkeley also reimplemented the `signal` call in terms of reliable signals (the examples in the previous section will work correctly on a 4.2BSD or 4.3BSD system). In System V, `signal` provides the old, unreliable mechanism (which nevertheless is adequate for most needs) for backward compatibility. This is true in SVR4 as well.

In this section, we examine the reliable signal implementation offered by SVR3 and SVR4. The Berkeley reliable signal implementation is discussed at the end of the chapter.

The following paragraphs provide the concepts underlying this implementation.

A signal is *generated* for a process when the event that causes the signal occurs. When the signal is generated, the operating system usually sets a flag of some sort in the process' state information.

A signal is *delivered* to a process when the action for that signal is actually taken. During the time between the generation of a signal and the time it is delivered, the signal is said to be *pending*.

In addition to the default disposition, ignoring a signal, and catching it, a process now also has the option of *blocking* a signal. If a blocked signal is generated for the process and that signal's disposition is either the default or to catch the signal, then the signal remains pending until the process either unblocks the signal or changes the disposition to ignore the signal. The action for a signal is determined when it is delivered, not when it is generated. This allows the process to change the signal's disposition before accepting its delivery.

If a blocked signal is generated more than once for a process before it is unblocked, the operating system has the option of either *queueing* the signals, or just delivering a single signal. Most UNIX systems choose the simpler of these approaches, and deliver the signal only once. If more than one signal is pending for a process, there is no specified order in which the signals should be delivered. However, POSIX does suggest that signals relating to the current state of the process (e.g., `SIGSEGV`) should be delivered first.

Each process has a *signal mask* that defines the set of signals currently being blocked. The signal mask is simply a set of bits, one for each signal. If the bit is on, the signal is blocked; if it is off, the signal may be delivered.

The sigset Function

The `sigset` function is the reliable signal mechanism's counterpart to the unreliable `signal` function:

```
#include <signal.h>

void (*sigset(int sig, void (*disp)(int)))(int);
```

NOTE

In order to make use of `sigset` in HP-UX 10.*x*, the `_SVR2` constant must be defined at compile time, and the program must be linked with *-lV3*.

As with `signal`, `sig` specifies the signal whose disposition is to be changed, and `disp` specifies a pointer to the signal handler function. As with `signal`, the `disp` parameter may be given one of the values `SIG_DFL` or `SIG_IGN`. It may also be given the value `SIG_HOLD`, in which case the signal is added to the process' signal mask and its disposition remains unchanged.

When a signal that is being caught is delivered, the operating system adds the signal to the process' signal mask, and then calls the signal handler function. When (if) the handler function returns, the signal mask is restored to its state prior to the delivery of the signal. The signal's disposition is no longer changed by the operating system, as it was with `signal`. This behavior solves the first problem mentioned in the previous section; the window of vulnerability has been eliminated.

Porting note

Recall from above that Berkeley, when implementing reliable signals, redefined their `signal` function in terms of the new mechanism. But `signal` does not provide reliable signals in SVR4; it provides the old, unreliable mechanism. This means that signal-handling code in programs that were written for Berkeley-based systems will not work properly on SVR4.

Fortunately, the `sigset` function accepts exactly the same arguments that `signal` does, and has the same return value. This means that, when porting code from Berkeley-based systems to SVR4, it is usually sufficient to add the line

```
#define signal sigset
```

to the top of the program. The only case in which this is not sufficient is when the program is working with `SIGCHLD`; properly handling that case requires use of the `sigaction` function, described later in this chapter.

Other Functions

The SVR3 reliable signal mechanism provides several other functions as well:

```
#include <signal.h>

int sighold(int sig);

int sigrelse(int sig);

int sigignore(int sig);

int sigpause(int sig);
```

The `sighold` function adds `sig` to the process' signal mask. The `sigrelse` function removes `sig` from the process' signal mask. The `sigignore` function sets the disposition of `sig` to `SIG_IGN`.

The `sigpause` function removes `sig` from the calling process' signal mask and then suspends the calling process until a signal is received. This is not the same as calling `sigrelse` followed by `pause`; `sigpause` is an atomic operation that cannot be interrupted in between the change in the signal mask and the suspension of the process.

We can use these functions to fix the second problem described in the previous section:

```
void handler(int);
int flag = 0;

int
main(void)
{
    ...
    sighold(SIGALRM);
    sigset(SIGALRM, handler);

    while (flag == 0)
        sigpause(SIGALRM);
    ...
}

void
handler(sig)
{
    flag = 1;
}
```

The initial call to `sighold` adds the alarm signal to the process' signal mask; this
means the signal can only be delivered when the process is ready for it. The call
to `sigpause` removes the alarm signal from the signal mask and suspends the
program. Because the signal is normally blocked, it is not possible for it to arrive
after the test of `flag` and before the call to `sigpause`.

Example 10-3 shows a reimplementation of our *signal* program using reliable signals.

Example 10-3: signal3

```c
#include <signal.h>
#include <stdio.h>

void handler(int);

int
main(void)
{
    /*
     * Send SIGUSR1 and SIGUSR2 to the handler function.
     */
    if (sigset(SIGUSR1, handler) == SIG_ERR) {
        fprintf(stderr, "cannot set handler for SIGUSR1\n");
        exit(1);
    }

    if (sigset(SIGUSR2, handler) == SIG_ERR) {
        fprintf(stderr, "cannot set handler for SIGUSR2\n");
        exit(1);
    }

    /*
     * Now wait for signals to arrive.
     */
    for (;;)
        pause();
}

/*
 * handler - handle a signal.
 */
void
handler(int sig)
{
    /*
     * Print out what we received.
     */
    psignal(sig, "Received signal");
}
```

```
% signal3 &
[1] 12345
% kill -USR1 12345
Received signal: Signal User 1
% kill -USR2 12345
Received signal: Signal User 2
% kill -USR1 12345
Received signal: Signal User 1
% kill -USR2 12345
Received signal: Signal User 2
% kill 12345
[1] + Terminated    signal3
```

Signals and System Calls

System calls (functions that call the operating system to perform some task on behalf of the program, such as transferring data to or from a disk) can be divided into two categories: those that are "slow" and those that aren't. A slow system call is one that can block forever. This category includes:

- *opens* of files that block until some condition occurs (e.g., an open of a terminal device that waits until a modem answers the phone)

- *reads* from certain types of files, such as pipes, terminal devices, and network connections, that can block forever if no data is present

- *writes* to these same types of files, that can block if the data cannot be immediately accepted

- the `pause` system call, which, by definition, blocks until a signal arrives

- the `wait` system call, which blocks until a child process completes

- certain `ioctl` operations (see Chapter 12)

- selected interprocess communications functions

Notice that operations pertaining to disk input and output are not considered slow system calls. Although these operations do block the caller temporarily while the data is moved to or from disk, unless a hardware failure occurs, the operation always returns and unblocks the caller quickly.

In earlier versions of UNIX, if a process caught a signal while it was blocked in one of these slow system calls, the system call was interrupted. It would return an error, and `errno` would contain EINTR. The thinking behind this is that if a signal arrives and the process is catching it, this is probably significant enough to justify breaking out of the system call.

The problem with interruptible system calls is that programs have to handle this case explicitly. If a system call can get interrupted every time a signal arrives, then anywhere the application doesn't want to be interrupted, it needs code like this:

```
again:
    if ((n = read(fd, buf, sizeof(buf))) < 0) {
        if (errno == EINTR)
            goto again;
        ...
    }
```

To ease the burden on programmers, 4.2BSD introduced the automatic restarting of certain system calls. The system calls that are automatically restarted are: `ioctl`, `read`, `readv`, `write`, `writev`, `wait`, and `waitpid`. If any of these calls is interrupted by a signal, it is automatically restarted when the signal handler function returns. Unfortunately, while this alleviated the need for writing code like that shown above, it broke just about every program that relied on the system call being interrupted! To solve this new problem, 4.3BSD allowed the programmer to disable this feature on a per-signal basis.

System V has, historically, never restarted system calls. However, in SVR4, a programmer can enable the automatic restart of system calls on a per-signal basis. This preserves backward compatibility with previous versions, yet allows the programmer access to the sometimes more desirable automatic restart behavior.

Using Signals for Timeouts

One of the more common uses for signals is the implementation of timeouts. For example, suppose that a process wants to stop for a short period of time, and then continue. This might be necessary in a program that prints a large amount of output—if an error occurs, the error message should be printed and then the program should pause for a moment to give the user time to read the error message before it disappears from the screen.

To do this, we can use the `alarm` function:

```
#include <unistd.h>

unsigned int alarm(unsigned int seconds);
```

The `alarm` function tells the operating system to deliver a `SIGALRM` signal to the process after `seconds` seconds have elapsed. There is only one alarm clock for each process; if a second call to `alarm` is made before the first one has expired, the clock is reset to the second value of `seconds`. If `seconds` is 0, any previously made alarm request is cancelled. The `alarm` function returns the amount of time remaining in the alarm clock from the previous request. Using `alarm`, we can implement our pause-after-an-error-message function:

```
#include <signal.h>
#include <unistd.h>

static void handler(int);

void
stop(int seconds)
{
    signal(SIGALRM, handler);
    alarm(seconds);
    pause();
}

void
handler(int sig)
{
    return;
}
```

By calling stop with the number of seconds we wish to pause, we can allow the user to read an error message. The function sets up a signal handler for SIGALRM, and then requests, using alarm, that the operating system send a SIGALRM after seconds seconds have elapsed. It then simply calls pause to suspend execution until the signal arrives. The signal handler doesn't actually have to do anything; it exists only so that we can get out of pause.

The stop function works, but is too primitive to be suitable for inclusion in a system programming library, for example. Some of the problems with this function include:

- The disposition of the SIGALRM signal is altered. If the programmer had already set up his own disposition for this signal, it is lost once he calls stop. A more polite function would save the old disposition of the signal (returned by the call to signal), and restore it when the function returns.

- If the caller has already scheduled an alarm with alarm, that alarm is erased by the call to alarm within stop. This can be corrected by saving the return value from alarm. If it is less than seconds, then we should wait only until the previously set alarm expires. If it is greater than seconds, then before returning we should reset the alarm to occur at its designated time.

- Finally, there is the problem of what happens when the alarm goes off and the signal handler is called before we call pause. If this happens, then stop will be aptly named; the program will stop "forever."

Because these problems tend to make implementing stop more difficult, especially in a portable fashion, all versions of UNIX provide a library routine that handles them for you. This routine is called sleep:

```
#include <unistd.h>

unsigned int sleep(unsigned int seconds);
```

This function causes the program to suspend itself for **seconds** seconds, and then return. The number of unslept seconds is returned. This value may be non-zero if another signal arrives while the process is suspended (since **pause** returns after the receipt of *any* signal, not just **SIGALRM**), or if the calling program had another alarm scheduled to go off before the end of the requested sleep.

Timeouts are also useful for breaking out of operations that would otherwise block indefinitely. For example, consider the following code fragment:

```
printf("Enter a string: ");
fgets(buf, sizeof(buf), stdin);
```

If the user walks away from the terminal, the program using this code will sit there forever, waiting for him to come back. But let's suppose that the program can assume a reasonable default value for the string, and if the user doesn't enter one of his own, the program can use that default. Now all that's necessary is to give the user a chance to enter his string, and if he doesn't do so in a certain amount of time, just continue about our business using the default value. Example 10-4 shows a program that does just that.

Example 10-4: timeout1

```
#include <signal.h>
#include <unistd.h>
#include <stdio.h>

int      flag = 0;

void     handler(int);

int
main(void)
{
    char buf[BUFSIZ];
    char *defstring = "hello";

    /*
     * Set up a timeout of 10 seconds.
     */
    signal(SIGALRM, handler);
    alarm(10);

    /*
     * Prompt for a string and remove the newline.
     */
    printf("Enter a string: ");
    fgets(buf, sizeof(buf), stdin);
    buf[strlen(buf)-1] = '\0';
```

Example 10–4: timeout1 (continued)

```
    /*
     * Turn off the alarm, they typed something.
     */
    alarm(0);

    /*
     * If flag is 1, the alarm went off.  Assume default string.
     */
    if (flag == 1) {
        strcpy(buf, defstring);
        putchar('\n');
    }

    /*
     * Display the string we're using.
     */
    printf("Using string \"%s\"\n", buf);
    exit(0);
}

/*
 * handler - catch alarm signal and set flag.
 */
void
handler(int sig)
{
    flag = 1;
}
```

```
    % timeout1
    Enter a string: howdy
    Using string "howdy"
    % timeout1
    Enter a string:
    Using string "hello"
```

This program uses `alarm` to set a ten-second timeout, and then prompts for the string. If the user enters a string, the read (`fgets`) returns, the alarm is turned off, the `flag` variable is still 0, and the program uses the string the user entered. However, if the user doesn't type anything, the alarm goes off, resulting in a call to `handler`, which sets `flag` to 1. The signal handler returns, the value of `flag` results in copying the default string value into `buf`, and the program continues.

Unfortunately, this program doesn't always work. If we try to use it on a system that offers automatic restarting of system calls, such as 4.2BSD or 4.3BSD, the read from the terminal will be restarted when `handler` returns, and we'll be right back where we started. Thus, for portability, we need some way to get out of the read even on systems that restart it after a signal arrives.

The setjmp and longjmp Functions

If C allowed us to `goto` a label in another function, we could solve this problem easily. Simply place a label after the call to `fgets`, and then instead of doing a `return` from `handler`, call `goto` with that label as an argument. Unfortunately, we can't do this.

UNIX does, however, provide two functions that do allow non-local branching:

```
#include <setjmp.h>

int setjmp(jmp_buf env);

void longjmp(jmp_buf env, int val);
```

The `setjmp` function is called first, and saves the current program state in the variable `env`. When called directly, `setjmp` returns 0. In order to return to the point in the program at which we called `setjmp`, the `longjmp` function is used. The first argument, `env`, is the same one we passed to `setjmp`. The second argument, `val`, is a non-zero value that becomes the return value from `setjmp`. This second argument allows us to have more than one `longjmp` for a single `setjmp`.

Example 10-5 shows a re-implementation of our *timeout* program, this time using `setjmp` and `longjmp`.

Example 10–5: timeout2

```
#include <signal.h>
#include <unistd.h>
#include <setjmp.h>
#include <stdio.h>

jmp_buf env;

void    handler(int);

int
main(void)
{
    char buf[BUFSIZ];
    char *defstring = "hello";

    /*
     * Set up signal handler.
     */
    signal(SIGALRM, handler);

    /*
     * If setjmp returns 0, we're going through the first time.
     * Otherwise, we're going through after a longjmp.
     */
    if (setjmp(env) == 0) {
```

Example 10–5: timeout2 (continued)

```
        /*
         * Set an alarm for 10 seconds.
         */
        alarm(10);

        /*
         * Prompt for a string and strip the newline.
         */
        printf("Enter a string: ");
        fgets(buf, sizeof(buf), stdin);
        buf[strlen(buf)-1] = '\0';

        /*
         * Turn off the alarm; they typed something.
         */
        alarm(0);
    }
    else {
        strcpy(buf, defstring);
        putchar('\n');
    }

    /*
     * Display the string we're using.
     */
    printf("Using string \"%s\"\n", buf);
    exit(0);
}

/*
 * handler - catch alarm signal and longjmp.
 */
void
handler(int sig)
{
    longjmp(env, 1);
}
```

```
    % timeout2
    Enter a string: howdy
    Using string "howdy"
    % timeout2
    Enter a string:
    Using string "hello"
```

The first time through the program, we call `setjmp`, which returns 0. This allows us to schedule our alarm and prompt for the string. If the user types something, we turn off the alarm and continue with the program. However, if the user doesn't type anything, we eventually receive a SIGALRM signal, and handler is called. In handler, we call longjmp with the val parameter equal to 1. This transfers control back to the if statement in main, and makes it appear to the program that setjmp has just returned 1. This causes us to take the else branch, and copy in the default string.

This version of *timeout* will work on any type of UNIX system, whether or not it restarts system calls. However, there is still another problem. If the program is used on a system that provides reliable signals, then recall that when handler is called, SIGALRM will be added to the process' signal mask. Since we don't actually return from handler, SIGALRM will still be blocked after the call to longjmp. This means that the process will no longer receive SIGALRM signals.

The 4.2BSD and 4.3BSD versions of setjmp and longjmp handle this case properly, by saving and restoring the signal mask. However, the SVR4 versions of these functions do not handle this case. One way to deal with it is to call sigrelse inside handler before doing the longjmp. Another way is to use the POSIX sigsetjmp and siglongjmp functions; these are described later in this chapter.

NOTE

Although the timeout mechanism shown here is viable, the select and poll functions described in Chapter 6, *Special-Purpose File Operations*, are more efficient and more flexible for this type of work.

Interval Timers

4.2BSD introduced a substantially more intricate version of timers and timeouts than those provided by alarm and sleep, called *interval timers*. These timers provide millisecond accuracy (subject to the resolution of the system's on-board clock). Interval timers have been carried forward into SVR4 as well. There are two basic functions for working with interval timers:

```
#include <sys/time.h>

int getitimer(int which, struct itimerval *value);

int setitimer(int which, struct itimerval *value,
        struct itimerval *ovalue);
```

The getitimer function looks up the current settings for the interval timer identified by which, and returns them in the area pointed to by value. The setitimer function makes the settings for the interval timer identified by which equal to those in value; if ovalue is non-null, the previous settings are returned.

There are four interval timers, identified by which:

ITIMER_REAL

> Decrements in real time ("clock on the wall" time). A SIGALRM signal is delivered to the process when this timer expires.

ITIMER_VIRTUAL

> Decrements in process virtual time. This timer runs only when the process is executing. A SIGVTALRM signal is delivered to the process when this timer expires.

ITIMER_PROF

> Decrements in both process virtual time and when the system is executing on behalf of the process. This timer is designed to be used by interpreters when statistically profiling the execution of interpreted programs. A SIGPROF signal is delivered to the process when this timer expires.

ITIMER_REALPROF

> Decrements in real time. This timer, designed to be used for real-time profiling of multithreaded programs, is specific to Solaris 2.*x*.

A timer is described by a structure of type struct itimerval:

```
struct itimerval {
        struct timeval     it_interval;
        struct timeval     it_value;
};
```

The it_value element of the structure specifies, in seconds and microseconds, the amount of time remaining until the timer expires. The it_interval element specifies a value to be used in reloading it_value when the timer expires. Thus, interval timers run over and over again, sending a signal each time they expire. Setting it_value to 0 disables a timer, regardless of the value of it_interval. Setting it_interval to 0 disables a timer after its next expiration (assuming it_value is non-zero). Example 10-6 shows another implementation of our *timeout* program, using interval timers.

Example 10–6: timeout3

```
#include <sys/time.h>
#include <signal.h>
#include <unistd.h>
#include <stdio.h>

int     flag = 0;

void    handler(int);

int
main(void)
{
    char buf[BUFSIZ];
```

Example 10–6: timeout3 (continued)

```
    struct itimerval itv;
    char *defstring = "hello";

    /*
     * Set up a timeout of 10 seconds.
     */
    signal(SIGALRM, handler);
    itv.it_interval.tv_usec = 0;
    itv.it_interval.tv_sec = 0;
    itv.it_value.tv_usec = 0;
    itv.it_value.tv_sec = 10;

    setitimer(ITIMER_REAL, &itv, (struct itimerval *) 0);

    /*
     * Prompt for a string and strip the newline.
     */
    printf("Enter a string: ");
    fgets(buf, sizeof(buf), stdin);
    buf[strlen(buf)-1] = '\0';

    /*
     * Turn off the alarm, they typed something.
     */
    itv.it_value.tv_usec = 0;
    itv.it_value.tv_sec = 0;

    setitimer(ITIMER_REAL, &itv, (struct itimerval *) 0);

    /*
     * If flag is 1, the alarm went off.  Assume default string.
     */
    if (flag == 1) {
        strcpy(buf, defstring);
        putchar('\n');
    }

    /*
     * Display the string we're using.
     */
    printf("Using string \"%s\"\n", buf);
    exit(0);
}

/*
 * handler - catch alarm signal and set flag.
 */
void
handler(int sig)
{
    flag = 1;
}
```

Example 10-6: timeout3 (continued)

```
% timeout3
Enter a string: howdy
Using string "howdy"
% timeout3
Enter a string:
Using string "hello"
```

Advanced Signal Handling

The POSIX standard specifies a substantially more complex mechanism for processing reliable signals. In return for the added complexity, the programmer gains significant new functionality. The POSIX mechanism is based, in large part, on the signal handling functions introduced in 4.2BSD. However, although the concepts and functionality are similar, the functions and their arguments are completely new.

The signal-processing functions introduced up to this point, while not POSIX-compliant, are adequate for most programmers. Unless POSIX-compliance is a requirement, the functions described so far are more desirable, because they allow portability to older systems. However, more and more operating systems are being made POSIX-compliant because of the additional functionality offered by the POSIX interface, and you should be familiar with it.

Signal Sets

Many of the functions in the POSIX signal interface work with *signal sets*, rather than individual signals. A signal set is simply a bit mask, with one bit for each signal. If the bit is 1, the corresponding signal is in the set; if the bit is 0, the corresponding signal is not in the set. Signal sets are called masks in the 4.2BSD signal interface.

Signal sets are described by the data type `sigset_t`, defined in the include file *signal.h*. There are five functions defined for manipulating signal sets:

```
#include <signal.h>

int sigemptyset(sigset_t *set);

int sigfillset(sigset_t *set);

int sigaddset(sigset_t *set, int sig);

int sigdelset(sigset_t *set, int sig);

int sigismember(sigset_t *set, int sig);
```

The `sigemptyset` function initializes the set pointed to by `set` to exclude all signals defined by the system; that is, it initializes the set to the empty set.

The `sigfillset` function initializes the set pointed to by `set` to include all signals defined by the system; that is, it initializes the set to the value "all signals."

The `sigaddset` function adds the individual signal identified by `sig` to the set pointed to by `set`. The `sigdelset` function does the opposite; it removes the individual signal identified by `sig` from the set pointed to by `set`.

The `sigismember` function returns 1 if the individual signal identified by `sig` is a member of the set pointed to by `set`, or 0 if it is not.

A signal set must be initialized by calling either `sigemptyset` or `sigfillset` before it can be used with any of the other functions. Upon successful completion all of the above functions (except `sigismember`) return 0; otherwise -1 is returned and `errno` is set to identify the error.

The sigaction Function

The principal workhorse of the POSIX signal mechanism is the `sigaction` function:

```
#include <signal.h>

int sigaction(int sig, const struct sigaction *act,
        struct sigaction *oact);
```

The purpose of `sigaction` is to examine or specify the action to be taken on delivery of a specific signal, identified by the `sig` parameter. If the `act` argument is not null, it points to a structure specifying the new action to be taken when delivering `sig`. If the `oact` argument is not null, it points to a structure where the action previously associated with `sig` is to be stored on return from the call to `sigaction`.

The `struct sigaction` structure is defined in *signal.h* and contains at least the following members:

```
struct sigaction {
    void        (*sa_handler)(int);
    void        (*sa_sigaction)(int, siginfo_t *, void *);
    sigset_t    sa_mask;
    int         sa_flags;
};
```

If the `SA_SIGINFO` flag in the `sa_flags` element of the structure is not set, the `sa_handler` element of the structure specifies the action to be associated with the signal specified in `sig`. It may take on any of the values `SIG_DFL`, `SIG_IGN`, or `SIG_HOLD`, or it may be the address of a signal handler function. In Solaris 2.*x*, if the `SA_SIGINFO` flag is set in `sa_flags`, then the `sa_sigaction` element of the structure specifies the signal handling function to be associated with `sig`. HP-UX 10.*x* and IRIX 5.*x* use the `sa_handler` field in this case, and do not define the `sa_sigaction` field.

The `sa_mask` element of the structure specifies a set of signals to be blocked while the signal handler is active; on entry to the signal handler this set of signals is added to the set of signals already being blocked when the signal is delivered. Additionally, the signal that caused the handler to be executed will be blocked, unless the `SA_NODEFER` flag has been set in `sa_flags`.

The `sa_flags` element of the structure specifies a set of flags that can be used to modify the delivery of the signal identified by `sig`. The value of `sa_flags` is formed by a logical *or* of the following values:

SA_ONSTACK
> If set and the signal is caught, and the process has defined an alternate signal stack with `sigaltstack`, the signal is processed on the alternate stack. Otherwise, the signal is processed on the process' main stack.

SA_RESETHAND
> If set and the signal is caught, the disposition of the signal is reset to `SIG_DFL` and the signal is not blocked on entry to the signal handler. This allows the old behavior of unreliable signals to be obtained.

SA_NODEFER
> If set and the signal is caught, the signal will not be automatically blocked by the kernel while the signal handler is executing. This flag is not available in HP-UX 10.*x*.

SA_RESTART
> If set and the signal is caught, a system call that is interrupted by the execution of this signal's handler will be restarted by the system when the signal handler returns. Otherwise, the system call will return with `errno` set to `EINTR`. This flag is not available in HP-UX 10.*x*.

SA_NOCLDWAIT
> If set and `sig` is `SIGCHLD`, the system will not create zombie processes when children of the calling process exit. If the calling process later issues a call to `wait`, it blocks until all of the calling process' child processes terminate, and then returns -1 with `errno` set to `ECHILD`. This flag, in conjunction with `SA_NOCLDSTOP`, allows the System V `SIGCLD` behavior to be obtained. This flag is not available in HP-UX 10.*x*.

SA_NOCLDSTOP

> If set and `sig` is SIGCHLD, SIGCHLD will not be sent to the calling process when its child processes stop or continue. In conjunction with SA_NOCLDWAIT, this flag allows the System V SIGCLD behavior to be obtained.

SA_WAITSIG

> If set and `sig` is SIGWAITING, then the system will send SIGWAITING to the process when all of its lightweight processes are blocked. This flag is not available in HP-UX 10.*x*.

SA_SIGINFO

> If not set and the signal identified by `sig` is caught, the function identified in `sa_handler` will be called, with `sig` as its only argument. If set and the signal is caught, pending signals of type `sig` will be reliably queued to the calling process, and the function identified in `sa_sigaction` will be called with three arguments. The first argument is the signal number, `sig`. The second argument, if non-null, points to a `siginfo_t` structure containing the reason why the signal was generated. The third argument points to a `ucontext_t` structure describing the receiving process' context when the signal was delivered. This flag is not available in HP-UX 10.*x*.

(The only one of these values defined by the POSIX standard is SA_NOCLDSTOP.)

On success, `sigaction` returns 0. On failure, it returns -1 and sets `errno` to indicate the error. If `sigaction` fails, no new signal handler will be installed.

The siginfo_t structure

If a process is catching a signal, it can ask the system to provide information about why it generated that signal. If the process is monitoring its child processes, it can ask the system to tell it why a child process changed state. In either case, this information is provided by means of a `siginfo_t` structure:

```
typedef struct {
    int           si_signo;
    int           si_errno;
    int           si_code;
    union sigval  si_value;
    pid_t         si_pid;
    uid_t         si_uid;
    caddr_t       si_addr;
    int           si_status;
    long          si_band;
} siginfo_t;
```

The `si_signo` element of the structure contains the system-generated signal number; when used with `waitid`, `si_signo` is always SIGCHLD.

If `si_errno` is non-zero, it contains an error number associated with the signal, as defined in the include file *errno.h*.

The `si_code` element of the structure contains a code identifying the cause of the signal. If the value of `si_code` is `SI_NOINFO`, then only the `si_signo` element of the structure is meaningful, and the value of all other elements of the structure is undefined.

If the value of `si_code` is less than or equal to 0, then the signal was generated by a user process (using one of the functions `kill`, `_lwp_kill`, `sigsend`, `abort`, or `raise`). If this is the case, then the `si_pid` element of the structure will contain the process ID of the process that sent the signal, and the `si_uid` element will contain the user ID of the process that sent the signal. When `si_code` is less than or equal to 0, it will contain one of the following values:

`SI_USER`
> The signal was sent by one of the functions `kill`, `sigsend`, `raise`, or `abort`.

`SI_LWP`
> The signal was sent by `_lwp_kill`, a function used with lightweight processes. This code is available only in Solaris 2.*x*.

`SI_QUEUE`
> The signal was sent by the `sigqueue` function, used in real-time programming.

`SI_TIMER`
> The signal was generated by the expiration of a timer set with the `timer_settime` function, used in real-time programming. This code is available only in Solaris 2.*x*.

`SI_ASYNCIO`
> The signal was generated by the completion of an asynchronous input/output request. This code is available only in Solaris 2.*x*.

`SI_MESGQ`
> The signal was generated by the arrival of a message on an empty message queue (used in real-time programming). This code is available only in Solaris 2.*x*.

In the latter four cases, the `si_value` element of the structure will contain the application-specified value that was passed to the signal-catching function when the signal was delivered.

If `si_code` contains a value greater than 0, it indicates the signal-specific reason that the system generated the signal, as shown in Table 10-1.

Table 10-1: Values of si_code

si_signo	si_code	Reason
SIGILL	ILL_ILLOPC	illegal opcode
	ILL_ILLOPN	illegal operand
	ILL_ILLADDR	illegal addressing mode
	ILL_ILLTRP	illegal trap
	ILL_PRVOPC	privileged opcode
	ILL_PRVREG	privileged register
	ILL_COPROC	co-processor error
	ILL_BADSTK	internal stack error
SIGFPE	FPE_INTDIV	integer division by 0
	FPE_INTOVF	integer overflow
	FPE_FLTDIV	floating point divide by 0
	FPE_FLTOVF	floating-point overflow
	FPE_FLTUND	floating-point underflow
	FPE_FLTRES	floating-point inexact result
	FPE_FLTINV	invalid floating-point operation
	FPE_FLTSUB	subscript out of range
SIGSEGV	SEGV_MAPERR	address not mapped to object
	SEGV_ACCERR	invalid permissions for mapped object
SIGBUS	BUS_ADRALN	invalid address alignment
	BUS_ADRERR	non-existent physical address
	BUS_OBJERR	object-specific hardware error
SIGTRAP	TRAP_BRKPT	process breakpoint
	TRAP_TRACE	process trace trap
SIGCHLD	CLD_EXITED	child has exited
	CLD_KILLED	child was killed
	CLD_DUMPED	child terminated abnormally
	CLD_TRAPPED	traced child has trapped
	CLD_STOPPED	child has stopped
	CLD_CONTINUED	stopped child has continued
SIGPOLL	POLL_IN	data input available
	POLL_OUT	output buffers available
	POLL_MSG	input message available
	POLL_ERR	I/O error

Table 10-1: Values of si_code (continued)

si_signo	si_code	Reason
	POLL_PRI	high priority input available
	POLL_HUP	device disconnected

In addition, other information may be provided for certain signals.

If the signal is SIGILL or SIGFPE, the si_addr element of the structure contains the address of the faulting instruction. If the signal is SIGSEGV or SIGBUS, si_addr contains the address of the faulting memory reference. (For some implementations the exact value of si_addr may not be available; in that case, si_addr is guaranteed to be on the same page as the faulting instruction or memory reference.)

If the signal is SIGCHLD, then the si_pid element of the structure will contain the process ID of the described child, and si_status will contain either the child's exit status (if si_code is CLD_EXITED) or the signal that caused the child to change state.

If the signal is SIGPOLL, the si_band element of the structure will contain the band event if si_code is equal to POLL_IN, POLL_OUT, or POLL_MSG.

Other Functions

Although the sigaction function is the most significant part of the POSIX signal mechanism, there are also a number of other functions defined. Some of these functions are simply souped-up versions of things we've already covered, while others are entirely new.

Sending signals

Although the kill function can still be used for sending signals to processes, SVR4 also defines two new functions that give the programmer somewhat more control over the set of processes the signal is delivered to:

```
#include <sys/types.h>
#include <sys/signal.h>
#include <sys/procset.h>

int sigsend(idtype_t idtype, id_t id, int sig);

int sigsendset(procset_t *psp, int sig);
```

The `sigsend` function sends the signal specified by `sig` to the process or set of processes identified by `idtype` and `id`. If `sig` is 0, error checking is performed but no signal is actually sent. The legal values for `idtype` and their meanings are:

P_PID

   The signal will be sent to the process with process ID set to `id`.

P_PGID

   The signal will be sent to any process with process group ID set to `id` (see Chapter 11).

P_SID

   The signal will be sent to any process with session ID set to `id` (see Chapter 11).

P_UID

   The signal will be sent to any process with effective user ID set to `id`.

P_GID

   The signal will be sent to any process with effective group ID set to `id`.

P_CID

   The signal will be sent to any process with scheduler class ID set to `id`. This value is not available in HP-UX 10.*x*.

P_ALL

   The signal will be sent to all processes; `id` is ignored.

If `id` is P_MYPID, the value of `id` is taken to be the calling process' process ID.

The `sigsendset` function provides an interesting way to send a signal to a set of processes. The signal is specified by `sig`, and the set of processes is specified by `psp`. The `psp` argument is a pointer to a structure of type `procset_t`:

```
typedef struct {
    idop_t      p_op;
    idtype_t    p_lidtype;
    id_t        p_lid;
    idtype_t    p_ridtype;
    id_t        p_rid;
} procset_t;
```

The `p_lidtype` and `p_lid` elements specify one set of processes (the "left" set), and the `p_ridtype` and `p_rid` elements specify another set (the "right" set). The `idtypes` and `ids` are specified in the same manner as for `sigsend`, described above.

The p_op element of the structure identifies an operation to be performed on the two sets of processes; the results of this operation are then used as the set of processes to which sig is delivered. Legal values for p_op are:

POP_DIFF
> Set difference. Processes in the left set that are not in the right set.

POP_AND
> Set intersection. Processes in both the left and right sets.

POP_OR
> Set union. Processes in either the left set, right set, or both.

POP_XOR
> Set exclusive-or. Processes in either the left or right set, but not both.

On success, sigsend and sigsendset return 0. On failure, they return -1 and errno will contain the reason for failure.

With both sigsend and sigsendset, the process with process ID set to 0 is always excluded, and the process with process ID 1 is excluded for all values of idtype except P_PID.

Also in both cases, the real or effective user ID of the calling process must match the real or effective user ID of the receiving process, unless the effective user ID of the sending process is that of the superuser, or sig is SIGCONT and the sending process has the same session ID as the receiving process.

Waiting for signals to occur

The POSIX standard provides two new functions for stopping a process until a signal occurs, sigsuspend and sigwait. The pause and sigpause functions, described earlier, may also be used for this purpose (however, sigpause should not be used with the POSIX signal functions, since it is part of a different signal mechanism).

```
#include <signal.h>

int sigsuspend(const sigset_t *set);

int sigwait(sigset_t *set);
```

The sigsuspend function replaces the process' signal mask with the set of signals pointed to by set, and then suspends the process until delivery of a signal whose action is either to execute a signal-catching function or to terminate the process. On return, the process' signal mask is restored to the set that existed before the call to sigsuspend.

The `sigwait` function selects a signal from the set pointed to by `set` that is pending for the process. If no signals in `set` are pending, then `sigwait` blocks until a signal in `set` becomes pending. The selected signal is cleared from the set of signals pending for the process, and the number of the signal is returned. The selection of a signal in `set` is independent of the process' signal mask. This means that a process can synchronously wait for signals that are being blocked by the signal mask.

Both `sigsuspend` and `sigwait` return -1 and set `errno` if an error occurs.

Printing signal information

The `psginal` function, described earlier, can still be used with the POSIX signal functions to print information about signals. SVR4 also provides a second function, for use with the `siginfo_t` structure:

```
#include <siginfo.h>

void psiginfo(siginfo_t *pinfo, char *s);
```

Like `psignal`, `psiginfo` prints the string pointed to by `s`, followed by a colon, followed by a string describing the signal (`pinfo->si_signo`). It then prints a description of the reason the signal was delivered, as indicated by the `siginfo_t` structure pointed to by `pinfo`.

The `psiginfo` function is not available in HP-UX 10.*x*.

Example 10-7 shows another version of our *signal* program that demonstrates the use of `psiginfo`.

Example 10-7: signal4

```
#include <signal.h>
#include <stdio.h>

void handler(int, siginfo_t *, void *);

int
main(void)
{
    struct sigaction sact;

    /*
     * Set up the sigaction structure.  We want to get the
     * extra information about the signal, so set SA_SIGINFO.
     */
    sact.sa_sigaction = handler;
    sact.sa_flags = SA_SIGINFO;
    sigemptyset(&sact.sa_mask);

    /*
```

Example 10–7: signal4 (continued)

```
        * Send SIGUSR1 and SIGUSR2 to the handler function.
        */
    if (sigaction(SIGUSR1, &sact, (struct sigaction *) NULL) < 0) {
        fprintf(stderr, "cannot set handler for SIGUSR1\n");
        exit(1);
    }

    if (sigaction(SIGUSR2, &sact, (struct sigaction *) NULL) < 0) {
        fprintf(stderr, "cannot set handler for SIGUSR2\n");
        exit(1);
    }

    /*
     * Now wait for signals to arrive.
     */
    for (;;)
        pause();
}

/*
 * handler - handle a signal.
 */
void
handler(int sig, siginfo_t *sinf, void *ucon)
{
    /*
     * Print out what we received.
     */
    psiginfo(sinf, "Received signal");
}
```

```
    % signal4 &
    [1] 12345
    % kill -USR1 12345
    Received signal: Signal User 1 (from process 678)
    % kill -USR2 12345
    Received signal: Signal User 2 (from process 678)
    % kill -USR1 12345
    Received signal: Signal User 1 (from process 678)
    % kill -USR2 12345
    Received signal: Signal User 2 (from process 678)
    % kill 12345
    [1] + Terminated     signal4
```

Manipulating the signal mask

The POSIX standard also specifies the way in which a process may examine and change its signal mask. This method is similar to, but less cumbersome than, the `sighold`/`sigrelse` method offered by SVR3.

```
#include <signal.h>

int sigprocmask(int how, const sigset_t *set, sigset_t *oset);
```

The `sigprocmask` function is used both to examine and change the signal mask. If `set` is non-null, then the signal set it points to modifies the signal mask according to the value of `how`:

SIG_BLOCK
> The signal set pointed to by `set` is added to the current signal mask.

SIG_UNBLOCK
> The signal set pointed to by `set` is removed from the current signal mask.

SIG_SETMASK
> The signal set pointed to by `set` replaces the current signal mask.

If `oset` is non-null, the previous value of the signal mask is stored in the area it points to. If `set` is null, the value of `how` is ignored and the signal mask is not changed; this enables the process to inquire about its current signal mask.

If there are any pending unblocked signals after the call to `sigprocmask`, at least one of those signals will be delivered to the process before `sigprocmask` returns.

On success, `sigprocmask` returns 0. On failure, it returns -1 and `errno` will contain the reason for failure.

Examining the list of pending signals

POSIX provides the `sigpending` function to obtain the list of signals a process has pending:

```
#include <signal.h>

int sigpending(sigset_t *set);
```

The function returns the list of signals that have been sent to the process but are being blocked from delivery by the signal mask, and stores them in the area pointed to by `set`. On success, `sigpending` returns 0; if it fails, it returns -1 and stores the reason for failure in `errno`.

The setjmp and longjmp functions, revisited

Recall that, when we discussed the `setjmp` and `longjmp` functions, we mentioned that they had one particularly annoying problem. Because the `longjmp` function is usually called from within a signal handler, and transfers control out of the signal handler without the handler ever returning, the signal that originally caused the handler to be invoked remains blocked in the process' signal mask.

To get around this problem, POSIX defines two new functions:

```
#include <setjmp.h>

int sigsetjmp(sigjmp_buf env, int savemask);

void siglongjmp(sigjmp_buf env, int val);
```

These two functions are identical to `setjmp` and `longjmp`, except that they use a `sigjmp_buf` data type instead of a `jmp_buf` data type, and `sigsetjmp` takes an additional argument. If the value of **savemask** is non-zero, then `sigsetjmp` saves the process' signal mask and scheduling parameters, and they will be restored when `siglongjmp` is called.

The POSIX signal mechanism is substantially more powerful than either the Version 7 or SVR3 mechanisms, particularly for complex applications in which signals must be blocked or detailed information about why a signal was delivered is needed. However, as mentioned before, it's somewhat more than the average programmer usually needs.

Porting Berkeley Signals to SVR4

Berkeley signals are both a blessing and a curse. They are a blessing because they introduced several important concepts such as reliable signals and restartable system calls. They are a curse because they are different from every other version of UNIX.

4.2BSD was the first version of UNIX to overhaul the signal mechanism; it is here that the concepts of reliable signals and restartable system calls were both introduced. In this section, we examine the 4.2BSD and 4.3BSD signal mechanisms in detail, as they pertain to porting programs that use them to SVR4.

It is important to understand that the way in which Berkeley implemented the new signal mechanism not only provided a number of new functions that will be described shortly, but it also changed the behavior of the standard `signal` function. Thus, *any* program being ported from 4.2BSD or 4.3BSD to SVR4 will need to have its signal handling code examined, not just those programs that use the new functions.

Fortunately, however, most programmers avoided the new Berkeley signal functions, and continued to simply use `signal`. Because they did not take advantage of any of the special features, the porting effort will usually be simple. The thing to remember in this case is that in Berkeley UNIX, the `signal` function provides reliable signals, while in SVR4 it does not. However, in SVR4, the `sigset` function provides reliable signals. So, most programs that use `signal` can be ported from Berkeley UNIX simply by placing the line

```
#define signal sigset
```

at the top of the program. The only exception to this rule occurs when the program handles SIGCHLD; recall that the `sigset` function implements the System V semantics for this signal. In this case, the program must be modified to use `sigaction`.

For those programs that do make use of the Berkeley signal functions, the rest of this chapter provides a basic description of these functions and how they work.

The sigvec Function

The primary function for handling signals in Berkeley UNIX is called `sigvec`:

```
#include <signal.h>

int sigvec(int sig, struct sigvec *vec, struct sigvec *ovec);
```

The function sets the disposition for the signal identified in `sig` to the information provided in `vec` if it is non-null; if `ovec` is non-null, the previous disposition information is returned.

The `struct sigvec` structure is defined this way in 4.2BSD:

```
struct sigvec {
    int     (*sv_handler)(int, int, struct sigcontext *);
    int     sv_mask;
    int     sv_onstack;
};
```

The `sv_handler` element of the structure is a pointer to the handler function; it may also take on the values SIG_DFL and SIG_IGN. The `sv_mask` element specifies a signal mask (see below) of signals that should be blocked for the duration of the signal handler. The `sv_onstack` element, if non-zero, indicates that the signal should be handled on an alternate signal stack instead of the process' main stack.

In 4.3BSD, the structure was changed to:

```
struct sigvec {
    int     (*sv_handler)(int, int, struct sigcontext *);
    int     sv_mask;
    int     sv_flags;
};
```

The `sv_flags` element could take on the values `SV_ONSTACK` to indicate the alternate signal stack, and `SV_INTERRUPT` to specify that the signal should interrupt system calls rather than restart them.

Generally speaking, if `sv_mask` and `sv_flags` (sv_onstack) are not used, calls to `sigvec` can be replaced with analogous calls to `sigset`. If the `sv_mask` element of the structure is used, `sigaction` should be used, with the `sa_mask` element of the `sigaction` structure. If the alternate signal stack is used (which it rarely, if ever, was), the `sigaction` function must be used, in conjunction with `sigaltstack` (not described in this book).

Handler Calling Conventions

Signal handlers in Berkeley UNIX use three arguments:

```
int (*handler)(int sig, int code, struct sigcontext *context);
```

The `sig` parameter is the signal number, just as in all other versions of UNIX. The `code` parameter related the signal to a hardware trap; this information is provided by SVR4 in the `si_info` element of the `siginfo_t` structure. The `context` parameter describes the program context to be restored on return from the signal handler; this information can be obtained by using the `sa_sigaction` handler with `sigaction`.

Signal Masks

Berkeley UNIX provides the concept of signal masks just as SVR4 does. A signal mask defines the set of signals currently blocked from delivery. If the *i*th bit in the mask is 1, then signal number *i* is blocked. The *i*th bit is set by *or*ing in a 1 shifted left *i*-1 places:

```
1 << (i-1)
```

4.3BSD defines a macro, `sigmask`, that performs this computation:

```
#include <signal.h>

int sigmask(int sig);
```

Calls to `sigmask` should be replaced with calls to `sigemptyset`, `sigfillset`, `sigaddset`, and `sigdelset`.

To install a new signal mask, use the `sigsetmask` function:

```
#include <signal.h>

int sigsetmask(int mask);
```

This returns the previous signal mask. You can, instead, call `sigprocmask` with `SIG_SETMASK` as the first argument.

To add a set of signals to the current signal mask, use the `sigblock` function:

```
#include <signal.h>

int sigblock(int mask);
```

The previous mask is returned. You can, instead, call `sigprocmask` with class="constant">SIG_BLOCK as the first argument, or `sighold`.

Waiting for Signals

Berkeley UNIX also provides a `sigpause` function:

```
#include <signal.h>

int sigpause(int mask);
```

The new mask is installed and the program blocked until a signal occurs. When `sigpause` returns, the old signal mask is restored. Note that this behavior is identical to the POSIX `sigsuspend` function, but that it is *not* the same as the SVR3 `sigpause` function.

The setjmp and longjmp Functions

In Berkeley UNIX, the `setjmp` and `longjmp` functions *do* save and restore the signal mask, unlike in the SVR4 version. Replace calls to `setjmp` and `longjmp` with calls to `sigsetjmp` and `siglongjmp`, respectively.

Chapter Summary

In this chapter, we learned how to process signals, and how to use signals to implement important functions such as timeouts. When writing systems-level programs, handling signals is almost always required to some extent, and knowledge of the material in this chapter is vital. In the next chapter we will learn how to handle processes, including how to implement job control. Job control demonstrates many of the complex interactions between processes and signals that the systems programmer sometimes has to deal with.

11

Processes

The UNIX operating system, unlike the operating systems on most personal computers, is a multiuser, multitasking operating system. The first term, *multiuser*, means that more than one person can use the system at the same time to get work done. The second term, *multitasking*, means that the system as a whole, and each user individually, can do more than one thing at a time. Contrast this with a personal computer, which supports one user at a time, using one program at a time.

But, this is all an illusion. On most computers, there is only one processor, and that processor can only do one thing at a time. (Some newer systems have more than one processor, but each processor can still do only one thing at a time.) The UNIX system creates the illusion that the computer is doing several things at once by *timesharing* the processor. The processor spends a few microseconds doing one task, and then switches to another. It spends a few microseconds there, and then switches to yet another task. Since microseconds are too short for most humans to deal with, it *appears* that all these tasks are taking place simultaneously. This scheme usually works well, because while some tasks are blocked (for example, waiting for the user to type something), other tasks can be processed. The illusion only breaks down when there are so many tasks waiting to be serviced that the system seems slow, and everyone starts to complain.

Processes are what the UNIX system uses to split work up into tasks. Each task is placed into a separate process, and the operating system timeshares the processor among all currently active processes. When a new task is started (by a user executing a command, for example), a new process is created. When the task is finished, the process associated with that task is destroyed. Many processes stand alone as individual tasks. Other processes may be interrelated, being subtasks of a larger task. In this chapter, we describe processes—how to create them, how to destroy them, and how to control them. We also examine the interrelationships among processes, and ways to use them.

Process Concepts

To manipulate processes successfully, you must understand a number of basic concepts. These concepts are described below.

Process Identifiers

Each process in the system has a unique process identifier, or *process ID*. The process ID is a positive integer, usually in the range from 0 to about 32,000. Each time a new process is created, the operating system assigns it the next sequential, unused process ID. When the maximum process ID is reached, the numbers wrap around to 0 again. The process ID is the only well-known (i.e., accessible outside the operating system itself) identifier of a process. A process can determine its process ID by using the `getpid` function:

```
#include <sys/types.h>
#include <unistd.h>

pid_t getpid(void);
```

The process ID is actually used as an index into an array of structures of type `struct proc` (see the include file *sys/proc.h*) called the *process table*. Each array element in the process table describes one process. Each `struct proc` structure contains all of the state information about a process, including its real and effective user- and group IDs, its signal mask, its list of pending signals, the command name, the amount of processor time used so far, pointers into the open file table, and all sorts of other information.

New processes come into being when existing processes create them. When a process creates another process, the new process is said to be a *child* of the existing process. Similarly, the existing process is said to be the *parent* of the new process. The *parent process ID* of a process is the process ID of the process that created it. A process can usually learn its parent's process ID by using the `getppid` function:

```
#include <sys/types.h>
#include <unistd.h>

pid_t getppid(void);
```

System processes

Generally, there is no direct correspondence between process IDs and programs. When a program is executed, it just gets the next available process ID. Execute the program more than once, and it will have a different process ID each time. However, there are a few, usually fewer than five, special processes that always have the same process ID. These processes are called *system processes*.

The process with process-id-0 is the *system scheduler,* usually called *sched* or *swapper.* It is responsible for allocating those few-millisecond time slices to all the other processes on the system. The scheduler is not a command in the usual sense; there is no corresponding program on the disk for it. It is a part of the operating system kernel itself.

The process with process-id-1 is the *init* process. This program is responsible for bringing the system up after a reboot. It executes the */etc/rc* files, and brings the system to a specific state (usually multiuser operation). The *init* process is a regular user-level process (i.e., it's a command that can be executed). After starting up the system, *init* stays around to perform some process-related bookkeeping tasks. If *init* is killed (or otherwise exits), the system will shut down.

On modern versions of UNIX that support virtual memory, the process with process-id-2 is usually the page daemon, called *pagedaemon* or *pageout.* This is a kernel process like the scheduler, and is responsible for moving unused pages of memory out to disk so that other programs may use them.

Termination Status

Eventually, most processes terminate normally, finishing whatever they're intended to do. There are three ways for a process to terminate normally; it may:

1. Execute a `return` from the `main` function.

2. Call the `exit` function (described later in this chapter). This function is defined by ANSI C; it calls any exit handlers that have been defined, and closes all *Standard I/O Library* streams.

3. Call the `_exit` function. This function is not usually called directly, but is called by `exit`. It is responsible for cleaning up operating system-specific resources used by the process; since ANSI C is operating system-independent, it cannot specify these functions.

There are also two ways in which a process can terminate abnormally; it may:

1. Call the `abort` function (see Chapter 16, *Miscellaneous Routines*).

2. Receive a signal from itself, from another process, or from the operating system. The signal can cause the program to terminate, sometimes with an accompanying core dump.

When a program terminates, the operating system provides a *termination status* to the process' parent. The termination status indicates whether the process terminated normally or abnormally. If the process terminated normally, the termination status provides the parent process with an *exit status* for the process; the exit status is used by some programs to indicate success, failure, and other events. If the process terminated abnormally, the termination status includes information about how the program terminated (what signal it received) and whether or not a core dump was produced.

The termination status of a child process is returned to the parent process when the parent calls the `wait` function, or one of its derivatives. These functions are described later in the chapter. The important point to understand here is that it is up to the parent to ask for the termination status of a child—it can do this as soon as the child terminates, several minutes or hours later, or even not at all.

Zombie processes

Since it is up to the parent process to request the termination status of a child process, what happens when the child process terminates? The system can't keep the entire process around; resources such as memory, open files, process table slots (process IDs), and so forth would rapidly be exhausted. On the other hand, it can't get rid of the process entirely, either, because then the termination status would not be available to return to the parent process.

To resolve this dilemma, UNIX compromises. When a process terminates, the operating system frees up all of the resources used by the process *except* the process table entry. The termination status of the process is stored in the process table entry, where it can be retrieved later by the parent. When the parent process finally does issue a call to `wait` or a similar function, the termination status is returned and the process table slot can be freed for reuse.

During the time between when a process terminates and the parent picks up its termination status, the process is called a *zombie process*. All of its resources have been freed except for the process table entry, and thus it is dead, still walking around in the system. Zombie processes are usually labeled as "<defunct>" in the output from the *ps* command and have a process status of "Z."

Orphaned processes

When a process terminates before its parent, it becomes a zombie process until the parent picks up its termination status. But what happens when the parent terminates before the child process? This is not an abnormal event; in fact, it happens all the time. Does the child process still have a parent? What happens if the child calls `getppid`?

UNIX handles this situation by arranging for the *init* process to become the new parent process of any process whose real parent terminates. When a process terminates, the operating system goes through the list of all active processes, looking for any whose parent is the terminating process. If it finds any, it sets those processes' parent process ID to 1 (the *init* process).

What happens when a process that has been inherited by *init* terminates? Since its original parent is no longer around to pick up its termination status, does it become a zombie forever? Fortunately, no. One of the functions of the *init* process is to call one of the `wait` functions each time one of its child processes terminates. In this way it picks up these orphaned processes' termination statuses (it simply discards them), and keeps the system from becoming clogged with zombie processes.

Process Groups

In addition to having a process ID, each process is also a member of a *process group*. A process group is a collection of one or more processes, and is identified by a unique positive integer called a process group ID. A process may obtain its process group ID by calling the `getpgrp` function:

```
#include <sys/types.h>
#include <unistd.h>

pid_t getpgrp(void);
```

The processes in a process group are usually related in some way. Process groups were introduced in Berkeley UNIX to implement job control. Shells that perform job control, such as the C shell or the Korn shell, usually place all of the commands in a pipeline into a single process group. For example, in the command

```
% eqn myreport | tbl | troff | psdit | lp
```

each program (*eqn, tbl, troff, psdit,* and *lp*) would be running as a separate process with a separate process ID (e.g., 123, 124, 125, 126, and 127). However, all five processes would have the same process group ID, e.g., 127. This allows the shell to treat those five processes as a single entity (a "job") for purposes of stop-ping them, continuing them, and moving them between the foreground and the background.

The process group leader

Each process group starts out with a process group leader. This is the process whose process group ID is equal to its process ID. It is, of course, possible for the process group leader to terminate at any time. The process group, however, remains in existence until the last process in that process group terminates. When a process group is created as the result of a pipeline, the last process in the pipeline is usually the process group leader. There is no deep and meaningful rea-son for this; it is simply a side effect of the way pipelines are created.

Sessions

The POSIX standard introduced still another construct, called a *session*. A session is a collection of one or more process groups. The idea is that while each process group is a group of related processes (such as a pipeline), a session is a group of related process groups (such as all the jobs currently being run by the user logged in on a particular terminal). Sessions exist only for job control, serving mainly to fix some deficiencies in the Berkeley job control implementation (which only used process groups).

The session leader

When a process creates a new session, it becomes the *leader* of that session. The session leader has certain privileges that other members of the session do not (see below).

In the POSIX standard, there is no concept of a session ID like that of the process ID and process group ID. However, SVR4 defines such an identifier; it is equal to the process ID of the session leader. A process can be identified as a session leader if its process ID, process group ID, and session ID are all equal. To make this identification process easier, SVR4 provides the `getsid` function:

```
#include <sys/types.h>

pid_t getsid(void);
```

This function is not part of the POSIX standard.

The Controlling Terminal

A *controlling terminal* can be associated with a session; in the case of interactive logins, the controlling terminal is usually the device on which the user is logged in. When a session is initially created, it has no controlling terminal. A controlling terminal is allocated for a session when the session leader opens a terminal device that is not already associated with a session, unless the session leader supplies the O_NOCTTY flag on the call to open (see Chapter 3, *Low-Level I/O Routines*). The session leader that establishes the connection to the controlling terminal is called the *controlling process.*

When a session has a controlling terminal associated with it, a number of things can happen. At all times, the controlling terminal is associated with a process group. When one of the session's process groups has the same process group ID as that of the controlling terminal, that process group is said to be in the *foreground*. If the process group's process group ID is not the same as that of the controlling terminal, the process group is said to be in the *background*. The foreground or background status of a process group has a number of interesting effects.

Whenever a user presses the interrupt key (usually CTRL-C) or quit key (usually CTRL-\) on the controlling terminal, a signal (either SIGINT or SIGQUIT) is delivered to all processes in the foreground process group. If job control is enabled, pressing the suspend key (usually CTRL-Z) on the controlling terminal sends a SIGTSTP signal to all processes in the foreground process group. Whenever a modem disconnect on the controlling terminal is detected by the system, the SIGHUP signal is sent to the controlling process (session leader).

When job control is enabled, only a process in the foreground process group may read from the terminal. Processes in background process groups will be stopped with a SIGTTIN signal if they attempt to read from the controlling terminal. If the TOSTOP mode is set on the controlling terminal (see Chapter 12, *Terminals*), only processes in the foreground process group may write to the controlling terminal. If a process in a background process group attempts to write to the controlling terminal, it will be stopped with a SIGTTOU signal.

Job control shells, such as the C shell and Korn shell, use the controlling terminal to implement job control. In order to move a job into the foreground, the shell changes the process group of the controlling terminal to the process group ID of that job and, if necessary, starts the job running again by sending the processes in that process group a SIGCONT signal. Each time a different job is placed into the foreground, the controlling terminal's process group is changed to the process group of that job.

Sometimes, a program wishes to talk to the controlling terminal, regardless of whether or not the standard input or standard output have been redirected. For example, the *passwd* program insists on reading a new password from the keyboard; it does not want to read it from a file (if the password is stored in a file, it is probably not secret any more). When this is necessary, the process can open the special file */dev/tty*. This special filename is translated within the kernel to refer to the controlling terminal for the process. Only a process with a controlling terminal can open */dev/tty*.

Priorities

The UNIX scheduler is responsible for allocating slices of the processor's time to processes in the system. In order to do this fairly, the scheduler computes a *priority* for each process in the system. These priorities are recalculated frequently, based on a complex formula that takes into account such things as the amount of memory the process is using, the amount of input and output it is performing, and how long it's been since the last time the process got any processor time. The calculation varies among different versions of UNIX, but the end result is the same— an ordered list of processes, sorted by priority. Generally speaking, processes with a high priority execute more often and/or for longer time slices.

A process cannot set or change its priority; this calculation is performed by the operating system. However, the process can influence the priority calculation slightly. One of the parameters of the scheduler's priority calculation is a process' *nice* value. This is a number that ranges from 0 to 40, with the default value being 20. A process can lower its priority (allow other processes to take precedence) by increasing its nice value to something between 20 and 40. (This is where the name "nice" comes from—large jobs are supposed to be nice to the system by increasing their nice value.) To raise its priority (take precedence over other processes), a process decreases its nice value to something between 0 and 20. Usually, any process may increase its nice value (give itself a worse priority), but only processes with superuser privileges may lower their nice values. To change the nice value, use the `nice` function:

```
#include <unistd.h>

int nice(int incr);
```

When called, `nice` adds `incr`, which may be positive or negative, to the process' current nice value.

Program Termination

As mentioned above, the operating system saves the termination status of a process that terminates. The termination status can be retrieved later by the parent process (we will describe how to do this later in the chapter). The termination status contains information about whether the process terminated normally or abnormally, and, if it terminated abnormally, the reason for termination.

When a process terminates normally, it may optionally return an *exit status* to the parent process. The exit status is a small integer value that can communicate information about how things went. Convention dictates that a zero exit status be used to indicate that everything went fine, no errors occurred. A non-zero exit status usually indicates that something went wrong, although this is not always the case. It is up to the programmer to define the meanings for non-zero exit status values. Many programs simply use exit status 1 to indicate something went wrong, without being more specific (error messages usually supplement this). But some programs have several different exit status values, with special meaning assigned to each one. For example, the *grep* utility exits with status 0 if matches were found, status 1 if no matches were found, and status 2 if the pattern specification was erroneous. For an example of even more special meanings, look at the manual page for the *fsck* program.

A program provides an exit status to the parent process by using the `exit` function:

```
#include <stdlib.h>

void exit(int status);
```

The `status` argument is the exit status. The function sets the exit status, and then causes the program to terminate.

The `exit` function is a library routine, defined by ANSI C, that closes all the *Standard I/O Library* streams the process has open, and then calls another function, `_exit`. The `_exit` function does a number of things, including closing all the process' open files, sending a `SIGCHLD` signal to the parent process, setting the process' child processes' parent process IDs to 1, freeing up any interprocess communication resources used by the process, and so forth. The reason that these chores are not performed by `exit` itself is that ANSI C does not specify operating system-dependent functionality, and thus cannot specify everything `exit` should do.

The `exit` function exists in all versions of UNIX. UNIX implementations that support ANSI C also allow the programmer to register up to 32 functions to be called automatically at the time the program exits, either by calling `exit` or by returning from `main`. These functions are registered by using the `atexit` function:

```
#include <stdlib.h>

int atexit(void (*func)(void));
```

Each function registered is called, with no arguments, when the program exits. The functions are called in the reverse order of their registration. Again, this functionality is only available in ANSI C.

Simple Program Execution

The simplest way to execute a program from within your program is to use the `system` function:

```
#include <stdlib.h>

int system(const char *string);
```

The `system` function uses the Bourne shell (*/bin/sh*) with its *-c* option to execute the shell command contained in `string`, waits for the command to complete, and then returns the termination status (which includes the exit status) of the command. Example 11-1 demonstrates the use of `system`.

Example 11–1: system

```
#include <stdlib.h>
#include <stdio.h>

struct {
    char    *abbrev;
    char    *fullname;
} days[] = {
    "Sun",   "Sunday",
    "Mon",   "Monday",
    "Tue",   "Tuesday",
    "Wed",   "Wednesday",
    "Thu",   "Thursday",
    "Fri",   "Friday",
    "Sat",   "Saturday",
    0,       0
};

int
main(void)
{
    int i;
    int status;
    char command[BUFSIZ];
```

Example 11-1: system (continued)

```
    /*
     * For each day, construct a command.
     */
    for (i=0; days[i].abbrev != NULL; i++) {
        /*
         * Run the date command, and use grep to search for
         * the day's abbreviated name.  Redirect the output
         * to /dev/null; we'll use the exit status to find
         * what we want.
         */
        sprintf(command, "date | grep %s > /dev/null", days[i].abbrev);

        /*
         * Run the command.  The termination status is returned
         * in status.
         */
        status = system(command);

        /*
         * The exit status is in the second byte of the
         * termination status.
         *
         * Grep returns 0 if a match was found, 1 if no
         * match was found, and 2 if an error occurred.
         */
        switch ((status >> 8) & 0xff) {
        case 0:
            printf("Today is %s.\n", days[i].fullname);
            break;
        case 1:
            printf("Today is not %s.\n", days[i].fullname);
            break;
        case 2:
            printf("Error in pattern specification.\n");
            exit(1);
        }
    }

    /*
     * Exit with a status of 0, indicating that
     * everything went fine.
     */
    exit(0);
}


    % system
    Today is not Sunday.
    Today is not Monday.
    Today is not Tuesday.
    Today is Wednesday.
    Today is not Thursday.
```

```
Today is not Friday.
Today is not Saturday.
```

For each day of the week, the program constructs a command to execute *date*, sending the output from that to *grep*, to search for the abbreviated day name. Each time, we save the termination status of *grep* (in a pipeline, the termination status of the entire pipeline is defined by the termination status of the last command in the pipeline) in the variable `status`. Next, we extract the exit status from the termination status, figure out what *grep* was telling us, and print an appropriate message.

The example extracts the exit status from the termination status in a non-portable fashion. As it turns out, this example will work on all versions of UNIX; the exit status is always in the second byte of the termination status. A more portable way to examine the termination status and extract information from it is shown in the next section.

Finally, notice that the commands we build redirect their output to */dev/null* (the "bit bucket"). We can do this because we are interested only in whether or not *grep* found anything, not what it found, and *grep* tells us this with its exit status. If we did not redirect the output to */dev/null*, then when we found a match, the output from *date* (as printed by *grep*) would appear in the middle of the output from our program. Try removing the redirection from the command to see the difference.

There are three final points to make about `system`:

1. Although convenient, `system` is also terribly inefficient. Each time it is called, it starts not only the command you want to execute, but also a copy of the shell. If your program executes many commands, you should execute them yourself directly, rather than via `system`. The means to do this are described in the next section.

2. System calls and library routines are always more efficient than using `system` to do the same thing. For example, instead of calling

    ```
    system("rm -f file");
    system("mkdir foo");
    system("mv oldfile newfile");
    ```

    you could include in your program functions we have discussed in previous chapters:

    ```
    unlink("file");
    mkdir("foo");
    rename("oldfile", "newfile");
    ```

3. The `system` function should *never*, under any circumstances, be used in programs that will be run with superuser permissions, or with the set-user-id bit set. Because `system` uses the shell to execute commands, there may be ways in which an unethical person can fool your program into executing a command other than the one you intended. This may enable the person to circumvent the security of your computer system.

Advanced Program Execution

In this section, we will examine the procedures used to create new processes, execute other programs, and retrieve processes' termination statuses. All three of these procedures are used in the construction of the `system` function, described above; at the end of this section we will show how `system` can be written.

Creating a New Process

The first step in executing a program is to create a new process. The function to do this is called `fork`:

```
#include <sys/types.h>
#include <unistd.h>

pid_t fork(void);
```

The `fork` function creates an exact copy of the calling process. This means that the child process inherits a number of characteristics from the parent process:

- The real user ID, real group ID, effective user ID, and effective group ID of the parent process

- The set-user-id and set-group-id mode bits of the parent process

- The supplementary group ID list of the parent process

- The saved user ID and saved group ID of the parent process

- All of the parent process' environment variables (see Chapter 16)

- All of the parent process' open file descriptors and file offsets

- Any file descriptor close-on-exec flags (see Chapter 6, *Special-Purpose File Operations*) set by the parent process

- The file mode creation mask (*umask*) of the parent process

- Any signal handling dispositions (`SIG_DFL`, `SIG_IGN`, `SIG_HOLD`, or a handler function address) set by the parent process

- The session ID and process group ID of the parent process

- The parent process' controlling terminal

- The parent process' nice value (see above)

- The current working directory of the parent process

- The parent process' resource limits

The child process will differ from the parent process in the following ways:

- The child process will have a unique process ID.

- The child process will have a different parent process ID.

- The child process will have its own copy of the parent's open file descriptors. It may close these file descriptors without affecting the parent. However, the parent and child will share the file offset for each descriptor; this means that if they both write to the file at the same time, the output will be intermixed. Likewise, if they both read from the file, they will each receive only part of the data.

- The child process will not have any of the file locks its parent may have created.

- The set of pending signals for the child process is initialized to the empty set.

The `fork` function is interesting in that it returns twice—once in the parent, and once in the child. In the parent process, `fork` returns the process ID of the child process (it returns -1 if a child process could not be created). In the child process, however, `fork` returns 0. In this way, the parent and child can distinguish themselves from one another.

As soon as `fork` returns, there are two nearly identical copies of the program running. There is no guarantee that the child will run before the parent or vice-versa; this must be taken into account to avoid a deadlock condition in which each process is waiting on the other to do something.

Example 11-2 is a program that creates a child process. The child process writes out the lowercase letters in alphabetical order ten times; the parent process writes out the uppercase letters in alphabetical order ten times. Notice that running the program multiple times may not produce the same output each time; this is because two processes are performing the task, and the order in which they execute is dependent on the system scheduler, how many other processes are running on the system, and other parameters outside of the program's control.

Example 11-2: fork

```c
#include <sys/types.h>
#include <unistd.h>

int
main(void)
{
    int i;
    char c;
    pid_t pid;

    /*
     * Create a child process.
     */
    if ((pid = fork()) < 0) {
        perror("fork");
        exit(1);
    }

    if (pid == 0) {
        /*
         * This code executes in the child process
         * (fork returned zero).
         */
        for (i=0; i < 10; i++) {
            for (c = 'a'; c <= 'z'; c++)
                write(1, &c, 1);
        }
    }
    else {
        /*
         * This code executes in the parent process.
         */
        for (i=0; i < 10; i++) {
            for (c = 'A'; c <= 'Z'; c++)
                write(1, &c, 1);
        }
    }

    /*
     * This code executes in both processes (i.e.,
     * it gets executed twice).
     */
    write(1, "\n", 1);
    exit(0);
}
```

% fork
abcdefghijklmnopqrstuvwxyzabcdefghijklmnopqrstuvwxyzabcdefghijklmnABCDEFG
HIJKLMNOPQRSTUVWXYZABCDEFGHIJKLMNOPQRSTUVWXYZABCDEFGHIJKLMNOPQRSTUVWXYZAB
CDEFGHIJKLMNOPQRSTUVWXYZABCDEFGHIJKLMNOPQRSTUVWXYZABCDEFGHIJKLMNOPQRSTUVW
XYZABCDEFopqrstuvwxyzabcdefghijklmnopqrstuvwxyzabcdefghijklmnopqrstuvwxyz

```
abcdefghijklmnopqrstuvwxyzabcdefghijklmnopqrstuvwxyzabcdefghijklmnopqrstu
vwxyzabcdefghijklmnopqGHIJKLMNOPQRSTUVWXYZABCDEFGHIJKLMNOPQRSTUVWXYZABCDE
FGHIJKLMNOPQRSTUVWXYZABCDEFGHIJKLMNOPQRSTUVWXYZ
% fork
abcdefghijklmnopqrABCDEFGHIJKLMNOPQRSTUVWXYZABCDEFGHIJKLMNOPQRSTUVWXYZABC
DEFGHIJKLMNOPQRSTUVWXYZABCDEFGHIJKLMNOPQRSTUVWXYZABCDEFGHIJKLMNOPQRSTUVWX
YZABCDEFGHIJKLMNstuvwxyzabcdefghijklmnopqrstuvwxyzabcdefghijklmnopqrstuvw
xyzabcdefghijklmnopqrstuvwxyzabcdefghijklmnopqrstuvwxyzabcdefghijklmnopqr
stuvwxyzabcOPQRSTUVWXYZABCDEFGHIJKLMNOPQRSTUVWXYZABCdefghijklmnopqrstuvwx
yzabcdefghijklmnopqrstuvwxyzabcdefghijklmnopqrstuvwxyzabcdefghijkDEFGHIJK
LMNOPQRSTUVWXYZABCDEFGHIJKLMNOPQRSTUVWXYZABCDEFGHIJKLMNOPQRSTUVWXYZ
```

Executing a Program

The second step in executing a program is to bring the program into memory and begin executing its instructions. To do this, use any of several routines, all generically referred to as the **exec** functions:

```
#include <unistd.h>

int execl(const char *path, const char *arg0, ..., const char *argn,
     char * /*NULL*/);

int execv(const char *path, const char *argv[]);

int execle(const char *path, const char *arg0, ..., const char *argn,
     char * /*NULL*/, const char *envp[]);

int execve(const char *path, const char *argv[], const char *envp[]);

int execlp(const char *file, const char *arg0, ..., const char *argn,
     char * /*NULL*/);

int execvp(const char *file, const char *argv[], const char *envp[]);
```

In all its forms, **exec** overlays the image of the calling process with the image of a new program. The new process image is constructed from an ordinary executable file, either an object file as produced by a compiler, or a file of data for an interpreter, such as the shell. If **exec** succeeds, it never returns, because the calling process is overlaid by the new process image (and thus no longer exists).

On most modern UNIX systems, shell scripts and other files of interpreted commands may begin with a line of the form

```
#!pathname [argument]
```

Where `pathname` is the full pathname to the interpreter, and `argument` is an optional argument. For example, "`#!/bin/sh`" is common in shell scripts. When one of these files is the target of an exec, the interpreter is invoked with its zeroth argument equal to pathname, and if present, its first argument equal to argument. The remaining arguments to the interpreter are the arguments specified in the call to exec. Most UNIX systems limit the length of this line to about 32 characters.

When an object file is executed, it is called as follows:

```
int main(int argc, char *argv[], char *envp[]);
```

where argc is the argument count, argv is an array of character pointers to the arguments themselves, and envp is an array of character pointers to the environment strings (see Chapter 16). The argc parameter is always at least 1, and the first element of argv points to the name of the executable file.

The execl and execle functions execute the file named by the pathname in path, with the strings pointed to by arg0 through argn as arguments. The argument following argn should be a null pointer, to indicate the end of the argument list. By convention, arg0 should always be present; it will become the name of the process as displayed by the *ps* command. Usually, arg0 is given as the pathname of the executable file, or the last component of the pathname. A program executed by execl will inherit the calling process' environment strings; execle allows the calling process to provide a new set of environment strings in envp.

The execv and execve functions execute the file named by the pathname in path, with the strings pointed to by the array of pointers in argv as arguments. By convention, argv should always contain at least one member, which will become the name of the process as displayed by the *ps* command. Usually, argv[0] is given as the pathname of the executable file, or the last component of the pathname. A program executed by execv will inherit the calling process' environment strings; execve allows the calling process to provide a new set of environment strings in envp.

The execlp and execvp functions are identical to execl and execv, except that instead of requiring a path name to the executable file, you supply only the file's name. These functions then search the directories in the calling process' search path (as defined by the PATH environment variable), looking for an executable file of the same name. The first such file encountered is then executed. If the target file is not an object file or executable interpreter script as described above, the contents of the file are used as input to the Bourne shell (*/bin/sh*).

An exec causes the new process to inherit the open file descriptors of the calling process, except those with the close-on-exec flag set (see Chapter 6). For those file descriptors that remain open, the file offset is unchanged. Signals that are being caught by the calling process are reset to their default dispositions in the new process; all other signal dispositions remain the same. If a call to **exec** fails, it returns -1 and places the reason for failure in **errno**.

Example 11-3 shows a program that creates a child process, after which both the child and parent processes execute other commands.

Example 11–3: forkexec

```
#include <sys/types.h>
#include <unistd.h>

int
main(void)
{
    pid_t pid;
    char *args[4];

    /*
     * Create a child process.
     */
    if ((pid = fork()) < 0) {
        perror("fork");
        exit(1);
    }

    if (pid == 0) {
        /*
         * This code executes in the child process
         * (fork returned zero).
         */
        execl("/bin/echo", "echo", "Today's", "date", "is:", 0);

        /*
         * If the exec succeeds, we'll never get here.
         */
        perror("exec");
        exit(1);
    }


    /*
     * This code executes in the parent process.
     */
    args[0] = "date";
    args[1] = "+%A, %B %d, %Y";
    args[2] = NULL;

    execv("/bin/date", args);

    /*
     * If the exec succeeds, we'll never get here.
     */
```

Example 11–3: forkexec (continued)

```
    perror("exec");
    exit(1);
}
```

```
% forkexec
Today's date is:
Wednesday, November 30, 1994
% forkexec
Wednesday, November 30, 1994
Today's date is:
```

Note that this program suffers from the same plight that our last example did—because there is no guarantee that the child process will execute before the parent process, the output can come out in the wrong order (you may have to run the program several times to see this behavior). To get around this, we could place a call to `sleep` in the parent right before the call to `exec`. However, if we use a small sleep value, there is no guarantee, on a heavily loaded system, that the child will get to execute in that amount of time. But if we use anything much larger than one or two seconds, the program will have an uncomfortable delay between printing "`Today's date is:`" and actually printing the date. In the next section, we will see how to solve this problem.

Collecting the Process Termination Status

The last step in executing a program is to wait for it to complete, and collect the termination status of the process. This is an optional step; if it is not performed, the child process will become a zombie while the parent process still exists, and if the parent process exits, the child process will be inherited by *init*.

The basic function used to wait for a child process to complete, and retrieve its termination status, is called `wait`:

```
#include <sys/types.h>
#include <sys/wait.h>

pid_t wait(int *status);
```

The `wait` function suspends the calling process until one of its immediate child processes terminates. (It also returns if a child process that is being traced is stopped due to the receipt of a signal, but that is beyond the scope of this book.) The termination status of the child process is stored in the integer pointed to by `status`. If the calling process does not care about the termination status, and is only interested in waiting until the child process terminates, status may be given as the null pointer. If a child process has terminated prior to the call to wait, wait returns immediately with the status for that process. The process ID of the process that terminated is returned by wait; if there are no unwaited-for child processes, wait returns -1.

The following macros, defined in the include file *sys/wait.h*, assist in decoding the termination status returned by wait. Each of them takes a single argument, the integer containing the termination status.

WIFEXITED
>   Evaluates to a non-zero value if the process terminated normally.

WEXITSTATUS
>   Evalutes to the exit code the process passed to exit or returned from main if WIFEXITED evalutes to a non-zero value (indicating normal termination).

WIFSIGNALED
>   Evaluates to a non-zero value if the process terminated due to the receipt of a signal.

WTERMSIG
>   Evaluates to the number of the signal that caused the process to terminate if WIFSIGNALED evaluates to a non-zero value (indicating termination due to a signal).

WIFSTOPPED
>   Evaluates to a non-zero value if the process is currently stopped.

WSTOPSIG
>   Evalutes to the number of the signal that caused the process to stop if WIF-STOPPED evaluates to a non-zero value (indicating the process is stopped).

WIFCONTINUED
>   Evaluates to a non-zero value if the process has been continued from a stopped state. This macro is not defined in HP-UX 10.*x.*

WCOREDUMP
>   Evaluates to a non-zero value if a core image of the process was created and if WIFSIGNALED evaluates to a non-zero value (indicating termination due to a signal).

Example 11-4 shows how to modify the program from Example 11-3 so that it always prints things in the right order. The only difference is the addition of the call to wait in the parent.

Example 11-4: forkexecwait

```c
#include <sys/types.h>
#include <unistd.h>

int
main(void)
{
    pid_t pid;
    char *args[4];

    /*
     * Create a child process.
     */
    if ((pid = fork()) < 0) {
        perror("fork");
        exit(1);
    }

    if (pid == 0) {
        /*
         * This code executes in the child process
         * (fork returned zero).
         */
        execl("/bin/echo", "echo", "Today's", "date", "is:", 0);

        /*
         * If the exec succeeds, we'll never get here.
         */
        perror("exec");
        exit(1);
    }

    /*
     * Wait for the child process to complete.  We
     * don't care about the termination status.
     */
    while (wait((int *) 0) != pid)
        continue;

    /*
     * This code executes in the parent process.
     */
    args[0] = "date";
    args[1] = "+%A, %B %d, %Y";
    args[2] = NULL;

    execv("/bin/date", args);

    /*
     * If the exec succeeds, we'll never get here.
     */
    perror("exec");
    exit(1);
```

Example 11-4: forkexecwait (continued)

```
}
```

```
% forkexecwait
Today's date is:
Wednesday, November 30, 1994
% forkexecwait
Today's date is:
Wednesday, November 30, 1994
```

Two variants of the `wait` function provide additional functionality:

```
#include <sys/types.h>
#include <sys/wait.h>

pid_t waitpid(pid_t pid, int *status, int options);

pid_t waitid(idtype_t idtype, id_t id, singinfo_t *info,
        int options);
```

The `waitpid` function is specified by the POSIX standard. It allows the programmer greater control over waiting for processes, by assigning several meanings to the values in the `pid` argument:

- If `pid` is equal to -1, the status is requested for any child process (in this case, `waitpid` is equivalent to `wait`).

- If `pid` is greater than 0, the status is requested for the process whose process ID is equal to `pid`. The process identified by `pid` must be a child of the calling process.

- If `pid` is 0, the status is requested for any process in the same process group as the calling process.

- If `pid` is less than -1, the status is requested for any process whose process group ID is equal to the absolute value of `pid`. The processes in that process group must be children of the calling process.

The `waitid` function, which is not specified by the POSIX standard, allows the list of processes to be waited for to be specified in much the same way as for the `sigsend` and `sigsendset` functions described in the last chapter. The `idtype` and `id` parameters specify which processes `waitid` should wait for:

- If `idtype` is P_PID, `waitid` waits for the child with process ID `id`.

- If idtype is P_PGID, waitid waits for any child process with process group ID id.

- If idtype is P_ALL, waitid waits for any child process, and id is ignored.

The waitid function is not available in HP-UX 10.*x*.

Both waitpid and waitid use the options parameter to allow the programmer to specify the state changes that are of interest. The value of the options parameter is constructed from the logical *or* of the following values:

WCONTINUED

Returns the status of any specified process that has continued, and whose status has not been reported since it continued (waitid only).

WEXITED

Wait for processes to exit (waitid only).

WNOHANG

Do not cause the calling process to block. If no status is immediately available, -1 is returned with errno set to ECHILD. This allows a process to poll for status information periodically while otherwise performing other tasks.

WNOWAIT

Keep the process whose status is returned in a waitable state. The process may be waited for again with identical results. This option is not available in IRIX 5.*x*.

WSTOPPED

Wait for and return the status of any process that has been stopped due to a signal (waitid only).

WTRAPPED

Wait for traced processes to become trapped or reach a breakpoint (waitid only).

WUNTRACED

Report the status of any specified child processes that are stopped, and whose status has not yet been reported since they stopped (waitpid only).

If we put all three of these steps together, we can construct a function much like system. Example 11-5 shows our function, called shellcmd, and also demonstrates the use of the macros described above.

Example 11-5: shellcmd

```
#include <sys/types.h>
#include <sys/wait.h>
#include <signal.h>
#include <unistd.h>
#include <string.h>
#include <errno.h>
#include <stdio.h>

int     shellcmd(char *);
void    prstat(int);

int
main(void)
{
    int status;
    char command[BUFSIZ];

    /*
     * Forever...
     */
    for (;;) {
        /*
         * Prompt for a command.
         */
        printf("Enter a command: ");

        /*
         * Read a command.  If NULL is returned, the
         * user typed CTRL-D, so exit.
         */
        if (fgets(command, sizeof(command), stdin) == NULL) {
            putchar('\n');
            exit(0);
        }

        /*
         * Strip off the trailing newline character
         * left by fgets.
         */
        command[strlen(command)-1] = '\0';

        /*
         * Execute the command and print the termination
         * status.
         */
        status = shellcmd(command);
        prstat(status);
        putchar('\n');
    }
}

/*
```

Example 11-5: shellcmd (continued)

```c
 * shellcmd - start a child process, and pass command to the shell.
 */
int
shellcmd(char *command)
{
    int status;
    pid_t p, pid;
    extern int errno;
    sigset_t mask, savemask;
    struct sigaction ignore, saveint, savequit;

    /*
     * Set up a sigaction structure to ignore signals.
     */
    sigemptyset(&ignore.sa_mask);
    ignore.sa_handler = SIG_IGN;
    ignore.sa_flags = 0;

    /*
     * Ignore keyboard signals; save old dispositions.
     */
    sigaction(SIGINT, &ignore, &saveint);
    sigaction(SIGQUIT, &ignore, &savequit);

    /*
     * Block SIGCHLD.
     */
    sigemptyset(&mask);
    sigaddset(&mask, SIGCHLD);
    sigprocmask(SIG_BLOCK, &mask, &savemask);

    /*
     * Start a child process.
     */
    if ((pid = fork()) < 0)
        status = -1;

    /*
     * This code executes in the child process.
     */
    if (pid == 0) {
        /*
         * Restore signals to their original dispositions,
         * and restore the signal mask.
         */
        sigaction(SIGINT, &saveint, (struct sigaction *) 0);
        sigaction(SIGQUIT, &savequit, (struct sigaction *) 0);
        sigprocmask(SIG_SETMASK, &savemask, (sigset_t *) 0);

        /*
         * Execute a shell with the command as argument.
         */
```

Example 11–5: shellcmd (continued)

```
        execl("/bin/sh", "sh", "-c", command, 0);
        _exit(127);
    }

    /*
     * Wait for the child process to finish.
     */
    while (waitpid(pid, &status, 0) < 0) {
        /*
         * EINTR (interrupted system call) is okay; otherwise,
         * we got some error that we need to report back.
         */
        if (errno != EINTR) {
            status = -1;
            break;
        }
    }

    /*
     * Restore signals to their original dispositions,
     * and restore the signal mask.
     */
    sigaction(SIGINT, &saveint, (struct sigaction *) 0);
    sigaction(SIGQUIT, &savequit, (struct sigaction *) 0);
    sigprocmask(SIG_SETMASK, &savemask, (sigset_t *) 0);

    /*
     * Return the child process' termination status.
     */
    return(status);
}

/*
 * prstat - decode the termination status.
 */
void
prstat(int status)
{
    if (WIFEXITED(status)) {
        printf("Process terminated normally, exit status = %d.\n",
            WEXITSTATUS(status));
    }
    else if (WIFSIGNALED(status)) {
        printf("Process terminated abnormally, signal = %d (%s)",
            WTERMSIG(status), strsignal(WTERMSIG(status)));

        if (WCOREDUMP(status))
            printf(" -- core file generated.\n");
        else
            printf(".\n");
    }
    else if (WIFSTOPPED(status)) {
```

Example 11–5: shellcmd (continued)

```
        printf("Process stopped, signal = %d (%s).\n",
                WSTOPSIG(status), strsignal(WSTOPSIG(status)));
    }
    else if (WIFCONTINUED(status)) {
        printf("Process continued.\n");
    }
}
```

We then run the program.

```
% shellcmd
Enter a command: date
Wed Nov 30 17:15:24 EST 1994
Process terminated normally, exit status = 0.

Enter a command: date | grep Wed
Wed Nov 30 17:15:42 EST 1994
Process terminated normally, exit status = 0.

Enter a command:  date | grep Thu
Process terminated normally, exit status = 1.

Enter a command:  sleep 5
^CProcess terminated normally, exit status = 130.

Enter a command:  sleep 5
^\Quit - core dumped
Process terminated normally, exit status = 131.

Enter a command: exec sleep 5
^CProcess terminated abnormally, signal = 2 (Interrupt).

Enter a command: exec sleep 5
^\Process terminated abnormally, signal = 3 (Quit)--core file generated.
Enter a command: ^D
```

First, we execute the command *date*, which terminates normally with an exit status of 0. Then, we execute the *date* command and send the output into *grep*, searching for the string "Wed." The *grep* command finds the string, prints the line on which it occurs, and exits with status 0, indicating a match was found. In the third case, we repeat this experiment, but search for the string "Thu." This time, *grep* exits with status 1, meaning no matches were found.

The next two runs demonstrate what happens when we press the interrupt (CTRL-C) and quit (CTRL-\) keys on the keyboard. We would expect the command to terminate abnormally, and we should learn what signal terminated it. But this doesn't happen. Instead, we find out that the command terminated *normally*! The problem here is that our `shellcmd` function is using the Bourne shell to execute our command, rather than executing it directly. The shell is waiting for our command to complete, catching the fact that it terminated abnormally (that's where the "Quit—core dumped" message comes from), and then the *shell* is exiting normally. But the shell indicates in its exit status that the command terminated abnormally, and with what signal it terminated, by adding the signal's number to a base value of 128.

In the last two runs, we accomplish what we wanted to do in the previous two. All UNIX shells have a built-in command called *exec* that tells them to execute the following command *without* starting a child process. This overlays the shell with the new command, and when the new command exits, the shell is just gone. By using the *exec* command here, we can eliminate the shell's checking of our command's termination status, allowing us to obtain it directly.

Now let's look at the program itself, specifically the `shellcmd` function.

The first thing the function does is set the disposition of the two keyboard interrupt signals, `SIGINT` and `SIGQUIT` to be ignored. Recall that the keyboard-generated signals are delivered to all foreground processes—that means that both the child process (which we meant to interrupt) *and* the parent process (which we didn't mean to interrupt) will receive the signal. As an experiment, try commenting out the first two calls to `sigaction` and see what happens when you press CTRL-C or CTRL-\.

The next thing `shellcmd` does is set up a signal mask to block `SIGCHLD`. This is not really necessary in our example here, but it is necessary in the real `system` function. If `system` did not block `SIGCHLD` from delivery, and the calling process was catching `SIGCHLD` for its own purposes, its signal handler would be called when the child process started by `system` terminates. But since the parent process is presumably catching `SIGCHLD` because it is interested in processes it started itself, it might get confused if it received the signal for a process that `system` started instead.

After setting up the signal handling, `shellcmd` creates a child process with `fork`. The first thing the child process does is restore the two keyboard signals to their original dispositions (we *want* them to interrupt the child process), and reset the signal mask to its original value. We reset the signal mask so that if the command we execute needs `SIGCHLD`, it will be available. Then the child process executes the shell, passing the `command` string as an argument. The last thing we do in the child is call `_exit`; if the `exec` succeeds, this will never happen. But if the `exec` fails, the child process still needs to exit, or the parent will block indefinitely waiting for it to terminate. We call `_exit` instead of `exit` so that we don't call any exit handlers that may have been registered with `atexit`.

While the child process is doing all that, the parent is patiently sitting in the call to `waitpid`, waiting until the child process is done. The advantage to using `waitpid` here is that we are guaranteed that we will only receive the termination status of the process we started ourselves. If we used `wait` instead, we might receive the status of some process started by our caller; this would then make that status unavailable to the caller when it tries to get it later. If our call to `waitpid` is interrupted by a signal, we continue to wait. Finally, we restore our signal dispositions to their original values, restore the signal mask, and then return the child process' termination status.

The vfork Function

Most versions of UNIX that implement virtual memory also provide a function called `vfork`. This function creates a child process but, unlike `fork`, does not copy the entire address space of the calling process. Rather, the child process executes using the parent's address space, and thus the parent's memory and thread of control.

The purpose of `vfork` is to provide a more efficient method of creating a child process when the purpose is to execute another program via `exec`. Since the call to `exec` will overwrite the calling process' address space anyway, there is little point in copying everything first. Needless to say, great havoc can result if `vfork` is used to create a process that does not immediately call `exec`.

The need for `vfork` has diminished as more recent versions of UNIX implement copy-on-write in `fork`. That is, the address space of the parent is not copied for the child unless and until the child tries to modify that address space. The use of `vfork` in new programs is discouraged since it is non-standard, but it may crop up from time to time when porting older software.

The `vfork` function is not available in IRIX 5.*x*.

Redirecting Input and Output

One of the most useful features of the UNIX shells, aside from their obvious ability to execute commands, is their ability to redirect input and output. For example, the command

```
ls > listing
```

places the output from the *ls* command into the file *listing* instead of sending it to the screen. Likewise, the command

```
a.out < data
```

tells the *a.out* command to read its input from the file *data* instead of from the keyboard. How does the shell arrange for this to work?

Earlier in the chapter, we said that files remain open across a call to **exec**. Thus, if we can arrange for the standard input (file descriptor 0) and the standard output (file descriptor 1) to refer to the files we want to use for input and output before calling **exec**, the newly-executed program will read from and write to these files.

In Chapter 3, we described the **dup** and **dup2** functions:

```
#include <unitstd.h>

int dup(int fd);

int dup2(int fd, int fd2);
```

As you may recall, **dup** returns a new file descriptor that references the same file as **fd**. The new descriptor has the same access mode (read, write, or read/write) and the same read/write offset as the original. The file descriptor returned will be the lowest numbered one available. **dup2** causes the file descriptor **fd2** to refer to the same file as **fd**. If **fd2** refers to an already-open file, that file is closed first.

NOTE

The **bufsplit** function is broken in some versions of Solaris 2.4. If this example does not work for you, edit the example program and remove the "**#ifdef notdef**" and "**#endif**" to enable the use of a locally-defined version of the function.

Thus, all that is necessary to perform input and output redirection in the shell is to have the shell open the files in question, call **dup** or **dup2** to attach those files to file descriptors 0 and 1, and then execute the command. Example 11-6 shows a rudimentary shell-like program that does just this.

Example 11-6: shell

```
#include <sys/types.h>
#include <sys/wait.h>
#include <libgen.h>
#include <signal.h>
#include <unistd.h>
#include <string.h>
#include <fcntl.h>
#include <errno.h>
```

Example 11–6: shell (continued)

```c
#include <stdio.h>

#define NARGS    64

int execute(char **, char *, char *);

int
main(void)
{
    char **cp;
    int n, status;
    char *args[NARGS];
    char command[BUFSIZ];
    char *infile, *outfile;

    /*
     * Set up bufsplit to parse the command line.
     */
    bufsplit(" \t\n", 0, NULL);

    /*
     * Forever...
     */
    for (;;) {
        /*
         * Prompt for a command.
         */
again:  printf("--> ");

        /*
         * Read a command.  If NULL is returned, the
         * user typed CTRL-D, so exit.
         */
        if (fgets(command, sizeof(command), stdin) == NULL) {
            putchar('\n');
            exit(0);
        }

        /*
         * Split the command into words.
         */
        n = bufsplit(command, NARGS, args);
        args[n] = NULL;

        /*
         * Ignore blank lines.
         */
        if (**args == '\0')
            continue;

        /*
         * Find any input and output redirections.
```

Example 11-6: shell (continued)

```
                 */
            infile = NULL;
            outfile = NULL;

            for (cp = args; *cp != NULL; cp++) {
                if (strcmp(*cp, "<") == 0) {
                    if (*(cp+1) == NULL) {
                        fprintf(stderr, "You must specify ");
                        fprintf(stderr, "an input file.\n");
                        goto again;
                    }

                    *cp++ = NULL;
                    infile = *cp;
                }
                else if (strcmp(*cp, ">") == 0) {
                    if (*(cp+1) == NULL) {
                        fprintf(stderr, "You must specify ");
                        fprintf(stderr, "an output file.\n");
                        goto again;
                    }

                    *cp++ = NULL;
                    outfile = *cp;
                }
            }

            /*
             * Execute the command.
             */
            status = execute(args, infile, outfile);
        }
}

/*
 * execute - execute a command, possibly with input/output redirection
 */
int
execute(char **args, char *infile, char *outfile)
{
    int status;
    pid_t p, pid;
    int infd, outfd;
    extern int errno;
    sigset_t mask, savemask;
    struct sigaction ignore, saveint, savequit;

    infd = -1;
    outfd = -1;

    /*
     * If an input file was given, open it.
     */
```

Example 11–6: shell (continued)

```
       */
      if (infile != NULL) {
          if ((infd = open(infile, O_RDONLY)) < 0) {
              perror(infile);
              return(-1);
          }
      }

      /*
       * If an output file was given, create it.
       */
      if (outfile != NULL) {
          if ((outfd = creat(outfile, 0666)) < 0) {
              perror(outfile);
              close(infd);
              return(-1);
          }
      }

      /*
       * Set up a sigaction structure to ignore signals.
       */
      sigemptyset(&ignore.sa_mask);
      ignore.sa_handler = SIG_IGN;
      ignore.sa_flags = 0;

      /*
       * Ignore keyboard signals; save old dispositions.
       */
      sigaction(SIGINT, &ignore, &saveint);
      sigaction(SIGQUIT, &ignore, &savequit);

      /*
       * Block SIGCHLD.
       */
      sigemptyset(&mask);
      sigaddset(&mask, SIGCHLD);
      sigprocmask(SIG_BLOCK, &mask, &savemask);

      /*
       * Start a child process.
       */
      if ((pid = fork()) < 0)
          status = -1;

      /*
       * This code executes in the child process.
       */
      if (pid == 0) {
          /*
           * Restore signals to their original dispositions,
           * and restore the signal mask.
```

Example 11-6: shell (continued)

```
         */
        sigaction(SIGINT, &saveint, (struct sigaction *) 0);
        sigaction(SIGQUIT, &savequit, (struct sigaction *) 0);
        sigprocmask(SIG_SETMASK, &savemask, (sigset_t *) 0);

        /*
         * Perform output redirection.
         */
        if (infd > 0)
            dup2(infd, 0);

        if (outfd > 0)
            dup2(outfd, 1);

        /*
         * Execute the command.
         */
        execvp(*args, args);
        perror("exec");
        _exit(127);
    }

    /*
     * Wait for the child process to finish.
     */
    while (waitpid(pid, &status, 0) < 0) {
        /*
         * EINTR (interrupted system call) is okay; otherwise,
         * we got some error that we need to report back.
         */
        if (errno != EINTR) {
            status = -1;
            break;
        }
    }

    /*
     * Restore signals to their original dispositions,
     * and restore the signal mask.
     */
    sigaction(SIGINT, &saveint, (struct sigaction *) 0);
    sigaction(SIGQUIT, &savequit, (struct sigaction *) 0);
    sigprocmask(SIG_SETMASK, &savemask, (sigset_t *) 0);

    /*
     * Close file descriptors.
     */
    close(outfd);
    close(infd);

    /*
     * Return the child process' termination status.
```

Example 11-6: shell (continued)

```
    */
    return(status);
}

/*
 * The bufsplit() function on Solaris 2.4 is broken.  Remove the
 * "#ifdef notdef" and "#endif" lines to enable this version.
 */
#ifdef notdef
size_t
bufsplit(char *buf, size_t n, char **a)
{
    int i, nsplit;
    static char *splitch = "\t\n";

    if (buf != NULL && n == 0) {
        splitch = buf;
        return(1);
    }

    nsplit = 0;
    while (nsplit < n) {
        a[nsplit++] = buf;

        if ((buf = strpbrk(buf, splitch)) == NULL)
            break;

        *(buf++) = '\0';

        if (*buf == '\0')
            break;
    }

    buf = strrchr(a[nsplit-1], '\0');

    for (i=nsplit; i < n; i++)
        a[i] = buf;

    return(nsplit);
}
#endif


    % shell
    --> ls > listing
    --> cat listing
    Makefile
    fork.c
    forkexec.c
    forkexecwait.c
    listing
    shell.c
```

```
shellcmd.c
system.c
-->    sort -r < listing > listing2
-->    cat listing2
system.c
shellcmd.c
shell.c
listing
forkexecwait.c
forkexec.c
fork.c
Makefile
-->    ^D
```

Technically, the files could be opened in the child process just as well as in the parent; this would save the parent from having to close them later. However, the method used in the example is preferable, because it does not waste a call to fork if one of the files is inaccessible.

Job Control

As discussed at the beginning of the chapter, sessions and process groups exist for the purposes of performing job control. A process group is a group of related processes, such as those in a pipeline. A session is a group of related process groups, such as all of the jobs currently being run by a user on a specific terminal. Usually, sessions are created by the system login process and process groups are managed by a job control shell; the average program doesn't have to worry about them. However, sometimes it is desirable to be able to manipulate them directly.

A new session is created with the setsid function:

```
#include <sys/types.h>
#include <unistd.h>

pid_t setsid(void);
```

If the process is not already a process group leader, three things happen when setsid is called:

1. The process becomes the session leader of a new session. The session ID of this new session will be the same as the process' process ID.

2. The process becomes the process group leader of a new process group. The process group ID of this new process group will be the same as the process' process ID (and thus the session ID).

3. If the calling process was associated with a controlling terminal, that association is broken. If the process later opens a terminal device, the first device opened will become the process' controlling terminal.

A process that is already a process group leader may not call `setsid`. To make sure, call `fork` and have the parent process terminate and the child process continue. If a new session is created, `setsid` returns the session ID of the session. Otherwise, -1 is returned and `errno` is set to the error condition.

A process may create a new process group, or join an existing one, by calling `setpgid`:

```
#include <sys/types.h>
#include <unistd.h>

int setpgid(pid_t pid, pid_t pgid);
```

This function sets the process group ID of the process with process ID `pid` to `pgid`. If `pgid` is equal to `pid`, the process becomes a process group leader. A process may only change the process group of itself and its children. If `setpgid` succeeds, it returns 0. Otherwise, it returns -1 and stores the reason for failure in `errno`.

Timing Process Execution

If you want to be able to determine how much processor time a process has consumed, use the `times` function. You may need this value for accounting purposes, or to attempt to optimize a program. In UNIX, processor time is divided into two parts, *user time* and *system time*. User time is the amount of time the processor spends executing in user mode; that is, time spent executing the parts of the program written by the user such as loops and local functions. System time is the amount of time the processor spends executing operating system code on the user's behalf; that is, time spent in system calls such as `read` and `write`.

The `times` function is defined as:

```
#include <sys/times.h>
#include <limits.h>

clock_t times(struct tms *buffer);
```

The `struct tms` structure is defined as follows:

```
struct tms {
    clock_t     tms_utime;
    clock_t     tms_stime;
    clock_t     tms_cutime;
    clock_t     tms_cstime;
}
```

The information reported by `times` applies to the calling process and all of the terminated child processes for which it has called a `wait` function. (It is not possible to obtain information about processes that are still running.)

The `tms_utime` and `tms_stime` elements of the structure report the amount of user and system time, respectively, used by the calling process. The `tms_cutime` element represents the sum of the `tms_utime` and `tms_cutime` of the calling process' children (thus, a process inherits the times of its children). The `tms_cstime` element represents the sum of the `tms_stime` and `tms_cstime` of the calling process' children.

All times are reported in units called *clock ticks*. The value of a clock tick is defined by the `CLK_TCK` constant in the include file *limits.h*. To obtain a value in seconds, the element of interest in the structure should be divided by `CLK_TCK`.

On success, `times` returns the elapsed real time in clock ticks from some arbitrary point in the past (usually system boot time). This point does not change between calls to `times`, so by making two calls (say, before a call to `fork` and after a call to `wait`), it is possible to determine how long a process took to execute.

Porting Notes

In BSD-based versions of UNIX, the `getpgrp` function accepts a process ID as an argument, and returns the process group of that process. In SVR4, this can be accomplished by using the `getpgid` function:

```
#include <sys/types.h>
#include <unistd.h>

pid_t getpgid(pid_t pid);
```

BSD UNIX provides functions called `getpriority` and `setpriority` to get and set the priorities (nice values) of processes. There is no direct replacement for these functions in SVR4, although the `priocntl` function supplies much of the same functionality.

The `wait3` function offered by BSD UNIX is not present in SVR4 (except in the compatibility library). Its functionality can mostly be provided by `waitpid`, except that `waitpid` will not return resource usage statistics as `wait3` does.

The BSD `killpg` function, which sends a signal to a process group, can be replaced with a call to the `kill` function, specifying the process group ID as a negative number.

Calls to the BSD `setpgrp` function should be replaced with calls to `setsid`. Note that other changes will probably be necessary, since all versions of Berkley UNIX prior to 4.4BSD do not offer POSIX sessions.

In BSD UNIX, a process disassociated itself from the controlling terminal with the following code sequence:

```
        :
    pid = fork();

    if (pid == 0) {
        if ((fd = open("/dev/tty", 0)) >= 0) {
            ioctl(fd, TIOCNOTTY, 0);
            close(fd);
        }
            :
    }
        :
```

In the POSIX environment, this should be replaced with a call to `setsid`:

```
        :
    pid = fork();

    if (pid == 0) {
        setsid();
            :
    }
        :
```

The BSD implementation of `times` returns times in units of 1/`HZ` seconds, where `HZ` is defined in the include file *sys/param.h*.

Chapter Summary

In this chapter, we examined how to execute programs, which can be viewed as the primary purpose of the UNIX operating system. The most common tasks performed on a UNIX system require the ability to execute programs, although much of this is hidden from the user by the shell. Many of these same tasks require the ability to execute multiple programs and tie them together with pipelines or inter-process communications facilities; this is discussed in detail in Chapter 13, *Inter-process Communication*.

12

Terminals

Terminal I/O is probably the messiest topic in UNIX systems programming; it is certainly the biggest stumbling block to portability. The problem is that serial lines are used for so many different things, such as connecting terminals to the system, communicating with printers, hooking up modems, and talking to specialized devices. Each of these uses has its own needs, and while they all overlap to some extent, the terminal interface has had to be extended each time a new use arose. The end result is that things have gotten very complex—the interface is pretty straightforward, but the number of options has grown so large that it's difficult to know which ones to choose. This is true not just for UNIX, but for any operating system that allows the programmer to control serial port processing.

The other problem with terminal I/O control is that the UNIX community historically supported two different, and incompatible, interfaces. The original interface was developed for Version 7, and was based on the `stty` and `ioctl` functions. Berkeley later extended this interface to cover the additional functionality added by their versions of the operating system, and this interface is present in all versions of BSD UNIX save the last (which has adopted the POSIX interface). The other interface was first developed in System III, and has continued forward through all releases of System V, including SVR4 (although its presence there is primarily for backward compatibility; the POSIX interface is preferred).

When the System III interface first became public, many programmers (including the author) viewed it as a gratuitous change made solely for the purpose of being different. However, in reality, the change was made with the best of intentions. The original Version 7 interface, especially as extended by Berkeley, was showing its age. It was made up of several different data structures, each used for different purposes, representing, in a way, its rather piecemeal development process. The designers of System III recognized this and, more importantly, recognized that as other extensions became necessary in the future, they would probably have to be "grafted onto" the interface, rather than integrated with it. So, they designed a new interface that unified all of the parts from the old interface, as well as some new capabilities, into a single, coherent whole. Furthermore, they designed the interface in such a way that new functionality could be added within the existing framework, rather than by extending the interface in incompatible ways. Although the first versions of this new interface suffered from a few deficiencies, these have since been fixed, and the interface has indeed met the goals set for it by the designers, while the older interface has been all but discarded. Indeed, when the POSIX committee specified a terminal I/O control interface, they chose one based on (in fact, nearly identical to) the System III/System V interface.

In this chapter, we will examine the issue of terminal I/O control in detail. We begin by discussing the topic at a high level, in order to introduce many of the concepts necessary to understand the remainder of the chapter. We follow this with a discussion of the POSIX terminal control interface; this interface is perhaps the easiest to understand. After presenting the POSIX interface, we present the System V interface, on which it is based. And then, because there are so many programs that must be ported from the BSD environment to SVR4, we present the Berkeley interface in detail.

Overview of Terminal I/O

Terminal input and output is processed in one of two modes, *canonical mode* or *non-canonical mode.*

In canonical mode, terminal input is processed in units of lines. A line is delimited by a newline (ASCII LF), an end-of-file character (ASCII EOT), or an end-of-line character (user defined). This means that a program attempting to read from the terminal will be suspended until an entire line has been typed. Furthermore, no matter how many characters are requested in the read call, at most one line will be returned. It is, of course, not necessary to read an entire line all at once; one or a few characters may be read at a time, and the operating system will satisfy the reads from the buffered input line. But it is important to understand that the first read request, regardless of its size, will not be satisfied until an entire line has been typed.

When in canonical mode, certain keyboard characters enable special processing. The *erase* character allows one character at a time to be deleted from the input, to correct typing mistakes. The *kill* character allows the entire input line typed to this point to be discarded. Other keyboard characters provide advanced editing features; these are discussed below. Because input is processed a line at a time, the erase and kill processing is done before a program reading from the terminal sees the input; therefore, the average program does not have to deal with these issues.

Canonical mode input processing also allows certain keyboard sequences to generate signals that are sent to the processes in the terminal's process group. These keyboard sequences can cause a program to terminate, with or without a core dump, and, on systems that support job control, can cause a program to stop execution.

Finally, canonical mode enables certain output processing features such as the generation of delays after the output of certain characters such as newlines, tabs, and form feeds, the expansion of tabs to spaces, and the conversion of lowercase letters to uppercase (for very old, uppercase-only terminals).

In non-canonical mode, input characters are not assembled into lines, and erase and kill processing does not occur. Signal generation and output processing are still performed, although they may be disabled.

When in non-canonical mode, input characters are returned to a reading process based on either a minimum input threshold (reads return after some minimum number of characters has been typed), a maximum time (reads return after a timer expires), or some combination of these.

Version 7 and BSD UNIX use the terms *cooked* instead of canonical and *cbreak* instead of non-canonical. These terms are still in general use today, even when describing systems on which they do not apply. They are presented below.

Cooked Mode

> *Cooked mode* corresponds to canonical mode, above. Input is processed a line at a time, and input editing and signal generation is enabled. Output processing is also performed.

Cbreak Mode

> *Cbreak mode* is a sort of "half-cooked" mode in which input editing is disabled, and reads are satisfied one character at a time (input is not buffered). When in `cbreak` mode, signal generation and output processing are still performed.

Raw Mode

In *raw mode*, all input and output processing is disabled, as is all signal generation. Read requests are satisfied one character at a time. `raw` mode corresponds to non-canonical mode, above, with the addition of disabling keyboard signals and output processing.

Special Characters

Several characters have special meaning in canonical mode. Version 7 provided only a basic set of these characters; most of those in the list below were added by Berkeley, and then later adopted by POSIX and SVR4. Almost all of these characters can be changed under program control; the default values are shown in parentheses.

CR (Carriage Return)

This character cannot be changed. This character is recognized in canonical input mode. Usually, the CR character is translated to NL (newline) and has the same effect as an NL character. This character is returned to the reading process (perhaps after being translated to NL).

DISCARD (CTRL-O)

This character causes all subsequent output to be discarded, until another DISCARD character is entered or the discard condition is cleared. This character is discarded by the terminal driver when processed; it is not returned to the reading process. This character is not specified in the POSIX standard, nor is it available in HP-UX 10.*x*.

DSUSP (CTRL-Y)

This is the delayed-suspend character; it is recognized in canonical and basic non-canonical modes if job control is in effect. Like the SUSP character, this character sends the SIGTSTP signal to all processes in the foreground process group. However, the signal is not delivered when the character is typed, but when a process reads from the controlling terminal. This character is discarded by the terminal driver when processed; it is not returned to the reading process. This character is not specified in the POSIX standard.

EOF (CTRL-D)

This character is recognized on input in canonical mode. When this character is entered, all bytes remaining to be read are immediately passed to the reading process. If there are no bytes remaining, a count of zero is returned to the read. Entering an EOF character at the beginning of a line is the usual way to indicate an end-of-file to a program. This character is discarded by the terminal driver when processed; it is not returned to the reading process.

Some operating systems, such as MS-DOS, use a character to mark the end of a file (MS-DOS uses CTRL-Z). This character, when encountered during reading, indicates the end of the file. UNIX, on the other hand, signifies the end-of-file condition by causing `read` to return zero. The presence of an EOF character in the input stream *does not* indicate the end of a file. Its only purpose is to tell the terminal driver to generate the end-of-file condition for the reading process.

EOL (No default)

In POSIX, this character functions as an additional end-of-line delimiter when in canonical mode. It is not normally used. This character is returned to the reading process.

EOL2 (No default)

In SVR4, this character functions as still another end-of-line delimiter when in canonical mode. It is not normally used. This character is returned to the reading process.

ERASE (DEL or CTRL-H)

This character is recognized in canonical mode, and causes the previous character in the line to be erased. It is not possible to erase beyond the beginning of the line. This character is discarded by the terminal driver; it is not returned to the reading process.

INTR (CTRL-C or DEL)

This character is recognized in canonical and basic non-canonical mode. When received, it causes a SIGINT signal to be delivered to all processes in the foreground process group. This character is discarded by the terminal driver; it is not returned to the reading process.

KILL (CTRL-U)

This character is recognized in canonical mode, and erases the entire input line. It is discarded by the terminal driver; it is not returned to the reading process.

LNEXT (CTRL-V)

This character is recognized in canonical mode and causes the special meaning of the next character to be typed to be ignored ("LNEXT" stands for "literal next"). This allows the user to type any of the characters in this section to a program. This character is discarded when processed by the terminal driver, but the next character typed is passed to the reading process. This character is not specified by the POSIX standard.

NL (Newline)

This character is recognized in canonical mode and serves as the end-of-line delimiter. This character cannot be changed. This character is returned to the reading process.

QUIT (CTRL-\)

This character is recognized in canonical and basic non-canonical mode. It causes the SIGQUIT signal to be delivered to all processes in the foreground process group. This character is discarded when processed by the terminal driver; it is not returned to the reading process.

REPRINT (CTRL-R)

This character is recognized in canonical mode. It causes all unread input (the line as typed so far) to be reprinted. This character is discarded when processed; it is not returned to the reading process. This character is not specified by the POSIX standard, nor is it available in HP-UX 10.*x*.

START (CTRL-Q)

This character is recognized in canonical and basic non-canonical mode if flow control is enabled. When received, it causes output that has been suspended with a STOP character to start again. This character is discarded when processed; it is not returned to the reading process.

STOP (CTRL-S)

This character is recognized in canonical and basic non-canonical mode if flow control is enabled. When received, it causes output to be suspended (but not discarded) until a START character is received. This character is not returned to the reading process.

SUSP (CTRL-Z)

This character is recognized in canonical and basic non-canonical mode when job control is enabled. It causes a SIGTSTP signal to be delivered to all processes in the foreground process group. This character is discarded by the terminal driver; it is not returned to the reading process.

WERASE (CTRL-W)

This character is recognized in canonical mode. It causes the previous word to be erased. A "word" is delimited by whitespace. This character is not returned to the reading process.

BREAK

BREAK is not really a character but, rather, a condition that can be generated by the terminal hardware. Usually, BREAK is interpreted as a synonym for the INTR character, although this is not required.

Terminal Characteristics

Table 12-1 summarizes all the terminal characteristics that can be controlled on POSIX, System V, and BSD systems. Several vendors have added additional characteristics to this list; those additions are not discussed in this book. For each characteristic, the table gives a brief description and indicates the flag and option that controls this characteristic in each of the three versions. The flags and options are described in detail in the remaining sections of the chapter.

Table 12–1: Terminal Characteristics

Characteristic	POSIX	System V	BSD
Generate SIGINT on BREAK	BRKINT	BRKINT	(cooked, cbreak)
Ignore BREAK condition	IGNBRK	IGNBRK	(raw)
Map NL to CR on input	INLCR	INLCR	—
Map CR to NL on input	ICRNL	ICRNL	CRMOD
Ignore CR	IGNCR	IGNCR	—
Enable input parity checking	INPCK	INPCK	EVENP, ODDP
Ignore characters with parity errors	IGNPAR	IGNPAR	(cooked, cbreak)
Mark characters with parity errors	PARMRK	PARMRK	—
Strip eighth bit off input characters	ISTRIP	ISTRIP	LPASS8
Enable start/stop input flow control	IXOFF	IXOFF	TANDEM
Enable start/stop output flow control	IXON	IXON	(cooked, cbreak)
Enable any character to restart output	—	IXANY	LDECCTQ
Map uppercase to lowercase on input	—	IUCLC	LCASE
Ring terminal bell on input queue full	—	IMAXBEL	NTTYDISC
Perform output processing	OPOST	OPOST	LLITOUT
Backspace delay mask	—	BSDLY	BSDELAY
Carriage return delay mask	—	CRDLY	CRDELAY
Form feed delay mask	—	FFDLY	VTDELAY
Horizontal tab delay mask	—	TABDLY	TBDELAY
Newline delay mask	—	NLDLY	NLDELAY
Vertical tab delay mask	—	VTDLY	VTDELAY
Use fill character for delay	—	OFILL	—
Fill character is DEL, else NUL	—	OFDEL	—
Map CR to NL on output	—	OCRNL	—

Table 12–1: Terminal Characteristics (continued)

Characteristic	POSIX	System V	BSD
Map NL to CR-NL on output	—	ONLCR	CRMOD
NL performs CR function	—	ONLRET	—
No CR output at column zero	—	ONOCR	—
Map lowercase to uppercase on output	—	OLCUC	LCASE
Expand tabs to spaces	—	XTABS	XTABS
Baud rate	B0...B38400	B0...B38400	B0...B9600
Character size mask	CSIZE	CSIZE	—
Send two stop bits, else one	CSTOPB	CSTOPB	—
Enable parity	PARENB	PARENB	—
Odd parity, else even	PARODD	PARODD	ODDP, EVENP
Extended parity (mark and space)	—	PAREXT	—
Ignore modem status lines	CLOCAL	CLOCAL	—
No hangup when carrier drops	—	—	LNOHANG
Hangup on last close	HUPCL	HUPCL	TIOCHPCL
Flow control via carrier drops	—	—	LMDMBUF
Enable receiver	CREAD	CREAD	—
Convert ~ to ` on output (Hazeltine)	—	—	LTILDE
Canonical input	ICANON	ICANON	(cooked)
Enable extended input processing	IEXTEN	IEXTEN	NTTYDISC
Enable tty-generated signals	ISIG	ISIG	(cooked, cbreak)
Enable character echo	ECHO	ECHO	ECHO
Backspace on erase	—	—	LCRTBS
Visually erase with backspace-space-backspace	ECHOE	ECHOE	LCRTERA
Echo newline after kill	ECHOK	ECHOK	default
Visually kill with backspace-space-backspace	ECHOKE	—	LCRTKIL
Visual erase/kill for hardcopy terminals	—	ECHOPRT	LPRTERA
Echo control characters as ^X	—	ECHOCTL	LCTLECH
Echo NL even if ECHO is off	ECHONL	ECHONL	—
Output is being flushed	—	FLUSHO	LFLUSHO
Disable flush after interrupt/quit	NOFLSH	NOFLSH	—
Retype pending input on next character	—	PENDIN	LPENDIN

Table 12-1: Terminal Characteristics (continued)

Characteristic	POSIX	System V	BSD
Send SIGTTOU on output from background	TOSTOP	—	LTOSTOP
Canonical uppercase/lowercase presentation	—	XCASE	LCASE

Terminal-Related Functions

Functions and methods for examining and changing terminal attributes are often used in conjunction with the three procedures ctermid, ttyname, and isatty.

The ctermid function is defined by the POSIX standard to return the name of the calling process' controlling terminal:

```
#include <stdio.h>

char *ctermid(char *s);
```

The single parameter s should point to a character array of at least L_ctermid bytes; this constant is defined in the include file. The name of the terminal will be stored in this array, and the address of the array returned. If s is null, ctermid stores the terminal name in an internal static array that is overwritten on each call, and returns a pointer to that array. If the process has no controlling terminal, ctermid returns a null pointer.

In the previous chapter, we said that a program can always refer to the file */dev/tty* when it wants to reference the controlling terminal; this makes ctermid seem somewhat superfluous. However, this is only true for UNIX systems. Other POSIX-compliant systems, such as Digital's VMS, may use a different name. The ctermid function allows the name to be determined in a portable manner.

Use the ttyname function to obtain the name of the terminal attached to a specific file descriptor:

```
#include <stdlib.h>

char *ttyname(int fd);
```

The fd parameter should be an open file descriptor referencing a terminal device. A pointer to a static array containing the name of the terminal device associated with that file descriptor is returned. The null pointer is returned if the file descriptor does not refer to a terminal device. Note that ttyname will always return the real name of the terminal referenced by fd; it will never return */dev/tty*.

The `isatty` function determines if a file descriptor does refer to a terminal device:

```
#include <stdlib.h>

int isatty(int fd);
```

The `fd` parameter should be a file descriptor referencing an open file. If the file is a terminal device, `isatty` returns 1; it returns 0 otherwise.

POSIX Terminal Control

On POSIX-based systems, all of the terminal input and output modes are controlled via a `struct termios` structure and the functions described in this section. The `struct termios` structure is defined in the include file *termios.h*:

```
struct termios {
    tcflag_t    c_iflag;
    tcflag_t    c_oflag;
    tcflag_t    c_cflag;
    tcflag_t    c_lflag;
    cc_t        c_cc[CCS];
};
```

The `c_iflag` element of the structure contains flags controlling the input of characters by the terminal driver, the `c_oflag` element contains flags controlling the output of characters, the `c_cflag` element contains flags controlling the hardware interface, and the `c_lflag` element contains flags controlling the interface between the terminal driver and the user. The `c_cc` array contains the values of the various special characters described earlier.

The `c_cc` array is indexed by constants whose names are identical to the special characters' names with a 'V' prepended. For example, to set the line-kill character to CTRL-X, we might use:

```
#include <termios.h>
    ⋮
struct termios modes;

modes.c_cc[VKILL] = '\030';
```

where the octal value 030 is CTRL-X. To disable a special character, set it to a special value. The special value can be obtained by calling `pathconf` or `fpathconf` (see Chapter 9, *System Configuration and Resource Limits*) with the `_PC_VDISABLE` argument. For example, to disable the interrupt character, we might use:

```
#include <termios.h>
#include <unistd.h>
    ⋮
struct termios modes;
long vdisable;

vdisable = fpathconf(0, _PC_VDISABLE);
modes.c_cc[VINTR] = vdisable;
```

Each of the flag elements of the structure is constructed from the logical *or* of the attributes described in Table 12-1. To turn on a particular attribute, the flag value is *or*ed into the flag element. For example, to turn the ECHO attribute on, we might use this:

```
#include <termios.h>
    ⋮
struct termios modes;

modes.c_lflag |= ECHO;
```

To turn a feature off, the complement of the attribute is *and*ed into the flag element. For example, to turn the ECHO attribute off, we would use this:

```
#include <termios.h>
    ⋮
struct termios modes;

modes.c_lflag &= ~ECHO;
```

Table 12-1 lists all the available attributes, and provides a very brief description of what they do. Most of these attributes, however, are not used very often. Some of the more commonly used attributes are described in more detail below:

ICRNL (c_iflag)
> When set, this attribute tells the terminal driver to map the carriage return character to a newline character on input. Recall that UNIX uses the newline character as a line terminator; this attribute allows the user to use the carriage return key on the keyboard to signify the end of a line.

ISTRIP (c_iflag)
> When set, this attribute tells the terminal driver to strip the eighth bit off of all input characters (by making it zero). Since ASCII is a 7-bit code, this has the general effect of forcing input into the ASCII character set.

OPOST (c_oflag)
> When set, this attribute enables the output post-processing features of the terminal driver. This includes inserting delays after certain characters such as newline and tab for slow devices, mapping newline to carriage return-newline, and so forth.

ONLCR (`c_oflag`)

When set, this attribute tells the terminal driver to output a carriage return and a newline each time a newline character occurs in the output. Most terminal devices (and printers) will move "down" when a newline is received, but they will not move back to the leftmost column unless a carriage return is also received.

B0...B38400 (`c_cflag`)

The baud rate is set by turning on one of these attributes. For example, B9600 represents 9600 baud. The special rate B0 has the effect of turning off the Data Terminal Ready signal, effectively hanging up the phone line.

CREAD (`c_cflag`)

This attribute enables the receiver. If it is not set, characters cannot be received from the device.

ICANON (`c_lflag`)

When set, this attribute enables canonical input mode. This mode is described in detail below.

IEXTEN (`c_lflag`)

This attribute enables the processing of certain implementation-defined features. In SVR4, it enables the processing of the WERASE, REPRINT, DISCARD, and LNEXT special characters, and enables the processing of the TOSTOP, ECHOCTL, ECHOPRT, ECHOKE, FLUSHO, and PENDIN attributes.

ISIG (`c_lflag`)

When set, this attribute enables the signal-generating properties of some of the the special characters (DSUSP, INTR, QUIT, and SUSP).

ECHO (`c_lflag`)

When set, characters typed by the user are echoed (printed) back to the terminal. This attribute is normally turned off when prompting for passwords (and for other reasons).

ECHOE (`c_lflag`)

When set, characters are erased on receipt of the ERASE character by printing a backspace, a space, and another backspace. If not set, the user has to mentally keep track of how many characters were erased.

ECHOK (`c_lflag`)

When set, the terminal driver will echo a newline character when the KILL character is received; this makes things a little easier to read.

ECHOKE (c_cflag)

> When set, the line is erased on receipt of a KILL character by printing a sequence of backspace-space-backspace characters.

TOSTOP (c_cflag)

> When set, a process in the background that tries to perform output to the terminal will be stopped with a SIGTTOU signal until it is brought into the foreground. If not set, background processes can write to the terminal unimpeded; this usually has the effect of "messing up" whatever the user is doing at the moment.

Examining and Changing Terminal Attributes

Terminal attributes can be examined and changed with the tcgetattr and tcsetattr functions:

```
#include <termios.h>

int tcgetattr(int fd, struct termios *modes);

int tcsetattr(int fd, int action, struct termios *modes);
```

The tcgetattr function obtains the attributes for the terminal device referenced by the open file descriptor fd, and stores them in the area pointed to by modes. The tcsetattr function sets the attributes of the terminal device referenced by the open file descriptor fd to the attributes contained in the struct termios structure pointed to by modes. The value of action must be one of the following:

TCSANOW

> The change occurs immediately.

TCSADRAIN

> The change occurs after all pending output to the device has been transmitted. Use this function when changing parameters that affect output.

TCSAFLUSH

> The change occurs after all pending output to the device has been transmitted. All input that has been received but not read by a program is discarded before the change is made.

Both tcgetattr and tcsetattr return 0 on success; if fd does not refer to a terminal device, or another error occurs, they return -1 and set errno to indicate the error.

Note that because `tcsetattr` sets all terminal attributes, you must pass a completely filled-in `struct termios` structure. Conventionally, this is done by first calling `tcgetattr` to get the current attributes, making changes to the structure it returns, and then passing the result to `tcsetattr`.

Baud Rates

The term "baud rate" is outdated and should really be referred to now as "bits per second." However, most UNIX documentation and functions still refer to baud rate. The baud rate of a device is stored in the `struct termios` structure, but the POSIX standard does not specify where. This means that it's implementation-dependent, and there are functions provided to examine and change the baud rate in the structure:

```
#include <termios.h>

speed_t cfgetispeed(const struct termios *modes);

speed_t cfgetospeed(const struct termios *modes);

int cfsetispeed(struct termios *modes, speed_t speed);

int cfsetospeed(struct termios *modes, speed_t speed);
```

The `cfgetispeed` and `cfgetospeed` functions extract the input and output baud rates for the device from the `struct termios` structure pointed to by `modes`. Note that `tcgetattr` must be called first, to place meaningful information into the structure. These functions return one of the constants `B0...B38400`.

The `cfsetispeed` and `cfsetospeed` functions set the input and output baud rates (which may be different if the device supports it) in the `struct termios` structure pointed to by `modes` to the value passed in the `speed` parameter. This value should be one of the constants `B0...B38400`. Notice that these functions only make the settings in the structure; the change does not take effect on the device until `tcsetattr` is called.

Job Control Functions

Three functions let you manipulate session IDs and process group IDs of the terminal:

```
#include <sys/types.h>
#include <termios.h>

pid_t tcgetpgrp(int fd);
```

```
    int tcsetpgrp(int fd, pid_t pgid);

    pid_t tcgetsid(int fd);
```

The `tcgetpgrp` function returns the process group ID of the terminal referenced by the open file descriptor `fd`. The `tcgetsid` function returns the session ID of the terminal referenced by `fd`.

The `tcsetpgrp` function sets the process group ID of the terminal referenced by the open file descriptor `fd` to `pgid`. For this to succeed, the terminal must be the controlling terminal of the calling process, the controlling terminal must be associated with the session of the calling process, and `pgid` must be the process group ID of a process in the same session as the calling process.

On success, `tcsetpgrp` returns 0. On failure, all three functions return -1 and set `errno` to indicate the error.

Other Functions

The POSIX standard specifies four additional functions for manipulating terminal devices:

```
    #include <termios.h>

    int tcsendbreak(int fd, int duration);

    int tcdrain(int fd);

    int tcflush(int fd, int queue);

    int tcflow(int fd, int action);
```

The `tcsendbreak` function transmits a continuous stream of zero-valued bits (called a break condition) for the specified `duration`. The POSIX standard specifies that if `duration` is 0, the transmission lasts for between 0.25 and 0.50 seconds. But, it also specifies that if `duration` is non-zero, the result is implementation dependent. In SVR4, a non-zero value for `duration` means that no bits are transmitted at all—instead, the function behaves like `tcdrain`. In some other systems, a non-zero value may mean to transmit for duration×N, where N is between 0.25 and 0.50 seconds. Still other systems may provide other interpretations. Non-zero values for `duration` should probably be avoided for portability reasons.

The `tcdrain` function waits until all output written to the device referred to by `fd` has been transmitted, and then returns.

The `tcflush` function discards data written to the device referenced by `fd` but not transmitted, or data received but not read, depending on the value of `queue`:

TCIFLUSH

   Flush data received but not read.

TCOFLUSH

   Flush data written but not transmitted.

TCIOFLUSH

   Flush both data received but not read and data written but not transmitted.

The `tcflow` function suspends the transmission or reception of data on the device referred to by `fd`, depending on the value of `action`:

TCOOFF

   Suspend output.

TCOON

   Resume output.

TCIOFF

   Cause the system to transmit a STOP character to inform the device to stop transmitting data to the system.

TCION

   Cause the system to transmit a START character to inform the device to start transmitting data to the system.

Canonical Mode

Canonical mode is the usual mode in which terminals operate. All of our examples up to this point have used the terminal in canonical mode. In this mode, a program issues a read request, and the read returns when a line has been entered. It is not necessary for the program to read an entire line; if a partial line is read, the next read will start where the previous one left off.

For the most part, programs that interact with the user will keep the terminal in canonical mode—it's easier to deal with, since the operating system handles all the messy details of buffering the input, handling character erases and line kills, keeping track of typeahead (when the user types faster than the program is reading), and so forth.

There are times when, operating in canonical mode, a program might want to change some of a terminal's attributes. The most common situation in which this occurs is when reading a password. Passwords, because they are meant to be secret, should not be printed on the screen as they are typed. In order to accomplish this, the program reading the password should disable the character echo attribute on the terminal. Example 12-1 shows a program that does this.

Example 12-1: readpass

```c
#include <termios.h>
#include <signal.h>
#include <stdio.h>

int
main(void)
{
    char line[BUFSIZ];
    sigset_t sig, savesig;
    struct termios modes, savemodes;

    /*
     * Block keyboard signals.
     */
    sigemptyset(&sig);
    sigaddset(&sig, SIGINT);
    sigaddset(&sig, SIGQUIT);
    sigaddset(&sig, SIGTSTP);
    sigprocmask(SIG_BLOCK, &sig, &savesig);

    /*
     * Get current terminal attributes.
     */
    if (tcgetattr(0, &modes) < 0) {
        perror("tcgetattr");
        exit(1);
    }

    /*
     * Save a copy of them to restore later, and then
     * change the attributes to remove echo.
     */
    savemodes = modes;
    modes.c_lflag &= ~(ECHO | ECHOE | ECHOK | ECHOKE);

    /*
     * Make our changes take effect.
     */
    if (tcsetattr(0, TCSAFLUSH, &modes) < 0) {
        perror("tcsetattr");
        exit(1);
    }

    /*
     * Prompt for and read a line.
     */
    printf("Enter a line (will not echo): ");
    fgets(line, sizeof(line), stdin);
```

Example 12-1: readpass (continued)

```
        line[strlen(line)-1] = '\0';
        putchar('\n');

        /*
         * Restore original terminal attributes.
         */
        if (tcsetattr(0, TCSAFLUSH, &savemodes) < 0) {
            perror("tcsetattr");
            exit(1);
        }

        /*
         * Restore original signal mask.
         */
        sigprocmask(SIG_SETMASK, &savesig, (sigset_t *) 0);

        /*
         * Print out what the user typed.
         */
        printf("You entered \"%s\"\n", line);
        exit(0);
    }
```

```
    % readpass
    Enter a line (will not echo):
    You entered "test"
```

The program begins by setting up a signal mask to block the receipt of signals that can be generated from the keyboard. The reason for doing this is that one of these signals can cause the program to terminate or stop, leaving the terminal in an undesirable state (character echo turned off). The `tcgetattr` function is then used to obtain the current terminal attributes. These are saved, and then modified to remove the character echo attribute. We also remove all the "visual" erase attributes. The new attributes are set with `tcsetattr`, and then the user is prompted to enter a line of text. Once the line is read, the original terminal attributes and the original signal mask are restored, and the line is printed. Note that a newline character is output right after reading the input; because echo is turned off, the newline entered by the user will not be printed.

You can use this program to verify that even with echo turned off, everything else in canonical mode still works. Try entering a line of text and using your character erase and line kill characters, and verify that the output is what you'd expect.

Non-Canonical Mode

Some programs cannot use canonical mode. For example, consider the *vi* editor (or *emacs*, if you prefer). The editor's commands are single characters that must be acted upon immediately, without waiting for the user to press return. Thus, we need a way to obtain input from the user in units of characters, rather than lines. Furthermore, some of the commands used by the editor are special to the terminal driver and are not normally passed to the reading program (e.g., CTRL-D, the default EOF character, tells *vi* to scroll down half a screen, and CTRL-R, the REPRINT character, tells *emacs* to search in the reverse direction). So, we need a way to turn off these special meanings, as well.

This is what non-canonical mode is for. To enter non-canonical mode, turn off the ICANON attribute. When in non-canonical mode, all of the special characters except those that generate signals are disabled. If we also turn off the ISIG attribute, we can disable the signal-generating special characters as well. Non-canonical mode also stops the system from buffering the input into units of lines.

But, if non-canonical mode disables the line-by-line processing of input, how does the system know when to return to data to us? Older systems, which use raw or cbreak mode for non-canonical input, return the data one character at a time. Unfortunately, this requires a lot of overhead. To avoid this, POSIX allows us to tell the system to return input when either a specified amount of data has been read, or after a certain amount of time has passed. The implementation of this uses two variables in the c_cc array, MIN and TIME, indexed by VMIN and VTIME, respectively.

MIN specifies a minimum number of characters to be processed before a read returns. TIME specifies the time, in tenths of a second, to wait for input. There are four combinations of these two variables:

Case A: MIN > 0, TIME > 0

In this case, TIME serves as an inter-character timer that is activated after the first character is received, and reset after each subsequent character is received. If MIN characters are received before the timer expires, the read returns the bytes received. If the timer expires before MIN bytes have been read, the characters read so far are received. At least one character is guaranteed to be returned, because the timer does not start until the first character is processed.

Case B: MIN > 0, TIME = 0

> Since TIME is 0, there is no timer involved in this case. A read will not be satisfied until MIN characters have been received.

Case C: MIN = 0, TIME > 0

> In this case, since MIN is 0, TIME does not serve as an inter-character timer. Instead, it serves as a read timer that is started as soon as the read call is issued. A read is satisfied as soon as a single character is typed, or when the timer expires. Note that if the timer expires, no character is read, and read returns 0.

Case D: MIN = 0, TIME = 0

> In this case, return is immediate. If data is available, the read will return up to the number of characters requested. If no data is available, read returns 0.

Example 12-2 shows a program that uses non-canonical mode to read one character at a time.

Example 12-2: caseflip

```
#include <termios.h>
#include <signal.h>
#include <stdlib.h>
#include <ctype.h>

int
main(void)
{
    char c, lastc;
    sigset_t sig, savesig;
    struct termios modes, savemodes;

    /*
     * Block keyboard signals.
     */
    sigemptyset(&sig);
    sigaddset(&sig, SIGINT);
    sigaddset(&sig, SIGQUIT);
    sigaddset(&sig, SIGTSTP);
    sigprocmask(SIG_BLOCK, &sig, &savesig);

    /*
     * Get current terminal attributes.
     */
    if (tcgetattr(0, &modes) < 0) {
        perror("tcgetattr");
        exit(1);
    }

    /*
     * Save a copy of them to restore later, and then
     * change the attributes to set character-at-a-time
```

Example 12-2: caseflip (continued)

```
 * input, turn off canonical mode, and turn off echo.
 */
savemodes = modes;
modes.c_cc[VMIN] = 1;
modes.c_cc[VTIME] = 0;
modes.c_lflag &= ~ICANON;
modes.c_lflag &= ~(ECHO | ECHOE | ECHOK | ECHOKE);

/*
 * Make our changes take effect.
 */
if (tcsetattr(0, TCSAFLUSH, &modes) < 0) {
    perror("tcsetattr");
    exit(1);
}

/*
 * Read characters.
 */
while (read(0, &c, 1) > 0) {
    /*
     * Turn uppercase to lowercase and lowercase
     * to uppercase.
     */
    if (isupper(c))
        c = tolower(c);
    else if (islower(c))
        c = toupper(c);

    /*
     * Since non-canonical mode disables EOF,
     * we need to handle it ourselves.
     */
    if (c == savemodes.c_cc[VEOF] && lastc == '\n')
        break;

    /*
     * Output the new character and save
     * it.
     */
    write(1, &c, 1);
    lastc = c;
}

/*
 * Restore the original terminal attributes.
 */
if (tcsetattr(0, TCSAFLUSH, &savemodes) < 0) {
    perror("tcsetattr");
    exit(1);
}
```

Example 12–2: caseflip (continued)

```
    /*
     * Restore the original signal mask.
     */
    sigprocmask(SIG_SETMASK, &savesig, (sigset_t *) 0);
    exit(0);
}
```

As in our previous example, this program sets a signal mask to block keyboard interrupts. It then sets MIN and TIME for character-at-a-time input, turns off canonical mode, and disables character echo. The program then reads one character at a time. For each lowercase letter it encounters, it echos the uppercase equivalent. For each uppercase letter, it echos the lowercase equivalent. Because non-canonical mode disables most of the special characters, there is no way to signal an end-of-file from the keyboard to terminate this loop. Thus, the program must check the characters it reads to see if one of them is the EOF character (and that it occurs at the beginning of a line) and break out of the loop itself.

Emulating cbreak and raw modes

When porting software from BSD-based systems, it is common to encounter two modes not available in POSIX. These are cbreak mode, enabled by setting the CBREAK attribute, and raw mode, enabled by setting the RAW attribute. These modes were described in detail earlier.

To reproduce cbreak mode on a POSIX system:

- Enable non-canonical mode (turn off ICANON).
- Enable one character at a time input (set MIN to 1 and TIME to 0).

To reproduce raw mode:

- Enable non-canonical mode (turn off ICANON).
- Disable CR-to-NL mapping on input (turn off ICRNL).
- Disable input parity detection (turn off INPCK) and input parity checking (turn off PARENB).
- Disable stripping of the eighth bit on input (turn off ISTRIP).
- Disable output flow control (turn off IXON).
- Make sure characters are eight bits wide (turn on CS8).

- Disable all output processing (turn off OPOST).

- Enable one character at a time input (set MIN to 1 and TIME to 0).

Pre-POSIX Terminal Control

Depending on the program, porting code that manipulates terminal attributes from a pre-POSIX operating system to a POSIX platform may or may not be a simple task. In this section we examine the other two common interfaces to terminal input and output control, those of System V and BSD.

System V Terminal Control

POSIX terminal attribute control is based on the System V interface, and is almost identical to it from a data structure and flag name point of view. System V uses a struct termio instead of struct termios; this structure is defined as follows in the include file *termio.h*:

```
struct termio {
    unsigned short    c_iflag;
    unsigned short    c_oflag;
    unsigned short    c_cflag;
    unsigned short    c_lflag;
    char              c_line;
    unsigned char     c_cc[NCC];
};
```

The elements of this structure bear a one-to-one correspondence to their struct termios counterparts (the c_line element was for future expansion and never used). There are some differences in the attributes that can be stored in the flags; these are summarized in Table 12-1.

System V releases prior to SVR4 did not support job control or most of the other terminal driver features added by Berkeley. The list of special characters supported by these versions is much shorter: EOF, EOL, ERASE, INTR, KILL, QUIT, and SWTCH. (SWTCH was for System V's *layers* job control facility, which was abandoned by POSIX in favor of Berkeley-style job control.)

The biggest difference between the System V interface and the POSIX interface is that instead of using tcgetattr, tcsetattr, and the other functions described in the last section, the System V interface uses the ioctl system call:

```
#include <unistd.h>
#include <termio.h>

int ioctl(int fd, int request, /* arg */ ...);
```

The ioctl function is the traditional UNIX system call for manipulating I/O devices. It performs some operation, defined by the value of request, on the device referenced by the open file descriptor `fd`. Each operation may have one argument, a pointer to which is provided as the third parameter to `ioctl`. The principal reason for POSIX's abandonment of this interface is that the third argument may be a pointer to different data types, depending on the value of `request`, making type checking impossible. (POSIX actually does offer an `ioctl`-based interface to terminal control, but its use is discouraged.)

In the case of the System V terminal interface, the third argument to `ioctl` is always the address of a **struct termio** structure. The legal values for `request` are:

TCGETA

> The current terminal attributes are retrieved and stored in the **struct termio** structure pointed to by the third argument. This is like `tcgetattr`.

TCSETA

> The current terminal attributes are set to those stored in the **struct termio** structure pointed to by the third argument. This is like `tcsetattr` with the TCSANOW action.

TCSETAW

> The current terminal attributes are set to those stored in the **struct termio** structure pointed to by the third argument. The changes do not take effect until all characters written to the device have been transmitted. This is like `tcsetattr` with the TCSADRAIN action.

TCSETAF

> The current terminal attributes are set to those stored in the **struct termio** structure pointed to by the third argument. The changes do not take effect until all characters written to the device have been transmitted and all input that has been received but not read is discarded. This is like `tcsetattr` with the TCSAFLUSH action.

BSD Terminal Control

The BSD terminal control interface is much less organized than the System V and POSIX interfaces, with five different data structures, each of which manipulates part of the interface. However, the functionality of the BSD interface is comparable to that of the other two.

The BSD interface, like the System V one, is based on the `ioctl` function. In all cases, the third argument is a pointer to one of the five data structures; which structure is obvious from the value of the `request` argument. There are also two older functions called `gtty` and `stty`; these functions work only with the `struct sgttyb` structure, and are left over from the early days when that was the only structure that described terminal attributes. These two functions can be emulated as follows:

```
#include <sgtty.h>

int gtty(int fd, struct sgttyb *arg)
{
    return(ioctl(fd, TIOCGETP, arg));
}

int stty(int fd, struct sgttyb *arg)
{
    return(ioctl(fd, TIOCSETP, arg));
}
```

Line disciplines

Berkeley UNIX provides two *line disciplines*; essentially these are two different terminal drivers (although they are not implemented as such). The old line discipline resembles the original Version 7 terminal driver, and also the one provided by pre-SVR4 versions of System V. The new line discipline supports all the features added by Berkeley; most significantly job control. The new line discipline provides essentially the same set of features as the POSIX terminal driver.

To change between the two line disciplines, use the following `ioctl` actions:

TIOCGETD

Get the current line discipline and store it in the integer pointed to by the third argument.

TIOCSETD

Set the current line discipline to the value stored in the integer pointed to by the third argument.

The legal values for the line discipline are `OTTYDISC` for the old line discipline, and `NTTYDISC` for the new line discipline.

The struct sgttyb structure

The basic terminal driver modes, in both the old and new line disciplines, are set with a structure of type `struct sgttyb`, defined in the include file *sgtty.h*:

```
struct sgttyb {
    char    sg_ispeed;
    char    sg_ospeed;
    char    sg_erase;
    char    sg_kill;
    char    sg_flags;
};
```

The `sg_ispeed` and `sg_ospeed` elements contain the input and output baud rates, and values from the set B0...B9600. The `sg_erase` and `sg_kill` elements are the ERASE and KILL characters, respectively. The `sg_flags` element is a set of attribute flags that can be *or*ed together. These include:

ECHO

Enable character echo. This is identical to the POSIX ECHO.

CRMOD

Map carriage return to newline on input, and echo newline or carriage return as carriage return-newline on output. This is a mix of the POSIX ICRNL and ONLCR attributes.

RAW

Turn on `raw` mode, as described earlier. The POSIX equivalent of `raw` mode is described in the section on POSIX terminal control.

CBREAK

Turn on `cbreak` mode, as described earlier. The POSIX equivalent of `cbreak` mode is described in the section on POSIX terminal control.

The values of the `ioctl request` argument that take a pointer to a `struct sgttyb` structure are:

TIOCGETP

Get the current attributes and store them in the structure pointed to by the third argument.

TIOCSETP

Set the current attributes from the structure pointed to by the third argument. This does not take effect until queued output has drained, and it flushes pending input.

TIOCSETN

Set the current attributes from the structure pointed to by the third argument. Do not wait for output to drain, and do not flush input. (Input is always flushed when entering or leaving raw mode.)

TIOCFLUSH

Flush all pending input and output. The third argument is ignored. This can be replaced with the POSIX `tcflush` function.

TIOCHPCL

Enable or disable hangup-on-last-close mode, in which the last close of the device hangs up the terminal. If the integer pointed to by the third argument is non-zero, this mode is enabled; otherwise, it is disabled. This can be replaced by the POSIX HUPCL attribute.

FIONREAD

> Place the number of characters pending on the input queue that have been received but not read by the program in the integer to which the third argument points. There is no replacement for this in POSIX, although the functionality can be obtained with the `select` or `poll` functions, described in Chapter 6, *Special-Purpose File Operations*.

The struct tchars structure

The `struct tchars` structure sets special characters in both the old and new line disciplines. It is defined as follows in the include file *sys/ioctl.h*:

```
struct tchars {
    char    t_intrc;
    char    t_quitc;
    char    t_startc;
    char    t_stopc;
    char    t_eofc;
    char    t_brkc;
};
```

These characters correspond to the POSIX INTR, QUIT, START, STOP, EOF, and EOL characters, respectively.

The values of the `ioctl request` argument that take a pointer to a `struct tchars` structure are:

TIOCGETC

> Get the current set of characters and store them in the structure pointed to by the third argument.

TIOCSETC

> Set the current set of characters from the structure pointed to by the third argument.

The local mode word

The local mode word is an integer containing attribute flags used by the new line discipline only. These attributes are set by *or*ing them into the mode word. These attributes include:

LPRTERA

> Set printing terminal erase mode, like System V's ECHOPRT.

LCRTERA

Erase with backspace-space-backspace, like POSIX ECHOE.

LLITOUT

Suppress output translations, like turning off POSIX OPOST.

LTOSTOP

Send SIGTTOU to background programs attempting to write to the terminal, like POSIX TOSTOP.

LCRTKIL

Kill lines with backspace-space-backspace, like POSIX ECHOKE.

LPASS8

Pass all eight bits of each character through, like turning off POSIX ISTRIP.

LCTLECH

Echo control characters on input as "^X"; SVR4 (but not POSIX) offers this feature as ECHOCTL.

The values of the ioctl request argument that take a pointer to a local mode word integer are:

TIOCLGET

Get the current value of the local mode word and place it in the integer to which the third argument points.

TIOCLSET

Treat the third argument as a pointer to a mask of bits to replace the current contents of the local mode word.

TIOCLBIS

Treat the third argument as a pointer to a mask of bits to be set in the local mode word.

TIOCLBIC

Treat the third argument as a pointer to a mask of bits to be cleared in the local mode word.

The struct ltchars structure

The last structure used by the Berkeley terminal interface is the struct ltchars structure; this structure sets the additional special characters used by the new line discipline. It is defined in the include file *sys/ioctl.h*:

```
struct ltchars {
    char    t_suspc;
    char    t_dsuspc;
    char    t_rprntc;
    char    t_flushc;
```

```
        char    t_werasc;
        char    t_lnextc;
};
```

These elements correspond to the POSIX special characters SUSP, DSUSP, REPRINT, DISCARD, WERASE, and LNEXT, respectively.

The values of the `ioctl request` argument that take a pointer to a `struct ltchars` structure are:

TIOCGLTC

Get the current special characters and store them in the structure pointed to by the third argument.

TIOCSLTC

Set the current special characters to those stored in the structure pointed to by the third argument.

Terminal Window Size

Both BSD and SVR4 provide a method to keep track of the current terminal size (or window size). The kernel will notify the foreground process group whenever this information is changed (e.g., when the user resizes his window) by sending a SIGWINCH signal. (Background processes should check the window size when they are moved into the foregound, to be sure it hasn't changed.)

The window size is stored in a `struct winsize` structure, defined in the include file *termio.h* on SVR4 systems, and the include file *sys/ioctl.h* on BSD systems:

```
struct winsize {
    unsigned short    ws_row;
    unsigned short    ws_col;
    unsigned short    ws_xpixel;
    unsigned short    ws_ypixel;
};
```

The `ws_row` element contains the number of character rows (lines) on the terminal, while the `ws_col` element contains the number of character columns. The `ws_xpixel` and `ws_ypixel` elements contain the size of the window in pixels in the X (horizontal) and Y (vertical) directions, respectively.

The `struct winsize` structure is manipulated with the `ioctl` function described earlier. The second argument (`request`) may be one of:

TIOCGWINSZ

Get the current window size and store it in the structure pointed to by the third argument.

`TIOCSWINSZ`

Set the current window size to the values contained in the structure pointed to by the third argument. If these values are different from the current values, generate a `SIGWINCH` signal.

Chapter Summary

In this chapter, we examined the functions provided to the programmer for controlling terminal input and output functions. Although these functions are not needed for basic terminal input and output, any program that requires special services such as input without echo or character-at-a-time input must make use of them. Because of the evolution of the terminal interface over the years, the functions described in this chapter are also one of the stickiest points in porting software between different versions of UNIX, and between other operating systems as well. However, the POSIX interface has gone a long way toward simplifying this interface and alleviating the portability problems.

13

Interprocess Communication

One of the most important features of the UNIX operating system is its ability to allow two processes to communicate with each other by exchanging data. This allows simple programs to be combined to build complex tools. Modularity is a major UNIX philosophy—it is better to develop small tools that do one thing well and then combine them, rather than develop huge monolithic programs that attempt to do everything for everyone. With a modular design, you can add or change functionality by changing individual subprograms.

In this chapter, we examine the myriad ways in which two UNIX processes executing on the same computer can communicate with each other. In the next two chapters, we examine how processes running on different computers can communicate. We begin this chapter with a discussion of pipes, the most basic form of interprocess communication (IPC), one that has been around since UNIX was created. We move on to first-in first-out devices, usually called FIFOs or named pipes, and then to UNIX-domain sockets, which in some sense are the same thing implemented differently. We finish with a discussion of message queues, semaphores, and shared memory; these three ideas are often collectively referred to as System V IPC.

Pipes

A *pipe* provides an interface between two processes. It is a special pair of file descriptors that, rather than being connected to a file, is connected to another process. When process A writes to its pipe file descriptor, process B can read that data from its pipe file descriptor. Alternatively, when process B writes to its pipe file descriptor, process A can read the data from its pipe file descriptor. Thus, a pipe provides a unidirectional communications medium for two cooperating processes.

Once a pipe has been created, there is very little difference between a pipe file descriptor and a regular file descriptor. In fact, unless a program takes special steps to find out, there is no way for it to know that it is reading or writing a pipe instead of a file. The UNIX shell makes use of this fact all the time, when it creates pipeline commands. For example, consider the following shell commands:

```
% eqn report > out1
% tbl out1 > out2
% troff out2 > out3
% psdit out3 > out4
% lp out4
% rm out1 out2 out3 out4
```

Although we can certainly execute these programs in this fashion, it's not terribly efficient. There's a lot of typing involved, there are four temporary files created which must then be deleted, etc. However, with the knowledge that each of the above commands has been written as a *filter*, we can simplify things. A filter is a program that will read from its standard input (instead of from a disk file) and write to its standard output. Programs that have been written in this way can be joined together in pipelines by the shell. For example, we can combine the five commands above into a single command, as follows:

```
% eqn report | tbl | troff | psdit | lp
```

The *eqn* program reads its input from the file *report*, just as in the previous example. But, instead of storing its output in the file *out1*, we have told the shell to connect the standard output from *eqn* to the standard input of the *tbl* command. The *tbl* command, instead of reading its input from the file *out1*, reads it from standard input. The standard output from *tbl* has been connected to the standard input of *troff*. The standard output from *troff* has been connected to the standard input of *psdit*. And finally, the standard output from *psdit* has been connected to the standard input of *lp*. Thus, data flows from one program to the next, with no need for temporary files in between. The tool used to connect these programs together is a pipe. The programs themselves, however, have no knowledge of being used in this manner—they just know that if there are no filename arguments given to them on the command line, they should read from their standard input and write to their standard output. For all they know, the standard input could be a file and the standard output could be the terminal screen. Because pipes work just like file descriptors, there is no need for special code in each of these programs to handle them.

Simple Pipe Creation

The simplest way to create a pipe to another process is to use the **popen** function:

```
#include <stdio.h>

FILE *popen(const char *command, const char *type);
```

The **popen** function is similar to **fopen**, described in Chapter 4, *The Standard I/O Library*, except that instead of opening a file for reading or writing, it creates a pipe for reading from or writing to another command. The command, passed in the **command** string, may be any valid shell command; it is executed with the Bourne shell (*/bin/sh*) using the shell's *-c* option. The **type** argument contains one of the strings **r** (open the pipe for reading) or **w** (open the pipe for writing).

When called, **popen** creates a new process, and executes the command. It also creates a pipe to that process, and connects it to the process' standard input or standard output, depending on the value in the **type** argument. It then returns a file pointer to the calling process. The calling process may read from this file pointer to obtain output from the child process, or may write to the file pointer to provide input to the child process. If the command cannot be executed, or the pipe cannot be created, **popen** returns the constant **NULL**.

With one exception, all of the usual *Standard I/O Library* functions described in Chapter 4 may be used with the file pointer returned by **popen**. The one exception is the **fclose** function. Instead, the **pclose** function should be used:

```
#include <stdio.h>

int pclose(FILE *stream);
```

The **pclose** function closes the stream and frees up the buffers associated with it, just like **fclose**. However, it also issues a call to **waitpid** (see Chapter 11, *Processes*) to wait for the child process to terminate, and then returns the child's termination status to the caller.

Example 13-1 shows a different version of the program from Example 11-1 that prints out the day of the week; this one uses **popen**.

Example 13-1: popen

```
#include <stdio.h>

struct {
    char    *abbrev;
    char    *fullname;
} days[] = {
    "Sun",   "Sunday",
    "Mon",   "Monday",
    "Tue",   "Tuesday",
```

Example 13–1: popen (continued)

```
        "Wed",   "Wednesday",
        "Thu",   "Thursday",
        "Fri",   "Friday",
        "Sat",   "Saturday",
        0,       0
};

int
main(void)
{
    int i;
    FILE *pf;
    char line[BUFSIZ];

    /*
     * Open a pipe to the date command.  We will
     * be reading from the pipe.
     */
    if ((pf = popen("date", "r")) == NULL) {
        perror("popen");
        exit(1);
    }

    /*
     * Read one line of output from the pipe.
     */
    if (fgets(line, sizeof(line), pf) == NULL) {
        fprintf(stderr, "No ouput from date command!\n");
        exit(1);
    }

    /*
     * For each day, see if it matches the output
     * from the date command.
     */
    for (i=0; days[i].abbrev != NULL; i++) {
        if (strncmp(line, days[i].abbrev, 3) == 0)
            printf("Today is %s.\n", days[i].fullname);
        else
            printf("Today is not %s.\n", days[i].fullname);
    }

    /*
     * Close the pipe and pick up the command's
     * termination status (which we ignore).
     */
    pclose(pf);

    /*
     * Exit with a status of 0, indicating that
     * everything went fine.
     */
```

Example 13–1: popen (continued)

```
    exit(0);
}
```

```
% popen
Today is not Sunday.
Today is not Monday.
Today is not Tuesday.
Today is not Wednesday.
Today is Thursday.
Today is not Friday.
Today is not Saturday.
```

This program creates a pipe from the *date* command, and reads its output. It then compares that output to its list of day name abbreviations, and prints out the appropriate information. This version of the program is much more efficient than the version in Chapter 11, because it creates only one child process instead of seven.

Because it works in a similar way, we can make the same points about popen that we did about system:

- Although very convenient, popen is also quite inefficient. Each time it is called, it starts up not only a copy of the command you want to execute, but also a copy of the shell. If your program will be executing many commands, you should execute them yourself directly and do your own "plumbing," rather than using popen. The means to do this are described in the next section.

- System calls and library routines are always more efficient than using popen. In the example above, it would be much better to simply use the time and localtime functions described in Chapter 7, *Time of Day Operations*, and avoid the overhead of executing a child process to obtain the same information.

- The popen function should *never*, under any circumstances, be used in programs that will be run with superuser permissions, or with the set-user-id bit set. Because popen uses the shell to execute commands, there may be ways in which an unethical person can fool your program into executing a command other than the one you intended. This may enable the person to circumvent the security of your computer system.

Advanced Pipe Creation

In this section, we examine the procedures used to create pipes ourselves. Before reading this section, you should be familiar with the information in Chapter 11, on which it relies.

A pipe is created with the `pipe` function:

```
#include <unistd.h>

int pipe(int fd[2]);
```

This function creates two file descriptors; `fd[0]` is open for reading, and `fd[1]` is open for writing. The two file descriptors are joined like a pipe, such that data written to `fd[1]` can be read from `fd[0]`. If the pipe is successfully created, `pipe` returns 0. If it cannot be created, `pipe` returns -1, and places the reason for failure in `errno`.

After creating a pipe, the calling process normally calls `fork` to create a child process. The two processes can then communicate, in one direction, using the pipe. Notice that, because a pipe is a half-duplex communications channel (it can only be used to communicate in one direction), either the parent may send data to the child, or the child may send data to the parent, but not both. If both processes must be able to send data, two pipes must be created, one for the child to use to send data to the parent, and the other for the parent to use to send data to the child.

In SVR4, pipes are full-duplex communications channels. This means that both file descriptors are opened for both reading and writing. A read from `fd[0]` accesses the data written to `fd[1]`, and a read from `fd[1]` accesses the data written to `fd[0]`. However, this feature is peculiar to SVR4, and is not the way pipes work on other UNIX systems. The POSIX standard specifies the more common half-duplex pipe described in the previous paragraph, and that is what we describe in the rest of this section.

As long as both ends of a pipe are open, communication can take place. When one end of a pipe is closed, the following rules apply:

- If the write end of a pipe has been closed, any further reads from the pipe (after all the data remaining in the pipe has been read) will return 0, or end-of-file.

- If the read end of a pipe has been closed, any attempt to write to the pipe will result in a `SIGPIPE` signal being delivered to the process attempting the write.

Each pipe has a buffer size; this size is defined by the constant `PIPE_BUF`, described in the include file *limits.h*. A write of this many bytes or less is guaranteed not to be interleaved with the writes from other processes writing the same pipe. Writes of more than PIPE_BUF bytes, however, can get jumbled up in the pipe if more than one process is writing to it at the same time. (It is possible to have more than one process writing to a pipe by using dup or dup2 on the file descriptor.)

Example 13-2 shows a reimplementation of the program in Example 13-1; this time we create the pipe and execute *date* ourselves.

Example 13-2: pipedate

```c
#include <sys/types.h>
#include <unistd.h>

struct {
    char    *abbrev;
    char    *fullname;
} days[] = {
    "Sun",  "Sunday",
    "Mon",  "Monday",
    "Tue",  "Tuesday",
    "Wed",  "Wednesday",
    "Thu",  "Thursday",
    "Fri",  "Friday",
    "Sat",  "Saturday",
    0,      0
};

int
main(void)
{
    pid_t pid;
    int pfd[2];
    int i, status;
    char line[64];

    /*
     * Create a pipe.
     */
    if (pipe(pfd) < 0) {
        perror("pipe");
        exit(1);
    }

    /*
     * Create a child process.
     */
    if ((pid = fork()) < 0) {
        perror("fork");
        exit(1);
    }

    /*
```

Example 13-2: pipedate (continued)

```
    * The child process executes "date".
    */
   if (pid == 0) {
       /*
        * Attach standard output to the pipe.
        */
       dup2(pfd[1], 1);
       close(pfd[0]);

       execl("/bin/date", "date", 0);
       perror("exec");
       _exit(127);
   }

   /*
    * We will not be writing to the pipe.
    */
   close(pfd[1]);

   /*
    * Read the output of "date".
    */
   if (read(pfd[0], line, 3) < 0) {
       perror("read");
       exit(1);
   }

   /*
    * For each day, see if it matches the output
    * from the date command.
    */
   for (i=0; days[i].abbrev != NULL; i++) {
       if (strncmp(line, days[i].abbrev, 3) == 0)
           printf("Today is %s.\n", days[i].fullname);
       else
           printf("Today is not %s.\n", days[i].fullname);
   }

   /*
    * Close the pipe and wait for the child
    * to exit.
    */
   close(pfd[0]);
   waitpid(pid, &status, 0);

   /*
    * Exit with a status of 0, indicating that
    * everything went fine.
    */
   exit(0);
}
```

Example 13-2: pipedate (continued)

```
% pipedate
Today is not Sunday.
Today is not Monday.
Today is not Tuesday.
Today is not Wednesday.
Today is Thursday.
Today is not Friday.
Today is not Saturday.
```

The program begins by creating a pipe. It then calls **fork** to create a child process. The child process will be executing the *date* command, and we want the parent to be able to read the output from this command, so the child process calls **dup2** to attach its standard output to **pfd[1]**. Because the child process will not be reading from the pipe, it closes **pfd[0]**. The child process then calls **execl** to execute the *date* command. Meanwhile, the parent closes **pfd[1]**, since it will not be writing to the pipe. It then calls **read** to obtain the data it needs, and examines the data just as in the previous example. Finally, the parent closes the read side of the pipe since it's done with it, and calls **waitpid** to wait for the child process to terminate and pick up its termination status.

Example 13-3 shows another program; this one uses the pipe in the other direction, to allow the parent to send data to the child.

Example 13-3: pipemail

```c
#include <sys/types.h>
#include <unistd.h>
#include <stdio.h>

int
main(void)
{
    pid_t pid;
    int pfd[2];
    int i, status;
    char *username;

    /*
     * Obtain the user name of the person
     * running this program.
     */
    if ((username = cuserid(NULL)) == NULL) {
        fprintf(stderr, "Who are you?\n");
        exit(1);
    }

    /*
     * Create a pipe.
     */
```

Example 13-3: pipemail (continued)

```
if (pipe(pfd) < 0) {
    perror("pipe");
    exit(1);
}

/*
 * Create a child process.
 */
if ((pid = fork()) < 0) {
    perror("fork");
    exit(1);
}

/*
 * The child process executes "mail".
 */
if (pid == 0) {
    /*
     * Attach standard input to the pipe.
     */
    dup2(pfd[0], 0);
    close(pfd[1]);

    execl("/bin/mail", "mail", username, 0);
    perror("exec");
    _exit(127);
}

/*
 * We won't be reading from the pipe.
 */
close(pfd[0]);

/*
 * Write our mail message to the pipe.
 */
write(pfd[1], "Greetings and salutations,\n\n", 28);
write(pfd[1], "This is your program saying hello.\n", 35);
write(pfd[1], "Have a nice day.\n\n", 18);
write(pfd[1], "Bye.\n", 5);

/*
 * Close the pipe and wait for the child
 * to exit.
 */
close(pfd[1]);
waitpid(pid, &status, 0);

/*
 * Exit with a status of 0, indicating that
 * everything went fine.
 */
```

Example 13-3: pipemail (continued)

```
    exit(0);
}
```

```
% pipemail
% mailx
mailx version 5.0 Mon Sep 27 07:25:51 PDT 1993  Type ? for help.
"/var/mail/davy": 1 message 1 new
>N  1 David A. Curry     Thu Dec  8 11:43    19/383
? 1
Message  1:
From davy Thu Dec  8 11:43 EST 1994
Date: Thu, 8 Dec 1994 11:43:55 +0500
From: davy (David A. Curry)

Greetings and salutations,

This is your program saying hello.
Have a nice day.

Bye.


? d
? q
```

In this case, the child process executes the *mail* command, and the parent will be sending a message. Since *mail* reads from its standard input, the child process uses dup2 to attach its standard input to the read side of the pipe. Since it won't be writing to the pipe, it closes pfd[1]. The parent closes pfd[0] since it won't be reading from the pipe, and then writes a few strings to the child process by using pfd[1]. It then closes the write side of the pipe (this provides the end-of-file indication to the *mail* command), and waits for the child process to terminate.

NOTE

When you execute this program, depending on the load on your system, it may take anywhere from a few seconds to several minutes for the mail message to be delivered to your mailbox. Be patient before assuming the program doesn't work.

FIFOs

Pipes are extraordinarily useful, but suffer from one major limitation: they can only be used between related processes. To get around this limitation, the FIFO (first-in, first-out) was invented. FIFOs are often called *named pipes*, because they are associated with an entry in the filesystem. This name allows them to be used by processes that are not related to each other.

A FIFO differs from a pipe in that it is a bidirectional (full-duplex) communications channel. This means that two processes may both read and write the FIFO in order to exchange data. As with pipes, FIFOs can have multiple processes writing to them. However, if this is the case, each writer must be careful to keep his writes no larger than `PIPE_BUF` bytes, or the data from multiple processes will become intermixed.

FIFOs can be created on most System V systems with the `mknod` function, which is used for creating special device files of all types. However, the POSIX standard specifies a function just for creating FIFOs, called `mkfifo`:

```
#include <sys/types.h>
#include <sys/stat.h>

int mkfifo(const char *path, mode_t mode);
```

The `path` parameter provides a pathname to the FIFO to be created, which must not already exist. The `mode` argument contains a set of permission bits to set on the FIFO; these are modified by the process' `umask` value. Upon successful completion, `mkfifo` returns 0. If it fails, it returns -1 and sets `errno` to indicate the error.

You can also create a FIFO on most systems with the *mkfifo* command. This lets you create a FIFO using a shell command, and then access it using normal I/O redirection.

Once a FIFO has been created, it must be opened for use with the `open` function (see Chapter 3, *Low-Level I/O Routines*). When a FIFO is opened, the O_NONBLOCK option affects what happens:

- If O_NONBLOCK is not specified (the usual case), an open for reading only blocks until another process opens the FIFO for writing. Similarly, an open for writing only blocks until another process opens the FIFO for reading.

- If O_NONBLOCK is specified, an open for reading only returns immediately. But an open for writing only will return an error if no process has yet opened the FIFO for reading.

As with pipes, an attempt to write to a FIFO that has no process reading it will generate a SIGPIPE signal. When the last writer on a FIFO closes it, an end-of-file indication is generated for the reader.

Example 13-4 and Example 13-5 show two programs, a server and a client, that use a FIFO to communicate. The server simply prints any data it receives from the client.

Example 13-4: fifo-srvr

```
#include <sys/types.h>
#include <sys/stat.h>
#include <fcntl.h>

#define FIFONAME       "myfifo"

int
main(void)
{
    int n, fd;
    char buf[1024];

    /*
     * Remove any previous FIFO.
     */
    unlink(FIFONAME);

    /*
     * Create the FIFO.
     */
    if (mkfifo(FIFONAME, 0666) < 0) {
        perror("mkfifo");
        exit(1);
    }

    /*
     * Open the FIFO for reading.
     */
    if ((fd = open(FIFONAME, O_RDONLY)) < 0) {
        perror("open");
        exit(1);
    }

    /*
     * Read from the FIFO until end-of-file and
     * print what we get on the standard output.
     */
    while ((n = read(fd, buf, sizeof(buf))) > 0)
        write(1, buf, n);

    close(fd);
    exit(0);
}
```

Example 13–5: fifo-clnt

```
#include <sys/types.h>
#include <sys/stat.h>
#include <fcntl.h>

#define FIFONAME    "myfifo"

int
main(void)
{
    int n, fd;
    char buf[1024];

    /*
     * Open the FIFO for writing.  It was
     * created by the server.
     */
    if ((fd = open(FIFONAME, O_WRONLY)) < 0) {
        perror("open");
        exit(1);
    }

    /*
     * Read from standard input, and copy the
     * data to the FIFO.
     */
    while ((n = read(0, buf, sizeof(buf))) > 0)
        write(fd, buf, n);

    close(fd);
    exit(0);
}


% fifo-srvr &
% fifo-clnt < /etc/motd
Sun Microsystems Inc.  SunOS 5.3      Generic September 1993
```

The server process first uses unlink to delete any old FIFO, and then calls mkfifo to create a new one. This is not strictly necessary, but insures that the FIFO has the proper modes and ownership. The server then opens the FIFO for reading, and copies anything it receives to the standard output. The client opens the FIFO (which has been created by the server) for writing, and copies its standard input to the FIFO.

UNIX-Domain Sockets

UNIX-domain sockets are similar to named pipes, in that they provide an address in the filesystem that unrelated processes may use to communicate. They differ from named pipes in the way that they are accessed. Named pipes (FIFOs) are accessed just like any other file; in fact, a command executed from the shell whose input or output is redirected to a FIFO never need know that it is using a named pipe. On the other hand, UNIX-domain sockets are implemented using the Berkeley networking paradigm, usually called the *socket* interface. This interface has a set of specialized functions used to create, destroy, and transfer data over communications channels.

Interprocess communication with sockets is usually described in terms of the *client-server model*. In this model, one process is usually called the *server*; it is responsible for satisfying the requests made of it by other processes, called *clients*. A server usually has a *well-known address*; this address is always the same, so that client programs will know where to contact it. An analogy in the real world might be the telephone number 911, which, at least in the United States, contacts the police/fire/ambulance service wherever it is dialed.

In order to use the functions described in this section, a program must be linked with the *-lnsl* and *-lsocket* libraries on Solaris 2.*x*, and with the *-lnsl* library on IRIX 5.*x*.

Creating a Socket

The basic unit of communication in the Berkeley networking paradigm is the *socket*, created with the `socket` function:

```
#include <sys/types.h>
#include <sys/socket.h>

int socket(int domain, int type, int protocol);
```

The `domain` argument specifies the domain, or address family, in which addresses should be interpreted; it imposes certain restrictions on the length of addresses, and what they mean. In this section, we use the `AF_UNIX` domain, in which addresses are ordinary UNIX pathnames. In the next chapter, we look at the `AF_INET` domain, which is used for Internet addresses.

There are two types of communications channels supported by sockets, selected with the `type` argument:

SOCK_STREAM

This type of connection is usually called a *virtual circuit*. It is a bidirectional continuous byte stream that guarantees the reliable delivery of data in the order in which it was sent. No data can be sent until the circuit is established; the circuit then remains intact until the conversation is complete. A telephone call is a real-world example of a virtual circuit; a FIFO is another example.

SOCK_DGRAM

This type of connection is used to send distinct packets of information called *datagrams*. Datagrams are not guaranteed to be delivered to the remote side of the communications channel in the same order they were sent. In fact, they are not guaranteed to be delivered at all. (This is not as undesirable as it may sound; there are many applications for which it is perfectly suited.) The U.S. mail system is a real-world example of datagrams: each letter is an individual message, letters may arrive in a different order than they were sent, and some may even get lost.

The `protocol` parameter specifies the protocol number that should be used on the socket; it is usually the same as the address family. In this section we use the `PF_UNIX` protocol family; in the next chapter we examine the `PF_INET` family. The `protocol` parameter can usually be given as 0, and the system will figure it out.

When a socket is successfully created, a *socket descriptor* is returned. This is a small non-negative integer, similar to a file descriptor (but with slightly different semantics). If the socket cannot be created, -1 is returned and the error information is stored in `errno`.

A second method for creating sockets can be used by two related processes (parent and child) to establish a full-duplex communications channel:

```
#include <sys/types.h>
#include <sys/socket.h>

int socketpair(int domain, int type, int protocol, int sv[2]);
```

This creates an unnamed pair of sockets and places their descriptors in `sv[0]` and `sv[1]`. Each socket is a bidirectional communications channel. A read from `sv[0]` accesses the data written to `sv[1]`, and a read from `sv[1]` accesses the data written to `sv[0]`. If the socket pair is successfully created, `socketpair` returns 0. Otherwise, it returns -1 and stores the error code in `errno`.

Server-Side Functions

The server process needs to call the `bind`, `listen`, and `accept` functions, in order, if it is to exchange data with a client.

Naming a socket

After creating a socket, a server process must provide that socket with a name so that client programs can access it. The function to assign a name to a socket is called `bind`:

```
#include <sys/types.h>
#include <sys/socket.h>

int bind(int s, const struct sockaddr *name, int addrlen);
```

After completion, the communications channel referenced by the socket descriptor `s` will have the address described by `name`. In order for `bind` to succeed, the address must not already be in use. Because `name` may be of different sizes depending on the address family being used, `addrlen` is used to indicate its length. If `bind` succeeds, it returns 0. If it fails (often because the address is already in use), it returns -1 and stores an error code in `errno`.

In the UNIX domain, the `name` parameter is actually of type `struct sockaddr_un`, defined in the include file *sys/un.h*:

```
struct sockaddr_un {
    short    sun_family;
    char     sun_path[108];
};
```

The `sun_family` element is always set to `AF_UNIX`, identifying this address as being in the UNIX domain. The `sun_path` element contains the filesystem pathname of the socket. As a side effect of the implementation of UNIX-domain sockets, this file is actually created when it is bound. Before a server calls `bind`, it should make sure that this file does not exist and delete it if it does, or the bind will fail because the address is already in use.

Waiting for connections

If a server is providing a service via a stream-based socket, it must notify the operating system when it is ready to accept connections from clients on that socket. To do this, it uses the `listen` function:

```
#include <sys/types.h>
#include <sys/socket.h>

int listen(int s, int backlog);
```

This function tells the operating system that the server is ready to accept connections on the socket referenced by `s`. The `backlog` parameter specifies the number of connection requests that may be pending at any given time; most operating systems silently limit this to a maximum of five. If a connection request arrives when the queue of pending connections is full, the client will receive a connection-refused error.

Accepting connections

To actually accept a connection, the server uses the `accept` function:

```
#include <sys/types.h>
#include <sys/socket.h>

int accept(int s, struct sockaddr *name, int *addrlen);
```

When a connection request arrives on the socket referenced by `s`, `accept` returns a new socket descriptor. The server can use this new descriptor to communicate with the client; the old descriptor (the one bound to the well-known address) may continue to be used for accepting additional connections. When the connection is accepted, if `name` is not null, the operating system stores the address of the client there, and stores the length of the address in `addrlen`. If `accept` fails, it returns -1 and places the reason for failure in `errno`.

Connecting to a Server

In order to connect to a server using a stream-based socket, the client program calls the `connect` function:

```
#include <sys/types.h>
#include <sys/socket.h>

int connect(int s, struct sockaddr *name, int addrlen);
```

This function connects the socket referenced by `s` to the server at the address described by `name`. The `addrlen` parameter specifies the length of the address in `name`. If the connection is completed, `connect` returns 0. Otherwise, it returns -1 and places the reason for failure in `errno`.

A client may use `connect` to connect a datagram socket to the server as well. This is not strictly necessary, and does not actually establish a connection. However, it does enable the client to send datagrams on the socket without having to specify the destination address for each datagram.

Transferring Data

To transfer data on a stream-based connection, the client and server may simply use `read` and `write`. Two other functions are also used with stream-based sockets:

```
#include <sys/types.h>
#include <sys/socket.h>

int recv(int s, char *buf, int len, int flags);

int send(int s, const char *buf, int len, int flags);
```

These functions are like `read` and `write`, except that they have a fourth argument. This argument allows the program to specify flags that affect how the data is sent or received. Only one flag has any meaning in the UNIX domain:

MSG_PEEK

> If specified in a call to `recv`, the data is copied into `buf` as usual, but it is not "consumed." Another call to `recv` will return the same data. This allows a program to "peek" at the data before reading it, to decide how it should be handled.

When using datagram-based sockets, the server does not call `listen` or `accept`, and the client (generally) does not call `connect`. Thus, there is no way for the operating system to determine automatically where data on these sockets is to be sent. Instead, the sender must tell the operating system each time where the data is to be delivered, and the receiver must ask where it came from. Two other functions accomplish this:

```
#include <sys/types.h>
#include <sys/socket.h>

int recvfrom(int s, char *buf, int len, int flags,
        struct sockaddr *from, int *fromlen);

int sendto(int s, const char *buf, int len, int flags,
        struct sockaddr *to, int tolen);
```

The `sendto` function sends `len` bytes from `buf` via the socket referenced by `s` to the server located at the address given in `to`. The `tolen` parameter specifies the length of the address. The number of bytes actually transferred is returned, or -1 if an error occurred. There is no indication whether or not the data actually reaches its destination. The `recvfrom` function receives up to `len` bytes of data from the socket referenced by `s` and stores them in `buf`. The address from which the data came is stored in `from`, and `fromlen` is modified to indicate the length of the address. The number of bytes received is returned, or -1 if an error occurs.

Destroying the Communications Channel

One way to close a socket is with the `close` function, with the side effect that if the socket refers to a stream-based socket, the close will block until all data has been transmitted.

Another way is with the **shutdown** function:

```
#include <sys/types.h>
#include <sys/socket.h>

int shutdown(int s, int how);
```

This function shuts down either or both sides of the communications channel referenced by s, depending on the value of how. If how is 0, the socket is shut down for reading; all further reads from the socket return end-of-file. If how is 1, the socket is shut down for writing; all further writes to the socket will fail. This also informs the operating system that no effort need be made to deliver any outstanding data on the socket. If how is 2, then both sides of the socket are shut down and it essentially becomes useless.

Putting it All Together

Example 13-6 and Example 13-7 show small server and client programs that transfer data using a virtual circuit. These two programs are identical in operation to the programs in Example 13-4 and Example 13-5, except that they are implemented using UNIX-domain sockets.

Example 13-6: socket-srvr

```
#include <sys/types.h>
#include <sys/socket.h>
#include <sys/un.h>
#include <string.h>

#define SOCKETNAME  "mysocket"

int
main(void)
{
    char buf[1024];
    int n, s, ns, len;
    struct sockaddr_un name;

    /*
     * Remove any previous socket.
     */
    unlink(SOCKETNAME);

    /*
     * Create the socket.
     */
    if ((s = socket(AF_UNIX, SOCK_STREAM, 0)) < 0) {
        perror("socket");
        exit(1);
    }
```

Example 13-6: socket-srvr (continued)

```
    /*
     * Create the address of the server.
     */
    memset(&name, 0, sizeof(struct sockaddr_un));

    name.sun_family = AF_UNIX;
    strcpy(name.sun_path, SOCKETNAME);
    len = sizeof(name.sun_family) + strlen(name.sun_path);

    /*
     * Bind the socket to the address.
     */
    if (bind(s, (struct sockaddr *) &name, len) < 0) {
        perror("bind");
        exit(1);
    }

    /*
     * Listen for connections.
     */
    if (listen(s, 5) < 0) {
        perror("listen");
        exit(1);
    }

    /*
     * Accept a connection.
     */
    if ((ns = accept(s, (struct sockaddr *) &name, &len)) < 0) {
        perror("accept");
        exit(1);
    }

    /*
     * Read from the socket until end-of-file and
     * print what we get on the standard output.
     */
    while ((n = recv(ns, buf, sizeof(buf), 0)) > 0)
        write(1, buf, n);

    close(ns);
    close(s);
    exit(0);
}
```

Example 13-7: socket-clnt

```
#include <sys/types.h>
#include <sys/socket.h>
#include <string.h>
#include <sys/un.h>
```

Example 13–7: socket-clnt (continued)

```c
#define SOCKETNAME  "mysocket"

int
main(void)
{
    int n, s, len;
    char buf[1024];
    struct sockaddr_un name;

    /*
     * Create a socket in the UNIX
     * domain.
     */
    if ((s = socket(AF_UNIX, SOCK_STREAM, 0)) < 0) {
        perror("socket");
        exit(1);
    }

    /*
     * Create the address of the server.
     */
    memset(&name, 0, sizeof(struct sockaddr_un));

    name.sun_family = AF_UNIX;
    strcpy(name.sun_path, SOCKETNAME);
    len = sizeof(name.sun_family) + strlen(name.sun_path);

    /*
     * Connect to the server.
     */
    if (connect(s, (struct sockaddr *) &name, len) < 0) {
        perror("connect");
        exit(1);
    }

    /*
     * Read from standard input, and copy the
     * data to the socket.
     */
    while ((n = read(0, buf, sizeof(buf))) > 0) {
        if (send(s, buf, n, 0) < 0) {
            perror("send");
            exit(1);
        }
    }

    close(s);
    exit(0);
}
```

```
% socket-srvr &
% socket-clnt < /etc/motd
Sun Microsystems Inc.  SunOS 5.3      Generic September 1993
```

System V IPC Functions

Three types of interprocess communication—message queues, shared memory, and semaphores—are usually referred to collectively as System V IPC. System V IPC originated in SVR2, but has since been made available by most vendors, and is also available in SVR4.

Each type of IPC structure (message queue, shared memory segment, or semaphore) is referred to by a non-negative integer *identifier*. To make use of a message queue, for example, all the processes using that message queue must know its identifier. When an IPC structure is being created, the program doing the creation provides a *key* of type key_t. The operating system will convert this key into an IPC identifier.

Keys can be specified in one of three ways:

1. The server can create a new structure by specifying a key of IPC_PRIVATE. The creation procedure will return an identifier for the newly created structure. The problem with this is that in order for client programs to make use of the structure, they must know the identifier. Thus, the server has to place the identifier in a file somewhere for the clients to read it.

2. The server and clients can agree on a key value, for example, by defining it in a common header file. The server creates a new IPC structure with this key, and the clients use the key to access the structure. The problem with this is that the key may already be in use by some other group of programs, in which case the IPC structure cannot be created.

3. The server and clients can agree on a pathname to an existing file in the filesystem, and a project ID (a value between 0 and 255), and then call the ftok function to convert these two values into a key:

    ```
    #include <sys/types.h>
    #include <sys/ipc.h>

    key_t ftok(const char *path, int projectid);
    ```

    This key is then used as in step 2, above.

To create a new IPC structure, the server (usually) calls the appropriate "get" function, either with the key argument equal to IPC_PRIVATE, or with the key argument equal to some key and the `IPC_CREAT` bit set in the `flag` argument. A client accesses an existing IPC structure (created by the server) by calling the appropriate "get" function with the `key` argument equal to the appropriate key and with the `IPC_CREAT` bit cleared in the `flag` argument. To be sure that a new IPC structure is created, rather than referencing an existing one with the same identifier, the `IPC_EXCL` bit can be set in the `flag` argument to the "get" function. This causes the "get" function to return an error if the IPC structure already exists.

Each IPC structure has a permissions structure associated with it, defined in the include file *sys/ipc.h*:

```
struct ipc_perm {
    uid_t      uid;
    gid_t      gid;
    uid_t      cuid;
    gid_t      cgid;
    mode_t     mode;
    ulong      seq;
    key_t      key;
    long       pad[4];
};
```

The `cuid` and `cgid` elements identify the user who created the object, the `uid` and `gid` elements identify the owner of the object. The `mode` element is a set of read/write permission bits identical to those for files, that specify owner, group, and world permissions to examine and change the object. The "control" function for each type of IPC can be used to examine and change this structure.

The System V IPC mechanisms have one major problem. All of the IPC structures are global to the system, and do not have a reference count. This means that if a program creates one of these structures, and then exits without destroying it, the operating system has no way of knowing whether any other programs are using it. Thus, the operating system has no choice but to leave the structure there; it cannot delete it. These structures remain in the system until someone comes along and removes them, or until the system is rebooted. This can be a serious problem, because the system places a limit on how many of these structures may exist at any point in time. Aside from consuming space that could be used by other programs, the structures left around by improperly-behaving programs can eventually consume all available IPC resources.

Message Queues

A message queue is a linked list of messages, each of a fixed maximum size. Messages are added to the end of the queue so that the order in which they were sent is preserved. However, each message may have a type, allowing multiple message streams to be processed in the same queue.

Before using a message queue, a process must obtain the queue identifier for it. This is done using the msgget function:

```
#include <sys/types.h>
#include <sys/ipc.h>
#include <sys/msg.h>

int msgget(key_t key, int msgflg);
```

The key parameter specifies the key to use for this message queue; it may either be the value IPC_PRIVATE, in which case a new message queue will always be created, or a non-zero value. If key contains a non-zero value, msgget will either create a new message queue or return the identifier of an existing message queue, depending on whether or not the IPC_CREAT bit is set in the msgflg argument. The msgflg parameter is also used to specify the read/write permissions on the message queue, in the same manner as with open and creat. Upon successful completion, a message queue identifier is returned. If the queue does not exist or cannot be created, -1 is returned and errno will describe the error that occurred.

The msgctl function allows several different control operations to be performed on a message queue:

```
#include <sys/types.h>
#include <sys/ipc.h>
#include <sys/msg.h>

int msgctl(int msqid, int cmd, struct msqid_ds *buf);
```

The msqid parameter contains the message queue identifier of interest. The buf parameter points to a structure of type struct msqid_ds, which describes the message queue:

```
struct msqid_ds {
    struct ipc_perm    msg_perm;
    struct msg         *msg_first;
    struct msg         *msg_last;
    ulong              msg_cbytes;
    ulong              msg_qnum;
    ulong              msg_qbytes;
    pid_t              msg_lspid;
    pid_t              msg_lrpid;
    time_t             msg_stime;
    long               msg_pad1;
```

```
    time_t              msg_rtime;
    long                msg_pad2;
    time_t              msg_ctime;
    long                msg_pad3;
    kcondvar_t          msg_cv;
    kcondvar_t          msg_qnum_cv;
    long                msg_pad4[3];
};
```

The `msg_perm` element of this structure describes the permission bits on the queue, as described in the introduction to this section. The `msg_qnum`, `msg_cbytes`, and `msg_qbytes` elements contain the number of messages on the queue, number of bytes on the queue, and maximum number of bytes on the queue, respectively. The `msg_lspid` and `msg_lrpid` elements contain the process ID of the last process to send and receive a message on the queue, respectively. Finally, the `msg_stime`, `msg_rtime`, and `msg_ctime` elements contain the time of the last send on the queue, time of the last receive on the queue, and time of the last permissions change on the queue, respectively.

The `cmd` parameter to `msgctl` may be one of the following values:

IPC_STAT

> Place the current contents of the `struct msqid_ds` structure into the area pointed to by `buf`.

IPC_SET

> Change the `msg_perm.uid`, `msg_perm.gid`, `msg_perm.mode`, and `msg_qbytes` elements of the `struct msqid_ds` structure to the values found in the area pointed to by `buf`. This operation is restricted to processes with an effective user ID of the superuser, or one that is equal to either `msg_perm.cuid` or `msg_perm.uid`. The `msg_qbytes` element may be changed only by the superuser.

IPC_RMID

> Remove the message queue identifier specified by `msqid` from the system, and destroy the message queue and data structure. This command may be executed only by a process with an effective user ID of the superuser, or one that is equal to either `msg_perm.cuid` or `msg_perm.uid`.

If successful, `msgctl` returns 0. If an error occurs, `msgctl` returns -1 and stores the reason for failure in `errno`.

To send and receive messages on a message queue, use the `msgsnd` and `msgrcv` functions:

```
#include <sys/types.h>
#include <sys/ipc.h>
#include <sys/msg.h>
```

```
int msgsnd(int msqid, const void *msgp, size_t msgsz, int msgflg);

int msgrcv(int msqid, void *msgp, size_t msgsz, long msgtype, int msgflg);
```

The `msgsnd` function sends a message, pointed to by `msgp` and of size `msgsz`, on the message queue identified by `msqid`. A message has the following structure:

```
struct msgbuf {
    long     mtype;
    char     mtext[];
};
```

The `mtype` element of this structure is a positive integer that can be used by the receiving process for message selection. The `mtext` element of the structure is a buffer of `msgsz` bytes; `msgsz` may be any value from 0 to some system-imposed maximum (usually 2048). If successful, `msgsnd` returns 0; otherwise it returns -1 and places an error code in `errno`.

The `msgrcv` function retrieves a message from the message queue specified by `msqid`, and stores it in the area pointed to by `msgp`, which is large enough to hold a message of `msgsz` bytes. The message retrieved is controlled by the `msgtype` parameter:

- If `msgtype` is 0, the next message on the queue is returned.

- If `msgtype` is greater than 0, the next message on the queue with `mtype` equal to `msgtype` is returned.

- If `msgtype` is less than 0, the next message on the queue with `mtype` less than or equal to the absolute value of `msgtype` is returned.

If a message is successfully received, `msgrcv` returns the number of bytes stored in `msgp`. If an error occurs, -1 is returned and `errno` will indicate the error.

For both `msgsnd` and `msgrcv`, the `msgflg` argument may contain the constant `IPC_NOWAIT`. This causes `msgsnd` to return an error immediately if the message queue is full, instead of blocking until space is available. It causes `msgrcv` to return an error immediately if no message of the specified type is available, instead of blocking until one arrives.

Example 13-8 and Example 13-9 show a small server and a client program that transfers data using message queues.

Example 13-8: msq-srvr

```c
#include <sys/types.h>
#include <sys/ipc.h>
#include <sys/msg.h>

#define MSQKEY      34856
#define MSQSIZE     32

struct mymsgbuf {
    long    mtype;
    char    mtext[MSQSIZE];
};

int
main(void)
{
    key_t key;
    int n, msqid;
    struct mymsgbuf mb;

    /*
     * Create a new message queue.  We use IPC_CREAT to create it,
     * and IPC_EXCL to make sure it does not exist already.  If
     * you get an error on this, something on your system is using
     * the same key - change MSQKEY to something else.
     */
    key = MSQKEY;
    if ((msqid = msgget(key, IPC_CREAT | IPC_EXCL | 0666)) < 0) {
        perror("msgget");
        exit(1);
    }

    /*
     * Receive messages.  Messages of type 1 are to be printed
     * on the standard output; a message of type 2 indicates that
     * we're done.
     */
    while ((n = msgrcv(msqid, &mb, MSQSIZE, 0, 0)) > 0) {
            switch (mb.mtype) {
            case 1:
                write(1, mb.mtext, n);
                break;
            case 2:
                goto out;
            }
    }

out:
    /*
     * Remove the message queue from the system.
     */
    if (msgctl(msqid, IPC_RMID, (struct msqid_ds *) 0) < 0) {
        perror("msgctl");
```

Example 13-8: msq-srvr (continued)

```
        exit(1);
    }

    exit(0);
}
```

Example 13-9: msq-clnt

```
#include <sys/types.h>
#include <sys/ipc.h>
#include <sys/msg.h>

#define MSQKEY      34856
#define MSQSIZE     32

struct mymsgbuf {
    long    mtype;
    char    mtext[MSQSIZE];
};

int
main(void)
{
    key_t key;
    int n, msqid;
    struct mymsgbuf mb;

    /*
     * Get a message queue.  The server must have created it
     * already.
     */
    key = MSQKEY;
    if ((msqid = msgget(key, 0666)) < 0) {
        perror("msgget");
        exit(1);
    }

    /*
     * Read data from standard input and send it in
     * messages of type 1.
     */
    mb.mtype = 1;
    while ((n = read(0, mb.mtext, MSQSIZE)) > 0) {
        if (msgsnd(msqid, &mb, n, 0) < 0) {
            perror("msgsnd");
            exit(1);
        }
    }

    /*
     * Send a message of type 2 to indicate we're done.
```

Example 13-9: msq-clnt (continued)

```
     */
    mb.mtype = 2;
    memset(mb.mtext, 0, MSQSIZE);
    if (msgsnd(msqid, &mb, MSQSIZE, 0) < 0) {
        perror("msgsnd");
        exit(1);
    }

    exit(0);
}


% msq-srvr &
% msq-clnt < /etc/motd
Sun Microsystems Inc.   SunOS 5.3        Generic September 1993
```

The server creates a new message queue that may be read and written by anyone.
(We use IPC_EXCL here to insure that nothing else in the system is using this key
value—if you get an error when you try to start the server, use a different key
value.) The server then receives messages from the queue. Messages of type 1 are
data, and are printed on the standard output. Since there is no concept of end-of-
file on a message queue, we use a message of type 2 to tell the server there is no
more data. The client simply obtains the message queue identifier, and then reads
from its standard input, sending the data in messages of type 1. It sends a final
message of type 2 to tell the server there is no more data.

Shared Memory

Shared memory allows two or more processes to share a region of memory, so
that they may all examine and change its contents. Obviously, some type of synchronization between the processes is required, to ensure that one process does
not change the memory while another is accessing it.

Before using a shared memory segment, a process must obtain the queue identifier for it. This is done using the shmget function:

```
#include <sys/types.h>
#include <sys/ipc.h>
#include <sys/shm.h>

int shmget(key_t key, int size, int shmflg);
```

The size parameter specifies the size of the desired segment, in bytes. The key
parameter specifies the key to use for this memory segment; it may either be the
value IPC_PRIVATE, in which case a new segment will always be created, or a

non-zero value. If key contains a non-zero value, msgget will either create a new memory segment or return the identifier of an existing segment, depending on whether or not the IPC_CREAT bit is set in the shmflg argument. The shmflg parameter is also used to specify the read/write permissions on the memory segment, in the same manner as with open and creat. Upon successful completion, the function returns a shared memory segment identifier. If the segment does not exist or cannot be created, -1 is returned and errno indicates the error that occurred.

The shmctl function allows several different control operations to be performed on a shared memory segment:

```
#include <sys/types.h>
#include <sys/ipc.h>
#include <sys/shm.h>

int shmctl(int shmid, int cmd, struct shmid_ds *buf);
```

The shmid parameter contains the shared memory segment identifier of interest. The buf parameter points to a structure of type struct shmid_ds, which describes the memory segment:

```
struct shmid_ds {
    struct ipc_perm     shm_perm;
    int                 shm_segsz;
    struct anon_map     *shm_amp;
    ushort              shm_lkcnt;
    pid_t               shm_lpid;
    pid_t               shm_cpid;
    ulong               shm_nattch;
    ulong               shm_cnattch;
    time_t              shm_atime;
    long                shm_pad1;
    time_t              shm_dtime;
    long                shm_pad2;
    time_t              shm_ctime;
    long                shm_pad3;
    kcondvar_t          shm_cv;
    char                shm_pad4[2];
    struct as           *shm_sptas;
    long                shm_pad5[2];
};
```

The shm_perm element of this structure describes the permission bits on the segment, as described in the introduction to this section. The shm_segsz element contains the size of the segment, in bytes. The shm_lpid and shm_cpid elements contain the process ID of the last process to modify the segment, and the process ID that created the segment, respectively. The shm_lkcnt element contains the number of locks on this segment. The `shm_nattch` element contains the number of processes that currently have this memory segment attached. Finally, the `shm_atime`, `shm_dtime`, and `shm_ctime` elements contain the time of the last attachment of the segment, time of the last detachment of the segment, and time of the last permissions change on the segment, respectively.

The `cmd` parameter to `shmctl` may have one of the following values:

IPC_STAT

> Place the current contents of the `struct shmid_ds` structure into the area pointed to by `buf`.

IPC_SET

> Change the `shm_perm.uid`, `shm_perm.gid`, and `shm_perm.mode` elements of the `struct shmid_ds` structure to the values found in the area pointed to by `buf`. This operation is restricted to processes with an effective user ID of the superuser, or one that is equal to either `shm_perm.cuid` or `shm_perm.uid`.

IPC_RMID

> Remove the shared memory identifier specified by `shmid` from the system, and destroy the memory segment and data structure associated with it. This command may only be executed by a process with an effective user ID of the superuser, or one that is equal to either `shm_perm.cuid` or `shm_perm.uid`.

SHM_LOCK

> Lock the shared memory segment specified by `shmid` into memory. This requires superuser status.

SHM_UNLOCK

> Unlock the shared memory segment specified by `shmid`. This requires superuser status.

If successful, `shmctl` returns 0. If an error occurs, `shmctl` returns -1 and stores the reason for failure in `errno`.

Before a process may use a shared memory segment, it must *attach* that segment; that is, it must map the segment into the process' address space. The function to attach a shared memory segment is called `shmat`:

```
#include <sys/types.h>
#include <sys/ipc.h>
#include <sys/shm.h>

void *shmat(int shmid, void *shmaddr, int shmflg);
```

The `shmid` parameter specifies the identifier of the segment to be attached. The `shmaddr` parameter specifies the address at which the memory should be attached; normally this is specified as 0 (allowing the system to choose) unless special circumstances prevail. If `shmflg` contains the constant `SHM_RDONLY` the memory segment is attached read-only, otherwise it is attached read-write. If the memory segment is successfully attached, `shmat` will return the address at which it starts. Otherwise, it returns `(void *)` -1 and the reason for failure is stored in `errno`.

Once a program is done using a shared memory segment, it may call `shmdt` to detach it:

```
#include <sys/types.h>
#include <sys/ipc.h>
#include <sys/shm.h>

int shmdt(void *shmaddr);
```

The `shmaddr` parameter should contain the value returned by `shmat`.

Semaphores

Semaphores do not exchange data between processes. They are counters that are used to provide synchronized access to a shared data object among multiple processes. To obtain access to a shared resource, a process:

1. Tests the value of the semaphore that controls access to the resource.

2. If the value is greater than 0, the process can use the resource. It decrements the semaphore by 1, indicating that it is using one unit of the resource.

3. If the value of the semaphore is 0, the process goes to sleep until the value is greater than 0. When the process wakes up, it returns to step 1.

When a process is done using a shared resource controlled by a semaphore, the semaphore's value is incremented by 1. If any processes are stuck in step 3 above, one of them is awakened. Most semaphores are *binary*, and their values are initialized to 1. However, any positive value can be used, with the value indicating how many units of the resource are available for sharing.

For semaphores to work properly, you must be able to test the value of a semaphore and decrement it in a single operation. For this reason, semaphores are usually implemented in the kernel.

The System V IPC version of semaphores operates on semaphore sets, rather than individual semaphores. Before using a semaphore set, a process must obtain the identifier for it. This is done using the `semget` function:

```
#include <sys/types.h>
#include <sys/ipc.h>
#include <sys/sem.h>
```

```
int semget(key_t key, int nsems, int semflg);
```

The `nsems` parameter specifies the number of semaphores in the set. The `key` parameter specifies the key to use for this semaphore set; it may either be the value `IPC_PRIVATE`, in which case a new set will always be created, or a non-zero value. If `key` contains a non-zero value, `msgget` will either create a new semaphore set or return the identifier of an existing set, depending on whether or not the `IPC_CREAT` bit is set in the `semflg` argument. The `semflg` parameter is also used to specify the read/write permissions on the semaphores in the set, in the same manner as with `open` and `creat`. Upon successful completion, a semaphore set identifier is returned. If the set does not exist or cannot be created, -1 is returned and `errno` will describe the error that occurred.

The `semctl` function allows several different control operations to be performed on a semaphore set:

```
#include <sys/types.h>
#include <sys/ipc.h>
#include <sys/sem.h>

int semctl(int semid, int semnum, int cmd, union semun arg);

union semun {
    int             val;
    struct semid_ds *buf;
    ushort          *array;
};
```

The `semid` parameter contains the identifier of the semaphore set, while the `semnum` parameter contains the number of the specific semaphore of interest. The `arg` parameter is a union of type `union semun`; its use is described below. A structure of type `struct semid_ds` describes the semaphore set:

```
struct semid_ds {
    struct ipc_perm sem_perm;
    struct sem      *sem_base;
    ushort          sem_nsems;
    time_t          sem_otime;
    long            sem_pad1;
    time_t          sem_ctime;
    long            sem_pad2;
    long            sem_pad3[4];
};
```

The `sem_perm` element of this structure describes the permission bits on the set, as described in the introduction to this section. The `sem_nsems` element contains the number of semaphores in the set. The `sem_otime` and `shm_ctime` elements contain the time of the last semaphore operation and the time of the last permissions change on the set, respectively.

Each semaphore in the set is described by a structure of type `struct sem`:

```
struct sem {
    ushort       semval;
    pid_t        sempid;
    ushort       semncnt;
    ushort       semzcnt;
    kcondvar_t   semncnt_cv;
    kcondvar_t   semzcnt_cv;
};
```

The `semval` element contains the semaphore's current value. The `sempid` element contains the process ID of the last process to operate on this semaphore. The `semncnt` and `semzcnt` elements contain the number of processes waiting for the semaphore's value to become greater than its current value, and to become zero, respectively.

The `cmd` parameter to `semctl` may have one of the following values:

IPC_STAT

Place the current contents of the `struct semid_ds` structure into the area pointed to by `arg.buf`.

IPC_SET

Change the `sem_perm.uid`, `sem_perm.gid`, and `sem_perm.mode` elements of the `struct semid_ds` structure to the values found in the area pointed to by `arg.buf`. This operation is restricted to processes with an effective user ID of the superuser, or one that is equal to either `sem_perm.cuid` or `sem_perm.uid`.

IPC_RMID

Remove the semaphore set identifier specified by `semid` from the system, and destroy the set of semaphores and data structure associated with it. This command may only be executed by a process with an effective user ID of the superuser, or one that is equal to either `sem_perm.cuid` or `sem_perm.uid`.

GETVAL

Return the value of `semval` for the specified semaphore.

SETVAL

Set the value of `semval` for the specified semaphore to `arg.val`.

GETPID

Return the value of `sempid` for the specified semaphore.

GETNCNT

Return the value of `semncnt` for the specified semaphore.

GETZCNT

Return the value of `semzcnt` for the specified semaphore.

GETALL

Store the value of `semval` for all semaphores in the set in the array pointed to by `arg.array`.

SETALL

Set the value of `semval` for all semaphores in the set to the values in the array pointed to by `arg.array`.

If successful, `semctl` returns a positive value for the GETVAL, GETPID, GET-NCNT, and GETZCNT commands, and 0 otherwise. If an error occurs, `semctl` returns -1 and stores the reason for failure in `errno`.

Semaphores are operated on with the `semop` function:

```
#include <sys/types.h>
#include <sys/ipc.h>
#include <sys/sem.h>

int semop(int semid, struct sembuf *ops, size_t nops);

struct sembuf {
    ushort      sem_num;
    short       sem_op;
    short       sem_flg;
};
```

The `semid` argument specifies the semaphore set of interest, and `ops` points to a list of `nops` structures of type `struct sembuf`. Within each structure, `sem_num` specifies the number of the semaphore to be manipulated, `sem_op` specifies the operation to be performed, and `sem_flg` specifies any flags for the operation:

- If `sem_op` is positive, its value is added to the semaphore's value. This corresponds to releasing a shared resource the program was using.

- If `sem_op` is negative, this indicates the program wants to obtain resources controlled by the semaphore.

If the semaphore's value is greater than or equal to the absolute value of `sem_op` (the resources are available), the absolute value of `sem_op` is subtracted from the semaphore's value.

If the semaphore's value is less than the absolute value of `sem_op` (the resources are not available), `semop` either returns immediately with an error (if `IPC_NOWAIT` was specified in `sem_flg`), or puts the process to sleep until the semaphore's value becomes greater than or equal to the absolute value of `sem_op`.

* If `sem_op` is 0, `semop` blocks until the semaphore's value becomes 0 (unless `IPC_NOWAIT` is specified in `sem_flg`).

Chapter Summary

In this chapter, we examined a number of techniques that allow two processes on the same computer to communicate. For related processes (parent and child), pipes are the most common and widespread solution, although others may be used. For unrelated processes, FIFOs (in the System V world) and UNIX-domain sockets (in the Berkeley world) are the most common. The so-called System V IPC functions, while sometimes convenient, have a number of drawbacks, and should probably be avoided unless absolutely necessary.

14

Networking with Sockets

These days, nearly every UNIX system is connected to some type of network. Desktop systems are connected via a network to file servers, and they use the network to access system and user files. Most universities and government organizations, and more and more companies, are connected to the Internet, and use the network to communicate with users, access data, and distribute information worldwide. Even many home computers now connect to the Internet or a private network via dial-up networking.

The *de facto* standard network protocol suite in use today is called TCP/IP, for *Transmission Control Protocol/Internet Protocol.* This protocol suite was developed by the Internet Engineering Task Force, and is the protocol suite used world-wide by hosts connected to the Internet. TCP/IP is also used for most UNIX-based local-area networking applications such as remote login and network file service. Another international standard protocol suite, usually called OSI (*Open Systems Interconnect*), has been standardized by the International Standards Organization (ISO). Although fairly popular in Europe, this protocol suite has never caught on in the United States, for a wide variety of both technical and political reasons. Although there was much talk of TCP/IP becoming obsolete when the ISO/OSI standards were first released, it is now clear that TCP/IP is here to stay, and even organizations that use ISO/OSI internally must also support TCP/IP if they want to connect to the outside world and the Internet.

Because TCP/IP development was funded by the U.S. Defense Advanced Research Projects Agency (DARPA), and DARPA also provided principal funding for the development of Berkeley UNIX, BSD UNIX was the first version of the operating system to support internetworking via TCP/IP. The Berkeley networking paradigm, usually called the *socket* interface, has since spread to nearly every other version of UNIX, SVR4 included.

In Chapter 13, *Interprocess Communication*, we introduced the Berkeley socket interface as it applied to UNIX-domain sockets, used for communicating between two or more processes on the same machine. In this chapter, we will again examine the socket interface, but this time as it applies to Internet-domain sockets, used for communicating between two or more processes on *different* machines. In the next chapter, we will examine the *Transport Layer Interface* (TLI), an alternate interface to the network first introduced in SVR3.

All programs that make use of the socket library functions must be linked with the *-lnsl* and *-lsocket* libraries on Solaris 2.*x*, and with the *-lnsl* library on IRIX 5.*x*.

Networking Concepts

Before discussing how network programs are written, we define a number of the underlying concepts.

Host Names and Addresses

Humans use host names to communicate with a host. Programs use host addresses.

Host names

Each host on the network has a unique *host name*. On a private network, host names can be simple, such as "fred" or "wilma." On the Internet, however, a host name must be a *fully qualified domain name*, such as "fred.some.college.edu" or "wilma.company.com."

The Internet Domain Name System allows the host name space to be subdivided into a number of logical areas, or domains. This allows the administration of the host name space to be spread out such that in general, each organization on the Internet can administer its own name space. In olden days, the entire host name space was controlled by the Network Information Center, and any time a new host was added to the network, it had to be registered with them. With over nine million hosts on the Internet as of January 1996, this is obviously no longer workable. Another reason for subdividing the name space is to allow host names to be re-used in different areas of the name space. Before the domain name system, there could be one and only one host named "fred" on the entire Internet. Again, with over nine million hosts, this rapidly becomes unworkable unless we all use host names such as "aaaaaaa," "aaaaaab," and so forth. The domain name system allows the "fred" host name to be used in each logical area. There can still be one and only one "fred" within a logical area, but two different logical areas can each have a "fred."

At the top level of the system are the largest domains; each country has a two-letter domain. For example, "us" is the United States, "se" is Sweden, and "mx" is Mexico. In the United States, there are four other top-level domains: "edu" is educational institutions (mostly colleges and universities), "mil" is military organizations, "gov" is non-military government organizations, and "com" is commercial organizations. These domains should really be under the "us" domain, since they are specific to the United States, but historical reasons make it otherwise.

Each top-level domain is subdivided into other domains. For example, the "edu" domain is divided into domains for each college or university: "mit.edu," "purdue.edu," "berkeley.edu," and so on. These domains can then be subdivided even further, for example, "cs.purdue.edu" for the Computer Science department, "cc.purdue.edu" for the Computer Center, and "physics.purdue.edu" for the Physics department. There is, generally speaking, no practical limit to how many times a domain may be subdivided, although most are not broken up beyond three or four levels.

The last subdivision of a domain is the host name. For example, "fred.cs.berkeley.edu" and "wilma.cs.berkeley.edu." On hosts within the "cs.berkeley.edu" domain, these hosts can be referred to as simply "fred" and "wilma." However, from a host not in the "cs.berkeley.edu" domain, the fully-qualified domain name ("fred.cs.berkeley.edu" or "wilma.cs.berkeley.edu") must be used. Note that because the domain name is part of the host name, "fred.cc.purdue.edu," "fred.mit.edu," "fred.army.mil," "fred.se," and "fred.co.ac.uk" all refer to different hosts.

To get the local host's name, you can use the **uname** function, described in Chapter 9, *System Configuration and Resource Limits*. For portability reasons, though, when using the Berkeley socket interface, it is more common to obtain the host name using the **gethostname** function:

```
int gethostname(char *name, int len);
```

This function places the local host's name into the character array pointed to by **name**, which is **len** bytes in size. It returns 0 on success; on failure it returns -1 and stores the reason for failure in **errno**. Depending on the particular configuration of your host, **gethostname** may or may not return the fully-qualified domain name for the host.

Host addresses

Host names are a useful way to identify hosts to other human beings, but they do not provide enough information in and of themselves to allow the networking software to make much use of them. For this reason, each host also has a *host address*. A host address is a unique 32-bit number; each host on the network has a different address.

Host addresses, also called network addresses or Internet addresses, are usually written in "dotted-quad" notation, in which each byte of the address is converted to an unsigned decimal number and separated from the next by a period (dot). For example, the hexadecimal network address 0x7b2d4359 would be written as 123.45.67.89.

Each network address consists of two parts: a network number and a host number. There are different types of addresses: Class A network addresses use one byte for the network number and three bytes for the host number; Class B network addresses use two bytes for the network number and two bytes for the host number; Class C addresses use three bytes for the network number and one byte for the host number. It is also possible to divide the host number part of an address further; part of it can be used to represent a subnetwork number, and the rest of it can be used to represent the host number on that subnetwork.

The network number part of an address is used by the network routing software to decide how to deliver data from one network (say, the one at Berkeley) to another (say, the one at Harvard). It corresponds in some ways to the area code part of a telephone number that tells the telephone switches how to route the call from one area of the country to another. The subnetwork number tells the network routing software within a given network what part of the network to deliver the data to. For example, within Berkeley, the subnetwork number would indicate whether the data should go to the Computer Science department or the English department. It corresponds in some ways to the exchange part of a telephone number in the United States, which tells the telephone system which central office should receive the data. Finally, the host number part of an address indicates the specific host that is to receive the data, just as the last part of a telephone number identifies the specific telephone to ring.

To translate between host names and host addresses, several functions are provided:

```
#include <sys/types.h>
#include <sys/socket.h>
#include <netdb.h>
#include <netinet/in.h>

struct hostent *gethostent(void);

struct hostent *gethostbyname(const char *name);

struct hostent *gethostbyaddr(const char *addr, int len, int type);
```

```
int sethostent(int stayopen);

int endhostent(void);
```

These functions look up host names and host addresses in one of several different databases, depending on how your system is configured. The */etc/hosts* file lists host name and address pairs, and is usually used only for local area addresses. The *Network Information Service* (Yellow Pages) provides a different interface to the */etc/hosts* file. Finally, the name server provides a distributed (by domain) database of host name and address information. On SVR4, the file */etc/nsswitch.conf* controls which databases are used, and the order in which they are searched.

The `sethostent` function opens the database and sets the "current entry" pointer to the beginning of the file. The `stayopen` parameter, if non-zero, indicates that the database should remain open across calls to the other functions; this cuts down on the number of system calls used to open the database. The `endhostent` function closes the database.

The `gethostent` function reads the next host name and address from the database, and returns it. The `gethostbyname` function searches for the entry in the database for the host with name `name`, and returns its entry. The `gethostbyaddr` function searches for the entry in the database for the host with address `addr`, whose length is specified by `len`, and type is given by `type` and returns its entry. All three of these functions return NULL if the entry cannot be found or end of file is encountered. On success, they return a pointer to a structure of type `struct hostent`:

```
struct hostent {
    char     *h_name;
    char     **h_aliases;
    int      h_addrtype;
    int      h_length;
    char     *h_addr_list;
};
```

The `h_name` field will contain the official host name of the host (usually this is the fully-qualified domain name). The `h_aliases` element will contain pointers to any other names the host is known by. The `h_addrtype` field indicates the type of addresses these are. The `h_length` element indicates how long (in bytes) an address is. And finally, `h_addr_list` will contain a list of the addresses for that host.

NOTE

Older systems use a `h_addr` field in the structure instead of
`h_addr_list`; this was changed when it was realized that systems may
have more than one address. On newer systems, `h_addr` is usually
defined to refer to `h_addr_list[0]`, for backward compatibility.

Services and Port Numbers

On any given host on the network, a number of network services may be provided. For example, a single host may offer remote login, file transfer, and electronic mail delivery. To distinguish data sent to the file transfer service from data
sent to, say, the electronic mail service, each service is assigned a *port number*.
The port number is a small integer used to identify the service to which data is to
be delivered.

In order for two hosts to communicate using some service, they must agree on the
port number to be used for that service. If two hosts used different port numbers
for the same service, they would not be able to communicate. All standard Internet
protocols use *well-known ports* for this purpose. For example, if host "fred" wants
to transfer a file to host "wilma" using the File Transfer Protocol (FTP), it knows
that it should use port number 21. If "fred" tries to use some other port number for
this purpose, things won't work, because "wilma" is expecting FTP traffic on port
21. Likewise, if "fred" sends some other type of traffic (say, remote login) to port
21 on "wilma," things won't work, because "wilma" is expecting file transfer traffic
on that port.

Most versions of UNIX, SVR4 included, use the file */etc/services* to store the list of
well-known port numbers. This file lists the name of the service and the port number and protocol (TCP or UDP; see below) to be used for communicating with that
service. The */etc/services* file is read using the following functions:

```
#include <netdb.h>

struct servent *getservent(void);

struct servent *getservbyname(const char *name, char *proto);

struct servent *getservbyport(int port, char *proto);

int setservent(int stayopen);

int endservent(void);
```

The `setservent` function opens the services file and sets the "current entry" pointer to the start of the file. The `stayopen` parameter, if non-zero, indicates that the file should remain open across calls to the other functions. The `endservent` function closes the services file.

The `getservent` function reads the next entry in the file and returns it. The `getservbyname` function searches for the service with name `name` and returns the entry for it. The `getservbyport` function searches for the service with port number `port` and returns the entry for it. The `proto` argument to these two functions is either "tcp" or "udp." There are actually two sets of port numbers, one for TCP (streams-based) services and one for UDP (datagram-based) services; it is therefore necessary to indicate which port number is of interest. All three of these functions return `NULL` if the entry cannot be found or end-of-file is encountered. If they succeed, they return a pointer to a structure of type `struct servent`:

```
struct servent {
    char     *s_name;
    char     **s_aliases;
    int      s_port;
    char     *s_proto;
};
```

The `s_name` field indicates the official name of the service; the `s_aliases` field indicates any alternate names for the service. The `s_port` field provides the port number, and the `s_proto` field indicates the protocol to use when communicating with the service.

Network Byte Order

When implementing integer storage on a computer, manufacturers have two choices. They can place the most significant byte in the lowest memory address, with less significant bytes stored in higher addresses; this is called "big endian" notation. Or they can place the most significant byte in the highest memory address, with less significant bytes stored in lower addresses; this is called "little endian" notation. Intel chips (80x86, Pentium, etc.) and Digital Equipment Corporation VAX computers are well-known little-endian architectures; Motorola 680x0 chips and Sun SPARC systems are two well-known big-endian architectures.

A 32-bit integer value as stored on a big-endian machine looks different than one stored on a little-endian machine. To copy data from one type of host to the other, it is necessary to transform the data into the proper format. However, without knowing the notation used by both machines, it is impossible to do this. Since there is no way to tell which format a remote machine on the network uses, a *network byte order* has been defined. The network byte order (which happens to be big-endian) insures that all traffic arriving at a host from the network will be in the same format. The host can then convert from this standard format to whatever format it uses internally. Similarly, all traffic sent by the host is converted to network byte order before it leaves, insuring that whatever host receives it will know what format it is in.

The Berkeley networking paradigm specifies that each network program must perform these byte order conversions itself. (It would be difficult to do it anywhere else, since only the program knows the structure of the data it is transferring, and what parts need to be converted.) Four functions are provided to make these translations:

```
#include <sys/types.h>
#include <netinet/in.h>

u_long htonl(u_long hostlong);

u_short htons(u_short hostshort);

u_long ntohl(u_long netlong);

u_long ntohs(u_short netshort);
```

The `htonl` function converts the 32-bit `hostlong` value from host byte order to network byte order. The `htons` function converts the 16-bit `hostshort` value from host byte order to network byte order. The `ntohl` function converts the 32-bit `netlong` value from network byte order to host byte order. And the `ntohs` function converts the 16-bit `netshort` value from network byte order to host byte order. These functions are usually implemented as C preprocessor macros, and may be "no-ops," depending on the host architecture.

Remember to use these functions whenever integer data is exchanged across the network. Character strings do not need to be converted, since they are arrays of one-byte values. There is no network floating point format; floating point numbers should generally be exchanged only by converting them to integers or by printing them as character strings and then sending the strings to the remote side, where they are converted back into floating point numbers.

The `gethostby*` and `getservby*` functions return integer values in network byte order.

Creating a Socket

The basic unit of communication in the Berkeley networking paradigm is the *socket*, created with the `socket` function:

```
#include <sys/types.h>
#include <sys/socket.h>

int socket(int domain, int type, int protocol);
```

The `domain` argument specifies the domain, or address family, in which addresses should be interpreted; it imposes certain restrictions on the length of addresses, and what they mean. In the last chapter, we used the `AF_UNIX` domain, in which addresses are ordinary UNIX pathnames. In this chapter, we will look at the `AF_INET` domain, which is used for Internet addresses.

There are two types of communications channels supported by sockets, selected with the `type` argument:

SOCK_STREAM

> This type of connection is usually called a *virtual circuit*. It is a bidirectional continuous byte stream that guarantees the reliable delivery of data in the order in which it was sent. No data can be sent until the circuit is established; the circuit then remains intact until the conversation is complete. A telephone call is a real-world example of a virtual circuit; a FIFO is another example. Virtual circuits are implemented in the Internet domain using the Internet-standard *Transmission Control Protocol* (TCP).

SOCK_DGRAM

> This type of connection is used to send discrete packets of information called *datagrams*. Datagrams are not guaranteed to be delivered to the remote side of the communications channel in the same order they were sent. In fact, they are not guaranteed to be delivered at all. (This is not as undesirable as it may sound; there are many applications for which it is perfectly suited.) The U.S. mail system is a real-world example of datagrams: each letter is an individual message, letters may arrive in a different order than they were sent, and some may even get lost. Datagrams are implemented in the Internet domain using the Internet-standard *User Datagram Protocol* (UDP).

The `protocol` parameter specifies the protocol number that should be used on the socket; it is usually the same as the address family. In the last chapter we used the `PF_UNIX` protocol family; in this chapter we will use the `PF_INET` family. The `protocol` parameter can usually be specified as 0, and the system will figure it out.

When a socket is successfully created, a *socket descriptor* is returned. This is a small non-negative integer, similar to a file descriptor (but with slightly different semantics). If the socket cannot be created, -1 is returned and the error information is stored in `errno`.

Server-Side Functions

The server process needs to call each of these functions, in order, if it is to exchange data with a client.

Naming a Socket

After creating a socket, a server process must provide that socket with a name by which client programs can access it. The function to assign a name to a socket is called `bind`:

```
#include <sys/types.h>
#include <sys/socket.h>

int bind(int s, const struct sockaddr *name, int addrlen);
```

After completion of `bind`, the communications channel referenced by the socket descriptor `s` will have the address described by `name`. In order for `bind` to succeed, the address must not already be in use. Because `name` may be of different sizes depending on the address family being used, `addrlen` is used to indicate its length. If `bind` succeeds, it returns 0. If it fails (often because the address is already in use), it returns -1 and stores an error code in `errno`.

In the Internet domain, the `name` parameter is of type `struct sockaddr_in`, defined in the include file *netinet/in.h*:

```
struct sockaddr_in {
    short           sin_family;
    u_short         sin_port;
    struct in_addr  sin_addr;
};
```

The `sin_family` element is always set to `AF_INET`, identifying this address as being in the Internet domain. The `sin_port` element contains the port number associated with this socket. The `sin_addr` element contains the host address associated with the port.

When writing server processes, remember that the host on which the process is running may have more than one network interface and, therefore, more than one network address. To handle this, you can create more than one socket and bind a name to each socket, using the same value for `sin_port`, and different values for `sin_addr`, for each socket. An easier way is to use the wildcard address `INADDR_ANY` in the `sin_addr` element; this will allow a single socket to receive data from all network interfaces.

Waiting for Connections

If a server is providing a service via a stream-based socket, it must notify the operating system when it is ready to accept connections from clients on that socket. To do this, it uses the `listen` function:

```
#include <sys/types.h>
#include <sys/socket.h>

int listen(int s, int backlog);
```

This function tells the operating system that the server is ready to accept connections on the socket referenced by `s`. The `backlog` parameter specifies the number of connection requests that may be pending at any given time; most operating systems silently limit this to a maximum of five. If a connection request arrives when the queue of pending connections is full, the client will receive a "connection refused" error.

Accepting Connections

To accept a connection, the server uses the `accept` function:

```
#include <sys/types.h>
#include <sys/socket.h>

int accept(int s, struct sockaddr *name, int *addrlen);
```

When a connection request arrives on the socket referenced by `s`, `accept` returns a new socket descriptor. The server can use this new descriptor to communicate with the client; the old descriptor (the one bound to the well-known address) may continue to be used for accepting additional connections. When the connection is accepted, if `name` is not null the operating system stores the address of the client there, and will store the length of the address in `addrlen`. If `accept` fails, it returns -1 and places the reason for failure in `errno`.

Client-Side Functions

To communicate with a server process, a client process needs to call, in order, the functions described below.

Connecting to a Server

To connect to a server using a stream-based socket, the client program calls the `connect` function:

```
#include <sys/types.h>
#include <sys/socket.h>

int connect(int s, struct sockaddr *name, int addrlen);
```

This function connects the socket referenced by `s` to the server at the address described by `name`. The `addrlen` parameter specifies the length of the address in `name`. If the connection is completed, `connect` returns 0. Otherwise, it returns -1 and places the reason for failure in `errno`.

A client may also use `connect` to connect a datagram socket to the server. This is not strictly necessary, and does not actually establish a connection. However, it does enable the client to send datagrams on the socket without having to specify the destination address for each datagram.

Transferring Data

To transfer data on a stream-based connection, the client and server may simply use `read` and `write`. However, there are also two functions specifically used with stream-based sockets:

```
#include <sys/types.h>
#include <sys/socket.h>

int recv(int s, char *buf, int len, int flags);

int send(int s, const char *buf, int len, int flags);
```

These functions are exactly identical to `read` and `write`, except that they have a fourth argument. This argument allows the program to specify flags that affect how the data is sent or received. The flags are:

MSG_DONTROUTE

If specified in a call to `send`, this flag disables network routing of the data. It is only used by diagnostic and routing programs.

MSG_OOB

If specified in a call to `send`, the data is sent as *out-of-band* data. This data "jumps over" any other data that has been sent and not received. It is used, for example, to handle interrupt characters in a remote login session. If specified in a call to `recv`, any pending out-of-band data will be returned instead of "regular" data.

MSG_PEEK

> If specified in a call to `recv`, the data is copied into `buf` as usual, but it is not consumed. Another call to `recv` will return the same data. This allows a program to "peek" at the data before reading it, to decide how it should be handled.

When using datagram-based sockets, the server does not call `listen` or `accept`, and the client (generally) does not call `connect`. Thus, there is no way for the operating system to automatically figure out where data on these sockets is to be sent. Instead, the sender must tell the operating system each time where to deliver the data, and the receiver must ask where it came from. To do this, two other functions are defined:

```
#include <sys/types.h>
#include <sys/socket.h>

int recvfrom(int s, char *buf, int len, int flags,
        struct sockaddr *from, int *fromlen);

int sendto(int s, const char *buf, int len, int flags,
        struct sockaddr *to, int tolen);
```

The `sendto` function sends `len` bytes from `buf` via the socket referenced by `s` to the server located at the address given in `to`. The `tolen` parameter specifies the length of the address. The number of bytes actually transferred is returned, or -1 if an error occurred. There is no indication whether or not the data actually reaches its destination. The `recvfrom` function receives up to `len` bytes of data from the socket referenced by `s` and stores them in `buf`. The address from which the data came is stored in `from`, and `fromlen` is modified to indicate the length of the address. The number of bytes received is returned, or -1 if an error occurs.

Destroying the Communications Channel

Sockets may be closed with the `close` function, with the side effect that if the socket refers to a stream-based socket, the close will block until all data has been transmitted.

The `shutdown` function may also be used to shut down the communications channel:

```
#include <sys/types.h>
#include <sys/socket.h>

int shutdown(int s, int how);
```

This function shuts down either one or both sides of the communications channel referenced by s, depending on the value of how. If how is 0, the socket is shut down for reading; all further reads from the socket return end-of-file. If how is 1, the socket is shut down for writing; all further writes to the socket will fail. This also informs the operating system that no effort need be made to deliver any outstanding data on the socket. If how is 2, then both sides of the socket are shut down and it becomes essentially useless.

Putting It All Together

Example 14-1 and Example 14-2 are small server and client programs that transfer data between themselves using a virtual circuit. These two programs are identical in operation to the programs in Example 13-6 and Example 13-7, except they are implemented using Internet-domain sockets.

Example 14-1: server

```
#include <sys/types.h>
#include <sys/socket.h>
#include <netinet/in.h>
#include <string.h>

#define PORTNUMBER  12345

int
main(void)
{
    char buf[1024];
    int n, s, ns, len;
    struct sockaddr_in name;

    /*
     * Create the socket.
     */
    if ((s = socket(AF_INET, SOCK_STREAM, 0)) < 0) {
        perror("socket");
        exit(1);
    }

    /*
     * Create the address of the server.
     */
    memset(&name, 0, sizeof(struct sockaddr_in));

    name.sin_family = AF_INET;
    name.sin_port = htons(PORTNUMBER);
    len = sizeof(struct sockaddr_in);

    /*
     * Use the wildcard address.
```

Example 14–1: server (continued)

```
     */
    n = INADDR_ANY;
    memcpy(&name.sin_addr, &n, sizeof(long));

    /*
     * Bind the socket to the address.
     */
    if (bind(s, (struct sockaddr *) &name, len) < 0) {
        perror("bind");
        exit(1);
    }

    /*
     * Listen for connections.
     */
    if (listen(s, 5) < 0) {
        perror("listen");
        exit(1);
    }

    /*
     * Accept a connection.
     */
    if ((ns = accept(s, (struct sockaddr *) &name, &len)) < 0) {
        perror("accept");
        exit(1);
    }

    /*
     * Read from the socket until end-of-file and
     * print what we get on the standard output.
     */
    while ((n = recv(ns, buf, sizeof(buf), 0)) > 0)
        write(1, buf, n);

    close(ns);
    close(s);
    exit(0);
}
```

Example 14–2: client

```
#include <sys/types.h>
#include <sys/socket.h>
#include <netinet/in.h>
#include <string.h>
#include <netdb.h>
#include <stdio.h>

#define PORTNUMBER  12345
```

Example 14-2: client (continued)

```c
int
main(void)
{
    int n, s, len;
    char buf[1024];
    char hostname[64];
    struct hostent *hp;
    struct sockaddr_in name;

    /*
     * Get our local host name.
     */
    if (gethostname(hostname, sizeof(hostname)) < 0) {
        perror("gethostname");
        exit(1);
    }

    /*
     * Look up our host's network address.
     */
    if ((hp = gethostbyname(hostname)) == NULL) {
        fprintf(stderr, "unknown host: %s.\n", hostname);
        exit(1);
    }

    /*
     * Create a socket in the INET
     * domain.
     */
    if ((s = socket(AF_INET, SOCK_STREAM, 0)) < 0) {
        perror("socket");
        exit(1);
    }

    /*
     * Create the address of the server.
     */
    memset(&name, 0, sizeof(struct sockaddr_in));

    name.sin_family = AF_INET;
    name.sin_port = htons(PORTNUMBER);
    memcpy(&name.sin_addr, hp->h_addr_list[0], hp->h_length);
    len = sizeof(struct sockaddr_in);

    /*
     * Connect to the server.
     */
    if (connect(s, (struct sockaddr *) &name, len) < 0) {
        perror("connect");
        exit(1);
    }
```

Example 14-2: client (continued)

```
    /*
     * Read from standard input, and copy the
     * data to the socket.
     */
    while ((n = read(0, buf, sizeof(buf))) > 0) {
        if (send(s, buf, n, 0) < 0) {
            perror("send");
            exit(1);
        }
    }

    close(s);
    exit(0);
}


% server &
% client < /etc/motd
Sun Microsystems Inc.   SunOS 5.3       Generic September 1993
```

Example 14-3 shows a sample datagram client program that contacts the "daytime" service on every host named on the command line. The "daytime" service is an Internet standard service that returns the local time (to the server) in an ASCII string. It is defined for both TCP and UDP; try modifying the program to use TCP instead.

Example 14-3: daytime

```
#include <sys/types.h>
#include <sys/socket.h>
#include <netinet/in.h>
#include <string.h>
#include <netdb.h>
#include <stdio.h>

#define SERVICENAME "daytime"

int
main(int argc, char **argv)
{
    int n, s, len;
    char buf[1024];
    char *hostname;
    struct hostent *hp;
    struct servent *sp;
    struct sockaddr_in name, from;

    if (argc < 2) {
        fprintf(stderr, "Usage: %s hostname [hostname...]\n", *argv);
        exit(1);
```

Example 14-3: daytime (continued)

```
    }

    /*
     * Look up our service.  We want the UDP version.
     */
    if ((sp = getservbyname(SERVICENAME, "udp")) == NULL) {
        fprintf(stderr, "%s/udp: unknown service.\n", SERVICENAME);
        exit(1);
    }

    while (--argc) {
        hostname = *++argv;

        /*
         * Look up the host's network address.
         */
        if ((hp = gethostbyname(hostname)) == NULL) {
            fprintf(stderr, "%s: unknown host.\n", hostname);
            continue;
        }

        /*
         * Create a socket in the INET
         * domain.
         */
        if ((s = socket(AF_INET, SOCK_DGRAM, 0)) < 0) {
            perror("socket");
            exit(1);
        }

        /*
         * Create the address of the server.
         */
        memset(&name, 0, sizeof(struct sockaddr_in));

        name.sin_family = AF_INET;
        name.sin_port = sp->s_port;
        memcpy(&name.sin_addr, hp->h_addr_list[0], hp->h_length);
        len = sizeof(struct sockaddr_in);

        /*
         * Send a packet to the server.
         */
        memset(buf, 0, sizeof(buf));

        n = sendto(s, buf, sizeof(buf), 0, (struct sockaddr *) &name,
                   sizeof(struct sockaddr_in));

        if (n < 0) {
            perror("sendto");
            exit(1);
        }
```

Example 14-3: daytime (continued)

```
        /*
         * Receive a packet back.
         */
        len = sizeof(struct sockaddr_in);
        n = recvfrom(s, buf, sizeof(buf), 0, (struct sockaddr *) &from, &len);

        if (n < 0) {
            perror("recvfrom");
            exit(1);
        }

        /*
         * Print the packet.
         */
        buf[n] = '\0';
        printf("%s: %s", hostname, buf);

        /*
         * Close the socket.
         */
        close(s);
    }

    exit(0);
}
```

```
% daytime localhost
localhost: Mon Mar 20 15:50:54 1995
```

Other Functions

Several other functions can be used with sockets, although their use is less common than the routines described so far.

Socket "Names"

Two functions let you obtain the name bound to a socket:

```
#include <sys/types.h>
#include <sys/socket.h>

int getsockname(int s, struct sockaddr *name, int *namelen);

int getpeername(int s, struct sockaddr *name, int *namelen);
```

The `getsockname` function obtains the name bound to the socket `s`, and stores it in the area pointed to by `name`. Since `name` is of different sizes depending on the networking domain (i.e., it may point to a `struct sockaddr_un` or a `struct sockaddr_in`), the length of the name is stored in `namelen`. Note that `namelen` should be initialized to the size of the area pointed to by `name`; on return it will be set to the actual length of the `name`.

The `getpeername` function obtains the name of the peer connected to the socket `s`. In other words, it obtains the address and port number of the remote host. A server can use this information to find out who has connected to it. The `name` and `namelen` parameters are as described above.

Both `getsockname` and `getpeername` return 0 on success; on failure they return -1 and store an error code in `errno`.

Socket Options

A number of options may be set on a socket to control its behavior; there are two functions for manipulating these options:

```
#include <sys/types.h>
#include <sys/socket.h>

int getsockopt(int s, int level, int optname, char *optval, int *optlen);

int setsockopt(int s, int level, int optname, char *optval, int optlen);
```

The `getsockopt` function returns information about the state of options currently set on the socket `s`; `setsockopt` changes the state of those options.

Options may exist at multiple protocol levels. Therefore, it is necessary to specify the level at which the option in question resides. All of the options described in this section exist at the socket level; the `level` parameter should always be set to `SOL_SOCKET`.

The `optval` parameter specifies a pointer to a buffer that either contains the value to be set for the option, or is used to store the value of the option. The `optlen` parameter specifies the size of the area pointed to by `optval`; on return from `getsockopt`, `optlen` will be modified to indicate the actual size of the value.

The `optname` parameter specifies the option of interest:

SO_DEBUG
>   Enables or disables debugging in the underlying protocol module.

SO_REUSEADDR

Indicates that the rules used in validating addresses provided with calls to bind should be modified to allow re-use of local addresses.

SO_KEEPALIVE

Enables the periodic transmission of "are you there" messages on a connected socket. If the connected party fails to respond to these messages, the connection is considered broken and processes using the socket will receive a SIGPIPE signal the next time they try to use it.

SO_DONTROUTE

Indicates that outgoing messages should bypass the network routing facilities. This is used only for debugging and diagnostic purposes.

SO_LINGER

If SO_LINGER is set on a socket that guarantees reliable data delivery, and a close is performed on the socket, the system will block the process on the close until any unsent data has been transmitted, or until the transmission times out. The timeout in seconds is specified in the optval parameter to setsockopt. If SO_LINGER is disabled and a close is issued, the system will process it in a manner that allows the calling process to continue as quickly as possible.

SO_BROADCAST

Requests permission to send broadcast datagrams (datagrams to be received by all hosts) on the socket.

SO_OOBINLINE

On sockets that support out-of-band data, requests that when the out-of-band data arrives, it be placed in the normal input queue; this allows the data to be processed by read or recv calls without the MSG_OOB flag.

SO_SNDBUF, SO_RCVBUF

Adjust the size of the normal send and receive buffers, respectively. Generally speaking, for large data transfers, these buffers should be made as large as possible to make the transfer as efficient as possible. The maximum limit on the buffer size in SVR4 is 64 Kbytes.

SO_TYPE

Used with getsockopt only; returns the type of the socket (e.g., SOCK_STREAM).

SO_ERROR

> Used with `getsockopt` only; returns any pending error on the socket and clears the error status.

Address Conversion

Routines are provided to convert between the internal (binary) and external (character string) representations of Internet addresses:

```
#include <sys/types.h>
#include <sys/socket.h>
#include <netinet/in.h>
#include <arpa/inet.h>

unsigned long inet_addr(const char *cp);

char *inet_ntoa(const struct in_addr addr);
```

The `inet_addr` function takes a character string containing an Internet address in "dotted-quad" notation (e.g., 192.10.42.34) and returns the integer representation of that address. The `inet_ntoa` function takes an integer representation of an Internet address, and returns a character string representation of the address in dotted-quad notation.

The Berkeley "r" Commands

The functionality of the Berkeley *rsh* command, which contacts a remote host and passes a command to the shell, is accessible through the `rcmd` function:

```
int rcmd(char **ahost, unsigned short inport, char *luser,
        char *ruser, char *cmd, int *fd2p);

int rresvport(int *port);
```

The authentication scheme is based on *reserved port numbers*, defined to be port numbers less than 1024. On BSD UNIX systems (and other systems, such as SVR4, that support the concept), only a superuser can obtain a reserved port. On the server side, when a client connects, the server checks to see that the client is using a reserved port between 513 and 1024; port numbers less than or equal to 512 are not permitted. If the port number used by the client is greater than 1024, it is not a reserved port, and the server will not allow it. Note that the whole concept of reserved ports is specific to UNIX; it is not an Internet standard. This means that the authentication provided by this mechanism is dubious at best (for example, a personal computer running MS-DOS can create any port it wants, since there is no concept of a superuser).

A reserved port number is obtained using the `rresvport` function; it returns either a reserved port suitable for use as the `inport` parameter to `rcmd`, or -1 on error.

The `rcmd` function connects to the host named in `*aname`, which is modified to contain the official host name, using the reserved port given by `inport`. It returns a stream socket on success, or -1 on failure. The `luser` parameter should contain the name of the local user; the `ruser` parameter should contain the name of the user on the remote host whose account is to be used to execute the command. On the remote host, the *rshd* daemon will search `ruser`'s *.rhosts* file for a line specifying the connecting host and `luser`. If such a line is found, access is granted; otherwise, access is denied.

If access is granted, the shell command in `cmd` is executed. The standard input and output of the command is connected to the socket returned by `rcmd`. If `fd2p` is non-null, an auxilliary channel to a control process will be set up, and a descriptor for it placed in `*fd2p`. The control process returns the command's standard error output on this channel; it also accepts bytes on this channel as signal numbers to be delivered to the process group of the command. If `fd2p` is null, the standard error output of the command becomes the same as its standard output, and no provision for delivering signals to the process is made.

As mentioned above, `rcmd` may only be used by the superuser, since it requires a reserved port. Generally, this means that the program using it must either be executed by "root," or made set-user-id to "root." Obviously, for the average user, this presents a problem. The `rexec` function avoids this problem, to some extent:

```
int rexec(char **ahost, unsigned short inport, char *user,
        char *password, char *cmd, int *fd2p);
```

The usage and parameters of `rexec` are basically the same as those of `rcmd`. However, the `inport` parameter does not have to specify a reserved port, and instead of using *.rhosts*-based authentication, a login name and password for the remote host must be specified. The advantage of `rexec` is that is does not require a privileged port. However, this advantage is lost because a `rexec` now requires a password; it means that programs using `rexec` cannot safely be used in a non-interactive environment since compiling the password into the program would be unsafe.

A server can implement *.rhosts*-based authentication by calling the `ruserok` function:

```
int ruserok(char *rhost, int suser, char *ruser, char *luser);
```

The `rhost` parameter should be the name of the remote host, as returned by `gethostbyaddr`. The `ruser` parameter is the name of the calling user on the remote host, and the `luser` parameter is the name of the user on the local host (the user whose *.rhosts* file should be checked). The `suser` flag should be 1 if the `luser` name is that of the superuser and 0 otherwise; this bypasses the check of the */etc/hosts.equiv* file (which is not used if the local user is the superuser).

The inetd Super-Server

When Berkeley originally developed networking support, each service was served by a separate daemon server process. As the number of services increased, so did the number of daemons. Unfortunately, many of these daemons executed only rarely, since their services were relatively unused. So, the daemon processes sat around all the time consuming system resources and cluttering up the process table, and only rarely did anything useful.

The *inetd* program was created to solve this problem. *inetd* is a super-server. It reads a configuration file (*/etc/inetd.conf*, usually) and then opens a socket for each service listed in the file, and binds it to the appropriate port. When a connection or datagram comes in on one of these ports, *inetd* spawns a child process and executes the daemon responsible for handling that service. In this way, most of the time the only daemon running is *inetd*. All the other daemons run only when they have something to do, thus freeing up system resources.

When a daemon server is invoked via *inetd*, its standard input and output are connected to the socket. When the server reads from standard input, it is actually reading from the network, and when it writes to standard output, it is actually writing to the network. All of the calls to `socket`, `bind`, `accept`, and `listen` described above are unnecessary. The daemon can use the `getpeername` function if it needs to know who (what host) is connecting to it.

Generally speaking, servers should be written to operate out of *inetd*. This is usually more efficient, and it is always much simpler. The only exception to this rule is a server that receives a high volume of connections; the performance cost of having *inetd* fork and spawn a new copy of the server for each connection may outweigh the performance gained by not having another server out there all the time.

Chapter Summary

In this chapter, we examined the Berkeley networking paradigm, called sockets. This paradigm is used throughout the world when writing networking applications for UNIX systems. For the most part, is is portable to just about any version of UNIX, since most vendors simply adopted Berkeley's implementation. The only significant difference between versions are the socket options available via the `getsockopt` and `setsockopt` functions.

Network programming is actually fairly straightforward. The functions are relatively simple to understand, and there are no major "gotchas" to be wary of. For a more complete understanding of UNIX network programming, though, you should examine some of the actual network programs used on the typical UNIX system, such as *ping*, *tftp*, and *rlogin*. Seeing how commands that you use every day are written will help you to better understand just how all these pieces are glued together.

If you would like to conduct this examination on your own, the Berkeley 4.4BSD Lite operating system distribution is widely available on the Internet. It contains the full source code to a number of commonly used UNIX network programs, including *ping*, *rlogin*, *rsh*, *telnet*, *ftp*, *tftp*, *routed*, and *named*. Source code for the Linux, 386BSD, and FreeBSD operating systems is also available on the Internet; these operating systems are based, at least in part, on the Berkeley code, and also make good reference sources.

If you prefer to be guided through the examination, the definitive reference on the topic is W. Richard Stevens' *UNIX Network Programming*, published by Prentice-Hall. Stevens covers the network programming functions in detail, and then reinforces the dicsussion by examining the source code for a number of common UNIX networking programs, including *ping*, *tftp*, *lpr*, *rlogin*, and *rmt*. The discussion of these programs breaks them down almost line by line, explaining what they do. If you plan to be doing a substantial amount of network programming, you'll find this book indispensable.

15

Networking with TLI

Although the socket interface described in Chapter 13, *Interprocess Communication* and Chapter 14, *Networking with Sockets*, is both simple and popular, it is flawed in that it is not protocol-independent. Although sockets can be used with a wide variety of protocols, including UNIX IPC, TCP/IP, ISO/OSI, and XNS, a socket program written to use one of these protocols cannot be used with another protocol unless you change the source code. These changes, although usually minor, mean that it is not possible to have a single program that can simultaneously operate over any of the aforementioned protocols.

The *Transport Layer Interface* (TLI) attempts to solve this problem. The TLI is a library of functions that allow two programs to communicate using a *transport provider*. A transport provider is a device driver or other operating system interface that provides communications support. For example, the TCP/IP protocol support is a transport provider, while support for the Novell IPX protocol is another. The value of the TLI, though, is that, provided the programmer is careful to avoid taking any protocol-dependent actions, a single program written to the TLI can operate over any number of different transport providers without any source code changes. The program doesn't even need to be recompiled when a new transport provider is added.

The TLI library was introduced in System V Release 3. Unfortunately, although AT&T went to the trouble of developing this interface, they neglected to include a transport provider with SVR3, meaning that without purchasing a third-party product, the TLI had nothing to talk to. Until SVR4, which included a TCP/IP transport provider, was released, sockets continued to be the only viable interface for writing network programs. TLI fell by the wayside; it is next to impossible to find any programs, outside of the System V source code, that make use of the TLI.

Even though it is rarely used, the TLI is still worth learning about, especially if you will be supporting or maintaining System V systems. In this chapter, we examine the TLI functions, and discuss some of the differences between them and the socket interface. We will reimplement the examples from Chapter 14 here with TLI; you may find it useful to compare the two implementations.

Between SVR3 and SVR4, a number of improvements were made to the TLI library; most of these changes resulted in adding a network-independent method for handling host and service addresses. These changes were adopted by Sun and Silicon Graphics, and are included in Solaris 2.*x* and IRIX 5.*x*. Hewlett-Packard, on the other hand, for reasons of backward compatibility with their earlier releases, did not adopt these new functions. The TLI library in HP-UX 10.*x* is much more like the TLI library originally provided with SVR3 (and included in earlier versions of HP-UX). In this chapter, we describe the SVR4 TLI library and describe the differences between this and the library used on HP-UX 10.*x*.

All programs that make use of the TLI must be linked with the *-lnsl* library on Solaris 2.*x* and IRIX 5.*x*, and with the *-lnsl_s* library on HP-UX 10.*x*.

The netbuf Structure

Because TLI is protocol-independent, the data structures used by its functions are the same, regardless of the network protocol being used. However, at the transport provider interface, there is no standard for data formats, and indeed, different transport providers use different formats. For example, there is no standard for how a host address is to be represented—TCP/IP uses a 32-bit value, but ISO/OSI uses a 160-bit value.

At some point, TLI functions must deal with these different data formats. However, it must be done in such a manner that the functions are not troubled by the differences. In the socket interface described in the last two chapters, this was handled by using a generic `struct sockaddr` data type, and typecasting the protocol-dependent data structures (`struct sockaddr_un`, `struct sockaddr_in`, etc.) to this generic type. In the TLI, it is handled with a `struct netbuf` structure, defined in the include file *tiuser.h*:

```
struct netbuf {
    unsigned int    maxlen;
    unsigned int    len;
    char            *buf;
}
```

The buf element of the structure contains the data (network address, etc.), and the len element indicates the length, in bytes, of buf. For the cases in which a TLI function fills in a buf provided by the user, the maxlen element indicates the size of the buffer, so that the function does not overflow it.

The struct netbuf structure is used throughout the SVR4 TLI library. It is not available in HP-UX 10.*x.*

Network Selection

The advantage of the TLI is its ability to work, without changes, over different transport providers (network protocols). For example, a program that requires a virtual circuit connection doesn't really care if this connection is made via TCP/IP or ISO/OSI, as long as it can get the job done. When a programmer writes a program with sockets, he must decide which protocol he wants to use, and write the program accordingly. When a programmer writes a program with TLI, however, she only has to decide what type of service she wants—virtual circuit, datagram, etc. The program will work on any system that provides a transport provider (any transport provider) that offers that type of service. (Obviously, for processes on two machines to communicate, both machines must speak the same networking protocol.)

The network selection function in TLI is driven by the */etc/netconfig* file:

```
#
# NetID     Semantics    Flags Proto   Proto Network        Directory Lookup
#                              Family  Name  Device         Libraries
#
udp         tpi_clts     v     inet    udp   /dev/udp       switch.so,tcpip.so
tcp         tpi_cots_ord v     inet    tcp   /dev/tcp       switch.so,tcpip.so
rawip       tpi_raw      -     inet    -     /dev/rawip     switch.so,tcpip.so
ticlts      tpi_clts     v     loopback -    /dev/ticlts    straddr.so
ticotsord   tpi_cots_ord v     loopback -    /dev/ticotsord straddr.so
ticots      tpi_cots     v     loopback -    /dev/ticots    straddr.so
```

This file contains one entry for every network protocol installed on the system. Each entry has seven fields: the first field is a unique name for the network. The second field, called the network "semantics," describes the type of service provided by the network. There are currently four legal values for this field:

`tpi_clts`

Connectionless Transport Service (datagrams).

`tpi_cots`

Connection-Oriented Transport Service (virtual circuits).

`tpi_cots_ord`

Connection-Oriented Transport Service with Orderly Release. This differs from `tpi_cots` in what happens when a connection is terminated. If the transport provider discards any outstanding data (data that has been sent by the local end but not yet delivered over the network to the remote end), it is said to have *abortive release*. If, on the other hand, the transport provider reliably delivers any outstanding data to the other side before tearing down the connection, it is said to have an *orderly release*.

`tpi_raw`

A "raw" (low-level) interface to the networking protocols.

The next field in the entry is a flags word; the only flag currently defined is v, which indicates that the entry is visible to the NETPATH routines, described below. A dash may be used to make a network temporarily (or permanently) invisible to these routines.

The fourth field describes a name for the protocol family; all the Internet protocols, for example, are grouped under the name "inet." The fifth field specifies the name of the protocol itself; a dash may be used if the protocol has no name.

The sixth field provides the pathname of the device to use when accessing the network and the protocol. The last field is a comma-separated list of shared libraries that contain the network protocol's name-to-address translation functions.

There are two sets of functions for reading the */etc/netconfig* file, described in the following sections. Both of them use a `struct netconfig` structure to describe an entry:

```
#include <netconfig.h>

struct netconfig {
    char               *nc_netid;
    unsigned long       nc_semantics;
    unsigned long       nc_flag;
    char               *nc_protofmly;
    char               *nc_proto;
    char               *nc_device;
```

```
    unsigned long      nc_nlookups;
    char               **nc_lookups;
};
```

The `nc_netid`, `nc_protofmly`, `nc_proto`, and `nc_device` elements of the structure contain the network identifier, protocol family, protocol name, and network device name, as described above. The `nc_lookups` element contains the names of the name-to-address translation libraries; `nc_nlookups` indicates how many of these there are. The `nc_semantics` field of the structure contains one of `NC_TPI_CLTS`, `NC_TPI_COTS`, `NC_TPI_COTS_ORD`, or `NC_TPI_RAW`, as described above. The `nc_flag` element will contain either `NC_NOFLAG` or `NC_VISIBLE`.

The network selection functions described in the following two sections are part of the SVR4 TLI implementation, and are not provided in HP-UX 10.*x*.

The Network Configuration Library

The simplest way to read the */etc/netconfig* file is one entry at a time, or by looking for a specific entry by its network identifier. The functions to do this are contained in the network configuration library:

```
#include <netconfig.h>

void *setnetconfig(void);

int endnetconfig(void *handlep);

struct netconfig *getnetconfig(void *handlep);

struct netconfig *getnetconfigent(const char *netid);

void freenetconfigent(struct netconfig *netconfigp);

void nc_perror(const char *msg);

char *nc_sperror(void);
```

The `setnetconfig` function opens or rewinds the */etc/netconfig* file. It returns a pointer to a "handle" that must be used with some of the other functions. The `setnetconfig` function must be called before any calls to `getnetconfig`, but it does not have to be called before `getnetconfigent`. The `endnetconfig` function closes the network configuration database; `handlep` should contain the value returned by a call to `setnetconfig`.

The `getnetconfig` function takes a single argument, `handlep`, which should have the value returned from a call to `setnetconfig`. It returns the next entry in the network configuration database, or NULL when there are no more entries to read. The getnetconfigent function returns the entry whose network identifier is equal to netid, or NULL if no entry is found.

The memory returned by getnetconfig and getnetconfigent is dynamically allocated. The freenetconfigent function can be called to free this memory. Note that a call to endnetconfig will also free the memory allocated by any calls to these functions; care should be taken not to call it before the program is finished with this information.

The nc_perror function can be called when an error is returned by one of the other functions in the library; it prints the string contained in msg on the standard error output, followed by an error message describing the error that occurred. The nc_sperror function returns the error message string rather than printing it.

To make a TLI program portable, call getnetconfig repeatedly looking for any network with the desired semantics. For example, a datagram application might call it as follows:

```
void *handlep;
struct netconfig *ncp;

handlep = setnetconfig();
while ((ncp = getnetconfig(handlep)) != NULL) {
    if (ncp->nc_semantics == NC_TPI_CLTS)
        break;
}

if (ncp == NULL) {
    fprintf(stderr, "cannot find acceptable transport provider.\n");
    exit(1);
}

/* use the network described by ncp */
```

A program that uses getnetconfigent, on the other hand, is by definition not portable across different transport providers, since it is requesting a specific transport provider.

The NETPATH Library

The NETPATH library provides an alternate way to read the */etc/netconfig* file; this method gives the user some control over the networks chosen. To do this, the user sets the NETPATH environment variable to a colon-separated list of network identifiers in the order of preference. For example, if a user prefers TCP over ISO TP4, but prefers ISO TP0 over UDP, she would set her NETPATH environment variable as follows:

```
NETPATH=tcp:iso_tp4:iso_tp0:udp
```

There are three functions in the NETPATH library:

```
#include <netconfig.h>

void *setnetpath(void);

int endnetpath(void *handlep);

struct netconfig *getnetpath(void *handlep);
```

The setnetpath function opens or rewinds the */etc/netconfig* file, and returns a pointer to a "handle" describing the file. It must be called before any calls to get-netpath. The endnetpath function closes the file and releases all allocated resources returned by the routines.

The getnetpath function reads the network configuration file described by handlep, which should be the value returned by a call to setnetpath. However, rather than reading the file sequentially, getnetpath returns the entry for the next valid network identifier contained in the NETPATH environment variable. Thus, regardless of the order in which the networks are listed in the file, getnet-path will always return them in the order given by the environment variable. getnetpath silently ignores invalid or nonexistent network identifiers contained in NETPATH, and returns NULL when it runs out of NETPATH entries.

If the NETPATH variable is not set, then getnetpath returns the list of "default" networks; these are the networks listed as "visible" in the network configuration file. The networks will be returned in the order listed.

The use of the getnetpath function is essentially the same as that described above for getnetconfig: the program calls getnetpath repeatedly until it finds a network with the semantics it wants. However, by ordering the values in the NETPATH environment variable, the user can exert some control over which network is chosen when more than one network with the same semantics exists.

Network Selection in HP-UX 10.x

Network transport selection in HP-UX 10.*x* is performed at compile time, rather than at run time. There is no library of functions to let the programmer choose a network based on type of service requirements; the programmer has to know exactly what she wants and code the name of the network device directly into her program. Thus, a program that is written to use TCP as its connection-oriented transport service would have to be modified to use ISO TP4 instead.

From a technical standpoint, the solution offered by SVR4 is a better one—it is more portable, and can be moved between systems with different networking services with no modifications. From a practical standpoint, however, it probably doesn't matter. Almost every system that is connected to a network at all is connected to a TCP/IP network; thus the program is portable "by default." For those programs that use some other network transport, it's doubtful that they are intended to be portable outside their own local environment anyway.

Name-to-Address Translation

As explained in Chapter 14, host names are a useful way for people to refer to hosts, but network protocols prefer to use addresses. So, as in the case of the socket interface, TLI must provide a way to translate between hosts and addresses, and port names and port numbers:

```
#include <netdir.h>

int netdir_getbyname(const struct netconfig *config,
        const struct nd_hostserv *service,
        struct nd_addrlist **addrs);

int netdir_getbyaddr(const struct netconfig *config,
        struct nd_hostservlist **service,
        const struct netbuf *netaddr);

int netdir_options(const struct netconfig *netconfig,
        const int opt, const int fd, char *argp);

void netdir_free(void *ptr, const int struct_type);

void netdir_perror(char *s);

char *netdir_sperror(void);
```

Rather than treating host addresses and services (port numbers) independently as the socket interface does, TLI views them as integrated. Thus, an *address* is a tuple of (host address, port number).

The `netdir_getbyname` function looks up a host name and service name as given in the `service` argument, which is a pointer to type `struct nd_hostserv`:

```
struct nd_hostserv {
    char    *h_host;
    char    *h_serv;
};
```

The `h_host` field contains the name of the host, and the `h_serv` field contains the name of the service. For services that do not have names (e.g., some arbitrarily selected port number), `h_serv` should point to a character-string representation of the port number. The `h_host` element may contain some special values instead of a host name:

HOST_SELF
> Represents the address by which local programs may refer to the local host. This address is not meaningful outside the local host.

HOST_ANY
> Represents any host accessible by this transport provider. This is equivalent to the `INADDR_ANY` value in the socket interface.

HOST_SELF_CONNECT
> Represents the host address that can be used to connect to the local host.

HOST_BROADCAST
> Represents the address for all hosts reachable by this transport provider. Network requests to this address will be sent to all machines on the network.

The `netdir_getbyname` function returns a list of all valid addresses for the host and service in the `addrs` parameter, which points to an array of structures of type `struct nd_addrlist`:

```
struct nd_addrlist {
    int          n_cnt;
    struct netbuf     *n_addrs;
};
```

Each element of `n_addrs` contains one address; the `n_cnt` element indicates how many addresses there are.

The `netdir_getbyaddr` function looks up a host address and port number, as given in `netaddr`, and returns a list of host and service names in `service`, which is a pointer to an array of type `struct nd_hostservlist`:

```
struct nd_hostservlist {
    int          h_cnt;
    struct nd_hostserv     *h_hostservs;
};
```

Both `netdir_getbyname` and `netdir_getbyaddr` return 0 on success, or non-zero on failure. If they fail, the `netdir_perror` and `netdir_sperror` functions can be used to learn why.

The memory used by these functions can be freed by calling `netdir_free`. The first argument is a pointer to the memory, and the second is a constant indicating the type of structure to be freed:

ND_ADDR

> Free a `struct netbuf` structure.

ND_ADDRLIST

> Free a `struct nd_addrlist` structure.

ND_HOSTSERV

> Free a `struct hostserv` structure.

ND_HOSTSERVLIST

> Free a `struct nd_hostservlist` structure.

The `netdir_options` function allows the programmer to set or check various options on the address he chooses. The `fd` parameter is the transport endpoint, defined later. The `opt` parameter specifies the option, which may be one of the following:

ND_SET_BROADCAST

> If the transport provider supports broadcast, set the program up to send broadcast packets. The `argp` parameter is ignored.

ND_SET_RESERVEDPORT

> If the concept of a reserved port exists for the transport provider, allow the caller to bind a reserved port. If `argp` is NULL, an arbitrary reserved port will be chosen. If `argp` points to a `struct netbuf` structure, an attempt will be made to bind to the reserved port it describes.

ND_CHECK_RESERVEDPORT

> Checks whether or not the address contained in the `struct netbuf` structure pointed to by `argp` is on a reserved port or not.

ND_MERGEADDR

> Converts a "local" address to a "real" address that may be used by other clients. The `argp` parameter should point to a structure of type `struct nd_mergearg`:

```
struct nd_mergearg {
    char     *s_uaddr;
    char     *c_uaddr;
    char     *m_uaddr;
};
```

The `s_uaddr` element should point to the server's (local machine) address, and the `c_uaddr` element should point to the client's (remote machine) address. After the call completes, `m_uaddr` will contain an address that the client can use to contact the server. (It's not really clear that this option is useful for anything, since this information is all available through other means.)

The `netdir_options` function returns 0 on success, non-zero on failure.

The name-to-address translation functions are part of the SVR4 TLI library, and are not available in HP-UX 10.*x*.

Name-to-Address Translation in HP-UX 10.x

As mentioned in the beginning of the chapter, SVR3, where TLI was first introduced, did not provide a network transport. Thus, vendors who adopted SVR3 as their base operating system had to "graft" their existing transport layers onto TLI. Most vendors did this the same way—they made use of the existing data structures and library routines provided by their socket interface (described in Chapter 14), making only minor changes to support the differences between sockets and TLI.

As with network selection, this method of implementing things is inherently less portable. The data structures needed to deal with 32-bit TCP/IP addresses are different from those needed to deal with 160-bit ISO addresses. To make a program written for one transport provider work with another one would require some significant changes. From a practical standpoint, though, it probably doesn't matter. Almost every system that is connected to a network at all is connected to a TCP/IP network, and thus the program is portable "by default." For those programs that use some other network transport, it's doubtful that they are intended to be portable outside their own local environment anyway.

TLI Utility Functions

Three utility functions are frequently used in conjunction with the rest of the TLI library:

```
#include <tiuser.h>

void t_error(const char *errmsg);

char *t_alloc(int fd, int struct_type, int fields);

int t_free(char *ptr, int struct_type);
```

The `t_error` function is used to print error messages when TLI functions fail. TLI functions set the external integer `t_errno` to an error code; `t_error` prints the string contained in `errmsg`, followed by an error message describing the error, to the standard error output. If the failure is due to a system error (as opposed to a library error), `t_error` also prints the system error message.

The `t_alloc` function can be used to allocate structures for use with the rest of the TLI library. The `fd` parameter is the transport endpoint (see below). The `struct_type` parameter specifies the type of structure to be allocated:

`T_BIND`
    Allocate a `struct t_bind` structure.

`T_CALL`
    Allocate a `struct t_call` structure.

`T_DIS`
    Allocate a `struct t_discon` structure.

`T_INFO`
    Allocate a `struct t_info` structure.

`T_OPTMGMT`
    Allocate a `struct t_optmgmt` structure.

`T_UDERROR`
    Allocate a `struct t_uderror` structure.

`T_UNITDATA`
    Allocate a `struct t_unitdata` structure.

With the exception of the `struct t_info` structure, all of these structures contain one or more `struct netbuf` structures. The `fields` parameter is used to specify which, if any, of these buffers should be allocated as well. The `fields` parameter is the logical *or* of any of the following:

`T_ADDR`
    Allocate the `addr` field of the `t_bind`, `tcall`, `t_unitdata`, or `t_uderr` structures.

`T_OPT`
    Allocate the `opt` field of the `t_optmgmt`, `t_call`, `t_unitdata`, or `t_uderr` structures.

`T_UDATA`
    Allocate the `udata` field of the `t_call`, `t_discon`, or `t_unitdata` structures.

`T_ALL`

Allocate all relevant fields of a given structure.

The `t_alloc` function allocates the `buf` portion of the `struct netbuf` structure, and sets the `maxlen` field appropriately. This frees the application from having to know how big a buffer needs to be for any particular purpose. If a structure cannot be allocated, `t_alloc` returns `NULL`. Otherwise, it returns a pointer to the allocated structure.

The `t_free` function frees the structure pointed to by `ptr`, which should have been allocated with `t_alloc`. The `struct_type` parameter specifies the type of structure, as described above for `t_alloc`. If one of the fields of the structure is `NULL`, `t_alloc` will not attempt to free it; in this way, partially allocated structures can be freed.

Transport Endpoint Management

In the socket interface, a socket was used to refer to one end of a communications channel. The socket was simply a file descriptor, and could be used with `read` and `write`, as well as the special-purpose networking functions.

In the TLI, the end of a communications channel is called a *transport endpoint*. A transport endpoint is a file descriptor with some associated state information. Without some special preparations, described later in this chapter, transport endpoints cannot be be used with `read` and `write`; they must instead be accessed through TLI functions.

Creating a Transport Endpoint

To create a transport endpoint, use the `t_open` function:

```
#include <tiuser.h>
#include <fcntl.h>

int t_open(const char *path, int oflag, struct t_info *info);
```

The `path` parameter should be the path to the communications device; this will usually be the `nc_device` field of a `struct netconfig` structure. The `oflag` parameter specifies how the endpoint should be opened; it is specified using the same flags that are used with the `open` system call (see Chapter 3, *Low-Level I/O Routines*) and should include at least `O_RDWR`. The `info` parameter, if non-null, points to a structure of type `struct t_info` into which the characteristics of the underlying transport protocol will be stored. On success, `t_open` returns a valid file descriptor. On failure, it returns -1 and stores the reason for failure in `t_errno` (and perhaps `errno`).

Information about the characteristics of the underlying protocol may be obtained when the transport endpoint is created. It may also be obtained at any other time by using the t_getinfo function:

```
#include <tiuser.h>

int t_getinfo(int fd, struct t_info *info);
```

The fd parameter should refer to a transport endpoint, and info should point to a structure of type struct t_info:

```
struct t_info {
    long    addr;
    long    options;
    long    tsdu;
    long    etsdu;
    long    connect;
    long    discon;
    long    servtype;
};
```

The fields of this structure have the following meanings:

addr

> The maximum size of a transport protocol address; a value of -1 indicates that there is no maximum, and a value of -2 indicates that the user does not have access to transport protocol addresses.

options

> The maximum number of bytes of protocol-specific options supported by the provider; a value of -1 indcates that there is no maximum, and a value of -2 indicates that the transport provider does not support user-settable options.

tsdu

> The maximum size of a Transport Service Data Unit (TSDU). This is the maximum amount of data whose message boundaries are preserved from one transport endpoint to another. A value of 0 indicates that the transport provider does not support the concept of a TSDU, although it does support transferring data across a stream with no logical boundaries. A value of -1 indicates that there is no limit on the size of a TSDU; a value of -2 indicates that the transport provider does not support the transfer of normal data.

etsdu

> The maximum size of an Expedited Transport Service Data Unit (ETSDU), with the same meanings as for the TSDU. Expedited data is delivered immediately, without waiting for the delivery of previously-sent normal data. (The socket interface term for this is out-of-band data.)

`connect`

> The maximum amount of data that can be sent along with a connection request; -1 indicates there is no limit, and -2 indicates that data may not be sent with connection establishment functions.

`discon`

> The maximum amount of data that can be associated with the `t_snddis` and `t_rcvdis` functions. A value of -1 indicates no limit; a value of -2 indicates that data may not be sent with these functions.

`srvtype`

> The type of service supported by the transport provider; may be one of the following:

> `T_COTS`
>
> > Connection-oriented service, but without orderly release.

> `T_COTS_ORD`
>
> > Connection-oriented service with orderly release.

> `T_CLTS`
>
> > Connectionless service. For this type of service, `etdsu`, `connect`, and `discon` will contain -2.

On success, `t_getinfo` returns 0. On failure, it returns -1, and `t_errno` (and possibly `errno`) will be set to indicate the error.

Binding an Address to a Transport Endpoint

Before a transport endpoint can be used, it must be bound to an address. Unlike the socket interface, in which a client program only needs to bind its socket to an address if it wants to use a specific port number, TLI requires both the client and server processes to bind addresses to their transport endpoints.

An address is described by a structure of type `struct t_bind`:

```
struct t_bind {
    struct netbuf    addr;
    unsigned int     qlen;
};
```

The `addr` field contains the address to be bound, and the `qlen` field specifies the maximum number of outstanding connection requests a server will allow on the endpoint.

The `t_bind` function binds an address to a transport endpoint:

```
#include <tiuser.h>

int t_bind(int fd, struct t_bind *reqp, struct t_bind *retp);
```

The `fd` parameter is the transport endpoint. The `reqp` parameter specifies the requested address, and the `retp` parameter, if non-null, points to a location in which the actual address that is bound will be stored.

Notice that the actual address bound by `t_bind` may be different than the requested address; this occurs if an address is already in use. In the case of servers, which usually have to live at specific addresses, the benefit of this behavior is not clear. It would probably make more sense to just refuse to bind the address, and return an "address in use" error, like the socket interface does. At any rate, after performing the `t_bind`, a process that cares about the address to which it is bound should check to see that the address in `retp` is the same as that in `reqp`.

If `reqp` is `NULL`, the system will assume that the user doesn't care what address is used, and the system will choose an appropriate one. This is usually the case with client programs (except for those that use reserved ports).

On success, `t_bind` returns 0. On failure, it returns -1 and `t_errno` (and perhaps `errno`) will be set to indicate the error.

Closing a Transport Endpoint

The `t_unbind` function disables a transport endpoint:

```
#include <tiuser.h>

int t_unbind(int fd);
```

Upon return, the endpoint may no longer be used to transfer data. The endpoint may be bound to another address at this time. The `t_unbind` function returns 0 on success, or -1 on failure. If a failure occurs, the error indication will be stored in `t_errno` (and perhaps `errno`).

The `t_close` function closes a transport endpoint:

```
#include <tiuser.h>

int t_close(int fd);
```

This function should be called when the endpoint is in an unbound state (after a call to `t_unbind`), but can also be called when the endpoint is in any state. It frees any local library resources used by the endpoint, and closes the file descriptor. On success, `t_close` returns 0; on failure it returns -1 and stores the reason for failure in `t_errno` (and perhaps `errno`).

Transport Endpoint Options

Some transport providers let the user control certain protocol options. To examine and change these options, TLI provides the `t_optmgmt` function:

```
#include <tiuser.h>

int t_optmgmt(int fd, const struct t_optmgmt *req,
        struct t_optmgmt *ret);
```

The `fd` parameter is a bound transport endpoint. The `req` and `ret` parameters point to structures of type `struct t_optmgmt`:

```
struct t_optmgmt {
    struct netbuf    opt;
    long             flags;
};
```

The `opt` field contains the options (in `req`, `len` contains the number of bytes in the options string, and `buf` contains the options; in `ret`, `maxlen` contains the maximum size of `buf`). The `flags` field specifies the action to be taken with the following options:

T_NEGOTIATE

Negotiate the values of the options specified in `req` with the transport provider. The provider will examine the options and negotiate the values, and return the negotiated values through `ret`.

T_CHECK

Check whether the options specified in `req` are supported by the transport provider. On return, the `flags` field of `ret` will contain either `T_SUCCESS` or `T_FAILURE`.

T_DEFAULT

Retrieve the default options supported by the transport provider into `ret`. When making this call, the `len` field in `req` must be zero.

The actual structure and content of the options are imposed by the transport provider.

If `t_optmgmt` succeeds, it returns 0. If it fails, it returns -1, and places an error code in `t_errno` (and perhaps `errno`).

Connectionless Service

Connectionless (datagram) service is the simplest of the two types of communication that can be performed with the TLI. After the client and server have created their transport endpoints and bound them to addresses, they can exchange data using the t_sndudata and t_rcvudata functions:

```
#include <tiuser.h>

int t_sndudata(int fd, struct t_unitdata *data);

int t_rcvudata(int fd, struct t_unitdata *data, int *flags);
```

In both functions, fd is a transport endpoint, and data points to a structure of type struct t_unitdata:

```
struct t_unitdata {
    struct netbuf    addr;
    struct netbuf    opt;
    struct netbuf    udata;
};
```

In this structure, addr is the address to which the data is to be sent or from which it was received, opt contains any protocol-specific options associated with the data, and udata contains the data that was transferred. Notice that the maxlen field of all three of these structures must be set before calling t_rcvudata.

The flags parameter to t_rcvudata should point at an area in which flags can be set. This area should be initialized to 0. The only flag currently defined is T_MORE, which will be set if the size of the udata buffer is not large enough to retrieve all the available data. Subsequent calls to t_rcvudata can be used to retrieve the remaining data.

The t_sndudata and t_rcvudata functions return 0 on success, and -1 on failure. If a failure occurs, an error code will be stored in t_errno (and perhaps errno).

Some errors that occur when a program is receiving data interrupt the flow of data. In connectionless mode, the only error that does this is the failure of a previous attempt to send data with t_sndudata. If t_rcvudata fails and sets t_errno to TLOOK, the application must call t_rcvuderr to clear the error:

```
#include <tiuser.h>

int t_rcvuderr(int fd, struct t_uderr *uderr);
```

The struct t_uderr structure is defined as:

```
struct t_uderr {
    struct netbuf       addr;
    struct netbuf       opt;
    long                error;
};
```

The `maxlen` field of `addr` and `opt` must be set before the call. On return, `addr` will contain the address of the failed transmission, `opt` will contain any options associated with the transmission, and `error` will contain an implementation-dependent error code.

One has to wonder why, when using an inherently unreliable service in which datagrams may be lost or discarded, TLI's designers decided it was necessary to inform the user of this particular error condition (but not of others). There is little that can be done about it (since no indication of which datagram failed is provided, no retransmission can be done), and it complicates the implementation of connectionless service.

Example 15-1 shows a reimplementation of Example 14-3 using SVR4 TLI. This program contacts the "daytime" service, an Internet standard service that returns the local time as an ASCII string.

Example 15-1: daytime

```
#include <netconfig.h>
#include <netdir.h>
#include <tiuser.h>
#include <string.h>
#include <fcntl.h>
#include <stdio.h>

#define SERVICENAME "daytime"

extern int t_errno;

int
main(int argc, char **argv)
{
    int fd, flags;
    struct netconfig *ncp;
    struct nd_hostserv ndh;
    struct t_unitdata *udp;
    struct nd_addrlist *nal;

    if (argc < 2) {
        fprintf(stderr, "Usage: %s hostname [hostname...]\n", *argv);
        exit(1);
    }

    /*
     * Select the UDP transport provider.
     */
```

Example 15-1: daytime (continued)

```
    if ((ncp = getnetconfigent("udp")) == NULL) {
        nc_perror("udp");
        exit(1);
    }

    while (--argc) {
        ndh.h_host = *++argv;
        ndh.h_serv = SERVICENAME;

        /*
         * Get a host and service address for this host.
         */
        if (netdir_getbyname(ncp, &ndh, &nal) != 0) {
            netdir_perror(*argv);
            exit(1);
        }

        /*
         * Create a transport endpoint.
         */
        if ((fd = t_open(ncp->nc_device, O_RDWR, NULL)) < 0) {
            t_error("t_open");
            exit(1);
        }

        /*
         * Bind an arbitrary address to the transport
         * endpoint.
         */
        if (t_bind(fd, NULL, NULL) < 0) {
            t_error("t_bind");
            exit(1);
        }

        /*
         * Allocate a datagram.
         */
        udp = (struct t_unitdata *) t_alloc(fd, T_UNITDATA, T_ALL);

        if (udp == NULL) {
            t_error("t_alloc");
            exit(1);
        }

        /*
         * Construct the datagram.
         */
        memcpy(&udp->addr, &nal->n_addrs[0], sizeof(struct netbuf));
        udp->udata.len = 1;

        /*
         * Send a packet to the server.
```

Example 15-1: daytime (continued)

```
        */
       if (t_sndudata(fd, udp) < 0) {
           t_error("t_sndudata");
           exit(1);
       }

       /*
        * Receive a packet back.
        */
       if (t_rcvudata(fd, udp, &flags) < 0) {
           if (t_errno == TLOOK) {
               if (t_rcvuderr(fd, NULL) < 0) {
                   t_error("t_rcvuderr");
                   exit(1);
               }
           }
           else {
               t_error("t_rcvudata");
               exit(1);
           }
       }

       /*
        * Print the packet.
        */
       udp->udata.buf[udp->udata.len] = '\0';
       printf("%s: %s", *argv, udp->udata.buf);

       /*
        * Shut down the connection.
        */
       t_unbind(fd);
       t_close(fd);
   }

   exit(0);
}


   % daytime localhost
   localhost: Mon Mar 20 15:50:54 1995
```

Example 15-2 shows the same program as it is implemented in HP-UX 10.*x*. The primary differences are as follows:

1. Rather than using `netdir_getbyname` to obtain a host/service address, `getservbyname` is used to get the service address (port number), and `gethostbyname` is used to get the host address. These functions are described in Chapter 14.

2. Rather than using `getnetconfigent` to obtain the name of a suitable network device for use with `t_open`, the device name is specified in the source
   code. In this case, */dev/inet_clts* provides a connectionless transport service
   using the Internet protocol suite (TCP/IP).

3. Instead of using a transport-independent `struct nd_addrlist` structure
   for handling network addresses, a `struct sockaddr_in` structure (specific
   to the Internet protocol domain) is used. Creating the host and service address
   for the host is similar to what we did when using the socket interface.

Example 15–2: daytime

```c
#include <sys/types.h>
#include <sys/socket.h>
#include <netinet/in.h>
#include <tiuser.h>
#include <string.h>
#include <netdb.h>
#include <fcntl.h>
#include <stdio.h>

#define SERVICENAME "daytime"

extern int t_errno;

int
main(int argc, char **argv)
{
    int fd, flags;
    struct hostent *hp;
    struct servent *sp;
    struct t_unitdata *udp;
    struct nd_addrlist *nal;
    struct sockaddr_in rem_addr;

    if (argc < 2) {
        fprintf(stderr, "Usage: %s hostname [hostname...]\n", *argv);
        exit(1);
    }

    if ((sp = getservbyname(SERVICENAME, "udp")) == NULL) {
        fprintf(stderr, "%s/udp: unknown service\n", SERVICENAME);
        exit(1);
    }

    while (--argc) {
        if ((hp = gethostbyname(*++argv)) == NULL) {
            fprintf(stderr, "%s: unknown host\n", *argv);
            continue;
        }

        /*
         * Create a transport endpoint.
```

Example 15-2: daytime (continued)

```
    */
    if ((fd = t_open("/dev/inet_clts", O_RDWR, NULL)) < 0) {
        t_error("t_open");
        exit(1);
    }

    /*
     * Bind an arbitrary address to the transport
     * endpoint.
     */
    if (t_bind(fd, NULL, NULL) < 0) {
        t_error("t_bind");
        exit(1);
    }

    /*
     * Allocate a datagram.
     */
    udp = (struct t_unitdata *) t_alloc(fd, T_UNITDATA, T_ALL);

    if (udp == NULL) {
        t_error("t_alloc");
        exit(1);
    }

    /*
     * Create a host and service address for our host.
     */
    memset((char *) &rem_addr, 0, sizeof(struct sockaddr_in));
    memcpy((char *) &rem_addr.sin_addr.s_addr, (char *) hp->h_addr,
            hp->h_length);
    rem_addr.sin_port = sp->s_port;
    rem_addr.sin_family = AF_INET;

    /*
     * Construct the datagram.
     */
    udp->addr.maxlen = sizeof(struct sockaddr_in);
    udp->addr.len = sizeof(struct sockaddr_in);
    udp->addr.buf = (char *) &rem_addr;
    udp->opt.buf = (char *) 0;
    udp->opt.maxlen = 0;
    udp->opt.len = 0;
    udp->udata.len = 1;

    /*
     * Send a packet to the server.
     */
    if (t_sndudata(fd, udp) < 0) {
        t_error("t_sndudata");
        exit(1);
    }
```

Example 15-2: daytime (continued)

```
        /*
         * Receive a packet back.
         */
        if (t_rcvudata(fd, udp, &flags) < 0) {
            if (t_errno == TLOOK) {
                if (t_rcvuderr(fd, NULL) < 0) {
                    t_error("t_rcvuderr");
                    exit(1);
                }
            }
            else {
                t_error("t_rcvudata");
                exit(1);
            }
        }

        /*
         * Print the packet.
         */
        udp->udata.buf[udp->udata.len] = '\0';
        printf("%s: %s", *argv, udp->udata.buf);

        /*
         * Shut down the connection.
         */
        t_unbind(fd);
        t_close(fd);
    }

    exit(0);
}
```

Connection-Oriented Service

Connection-oriented service is more complicated than connectionless service, just
as it was for the socket interface.

Server-Side Functions

To be a server, a process must inform the operating system that it wishes to
receive connections, and then process those connection requests as they come in.

Waiting for connections

Unlike the socket interface, in which the server calls listen once and then loops
on calls to accept to be notified of incoming connections, in TLI the server loops
on calls to t_listen:

```
#include <tiuser.h>

int t_listen(int fd, struct t_call *call);
```

This function will block until a connection request arrives on the transport endpoint referenced by `fd`. When a connection request arrives, a description of the request will be placed in `call`, a pointer to a structure of type `struct t_call`:

```
struct t_call {
    struct netbuf     addr;
    struct netbuf     opt;
    struct netbuf     udata;
    int               sequence;
};
```

The `maxlen` field of `addr`, `opt`, and `udata` must be set before the call to `t_listen`. On return, `addr` will contain the address of the caller, `opt` will contain any protocol-specific options associated with the request, and `udata` will contain any data sent by the caller in the connection request (if the transport provider supports this). The `sequence` field will uniquely identify the connection request, allowing a server to listen for multiple connection requests before responding to any of them.

On success, `t_listen` returns 0. If a failure occurs, it returns -1 and the error indication is stored in `t_errno` (and perhaps `errno`).

Accepting and rejecting connections

Once a connection request has been received via `t_listen`, the server can either accept or reject that request. To accept the request, the server calls the `t_accept` function:

```
#include <tiuser.h>

int t_accept(int fd, int resfd, struct t_call *call);
```

The `fd` parameter refers to the transport endpoint, and the `call` parameter should be a pointer to the `struct t_call` structure returned by `t_listen`.

If `resfd` is equal to `fd`, the connection will be accepted on the same transport endpoint from which it arrived. This is permissible only when there are no outstanding connection indications on the endpoint that have not been responded to. If `resfd` is not equal to `fd`, it should refer to another bound endpoint that will be used to accept the connection. This allows the server to continue to receive connection requests on the original endpoint (which is the desired behavior for servers using well-known ports).

To reject a connection request, the server uses the `t_snddis` function:

```
#include <tiuser.h>

int t_snddis(int fd, struct t_call *call);
```

The `fd` parameter is the transport endpoint, and `call` should point to the `struct t_call` structure returned by `t_listen`.

Both `t_accept` and `t_snddis` return 0 on success, and -1 on failure. If an error occurs, its indication will be placed in `t_errno` (and perhaps `errno`).

Client-Side Functions

Before it can transfer data, a client program must connect to the server. To do this, it uses the `t_connect` function:

```
#include <tiuser.h>

int t_connect(int fd, struct t_call *sndcall,
        struct t_call *rcvcall);
```

The `fd` parameter refers to a bound transport endpoint. The `sndcall` and `rcvcall` parameters point to structures of type `t_call` (see above).

In `sndcall`, `addr` is the address of the server to connect to, `opt` contains any protocol-specific options, and `udata` may contain data to be transmitted along with the connection request if the transport provider supports this.

In `rcvcall`, the `maxlen` field of the `struct netbuf` structures must be set before the call. On return, the `addr` field will contain the address of the remote end of the connection, `opt` will contain any protocol-specific options, and `udata` will contain any data returned with the connection establishment or rejection. If `rcvcall` is NULL, no information will be returned.

If the connection request is rejected by the server, `t_connect` will fail with `t_errno` set to TLOOK. In this case, the client should then call `t_rcvdis`:

```
#include <tiuser.h>

int t_rcvdis(int fd, struct t_discon *discon);
```

The `fd` parameter specifies the transport endpoint, and the `discon` parameter points to a structure of type `struct t_discon`, which will contain the reason for rejection:

```
struct t_discon {
    struct netbuf    udata;
    int              reason;
```

```
    int           sequence;
};
```

The `udata` field will contain any data sent by the server along with the rejection. The `reason` parameter specifies an implementation-specific reason for the rejection, and `sequence` is unused in this case. If the client is not interested in the reason for rejection it can specify `discon` as `NULL`, but it must still make the call to `t_rcvdis`.

Both `t_connect` and `t_rcvdis` return 0 on success, and -1 on failure. If the operation fails, `t_errno` (and perhaps `errno`) will contain the error indication.

Transferring Data

Once a connection has been established, the client and server can exchange data using the `t_snd` and `t_rcv` functions:

```
#include <tiuser.h>

int t_snd(int fd, char *buf, unsigned nbytes, int flags);

int t_rcv(int fd, char *buf, unsigned nbytes, int *flags);
```

In both cases, `fd` is the transport endpoint. In `t_snd`, `buf` is the data to be transferred, and `nbytes` is the number of bytes to be transferred. In `t_rcv`, `buf` is the buffer in which to store received data, and `nbytes` specifies the size of the buffer.

In `t_snd`, the `flags` parameter specifies the following options on the send:

T_EXPEDITED
Send the data as expedited (out-of-band) data instead of as normal data.

T_MORE
The current TSDU is being sent in multiple `t_snd` calls. Each call with `T_MORE` set appends to the current TSDU; when a send without this flag is executed, the TSDU is sent.

In `t_rcv`, `flags` points to a flags word that will be modified to contain any flags from the call to `t_snd`.

On successful completion, `t_snd` and `t_rcv` return the number of bytes sent or received. On failure, they return -1 and store the error indication in `t_errno` (and perhaps `errno`).

Connection Release

If the connection supports orderly release, the server and client must negotiate the orderly release of the connection. This is done with the t_sndrel and t_rcvrel functions:

```
#include <tiuser.h>

int t_sndrel(int fd);

int t_rcvrel(int fd);
```

When the client or server has nothing more to send, it should call t_sndrel. When the client or server receives the notification of this (see below), it should call t_rcvrel to acknowledge its receipt. To shut down the connection completely in both directions, both sides should eventually call both of these functions.

Both of these functions return 0 on success, and -1 on failure. If they fail, an error indication will be stored in t_errno (and perhaps errno).

Examples 15-3 and 15-4 show reimplementations of the client and server programs from Examples 14-1 and 14-2 using TLI. These two programs exchange data using a virtual circuit.

Example 15–3: server

```
#include <sys/types.h>
#include <sys/socket.h>
#include <netinet/in.h>
#include <netconfig.h>
#include <tiuser.h>
#include <netdir.h>
#include <string.h>
#include <fcntl.h>
#include <stdio.h>

#define PORTNUMBER  12345

extern int t_errno;

int
main(void)
{
    int n, fd, flags;
    struct t_call *callp;
    struct netconfig *ncp;
    struct nd_hostserv ndh;
    struct nd_addrlist *nal;
    struct t_bind *reqp, *retp;
    char buf[1024], hostname[64];
```

Example 15-3: server (continued)

```
/*
 * Get our local host name.
 */
if (gethostname(hostname, sizeof(hostname)) < 0) {
    perror("gethostname");
    exit(1);
}

/*
 * Select the TCP transport provider.
 */
if ((ncp = getnetconfigent("tcp")) == NULL) {
    nc_perror("tcp");
    exit(1);
}

/*
 * Get a host and service address for our host.  Since our
 * port number is not registered in the services file, we
 * send down the ASCII string representation of it.
 */
sprintf(buf, "%d", PORTNUMBER);
ndh.h_host = hostname;
ndh.h_serv = buf;

if (netdir_getbyname(ncp, &ndh, &nal) != 0) {
    netdir_perror(hostname);
    exit(1);
}

/*
 * Create a transport endpoint.
 */
if ((fd = t_open(ncp->nc_device, O_RDWR, NULL)) < 0) {
    t_error("t_open");
    exit(1);
}

/*
 * Bind the address to the transport endpoint.
 */
retp = (struct t_bind *) t_alloc(fd, T_BIND, T_ADDR);
reqp = (struct t_bind *) t_alloc(fd, T_BIND, T_ADDR);

if (reqp == NULL || retp == NULL) {
    t_error("t_alloc");
    exit(1);
}

memcpy(&reqp->addr, &nal->n_addrs[0], sizeof(struct netbuf));
reqp->qlen = 5;
```

Example 15–3: server (continued)

```
    if (t_bind(fd, reqp, retp) < 0) {
        t_error("t_bind");
        exit(1);
    }

    if (retp->addr.len != nal->n_addrs[0].len ||
        memcmp(retp->addr.buf, nal->n_addrs[0].buf, retp->addr.len) != 0) {
        fprintf(stderr, "did not bind requested address.\n");
        exit(1);
    }

    /*
     * Allocate a call structure.
     */
    callp = (struct t_call *) t_alloc(fd, T_CALL, T_ALL);

    if (callp == NULL) {
        t_error("t_alloc");
        exit(1);
    }

    /*
     * Listen for a connection.
     */
    if (t_listen(fd, callp) < 0) {
        t_error("t_listen");
        exit(1);
    }

    /*
     * Accept a connect on the same file descriptor used for listening.
     */
    if (t_accept(fd, fd, callp) < 0) {
        t_error("t_accept");
        exit(1);
    }

    /*
     * Read from the network until end-of-file and
     * print what we get on the standard output.
     */
    while ((n = t_rcv(fd, buf, sizeof(buf), &flags)) > 0)
        write(1, buf, n);

    /*
     * Release the connection.
     */
    t_rcvrel(fd);
    t_sndrel(fd);

    t_unbind(fd);
    t_close(fd);
```

Example 15-3: server (continued)

```
    exit(0);
}
```

Example 15-4: client

```c
#include <sys/types.h>
#include <sys/socket.h>
#include <netinet/in.h>
#include <netconfig.h>
#include <tiuser.h>
#include <netdir.h>
#include <string.h>
#include <fcntl.h>
#include <stdio.h>

#define PORTNUMBER  12345

extern int t_errno;

int
main(void)
{
    int n, fd;
    struct t_call *callp;
    struct netconfig *ncp;
    struct nd_hostserv ndh;
    struct nd_addrlist *nal;
    char buf[32], hostname[64];

    /*
     * Get our local host name.
     */
    if (gethostname(hostname, sizeof(hostname)) < 0) {
        perror("gethostname");
        exit(1);
    }

    /*
     * Select the TCP transport provider.
     */
    if ((ncp = getnetconfigent("tcp")) == NULL) {
        nc_perror("tcp");
        exit(1);
    }

    /*
     * Get a host and service address for our host.  Since our
     * port number is not registered in the services file, we
     * send down the ASCII string representation of it.
     */
    sprintf(buf, "%d", PORTNUMBER);
```

Example 15-4: client (continued)

```
ndh.h_host = hostname;
ndh.h_serv = buf;

if (netdir_getbyname(ncp, &ndh, &nal) != 0) {
    netdir_perror(hostname);
    exit(1);
}

/*
 * Create a transport endpoint.
 */
if ((fd = t_open(ncp->nc_device, O_RDWR, NULL)) < 0) {
    t_error("t_open");
    exit(1);
}

/*
 * Bind an arbitrary address to the transport
 * endpoint.
 */
if (t_bind(fd, NULL, NULL) < 0) {
    t_error("t_bind");
    exit(1);
}

/*
 * Allocate a connection structure.
 */
callp = (struct t_call *) t_alloc(fd, T_CALL, 0);

if (callp == NULL) {
    t_error("t_alloc");
    exit(1);
}

/*
 * Construct the connection request.
 */
memcpy(&callp->addr, &nal->n_addrs[0], sizeof(struct netbuf));

/*
 * Connect to the server.
 */
if (t_connect(fd, callp, NULL) < 0) {
    if (t_errno == TLOOK) {
        if (t_rcvdis(fd, NULL) < 0) {
            t_error("t_rcvdis");
            exit(1);
        }
    }
    else {
        t_error("t_connect");
```

Example 15-4: client (continued)

```
            exit(1);
        }
    }



    /*
     * Read from standard input, and copy the
     * data to the network.
     */
    while ((n = read(0, buf, sizeof(buf))) > 0) {
        if (t_snd(fd, buf, n, 0) < 0) {
            t_error("t_snd");
            exit(1);
        }
    }

    /*
     * Release the connection.
     */
    t_sndrel(fd);
    t_rcvrel(fd);

    t_unbind(fd);
    t_close(fd);
    exit(0);
}


% server &
% client < /etc/motd
Sun Microsystems Inc.  SunOS 5.3       Generic September 1993
```

Examples 15-5 and 15-6 show the same programs as they are implemented in HP-UX 10.*x*. The primary differences are as follows:

1. The function `gethostbyname` is used rather than `netdir_getbyname` to get the host address, and the port number is already known. The `gethostbyname` function is described in Chapter 14.

2. Rather than using `getnetconfigent` to obtain the name of a suitable network device for use with `t_open`, the device name is specified in the source code. In this case, */dev/inet_cots* provides a connection-oriented transport service using the Internet protocol suite (TCP/IP).

3. Instead of using a transport-independent `struct nd_addrlist` structure for handling network addresses, a `struct sockaddr_in` structure (specific to the Internet protocol domain) is used. Creating the host and service address for the host is the same as with the socket interface.

Example 15-5: server

```c
#include <sys/types.h>
#include <sys/socket.h>
#include <netinet/in.h>
#include <tiuser.h>
#include <string.h>
#include <fcntl.h>
#include <stdio.h>

#define PORTNUMBER  12345

extern int t_errno;

int
main(void)
{
    int n, fd, flags;
    struct t_call *callp;
    struct t_bind *reqp, *retp;
    struct sockaddr_in loc_addr;
    char buf[1024], hostname[64];

    /*
     * Get our local host name.
     */
    if (gethostname(hostname, sizeof(hostname)) < 0) {
        perror("gethostname");
        exit(1);
    }

    /*
     * Create a host and service address for our host.
     */
    memset((char *) &loc_addr, 0, sizeof(struct sockaddr_in));
    loc_addr.sin_addr.s_addr = htonl(INADDR_ANY);
    loc_addr.sin_port = htons(PORTNUMBER);
    loc_addr.sin_family = AF_INET;

    /*
     * Create a transport endpoint.
     */
    if ((fd = t_open("/dev/inet_cots", O_RDWR, NULL)) < 0) {
        t_error("t_open");
        exit(1);
    }

    /*
     * Bind the address to the transport endpoint.
     */
    retp = (struct t_bind *) t_alloc(fd, T_BIND, T_ADDR);
    reqp = (struct t_bind *) t_alloc(fd, T_BIND, T_ADDR);

    if (reqp == NULL || retp == NULL) {
```

Example 15-5: server (continued)

```
        t_error("t_alloc");
        exit(1);
}

reqp->addr.maxlen = sizeof(struct sockaddr_in);
reqp->addr.len = sizeof(struct sockaddr_in);
reqp->addr.buf = (char *) &loc_addr;
reqp->qlen = 5;

if (t_bind(fd, reqp, retp) < 0) {
    t_error("t_bind");
    exit(1);
}

if (retp->addr.len != reqp->addr.len ||
    memcmp(retp->addr.buf, reqp->addr.buf, retp->addr.len) != 0) {
    fprintf(stderr, "did not bind requested address.\n");
    exit(1);
}

/*
 * Allocate a call structure.
 */
callp = (struct t_call *) t_alloc(fd, T_CALL, T_ALL);

if (callp == NULL) {
    t_error("t_alloc");
    exit(1);
}

/*
 * Listen for a connection.
 */
if (t_listen(fd, callp) < 0) {
    t_error("t_listen");
    exit(1);
}

/*
 * Accept a connect on the same file descriptor used for listening.
 */
if (t_accept(fd, fd, callp) < 0) {
    t_error("t_accept");
    exit(1);
}

/*
 * Read from the network until end-of-file and
 * print what we get on the standard output.
 */
while ((n = t_rcv(fd, buf, sizeof(buf), &flags)) > 0)
    write(1, buf, n);
```

Example 15-5: server (continued)

```
    /*
     * Release the connection.
     */
    t_rcvrel(fd);
    t_sndrel(fd);

    t_unbind(fd);
    t_close(fd);
    exit(0);
}
```

Example 15-6: client

```c
#include <sys/types.h>
#include <sys/socket.h>
#include <netinet/in.h>
#include <tiuser.h>
#include <string.h>
#include <netdb.h>
#include <fcntl.h>
#include <stdio.h>

#define PORTNUMBER  12345

extern int t_errno;

int
main(void)
{
    int n, fd;
    struct hostent *hp;
    struct t_call *callp;
    char buf[32], hostname[64];
    struct sockaddr_in rem_addr;

    /*
     * Get our local host name.
     */
    if (gethostname(hostname, sizeof(hostname)) < 0) {
        perror("gethostname");
        exit(1);
    }

    /*
     * Get the address of our host.
     */
    if ((hp = gethostbyname(hostname)) == NULL) {
        fprintf(stderr, "Cannot find address for %s\n", hostname);
        exit(1);
    }
```

Example 15-6: client (continued)

```
/*
 * Create a host and service address for our host.
 */
memset((char *) &rem_addr, 0, sizeof(struct sockaddr_in));
memcpy((char *) &rem_addr.sin_addr.s_addr, (char *) hp->h_addr,
        hp->h_length);
rem_addr.sin_port = htons(PORTNUMBER);
rem_addr.sin_family = AF_INET;

/*
 * Create a transport endpoint.
 */
if ((fd = t_open("/dev/inet_cots", O_RDWR, NULL)) < 0) {
    t_error("t_open");
    exit(1);
}

 /*
  * Bind an arbitrary address to the transport
  * endpoint.
  */
 if (t_bind(fd, NULL, NULL) < 0) {
    t_error("t_bind");
    exit(1);
 }

/*
 * Allocate a connection structure.
 */
callp = (struct t_call *) t_alloc(fd, T_CALL, T_ADDR);

if (callp == NULL) {
    t_error("t_alloc");
    exit(1);
}

/*
 * Construct the connection request.
 */
callp->addr.maxlen = sizeof(struct sockaddr_in);
callp->addr.len = sizeof(struct sockaddr_in);
callp->addr.buf = (char *) &rem_addr;
callp->udata.len = 0;
callp->opt.len = 0;

/*
 * Connect to the server.
 */
if (t_connect(fd, callp, NULL) < 0) {
    if (t_errno == TLOOK) {
        if (t_rcvdis(fd, NULL) < 0) {
            t_error("t_rcvdis");
```

Example 15-6: client (continued)

```
                exit(1);
            }
        }
        else {
            t_error("t_connect");
            exit(1);
        }
    }


    /*
     * Read from standard input, and copy the
     * data to the network.
     */
    while ((n = read(0, buf, sizeof(buf))) > 0) {
        if (t_snd(fd, buf, n, 0) < 0) {
            t_error("t_snd");
            exit(1);
        }
    }

    /*
     * Release the connection.
     */
    t_sndrel(fd);
    t_rcvrel(fd);

    t_unbind(fd);
    t_close(fd);
    exit(0);
}
```

Other Functions

Other useful functions provided in the TLI are described below.

Transport Endpoint Names

The t_getname function is used to obtain the address bound to the local or remote side of a connection. (Through an oversight, this function is not documented in SVR4.)

```
#include <tiuser.h>

int t_getname(int fd, struct netbuf *namep, int type);
```

The fd parameter is the transport endpoint. In the **struct netbuf** structure pointed to by **namep**, the **buf** and **maxlen** fields should be set accordingly. The **type** parameter may take on one of two values:

LOCALNAME

Return the address bound to the local transport endpoint.

REMOTENAME

Return the address bound to the remote transport endpoint.

The `t_getname` function returns 0 on success, and -1 on failure. If it fails, `t_errno` (and perhaps `errno`) will contain the error indication.

Connection State

The `t_getstate` function is used to obtain the current state of a transport endpoint:

```
#include <tiuser.h>

int t_getstate(int fd);
```

This function returns -1 if an error occurs and places the error indication in `t_errno` (and perhaps `errno`). On success, it returns one of the following constants, describing the state of the endpoint:

T_UNBND

The transport endpoint is not bound to an address.

T_IDLE

The transport endpoint is bound to an address, but is not connected to anything.

T_OUTCON

An outgoing connection request is pending on the endpoint.

T_INCON

An incoming connection request is pending on the endpoint.

T_DATAXFER

The endpoint is currently transferring data.

T_OUTREL

An orderly release has been sent on the endpoint.

T_INREL

An orderly release has been received on the endpoint.

One problem with the TLI is that the library state is lost after a call to `exec`. This makes it impossible to use the `t_getstate` function. To fix this, the `t_sync` function can be called to restore the library state:

```
#include <tiuser.h>

int t_sync(int fd);
```

On success, the current state as defined above is returned. On failure, -1 is returned and `t_errno` (and perhaps `errno`) will contain the error indication.

Asynchronous Events

A number of asynchronous events can occur on the communications channel that will cause TLI functions to return errors. Whenever they do, examine `t_errno`. If its value is TLOOK, then the `t_look` function should be called:

```
#include <tiuser.h>

int t_look(int fd);
```

This function returns -1 on error and stores the error indication in `t_errno` (and perhaps `errno`). On success, it returns an indication of which asynchronous event has occurred:

T_LISTEN
> A connection request has arrived on the endpoint.

T_CONNECT
> A connection confirmation has arrived on the endpoint.

T_DATA
> Normal data has arrived on the endpoint.

T_EXDATA
> Expedited data has arrived on the endpoint.

T_DISCONNECT
> A disconnect indication has arrived on the endpoint.

T_UDERR
> A datagram error indication has arrived on the endpoint.

T_ORDREL
> An orderly release indication has arrived on the endpoint.

Address Conversion

Two functions convert between the internal representation of an address and a character string. The character string is a set of decimal byte values, separated by periods. Note that the string includes both the host address and the service port number. The functions to perform these conversions are:

```
#include <netdir.h>

char *taddr2uaddr(const struct netconfig *config,
        const struct netbuf *addr);
```

```
struct netbuf *uaddr2taddr(const struct netconfig *config,
        const char *uaddr);
```

The `taddr2uaddr` function converts the TLI address in the `struct netbuf` structure pointed to by `addr` to a "universal address" in a character string and returns the character string. The `uaddr2taddr` function converts the universal address in `uaddr` to a TLI address and returns a pointer to it in a `struct netbuf`. Both functions must have the current network selection passed to them in the `config` parameter.

These functions are not available in HP-UX 10.*x*.

Using read and write with TLI

Earlier we said that `read` and `write` could not be used on transport endpoints without some special preparations. This is because TLI is implemented on top of the STREAMS subsystem, which is not discussed in this book. The original Streams subsystem was invented by Dennis Ritchie and included in Research UNIX Version 8. AT&T productized Streams by adding some additional functionality and changing the name to STREAMS, and released it for the first time in System V Release 3.0. However, SVR4 is the first release to fully support all devices with STREAMS drivers.

The STREAMS subsystem provides a raw data stream between the user and some device—a disk, a terminal, or a network interface. It removes the specialized drivers for each different type of device (there are still drivers, but they all have a common interface now). The user can add ("push") and remove ("pop") intermediate processing elements, called *modules*, to and from the data stream at will. The modules can be stacked so that more than one processes the data stream at the same time. This allows relatively simple, single-purpose modules to be combined in new and interesting ways to perform complex tasks, in the same manner as the UNIX shell allows complex tasks to be built out of simpler ones using pipelines.

STREAMS works by passing messages between adjacent processing elements. These messages are why `read` and `write` can't be used—they expect a plain byte stream, and do not know what to do with the message headers. In order to use `read` and `write` on a transport endpoint, it is necessary to push a processing module that essentially removes these message headers from the stream for the read side, and converts writes to messages on the write side. To push this module, the following call is used:

```
#include <sys/ioctl.h>
#include <sys/stropts.h>

    :
ioctl(fd, I_PUSH, "tirdwr");
    :
```

After the module has been pushed, `read` and `write` can be used to transfer data. However, while the module is on the stream, the TLI functions cannot be used (although some may work). To use a TLI function, the module must be popped back off the stream:

```
#include <sys/ioctl.h>
#include <sys/stropts.h>
    ⋮
ioctl(fd, I_POP, "tirdwr");
    ⋮
```

For all the hassles involved with this, it's probably not worth doing in the general case.

Chapter Summary

In this chapter, we examined the *Transport Layer Interface*, an alternative to the socket interface for UNIX networking. Although the TLI is, arguably, a better interface than the socket interface since it is protocol-independent, it is seldom used. If portability is a goal, the TLI should be avoided in favor of the socket interface.

The information in this chapter covers only the basics of using the TLI. For a thorough discussion of the interface, as well as the STREAMS subsystem on which it is based, consult Stephen A. Rago's book *UNIX System V Network Programming*, published by Addison-Wesley.

16

Miscellaneous Routines

In this last chapter of the book, we collect the miscellaneous utility routines that have not been discussed in the previous chapters. These functions are all quite useful, although less frequently used than the ones described in Chapter 2, *Utility Routines.*

Exiting When Errors Occur

When debugging a program, a core dump of the program's current state to examine with a debugger is invaluable. As discussed in Chapter 10, *Signals*, a number of events will cause the operating system to send a signal to a process that causes a core dump. But there are a wide variety of other circumstances when it would be nice to have a core dump and the operating system doesn't know anything is wrong.

The `abort` function can be used to generate a core dump at any time:

```
#include <stdlib.h>

void abort(void);
```

When called, `abort` attempts to close all open files, and then sends a `SIGABRT` signal to the calling process. If the process is not catching or ignoring this signal, a core dump results.

The `assert` function (actually, it's a preprocessor macro) provides an easy way to use `abort` in debugging:

```
#include <assrt.h>

void assert(int expression);
```

The `assert` macro evaluates `expression` and if it evaluates to false (0), prints a line on the standard error output containing the expression, the source filename, and the line number, and then calls `abort`.

Example 16-1 shows a small program that accepts numbers as arguments, adds them together, and prints the total. Before printing the total, it uses `assert` to check that the total is greater than 100. If it isn't, `assert` will print an error message and call `abort`.

Example 16-1: assert

```
#include <assert.h>
#include <stdio.h>

int
main(int argc, char **argv)
{
    int total;

    total = 0;

    while (--argc)
        total += atoi(*++argv);

    assert(total > 100);

    printf("%d\n", total);
    exit(0);
}
```

```
% assert 10 20 30 40 50
150
% assert 1 2 3 4 5
assert.c:14: failed assertion 'total > 100'
Abort (core dumped)
```

Error Logging

When systems programs encounter errors, it's often difficult to figure out where to print the error message. For commands executed by users, the answer is simple: print the message on the terminal screen. For daemons, programs run out of *at* or *cron*, and so forth, there's no obvious place. One method is simply to open */dev/console* (the machine's console terminal) and print the error there. Back in the days of console terminals such as Decwriters that had a printer instead of a screen, this made sense. But most machines now have a video screen for a console, if they have one at all. Once a message scrolls off the top of the screen, it is gone forever. If nobody sees it before it disappears, the error will never be noted and fixed.

In 4.2BSD, Berkeley introduced the *syslog* daemon, a technique that has since been adopted by most vendors. The *syslogd* program starts when the system boots, and remains active permanently. Programs (and the operating system itself) that have errors or other information to report send these messages to the daemon. The daemon follows the directions in its configuration file, usually stored in */etc/syslog.conf*, to handle the message:

- It can print the message on the system console. The message will be preceded by the current date and time, the name of the program that sent it, and, optionally, the program's process ID number.

- It can print the message to a log file. Different types of messages may be sent to the same log file, but they may also be sent to different files.

- It can send the message to a *syslogd* running on another host. The remote host will then process the message. It is common to configure client systems to send all their messages to the file server for logging, both because of the additional disk space on the server, and to reduce the number of places messages are logged.

- It can ignore the message. It is common to ignore debugging messages; when they are needed, *syslogd* can always be told to process them temporarily.

To log error messages via *syslogd*, a program must first call the `openlog` function:

```
#include <syslog.h>

void openlog(char *ident, int logopts, int facility);

void closelog(void);
```

The `ident` parameter is a name that identifies the program. Usually, it can just be the value of `argv[0]` with any leading pathname removed. The `logopts` parameter specifies several logging options that may be *or*ed together:

LOG_PID

Log the process ID with each message. This is frequently used in daemon processes to identify the particular instance of the daemon.

LOG_CONS

Write messages to the system console if they cannot be sent to *syslogd*. This is safe to do in daemon processes that have no controlling terminal, as `syslog` will spawn a child process to open the console.

LOG_NDELAY

Open the connection to *syslogd* immediately, instead of waiting until the first message is logged. This can be used in programs that need to manage the order in which file descriptors are allocated.

LOG_NOWAIT

Do not wait for child processes that have been spawned to write on the system console. This should be used by processes that receive notification of child exits via `SIGCHLD`, since `syslog` may otherwise block waiting for a child whose exit status has already been collected.

The `facility` parameter specifies a default facility (category) to be assigned to all messages that do not have a facility encoded in them. The facility is used in the *syslogd* configuration file to group messages of certain types together. The allowable facilities are:

LOG_KERN

Messages generated by the operating system kernel. These cannot be generated by user processes.

LOG_USER

Messages generated by user processes. This is the default facility if none is specified.

LOG_MAIL

Messages generated by the mail subsystem.

LOG_DAEMON

Messages generated by system daemon processes.

LOG_AUTH
Messages generated by the authentication subsystem (*login, su*, etc.).

LOG_LPR
Messages generated by the print spooler subsystem.

LOG_NEWS
Messages generated by the Usenet news subsystem. This facility is not available in HP-UX 10.*x*.

LOG_UUCP
Messages generated by the UUCP subsystem. This facility is not available in HP-UX 10.*x*.

LOG_CRON
Messages generated by *cron* and *at*. This facility is available only in Solaris 2.*x*.

LOG_LOCAL0 — LOG_LOCAL7
Reserved for local use. These can be assigned to any purpose the system administrator desires.

The `closelog` function closes the log file.

Messages are actually logged using the `syslog` function:

```
#include <syslog.h>

void syslog(int priority, char *mesg, /* args */ ...);

#include <stdarg.h>

int vsyslog(int priority, char *mesg, va_list ap);
```

The `mesg` parameter is a character string identical to that used by `printf`, with the additional conversion specification `%m`, which is replaced with a system error message (as would be printed by `perror`). The `args` parameters correspond to the conversion specifications in `mesg`, just as they do in `printf`.

The `priority` parameter is encoded as a facility and a level, *or*ed together. The facility part is as described above; if omitted, the facility declared in the call to `openlog` is used. The level part may be one of the following:

LOG_EMERG
A panic condition; messages at this level are usually broadcast to all logged-in users.

LOG_ALERT

A condition that should be corrected immediately, such as a corrupt system database.

LOG_CRIT

Critical conditions, such as hard device errors.

LOG_ERR

Errors such as non-existent files. This is the most frequently used level.

LOG_WARNING

Warning messages.

LOG_NOTICE

Conditions that are not errors, but may require special attention.

LOG_INFO

Informative messages.

LOG_DEBUG

Debugging messages. Normally only used when debugging a program.

The `vsyslog` function is to `syslog` as `vprintf` is to `printf` (see Chapter 4, *The Standard I/O Library*). It takes a variable-length argument list and breaks it apart with the `stdarg` functions. The `vsyslog` function is not available in HP-UX 10.*x*.

Finally, the `setlogmask` function can be used to control which messages actually get delivered to *syslogd*:

```
#include <syslog.h>

int setlogmask(int maskpri);
```

The function sets the current mask priority to `maskpri` and returns the previous priority. Messages whose priority is not contained in `maskpri` are not delivered to *syslogd*. The mask for an individual priority `pri` is calculated with the macro

```
LOG_MASK(pri)
```

The mask for all priorities up to and including `pri` is calculated with the macro

```
LOG_UPTO(pri)
```

One use of priorities is to include debugging messages in a program, but to print them only when debugging is enabled. This can be achieved with a code segment such as:

```
#include <syslog.h>
    .
    .
openlog(ident, logopt, facility);
```

```
if (debug)
    setlogmask(LOG_UPTO(LOG_DEBUG));
else
    setlogmask(LOG_UPTO(LOG_ERR));
```

Although it is a matter of local policy, it is usually appropriate for most system programs to log to the LOG_DAEMON or one of the LOG_LOCALn facilities. A program that generates a large amount of logging information should probably either have one of the LOG_LOCALn facilities reserved for its use so that the *syslogd* configuration file can be used to separate those messages from others, or it should simply open its own log file and not use syslog at all.

Searching

SVR4 provides a number of useful routines for performing standard types of searches in memory, including linear search, binary search, and hash tables. These tasks are performed frequently, and a set of library routines that provide good algorithmic implementations of them is a valuable addition to the UNIX programming library. Unfortunately, most other implementations do not provide these functions.

Linear Search

A linear search is the most inefficient of searches, but it is useful for small lists. The search begins at the front of the list, and compares each item in turn until the desired item is found. On average, $n/2$ comparisons are performed in each search, where n is the size of the list.

The linear search algorithm is implemented by the lsearch and lfind functions:

```
#include <search.h>

void *lsearch(const void *key, void *base, size_t *nelp,
        size_t width, int (*compar)(const void *, const void *));

void *lfind(const void *key, const void *base, size_t *nelp,
        size_t width, int (*compar)(const void *, const void *));
```

These functions implement *Algorithm S* from Donald Knuth's *The Art of Computer Programming, Volume 3, Section 6.1*, published by Addison-Wesley.

In both cases, key is the datum to be found in the table, base points to the first element in the table, nelp points to an integer containing the number of elements currently in the table, and width is the size of a table element in bytes. The `compar` parameter is a pointer to a function (e.g., `strcmp`) used to compare two elements of the table. The function must return 0 if the elements are equal, and non-zero otherwise.

The `lsearch` function searches for the key in the table, and returns a pointer to it. If the key is not found, it is added to the end of the table, `nelp` is incremented, and a pointer to the new entry is returned.

The `lfind` function searches for the key in the table, and returns a pointer to it. If the key is not found, a null pointer is returned instead.

The pointers to the key and the element at the base of the table may be of any type. The comparison function need not compare every byte of its arguments; this allows arbitrary data types (strings, integers, structures) to be searched. A side effect of using `lsearch` to create the table is to remove duplicates from a list, since it only adds an element to the list if it is not already present.

Example 16-2 shows a small program that demonstrates the use of `lsearch` and `lfind`. The program prompts the user for several strings, and adds them to a table. Since it uses `lsearch` to add them to the table, duplicates won't be added. The program then prints the resulting table, and lets the user search for strings. The searches are done with `lfind`, so that strings not in the table do not get added.

Example 16–2: lsearch

```c
#include <search.h>
#include <string.h>
#include <stdio.h>

#define TABLESIZE    10      /* max. size of the table       */
#define ELEMENTSIZE 16      /* max. size of a table element */

int compare(const void *, const void *);

int
main(void)
{
    int i;
    char *p;
    size_t nel;
    char line[ELEMENTSIZE];
    char table[TABLESIZE][ELEMENTSIZE];

    /*
     * Tell the user what to do.
     */
    printf("Enter %d strings, not all unique.\n\n", TABLESIZE);

    /*
```

Example 16–2: lsearch (continued)

```
 * Read in some strings.
 */
nel = 0;
for (i = 0; i < TABLESIZE; i++) {
    /*
     * Prompt for each string.
     */
    printf("%2d> ", i + 1);

    /*
     * Read the string.
     */
    if (fgets(line, sizeof(line), stdin) == NULL)
        exit(0);

    /*
     * Strip the newline.
     */
    line[strlen(line) - 1] = '\0';

    /*
     * Search for the string.  If it's not in the table,
     * lsearch will add it for us.
     */
    (void) lsearch(line, table, &nel, ELEMENTSIZE, compare);
}

/*
 * Print the contents of the table.
 */
printf("\nContents of the table:\n");

for (i = 0; i < nel; i++)
    printf("\t%s\n", table[i]);

/*
 * Let the user search for things.
 */
for (;;) {
    /*
     * Prompt for a search string.
     */
    printf("\nSearch for: ");

    /*
     * Read the search string.
     */
    if (fgets(line, sizeof(line), stdin) == NULL) {
        putchar('\n');
        exit(0);
    }
```

Example 16-2: lsearch (continued)

```
        /*
         * Strip the newline.
         */
        line[strlen(line) - 1] = '\0';

        /*
         * Search for the string.  lfind will return null
         * if it's not there.
         */
        p = (char *) lfind(line, table, &nel, ELEMENTSIZE, compare);

        /*
         * Print the search results.
         */
        if (p == NULL) {
            printf("String not found.\n");
        }
        else {
            printf("Found at location %d.\n",
                    ((int) p - (int) table) / ELEMENTSIZE + 1);
        }
    }
}

/*
 * compare - compare two strings, return 0 if equal, non-zero if not.
 */
int
compare(const void *a, const void *b)
{
    return(strcmp((char *) a, (char *) b));
}


    % lsearch
    Enter 10 strings, not all unique.
     1> abcdef
     2> ghijkl
     3> mnopqr
     4> stuvwx
     5> yz
     6> abcdef
     7> ghijkl
     8> mnopqr
     9> stuvwx
    10> yz
    Contents of the table:
            abcdef
            ghijkl
            mnopqr
            stuvwx
            yz
```

```
Search for: abc
String not found.
Search for: abcdef
Found at location 1.
Search for: ghijkl
Found at location 2.
Search for: mn
String not found.
Search for: yz
Found at location 5.
Search for: ^D
```

Binary Search

The binary search is one of the most efficient methods for searching large tables. Given a table of n entries, a binary search compares the item to be found against item n/2 in the table. If the item to be found is "less" than the item in the middle of the table, it then looks at the item halfway between the start of the table and the middle of the table. If the item to be found is "more" than the item in the middle of the table, it then looks at the item halfway between the middle of the table and the end of the table. This process continues, dividing the search space in half each time, until the item is found or not. In order for a binary search to work, the table must be sorted into increasing order. On average, $\log_2 n$ comparisons are performed to find any item in the table. Even for large tables, this is very efficient—a table of one million entries only requires 20 comparisons to find any item in the table.

The binary search algorithm is implemented by the **bsearch** function:

```
#include <stdlib.h>

void *bsearch(const void *key, const void *base, size_t nel,
        size_t size, int (*compar)(const void *, const void *));
```

This function implements *Algorithm B* from *Volume 3, Section 6.2.1* of *The Art of Computer Programming*.

The **key** parameter is the item to be found; **base** points to the beginning of the table to search. The table must be sorted into increasing order. The **nel** parameter gives the number of elements in the table, each of which is **size** bytes in size. The **compar** parameter must point to a function that compares two table entries and returns less than, equal to, or greater than 0 depending on whether the first item is to be considered less than, equal to, or greater than the second item. If the item is found, **bsearch** returns a pointer to it; if the item is not in the table, NULL is returned.

Example 16-3 shows a program that reads in the system spelling dictionary, */usr/dict/words*, and then searches it. The file is already sorted, but the sort is case-independent. For this reason, we use `strcasecmp` in our comparison function.

Example 16–3: bsearch

```c
#include <search.h>
#include <string.h>
#include <stdio.h>

#define TABLESIZE    32768        /* max. size of the table     */
#define ELEMENTSIZE 32            /* max. size of a table element */

int compare(const void *, const void *);

int
main(void)
{
    char *p;
    FILE *fp;
    size_t nel;
    char line[ELEMENTSIZE];
    char table[TABLESIZE][ELEMENTSIZE];

    /*
     * Open the file.
     */
    if ((fp = fopen("/usr/dict/words", "r")) == NULL) {
        perror("/usr/dict/words");
        exit(1);
    }

    printf("Reading the table... ");
    fflush(stdout);

    /*
     * Read in the file.
     */
    for (nel = 0; nel < TABLESIZE; nel++) {
        /*
         * Read a line.
         */
        if (fgets(table[nel], ELEMENTSIZE, fp) == NULL)
            break;

        /*
         * Strip the newline.
         */
        table[nel][strlen(table[nel]) - 1] = '\0';
    }

    printf("done.\n");
    fclose(fp);
```

Example 16-3: bsearch (continued)

```
    /*
     * Let the user search for things.
     */
    for (;;) {
        /*
         * Prompt for a search string.
         */
        printf("\nSearch for: ");

        /*
         * Read the search string.
         */
        if (fgets(line, sizeof(line), stdin) == NULL) {
            putchar('\n');
            exit(0);
        }

        /*
         * Strip the newline.
         */
        line[strlen(line) - 1] = '\0';

        /*
         * Do a binary search for the string.
         */
        p = (char *) bsearch(line, table, nel, ELEMENTSIZE, compare);

        /*
         * Print the search results.
         */
        if (p == NULL) {
            printf("String not found.\n");
        }
        else {
            printf("Found at location %d.\n",
                    ((int) p - (int) table) / ELEMENTSIZE);
        }
    }
}

/*
 * compare - compare two strings, return 0 if equal, non-zero if not.
 */
int
compare(const void *a, const void *b)
{
    return(strcasecmp((char *) a, (char *) b));
}
```

```
% bsearch
Reading the table... done.
Search for: mambo
Found at location 14113.
Search for: zip
Found at location 25121.
Search for: alpha
Found at location 722.
Search for: xyzzy
String not found.
Search for: ^D
```

Hash Tables

Hash tables are frequently used to manage symbol tables in compilers and other similar programs. They store items in a series of *buckets* (for example, one bucket for each letter of the alphabet) where they can be found with a minimum of searching. The advantage to using a hash table as opposed to a linear or binary search is that items can be inserted into the table in any order (unlike binary search), yet they can be found quickly (unlike linear search). The disadvantage is that without a good estimate of how large your table needs to be, hashing can be very inefficient.

Hash tables are implemented with the `hsearch`, `hcreate`, and `hdestroy` functions:

```
#include <search.h>

typedef struct {
    char    *key;
    char    *data;
} ENTRY;

typedef enum { FIND, ENTER } ACTION;

ENTRY *hsearch(ENTRY item, ACTION action);

int hcreate(size_t nel);

void hdestroy(void);
```

These functions implement *Algorithm D* from *Volume 3, Section 6.4* of *The Art of Computer Programming.*

A hash table is created with the `hcreate` function; the `nel` parameter is an estimate of the maximum number of entries the table will contain. A hash table is destroyed with the `hdestroy` function. Only one hash table may be in use at a time.

The hsearch function searches for item in the hash table, using strcmp to compare the item.key fields. The item.data field points to arbitrary data associated with the key. If action is FIND, hsearch returns a pointer to the item, or NULL if it is not in the table. If action is ENTER, hsearch searches for the item, and if it is found, returns a pointer to the item already in the table. If it is not found, the item is added to the table, and a pointer to its location returned. The hsearch function uses malloc to allocate space for the table entries.

Example 16-4 is a sample program that uses hsearch to manage a list of people and some personal data about them. The program prompts for some input data, stores that in the hash table, and then lets the user search the table.

Example 16–4: hsearch

```
#include <search.h>
#include <string.h>
#include <stdlib.h>
#include <stdio.h>

struct data {
    int age;
    int height;
    int weight;
};

int
main(void)
{
    char *p;
    ENTRY item;
    ENTRY *result;
    struct data *d;
    char buf[BUFSIZ];

    /*
     * Create the hash table.
     */
    hcreate(100);

    printf("Enter Name/age/height/weight; terminate with blank line.\n\n");

    /*
     * Read information until a blank line.
     */
    while (fgets(buf, sizeof(buf), stdin) != NULL) {
        /*
         * Blank line, all done.
         */
        if (*buf == '\n')
            break;

        /*
```

Example 16-4: hsearch (continued)

```
     * Allocate a data structure (we should check for
     * errors here).
     */
    d = (struct data *) malloc(sizeof(struct data));
    item.data = (char *) d;

    /*
     * Split up the data (we should check for errors
     * here).
     */
    p = strtok(buf, "/");
    item.key = strdup(p);

    p = strtok(NULL, "/");
    d->age = atoi(p);

    p = strtok(NULL, "/");
    d->height = atoi(p);

    p = strtok(NULL, "/");
    d->weight = atoi(p);

    /*
     * Add the item to the table.
     */
    (void) hsearch(item, ENTER);
}

/*
 * Let the user search for things.
 */
for (;;) {
    /*
     * Prompt for a search string.
     */
    printf("\nSearch for: ");

    /*
     * Read the search string.
     */
    if (fgets(buf, sizeof(buf), stdin) == NULL) {
        putchar('\n');
        hdestroy();
        exit(0);
    }

    /*
     * Strip the newline.
     */
    buf[strlen(buf) - 1] = '\0';

    /*
```

Example 16-4: hsearch (continued)

```
     * Look in the table for the item.
     */
    item.key = buf;
    result = hsearch(item, FIND);

    /*
     * Print the search results.
     */
    if (result == NULL) {
        printf("Entry not found.\n");
    }
    else {
        d = (struct data *) result->data;
        printf("Name: %s\nAge: %d\nHeight: %d\nWeight: %d\n",
               result->key, d->age, d->height, d->weight);
    }
  }
}
```

```
% hsearch
Enter Name/age/height/weight; terminate with blank line.
Dave/32/73/220
Cathy/34/64/120
Trevor/8/48/85
Sean/3/32/31

Search for: Cathy
Name: Cathy
Age: 34
Height: 64
Weight: 120
Search for: Trevor
Name: Trevor
Age: 8
Height: 48
Weight: 85
Search for: Fred
Entry not found.
Search for: ^D
```

Binary Trees

Binary trees are an efficient way to maintain a list of items in sorted order. At any given node in the tree, all of the items below and to the left of that node are "less" than that node, and all of the items below and to the right of that node are "greater" than that node. For a tree with n nodes, searches of the tree can be performed in $\log_2 n$ comparisons.

The binary tree algorithms are implemented with the `tsearch`, `tfind`, `tdelete`, and `twalk` functions:

```
#include <search.h>

typedef enum { preorder, postorder, endorder, leaf } VISIT;

void *tsearch(const void *key, void **rootp,
        int (*compar)(const void *, const void *));

void *tfind(const void *key, const void **rootp,
        int (*compar)(const void *, const void *));

void *tdelete(const void *key, void **rootp,
        int (*compar)(const void *, const void *));

void twalk(void *rootp, void(*action)(void **, VISIT, int));
```

These functions implement *Algorithm D* and *Algorithm T* from *Volume 3, Section 6.2.2* of *The Art of Computer Programming*.

The `compar` parameter to the first three functions is a pointer to a function that compares two items and returns less than, equal to, or greater than 0 depending on whether the first key should be considered less than, equal to, or greater than the second key.

The `tsearch` function is used to build and search the tree. It searches the tree for `key` and, if found, returns a pointer to it. If not found, `tsearch` adds it to the tree and returns a pointer to it. Only pointers are copied into the tree; the calling program is responsible for saving the data. The `rootp` function returns a pointer to a variable that points to the root of the tree; if the pointer is NULL, a new tree will be created.

The `tfind` function is almost identical to `tsearch`, except that instead of adding an item to the tree if it is not already there, `tfind` returns NULL in that case. Note that there is one level less redirection in `rootp` when used with `tfind`.

The `tdelete` function removes an item from the tree. It returns a pointer to the item's parent node, or NULL if the item was not in the tree.

The `twalk` function traverses the tree rooted at `rootp` (any node may be used as the root of the tree for a walk below that node). The `action` parameter is a pointer to a function that is called at each node. The function takes three arguments: a pointer to the node being visited, the number of times the node has been visited, and the level at which the node resides in the tree, with the root being level zero. The second argument is given as an enumerated type with the following values:

preorder

The node has been visited for the first time, before any of its children.

postorder

The node has been visited for the second time, after its left child but before its right child.

endorder

The node has been visited for the third time, after both of its children.

leaf

The node is a leaf; it has no children (and hence is only visited once).

An alternative notation for trees uses the terms "preorder," "inorder," and "postorder" for the same three node visits; this may cause some confusion with the different meanings of "postorder."

Example 16-5 shows a program that reads a number of strings from the standard input, storing them in a binary tree. It then prints the tree in alphabetical order.

Example 16–5: tsearch

```
#include <search.h>
#include <string.h>
#include <stdlib.h>
#include <stdio.h>

struct node {
    char    *string;
    int     length;
};

int     compareNode(const void *, const void *);
void    printNode(void **, VISIT, int);

int
main(void)
{
    void *root;
    struct node *n;
    char buf[BUFSIZ];

    root = NULL;

    /*
     * Read strings until end of file.
     */
    while (fgets(buf, sizeof(buf), stdin) != NULL) {
        /*
         * Strip the newline.
         */
        buf[strlen(buf) - 1] = '\0';
```

Example 16–5: tsearch (continued)

```
        /*
         * Allocate a node structure.
         */
        n = (struct node *) malloc(sizeof(struct node));

        if (n == NULL) {
            fprintf(stderr, "out of memory.\n");
            exit(1);
        }

        /*
         * Save the information in the node.
         */
        n->string = strdup(buf);
        n->length = strlen(buf);

        /*
         * Add the item to the tree.
         */
        (void) tsearch((void *) n, &root, compareNode);
    }

    /*
     * Print out the tree in alphabetical order.
     */
    twalk(root, printNode);

    exit(0);
}

/*
 * compareNode - compare the strings in two nodes.
 */
int
compareNode(const void *a, const void *b)
{
    struct node *aa, *bb;

    aa = (struct node *) a;
    bb = (struct node *) b;

    return(strcmp(aa->string, bb->string));
}

/*
 * printNode - print a node - we only print if this is the postorder
 *             (inorder) visit or a leaf; this results in
 *             alphabetical order.
 */
void
printNode(void **node, VISIT order, int level)
{
```

Example 16–5: tsearch (continued)

```
struct node *n;

n = *(struct node **) node;

if (order == postorder || order == leaf)
    printf("level=%d, length=%d, string=%s\n", level, n->length,
           n->string);
}
```

```
% tsearch
one
two
three
four
five
six
seven
eight
nine
ten
^D
level=3, length=5, string=eight
level=2, length=4, string=five
level=1, length=4, string=four
level=2, length=4, string=nine
level=0, length=3, string=one
level=4, length=5, string=seven
level=3, length=3, string=six
level=4, length=3, string=ten
level=2, length=5, string=three
level=1, length=3, string=two
```

Queues

Two functions are provided to manipulate queues built from doubly-linked lists:

```
#include <search.h>

void insque(struct qelem *elem, struct qelem *pred);

void remque(struct qelem *elem);
```

Each element in the list must be of type **struct qelem**:

```
struct qelem {
    struct qelem    *q_forw;
    struct qelem    *q_back;
    char            *q_data;
};
```

The `insque` function inserts the element pointed to by `elem` into the queue immediately after the element pointed to by `pred`. The `remque` function removes the element pointed to by `elem` from the queue.

HP-UX 10.*x* does not provide the `struct qelem` data type; instead the arguments to `insque` and `remque` are of type `void *`.

Sorting

Every version of UNIX provides the same function to sort a table of data "in place:"

```
#include <stdlib.h>

void qsort(void *base, size_t nel, size_t width,
           int (*compar)(const void *, const void *));
```

This function implements Quicksort, a reasonably efficient general-purpose sorting algorithm. The `base` parameter points to the first element of the table to be sorted; `nel` indicates the number of elements in the table, each of size `width`. The `compar` parameter is a pointer to a function that compares two elements of the table and returns less than, equal to, or greater than 0, depending on whether the first element is to be considered less than, equal to, or greater than the second element.

Example 16-6 shows a small program that sorts an array of numbers.

Example 16–6: qsort

```
#include <stdlib.h>

#define NELEM    10

int compare(const void *, const void *);

int
main(void)
{
    int i;
    int array[NELEM];

    /*
     * Fill the array with numbers.
     */
    for (i = 0; i < NELEM; i++)
        array[NELEM - i - 1] = (i * i) & 0xf;

    /*
     * Print it.
     */
    printf("Before sorting:\n\t");
```

Example 16–6: qsort (continued)

```
    for (i = 0; i < NELEM; i++)
        printf("%d ", array[i]);
    putchar('\n');

    /*
     * Sort it.
     */
    qsort(array, NELEM, sizeof(int), compare);

    /*
     * Print it again.
     */
    printf("After sorting:\n\t");

    for (i = 0; i < NELEM; i++)
        printf("%d ", array[i]);
    putchar('\n');

    exit(0);
}

/*
 * compare - compare two integers.
 */
int
compare(const void *a, const void *b)
{
    int *aa, *bb;

    aa = (int *) a;
    bb = (int *) b;

    return(*aa - *bb);
}


    % qsort
    Before sorting:
            1 0 1 4 9 0 9 4 1 0
    After sorting:
            0 0 0 1 1 1 4 4 9 9
```

Environment Variables

Each process has a set of associated variables. The variables are called *environment variables* and, together, constitute the process environment. These variables include the search path, the terminal type, and the user's login name. The UNIX shells provide a method for adding, changing, and removing environment variables.

As discussed in Chapter 11, *Processes*, a program is started by a call to `main`:

```
int
main(int argv, char **argv, char **envp)
```

The `argc` and `argv` parameters are the number of arguments passed to the program and the arguments themselves. The `envp` parameter is the array of environment variables. The `execve` and `execle` functions described in Chapter 11 can be used to execute a program with a new set of environment variables; the other `exec` functions allow the program to inherit its environment from the parent. Example 16-7 shows a small program that prints its environment variables.

Example 16-7: printenv

```
#include <stdio.h>

int
main(int argc, char **argv, char **envp)
{
    while (*envp != NULL)
        printf("%s\n", *envp++);

    exit(0);
}
```

```
% printenv
HOME=/home/foo
HZ=100
LOGNAME=foo
MAIL=/var/mail/foo
PATH=/usr/opt/bin:/usr/local/bin:/usr/bin
SHELL=/bin/sh
TERM=xterm
TZ=US/East-Indiana
```

To obtain the value of a specific environment variable, the `getenv` function is used:

```
#include <stdlib.h>

char *getenv(char *name);
```

The `name` parameter should be the name of the desired variable (the name to the left of the '=' in the example above). If the variable exists, its value (to the right of the '=') is returned; otherwise, `NULL` is returned.

Most newer versions of UNIX, SVR4 included, also provide the `putenv` function, which places a new variable into the environment:

```
#include <stdlib.h>

int putenv(char *string);
```

The `putenv` function uses `malloc` to allocate a new environment large enough for the old environment plus the string contained in `string`. The string contained in `string` should be of the form `name=value`; by convention, environment variable names are usually all uppercase. Note that the `string` variable should remain in existence for the life of the program; that is, it should be declared `static` or dyanmically allocated. Changing the value of `string` will change the value of the variable in the environment.

If the environment is successfully modified, `putenv` returns 0; otherwise it returns non-zero.

Passwords

UNIX password encryption is based on a modified version of the *Data Encryption Standard* (DES). Contrary to popular belief, the password itself is *not* encrypted. Rather, the password is used as the key to encrypt a block of zero-valued bytes. The result of this encryption is a 13-character string that is stored in either the password file or the shadow password file (see Chapter 8, *Users and Groups*).

When a user selects a password, the *passwd* program chooses two characters at random; this value is called the *salt*. It then prompts the user for his password, and passes this value and the salt to the `crypt` function:

```
#include <crypt.h>

char *crypt(const char *key, const char *salt);
```

The `crypt` function extracts seven bits from each character of the password, ignoring the parity bit, to form the 56-bit DES key. This implies that no more than eight characters are significant in the password. Next, one of the internal tables in the DES algorithm is permuted in one of 4,096 different ways depending on the value of the salt. The purpose of the salt is to make it more difficult to use DES chips or a precomputed list of encrypted passwords to attack the algorithm (although with current processor speeds and disk capacities, this deterrent is not as significant as it once was). The DES algorithm (with the modified table) is then invoked for 25 iterations on a block of zeros. The output of this encryption, which is 64 bits long, is then coerced into a 64-character alphabet (`A-Z`, `a-z`, `0-9`, '`.`', and '`/`'). Because this coercion involves translations in which several different values are represented by the same character, password encryption is essentially one way; the result cannot be decrypted. The resulting string returned by `crypt` contains the two-character salt followed by the eleven-character coerced result of the encryption.

When a program prompts the user for a password, it usually uses the `getpass` function:

```
#include <stdlib.h>

char *getpass(const char *prompt);
```

This function prints the string contained in **prompt**, turns off character echo on the terminal, reads the password, and then restores the terminal modes. The typed password is returned. Note that `getpass` truncates the typed password to at most eight characters.

After prompting for the password, the program looks up the user's password in the password file or shadow password file (if a shadow password file is used, the program must be running with superuser permissions). It then passes the value typed by the user to the `crypt` function, along with the salt, and compares the result with the value obtained from the password file. If they are the same the user's password was correct. This process is shown below:

```
#include <stdlib.h>
#include <crypt.h>

char *typed, *encrypted;

    .
    .
    .
encrypted = /* obtain the encrypted password */;
typed = getpass("Password: ");

if (strcmp(crypt(typed, encrypted), encrypted) == 0)
    /* okay... */
else
    /* not okay... */
```

Random Numbers

A number of applications occasionally require one or more random numbers. All versions of UNIX provide a pseudo-random number generator:

```
#include <stdlib.h>

int rand(void);

void srand(int seed);
```

Before requesting any random numbers, the generator should be *seeded* by calling `srand`. The **seed** parameter should be an integer type; the output of `getpid` or `time(0)` is usually a good value. Each time `srand` is called with the same seed, the output of the random number generator will be the same.

The `rand` function returns a random number in the range 0 to $2^{15}-1$.

Some versions of UNIX, usually those based on BSD, also supply `random` and `srandom`, with similar semantics.

System V versions of UNIX provide a number of other random number generators described in the `drand48` manual page; because they are not portable to all versions of the operating system, they are not frequently used.

Directory Trees

SVR4 provides three functions for traversing directory trees. Implementations of the `ftw` function are also available in the public domain.

```
#include <ftw.h>

int ftw(const char *path, int (*fn)(const char *,
        const struct stat *, int), int depth);

int nftw(const char *path, int (*fn)(const char *,
        const struct stat *, int, struct FTW *),
        int depth, int flags);

#include <libgen.h>

char *pathfind(const char *path, const char *name,
        const char *mode);
```

The `ftw` function recursively descends the directory hierarchy rooted at `path`. For each object in the directory, it calls the user-defined function `fn`. This function takes three arguments: the first argument is the name of the object, the second argument is a pointer to a `struct stat` structure (see Chapter 5, *Files and Directories*), and the third argument is a flag. Possible values of the flag are:

FTW_F
    The object is a file.

FTW_D
    The object is a directory.

FTW_DNR
    The object is a directory that cannot be read. Descendants of the directory will not be processed.

FTW_NS

> The call to stat on the object failed, either because of permissions problems
> or because it is a symbolic link pointing to a non-existent file. The contents of
> the struct stat structure are undefined.

The last parameter to ftw is depth, a limit on the number of file descriptors ftw
may use. It requires one file descriptor for each level in the tree. The traversal will
visit a directory (call fn on it) before it visits subdirectories of that directory.

The traversal continues until the fn function returns a non-zero value, or some
error occurs. If the tree is exhausted, ftw will return 0. If fn returns a non-zero
value, ftw stops the traversal and returns that value.

Example 16-8 shows an example of the use of ftw.

Example 16–8: ftw

```
#include <sys/types.h>
#include <sys/stat.h>
#include <unistd.h>
#include <stdio.h>
#include <ftw.h>

int process(const char *, const struct stat *, int);

int
main(int argc, char **argv)
{
    while (--argc) {
        printf("Directory %s:\n", *++argv);

        ftw(*argv, process, sysconf(_SC_OPEN_MAX) - 3);

        putchar('\n');
    }

    exit(0);
}

int
process(const char *path, const struct stat *st, int flag)
{
    printf("%-24s", path);

    switch (flag) {
    case FTW_F:
        printf("file, mode %o\n", st->st_mode & 07777);
        break;
    case FTW_D:
        printf("directory, mode %o\n", st->st_mode & 07777);
        break;
    case FTW_DNR:
```

Example 16–8: ftw (continued)

```
        printf("unreadable directory, mode %o\n", st->st_mode & 07777);
        break;
    case FTW_NS:
        printf("unknown; stat() failed\n");
        break;
    }

    return(0);
}
```

```
% ftw /tmp
Directory /tmp:
/tmp                    directory, mode 777
/tmp/.X11-UNIX          directory, mode 777
/tmp/.X11-UNIX/X0       file, mode 0
/tmp/ps_data            file, mode 664
/tmp/sh304.1            file, mode 640
/tmp/sh309.1            file, mode 640
/tmp/foo                file, mode 640
/tmp/jreca002Ll         file, mode 640
/tmp/zip                file, mode 640
/tmp/foo.ps             file, mode 640
/tmp/zip.ps             file, mode 640
/tmp/jovea002Ll         file, mode 600
/tmp/jreca0020w         file, mode 640
/tmp/jovea0020w         file, mode 600
```

The `nftw` function is similar to `ftw`, except that it takes an additional argument, `flags`, which may specify any of the following values, *or*ed together:

`FTW_PHYS`

Perform a "physical" walk; do not follow symbolic links. By default, `nftw` follows symbolic links.

`FTW_MOUNT`

Do not cross filesystem mount points.

`FTW_DEPTH`

Perform a depth-first search; visit subdirectories of a directory before visiting the directory itself.

`FTW_CHDIR`

Change to each directory before reading it.

The `fn` function also has an additional parameter, a structure of type `struct FTW`:

```
struct FTW {
    int    base;
    int    level;
};
```

The `base` field contains the offset of the filename in the pathname parameter, and the `level` field contains the current level in the tree.

The `nftw` function also allows two additional flags to be passed to `fn`:

FTP_DP

The object is a directory whose subdirectories have already been visited.

FTW_SL

The object is a symblic link to a non-existent file.

Example 16-9 shows a slightly different version of Example 16-8; this one uses `nftw` and shows the structure of the directory tree with indentation.

Example 16–9: nftw

```
#include <sys/types.h>
#include <sys/stat.h>
#include <unistd.h>
#include <stdio.h>
#include <ftw.h>

int process(const char *, const struct stat *, int, struct FTW *);

int
main(int argc, char **argv)
{
    while (--argc) {
        printf("Directory %s:\n", *++argv);

        nftw(*argv, process, sysconf(_SC_OPEN_MAX) - 3, 0);

        putchar('\n');
    }

    exit(0);
}

int
process(const char *path, const struct stat *st, int flag, struct FTW *info)
{
    int i;

    for (i = 0; i < info->level; i++)
        printf("   ");
```

Example 16-9: nftw (continued)

```
    printf("%-*s", 36 - 2 * info->level, &path[info->base]);

    switch (flag) {
    case FTW_F:
        printf("file, mode %o\n", st->st_mode & 07777);
        break;
    case FTW_D:
    case FTW_DP:
        printf("directory, mode %o\n", st->st_mode & 07777);
        break;
    case FTW_SL:
        printf("symbolic link to nowhere\n");
        break;
    case FTW_DNR:
        printf("unreadable directory, mode %o\n", st->st_mode & 07777);
        break;
    case FTW_NS:
        printf("unknown; stat() failed\n");
        break;
    }

    return(0);
}


% nftp /tmp
Directory /tmp:
tmp                             directory, mode 777
  .X11-UNIX                     directory, mode 777
    X0                          file, mode 0
  ps_data                       file, mode 664
  sh304.1                       file, mode 640
  sh309.1                       file, mode 640
  foo                           file, mode 640
  jreca002Ll                    file, mode 640
  zip                           file, mode 640
  foo.ps                        file, mode 640
  zip.ps                        file, mode 640
  jovea002Ll                    file, mode 600
  jreca0020w                    file, mode 640
  jovea0020w                    file, mode 600
```

The `pathfind` function is a library implementation of the *find* command. It could also be implemented fairly easily with `ftw` or `nftw`. To make use of the `pathfind` function, your program must be linked with the *-lgen* library.

```
#include <libgen.h>
```

```
char *pathfind(const char *path, const char *name, const char *mode);
```

The `pathfind` function searches the directories in `path`, which should be separated by colons, for a file whose name is `name`, and whose mode matches `mode`. The `mode` parameter is a string containing one or more of the following characters:

r   The object is readable by the user.

w   The object is writable by the user.

x   The object is executable by the user.

f   The object is a regular file.

b   The object is a block-special device file.

c   The object is a character-special device file.

d   The object is a directory.

p   The object is a FIFO (pipe).

u   The object has the set-user-id bit set.

g   The object has the set-group-id bit set.

k   The object has the "sticky" bit set.

s   The object has non-zero size.

If an item matching the requirements is found, `pathfind` returns the concatenation of `path` and `name`. If no object is found, `pathfind` returns `NULL`.

Example 16-10 shows a program that uses `pathfind` to tell the caller what version of a program he is using. The user's search path is used as the list of directories to search, and files with the execute bit set are of interest. This program is similar to the *which* command provided by most versions of UNIX.

The `pathfind` function is not available in HP-UX 10.*x*.

Example 16–10: pathfind

```
#include <stdlib.h>
#include <libgen.h>

int
main(int argc, char **argv)
{
    char *p, *path;

    if ((path = getenv("PATH")) == NULL) {
        fprintf(stderr, "cannot find path in environment.\n");
        exit(1);
    }

    while (--argc) {
```

Example 16–10: pathfind (continued)

```
        if ((p = pathfind(path, *++argv, "x")) == NULL)
            printf("%s: not found in search path.\n", *argv);
        else
            printf("%s: %s\n", *argv, p);
    }

    exit(0);
}


% pathfind ls
ls: /usr/bin/ls
```

Database Management

Most versions of UNIX provide a library to maintain a rudimentary database. This
database is basically an on-disk hash table (see above), designed for efficiency.
The routines can handle very large databases (up to a billion blocks), and require
only one or two filesystem accesses to retrieve an item.

Although not necessary on most versions of SVR4, HP-UX 10.*x* requires linking with
the *-lndbm* library to use these functions.

```
#include <ndbm.h>

DBM *dbm_open(char *file, int flags, int mode);

void dbm_close(DBM *db);

int dbm_store(DBM *db, datum key, datum content, int flags);

datum dbm_fetch(DBM *db, datum key);

int dbm_delete (DBM *db, datum key);

datum dbm_firstkey(DBM *db);

datum dbm_nextkey(DBM *db);

int dbm_clearerr(DBM *db);

int dbm_error(DBM *db);
```

Before using the other functions, the database must be opened with **dbm_open**.
The database is stored in two files, one with a ".*dir*" suffix and the other with a
".*pag*" suffix. The root name of the file (without the suffixes) should be passed to

dbm_open in the file parameter. The flags and mode arguments are given as for the open function. On success, dbm_open returns a pointer to type DBM; otherwise it returns NULL. A database can be closed with dbm_close.

Keys and contents are described with objects of type datum:

```
typedef struct {
    char    *dptr;
    int      dsize;
} datum;
```

The dptr field points to the data, and dsize indicates the size of the data. Note that both keys and contents may be arbitrary data types.

An item is stored in the database by calling dbm_store. The db argument is a pointer to an open database. The key parameter is the key under which the data in the content parameter is to be stored. The flags argument may be one of the following:

DBM_INSERT

Insert an item into the database. If an item with this key is already in the database, do not replace it with the new value. If an existing entry is found, dbm_store returns 1, otherwise it returns 0.

DBM_REPLACE

Insert an item into the database. If an item with this key is already in the database, replace it with the new value.

To retrieve an item from the database, the dbm_fetch function is used. The db parameter specifies an open database, and the key for the item is given in key. The content for that key is returned as a datum type; note that the structure itself is returned, not a pointer to the structure. If no item was found for the key, then the dptr field of the datum structure will be null.

To delete an item with key key from the database referred to by db, the dbm_delete function is used.

The dbm_firstkey and dbm_nextkey functions can be used to make a linear pass through all keys in the database as follows:

```
#include <ndbm.h>

    .
    .
    .
for (key = dbm_firstkey(db); key.dptr != NULL; key = dbm_nextkey(db)) {
    ...
    content = dbm_fetch(db, key);
    ...
}
    .
    .
    .
```

The dbm_error function returns non-zero when an error has occurred in reading or writing the database referenced by db; the dbm_clearerr function clears the error condition.

Porting Notes

Some particularly old versions of UNIX may offer the predecessor to the *-lndbm* library, called the *-ldbm* library. This version of the library uses functions with the same names, except without the leading dbm_. They do not accept a db argument, and handle only one open database at a time. Replacing these functions with the newer ones is straightforward.

Pattern Matching

Most of the UNIX shells and text editors allow the user to use wildcard characters to match a large set of items. For example, a* matches all filenames that begin with a in the shell, * being a wildcard. More sophisticated ways to abbreviate a search string are also supported. For example, ^whi[lnt]e.*sleeping$ matches all lines that begin with while, whine, or white and end in sleeping in a text editor.

The code that performs this type of matching is fairly complex, and would be difficult to reproduce each time a program needed these facilities. For this reason, library routines that implement these functions are provided.

Shell Pattern Matching

Pattern matching in the shell, also called *globbing*, is used primarily to generate lists of filenames. In a shell pattern, the following characters have special meaning:

*   Matches any string, including the null string.

?   Matches any single character.

[]   Matches any one of the enclosed characters. Two characters separated by –
     match any one character lexically between the two characters (i.e., [a-z]
     matches any of the characters a through z). If the first character after the [is
     !, then this matches any character *except* one of the enclosed characters.

These special characters, also called *metacharacters*, may be escaped with a backslash; i.e., \? matches the actual question mark character.

The gmatch function is used to perform shell pattern matching in a program. This function is contained in the *-lgen* library:

```
#include <libgen.h>

int gmatch(const char *str, const char *pattern);
```

The gmatch function returns non-zero if the shell pattern in **pattern** matches the string contained in **str**; it returns 0 if they do not match. The additional pattern matching characters provided by the C shell, most notably { }, are not supported by gmatch.

The gmatch function is not available in HP-UX 10.*x*. However, a similar function, fnmatch, is available. You can use fnmatch to emulate gmatch as follows:

```
int
gmatch(const char *str, const char *pattern)
{
        return(!fnmatch(pattern, str, 0));
}
```

Example 16-11 shows a program that uses gmatch to search a file given as its second argument for lines that match the pattern given as its first argument. Note that the pattern must be enclosed in quotes to prevent the shell from processing it.

Example 16–11: gmatch

```
#include <libgen.h>
#include <stdio.h>

int
main(int argc, char **argv)
{
    FILE *fp;
    char line[BUFSIZ];
    char *pattern, *filename;

    /*
     * Check arguments.
     */
    if (argc != 3) {
        fprintf(stderr, "Usage: %s pattern file\n", *argv);
        exit(1);
    }

    pattern = *++argv;
    filename = *++argv;

    /*
     * Open the file.
     */
    if ((fp = fopen(filename, "r")) == NULL) {
        perror(filename);
```

Example 16-11: gmatch (continued)

```
        exit(1);
    }

    /*
     * Read lines from the file.
     */
    while (fgets(line, sizeof(line), fp) != NULL) {
        /*
         * Strip the newline.
         */
        line[strlen(line) - 1] = '\0';

        /*
         * If it matches, print it.
         */
        if (gmatch(line, pattern) != 0)
            puts(line);
    }

    fclose(fp);
    exit(0);
}
```

```
% gmatch 'A????d' /usr/dict/words
Aeneid
Alfred
Arnold
Atwood
% gmatch 'z*[ty]' /usr/dict/words
zealot
zest
zesty
zippy
zloty
zoology
```

Regular Expressions

A *regular expression* specifies a set of strings, through the use of special characters. Most text editors support regular expressions in some form; the *grep* family of commands also supports them. The canonical definition of a regular expression is provided by the *ed* text editor, which was the first UNIX text editor to implement them.

In *ed*, a regular expression is defined as follows:

- A single character (except a special character; see below) is a one-character regular expression that matches itself.

- A backslash preceding a special character causes that character to lose its special meaning.

- A period (.) is a one-character regular expression that matches any single character.

- A string of characters enclosed in square brackets ([and]) is a one-character regular expression that matches any single character in the string, unless the first character of the string is a circumflex (^), in which case the string is a regular expression that matches any single character *not* in the string. The circumflex has special meaning only when it is the first character in the string.

  Within the string, a dash (-) may be used to specify a range of characters; e.g., [0-9] matches the same thing as [0123456789]. If the dash is the first character (following the circumflex) or last character in the string, it loses its special meaning.

  The right square bracket (]) may be included in the string only if it is the first character of the string.

  The other special characters have no special meaning within square brackets.

- Regular expressions may be concatenated to form larger regular expressions.

- A regular expression preceded by a circumflex (^) is constrained to match at the beginning of a line.

- A regular expression followed by a dollar sign ($) is constrained to match at the end of a line.

- A regular expression both preceded by a circumflex and followed by a dollar sign is constrained to match an entire line.

- A regular expression followed by an asterisk (*) matches zero or more occurrences of the regular expression. For example, ab*c matches ac, abc, abbc, and so forth. When a choice exists, the longest leftmost match will be chosen.

- A regular expression contained between \(and \) matches the same string that the unenclosed regular expression matches.

- The regular expression \n matches the same string that the nth regular expression enclosed in \(and \) in the same regular expression matches. For example, \(abc\)\1 matches the string abcabc.

- A regular expression followed by \{m\} matches *exactly* m occurrences of that regular expression. A regular expression followed by \{m,\} matches *at least* m occurrences of that regular expression. A regular expression followed by \{m,n\} matches *at least* m and *no more than* n occurrences of that regular expression.

  This notation was originally introduced in PWB UNIX, and from there made its way into System V. Versions of UNIX that do not have PWB UNIX as an ancestor (i.e., Berkeley-based versions) do not support this notation.

- A regular expression preceded by \< is constrained to match at the beginning of a line or to follow a character that is not a digit, underscore, or letter.

  A regular expression followed by \> is constrained to match at the end of a line or to precede a character that is not a digit, underscore, or letter.

  This allows a regular expression to be constrained to match words.

  This notation was introduced in the *ex* and *vi* editors. Versions of *ed* prior to the one in SVR4 do not support this notation.

The basic functions provided for using regular expressions in programs are `regcmp` and `regex`:

```
#include <libgen.h>

char *regcmp(const char *str1, /* const char *str2 */, ... , NULL);

char *regex(const char *re, const char *str, /* char *ret0 */, ...);

extern char *__loc1;
```

The `regcmp` function compiles the regular expression (consisting of its concatenated arguments) and returns a pointer to the compiled form. The memory to hold the compiled form is allocated with `malloc`; it is the user's responsibility to free this memory when it is no longer needed. If one of the arguments contains an error, `regcmp` returns NULL.

The `regex` function applies the compiled regular expression `re` to the string in `str`. Additional arguments may be given to receive values back (see below). If the pattern matches, a pointer to the next unmatched character in `str` is returned, and the external character pointer `__loc1` will point to the place where the match begins. If the pattern does not match, `regex` returns NULL.

HP-UX 10.*x* requires you to link with the *-lPW* library to use these functions.

The regular expressions used by `regcmp` and `regex` are somewhat different from those described above:

- The dollar sign ($) matches the end of the string; \n matches a newline.

- A regular expression followed by a plus sign (+) matches one or more occurrences of the regular expression.

- The curly-brace notation does not use backslashes to escape the curly braces. For example, while *ed* uses \{m\}, `regcmp` and `regex` use {m}.

- The parenthesis notation from *ed* (\(...\)) has been replaced with the following:

  (...)$n
  > The part of the string that matches the regular expression will be returned. The value will be stored in the string pointed to by the (n+1)th argument following `str` in the call to `regex`. Up to ten strings may be returned this way.

  (...)
  > Parentheses are used for grouping. The operators *, +, and { } can operate on a single character or on a regular expression contained in parentheses.

SVR4 provides a second set of functions for implementing regular expressions, called `compile`, `advance`, and `step`. These functions implement regular expressions just as they exist in *ed* and *grep*, but their usage is complicated, and, because they are not available in other versions of the operating system, not portable. For more information on them, consult the *regexpr*(5) manual page.

Example 16-12 shows a different version of the file-searching program than Example 16-11; this one uses regular expressions, much like the *grep* command. Notice again that the pattern must be enclosed in quotes to prevent the shell from trying to interpret it.

Example 16–12: regexp

```
#include <libgen.h>
#include <stdio.h>

int
main(int argc, char **argv)
{
    FILE *fp;
    char line[BUFSIZ];
    char *re, *pattern, *filename;

    /*
     * Check arguments.
```

Example 16-12: regexp (continued)

```
 */
if (argc != 3) {
    fprintf(stderr, "Usage: %s pattern file\n", *argv);
    exit(1);
}

pattern = *++argv;
filename = *++argv;

/*
 * Compile the regular expression.
 */
if ((re = regcmp(pattern, NULL)) == NULL) {
    fprintf(stderr, "bad regular expression.\n");
    exit(1);
}

/*
 * Open the file.
 */
if ((fp = fopen(filename, "r")) == NULL) {
    perror(filename);
    exit(1);
}

/*
 * Read lines from the file.
 */
while (fgets(line, sizeof(line), fp) != NULL) {
    /*
     * Strip the newline.
     */
    line[strlen(line) - 1] = '\0';

    /*
     * If it matches, print it.
     */
    if (regex(re, line) != NULL)
        puts(line);
}

fclose(fp);
exit(0);
}


% regexp 'A....d' /usr/dict/words
Aeneid
Alameda
Alfred
Alfredo
Amerada
```

```
Aphrodite
Arnold
Atwood
Avogadro
% regexp '^A....d$' /usr/dict/words
Aeneid
Alfred
Arnold
Atwood
% regexp 'b(an){2,}' /usr/dict/words
banana
```

Porting Notes

The `regcmp` and `regex` functions are available on System V-based systems only. BSD-based systems provide a slightly different set of functions:

```
char *re_comp(const char *re);
```

```
int re_exec(const char *str);
```

The `re_comp` function compiles the regular expression contained in `re` and stores the result internally. If the expression is compiled successfully, `re_comp` returns NULL; otherwise it returns a pointer to an error message describing the problem. The `re_exec` function compares the string `str` to the last compiled regular expression and returns 1 if they match, 0 if they don't, and -1 if an error occurs (such as calling `re_exec` before calling `re_comp`).

The BSD functions are more user-friendly than their System V counterparts in that they accept standard *ed* regular expressions. The System V functions allow you to use multiple regular expressions simultaneously without having to recompile them, and they allow the program to obtain the parts of the string that matched the regular expression.

If portability is a concern, it is necessary to write code that is compatible with either set of regular expression functions. The lack of support for simultaneous use of multiple regular expressions in the BSD functions can make this difficult, however. Another approach is to obtain a free or public-domain implementation of regular-expression functions and simply include those with the program.

Henry Spencer offers a wonderful public domain implementation of the regular expression functions included in Research UNIX Version 8; his package includes not only the `compile` and `match` functions, but also a function to perform substitutions in strings much like a text editor does. The package is available from *ftp://ftp.cs.toronto.edu/pub/regexp.shar.Z*. The GNU Project also provides a fairly robust implementation of the regular expression functions; their implementation is covered by the GNU General Public License. The package is available from *ftp://prep.ai.mit.edu/pub/gnu/regex-0.12.tar.gz.*

Internationalization

For years, UNIX used the ASCII character set. ASCII, being the *American* Standard Code for Information Interchange, works great in the United States. But in England, where the monetary symbol is '£,' a non-ASCII character, a problem arises. In countries that use diacritical marks with their letters, e.g., â, ç, ì, õ, and ü, the problem is even worse. And in countries like Japan, where the character set is not even remotely Latin in origin, ASCII is completely hopeless.

In recent years, as UNIX has spread throughout the world, so has interest in internationalizing it. All programs should handle the local country's character set, whatever that is. Programs that print dates and times should print them in the commonly accepted format of the local country. Programs that print formatted numbers should use the proper character to mark the decimal point, and so forth.

Internationalization is too complex a topic to cover in this book. Instead, we present only a few of the many functions available for internationalization.

Programs using the functions described in this section must be linked with the *-lintl* library.

Defining the Locale

A *locale* defines the characteristics of the environment, from an internationalization standpoint, that a program is operating in. The "UNIX" locale is named "C." Other locales generally use a two-character name, usually the ISO standard two-letter abbreviation for the country name. For example, "de" is the German locale, "fr" is the French locale, and "ja" is the Japanese locale.

The setlocale function sets a program's locale for any of several different categories:

```
#include <locale.h>

char *setlocale(int category, const char *locale);
```

The locale parameter contains the name of the locale; this will be used by the internationalization functions to look at various databases contained in the subdirectory of the same name in */usr/lib/locale*. If locale contains the empty string, the value will be taken from environment variables. If locale is NULL, the current locale will be returned and no changes made.

The `category` parameter must be one of the following:

LC_CTYPE

Affects the behavior of the character type functions such as `isdigit` and `tolower`.

LC_NUMERIC

Affects the decimal point character and the thousands digit separator character for formatted input/output functions (`scanf`, `printf`, etc.) and string conversion functions (`strtol`, etc.).

LC_TIME

Affects the date and time formats delivered by `ascftime`, `cftime`, `getdate`, and `strftime`.

LC_COLLATE

Affects the sort order produced by `strcoll` and `strxfrm` (see below).

LC_MONETARY

Affects the monetary formatting information returns by `localeconv` (see below).

LC_MESSAGES

Affects the behavior of `dgettext`, `gettext`, and `gettxt` (not discussed in this book).

LC_ALL

A shorthand way to specify all of the above categories.

If `setlocale` succeeds, it returns `locale`. If it fails, it returns NULL.

Formatting Numbers

A number of factors affect formatting numbers in different countries. Aside from the obvious differences in monetary symbols, there are also differences in the character used for a decimal point (some countries use a period, others use a comma), the character used to separate thousands groups (some countries use a comma, others use a period), and so forth.

The `localeconv` function returns information about how to format numbers in the program's current locale:

```
#include <locale.h>

struct lconv *localeconv(void);
```

The function returns a pointer to a structure of type `struct lconv`:

```
struct lconv    {
    char    *decimal_point;
    char    *thousands_sep;
    char    *grouping;
    char    *int_curr_symbol;
    char    *currency_symbol;
    char    *mon_decimal_point;
    char    *mon_thousands_sep;
    char    *mon_grouping;
    char    *positive_sign;
    char    *negative_sign;
    char     int_frac_digits;
    char     frac_digits;
    char     p_cs_precedes;
    char     p_sep_by_space;
    char     n_cs_precedes;
    char     n_sep_by_space;
    char     p_sign_posn;
    char     n_sign_posn;
};
```

The fields of this structure are:

`decimal_point`

The decimal point character used to format non-monetary quantities.

`thousands_sep`

The character used to separate groups of digits to the left of the decimal point in non-monetary quantities.

`grouping`

A string in which each byte is taken as an integer that indicates the number of digits comprising the current group in a formatted non-monetary quantity. Each integer is interpreted according to the following:

CHAR_MAX

No further grouping should be performed.

0   The previous element is to be used repeatedly for the remainder of the digits.

other

The value is the number of digits that comprise the current group. The next element is examined to determine the size of the next group of digits to the left of the current group.

`int_curr_symbol`

    The international currency symbol applicable to the current locale.

`currency_symbol`

    The local currency symbol applicable to the current locale.

`mon_decimal_point`

    The decimal point character to be used in formatting monetary quantities.

`mon_grouping`

    A string in which each byte is taken as an integer that indicates the number of digits comprising the current group in a formatted monetary quantity. Each integer is interpreted according to the rules described above.

`positive_sign`

    The string used to indicate a non-negative formatted monetary quantity.

`negative_sign`

    The string used to indicate a negative formatted monetary quantity.

`int_frac_digits`

    The number of decimal places to the right of the decimal to display in internationally formatted monetary quantities.

`frac_digits`

    The number of decimal places to the right of the decimal to display in locally formatted monetary quantities.

`p_cs_precedes`

    Set to 1 or 0 to indicate whether the currency symbol precedes (1) or succeeds (0) the value for non-negative formatted monetary quantities.

`p_sep_by_space`

    Set to 1 or 0 to indicate whether the currency symbol is (1) or is not (0) separated by a space from the value for a non-negative formatted monetary quantity.

`n_cs_precedes`

    Set to 1 or 0 to indicate whether the currency symbol precedes (1) or succeeds (0) the value for negative formatted monetary quantities.

`n_sep_by_space`

    Set to 1 or 0 to indicate whether the currency symbol is (1) or is not (0) separated by a space from the value for a negative formatted monetary quantity.

`p_sign_posn`

Indicates how to position the positive sign for a non-negative formatted monetary quantity, as follows:

0 Parentheses surround the quantity and currency symbol.

1 The sign string precedes the quantity and currency symbol.

2 The sign string follows the quantity and currency symbol.

3 The sign string immediately precedes the currency symbol.

4 The sign string immediately follows the currency symbol.

`n_sign_posn`

Indicates the positioning of the negative sign for a negative formatted monetary quantity. The possible values are as described above for `p_sign_posn`.

Collating Sequences

Functions such as `strcmp` compare strings based on the ASCII collating sequence, which in general is the same as alphabetical order. However, these functions do not work properly for character sets other than ASCII. Thus, when working in an international environment, `qsort` cannot be used with `strcmp` to sort strings into the proper order.

The `strcoll` and `strxfrm` functions can be used instead to make these comparisons:

```
#include <string.h>

int strcoll(const char *s1, const char *s2);

size_t strxfrm(char *dst, const char *src, size_t n);
```

The `strcoll` function compares strings `s1` and `s2`. If `s1` is less than `s2`, the function returns less than 0; if `s1` is greater, it returns 0, and if `s1` is greater than `s2`, it returns a greater than 0 value. The strings are interpreted in the program's locale for the LC_COLLATE category.

The `strxfrm` function transforms the string `src`, placing the result in `dst`. If `strcmp` is applied to two transformed strings, it will return the same result as if `strcoll` had been applied to the original strings. No more than `n` bytes will be placed into `dst`, including the terminating null character. If `dst` is null and `n` is 0, `strxfrm` will return the number of bytes required to store the transformed string. The length of the transformed string is returned by `strxfrm`; if this is greater than `n`, the contents of `dst` are undefined.

The `strcoll` function calls `strxfrm` on `s1` and `s2` and then returns the result of comparing them with `strcmp`. If a large number of strings is to be compared against a single string for a match, it is more efficient to call `strxfrm` and `strcmp` yourself.

As mentioned previously, there are many more internationalization-support functions. Functions and libraries are also available to help the programmer implement multilingual error messages, handle multi-byte characters (for languages such as Japanese), and so forth. For a complete discussion of the issues involved in internationalization and the functions provided to work around them, consult one of the several books devoted to the topic.

Chapter Summary

Just as we began this book with a discussion of the numerous little functions that you've probably used every day, we finish the book with a discussion of a number of functions that you may not use every day, but that are just as useful. The number of functions available to the systems programmer grows with every release of UNIX. Some of the new functions are useful, and others are less so. As new functions are added, some of them catch on and start to show up in lots of programs. These functions tend to start propagating to other versions of UNIX, as programmers demand them. Other functions are added and then later removed, as their use never catches on or as better replacements are developed.

Most of the functions described in this chapter are available in most newer versions of UNIX. The exception to this rule, unfortunately, are the search functions, which are available only in System V-based versions. Hopefully, as more vendors standardize on (or at least adopt parts of) SVR4, this will become less of a portability problem.

Significant Changes in ANSI C

From its inception, the C programming language was defined by the book *The C Programming Language* by Brian Kernighan and Dennis Ritchie. Unfortunately, while the book was an excellent tool for learning the language, it was not an unambiguous specification of the language. This resulted in a variety of compilers which, while mostly compatible, would do different things with certain constructs, creating a portability nightmare. Furthermore, a few extensions were added to the language at various points (enumerated types, the void type, and structures as function arguments and return values) but never sufficiently documented, resulting in different levels of support in different compilers.

In the late 1980s, the American National Standards Institute set out to remedy this situation. The X3J11 Technical Committee was charged with developing a standard for the C programming language that clarified the ambiguities in the language, and solved the problems of divergent implementations. For the most part, the committee attempted to codify existing practice, rather than invent new language mechanisms. However, where it seemed valuable, the committee did define some new features that were thought to be generally useful. Overall, they did a pretty good job (although there are some surprising lapses).

In 1989, ANSI Standard X3.159 was released, and became the standard for the C programming language. Most modern C compilers implement the ANSI version of the language, including the compilers described in Chapter 1, *Introduction to SVR4*. In this appendix, we describe some of the more significant changes made in ANSI C. This is not an exhaustive list; if you need more information, you should consult the standard itself, or one of the numerous books on the topic (Kernighan and Ritchie, Second Edition, is the definitive reference). If you are already a proficient C programmer, you may wish to examine *A C User's Guide to ANSI C*, by Ken Arnold and John Peyton, published by Addison-Wesley. This book presents all the changes in a concise manner for readers who already know the pre-ANSI version of the language.

Tokens

Tokens are the smallest recognizable units of the language. Tokens include operators, variable names, keywords, and constants.

String Concatenation

The ANSI C standard says that adjacent string constants with no operators between them should simply be concatenated. This means that

```
"foo" "bar"
```

is equivalent to

```
"foobar"
```

This is useful in situations in which a long string needs to be defined. For example:

```
char *usage = "Usage: thisprogram [-b] [-g] [-l] files...\n"
              "       -b    babble incessantly about everything\n"
              "       -g    babble in ancient greek\n"
              "       -l    babble in latin\n";
```

Escape Sequences

The ANSI C standard has defined some new backslash escape sequences:

\a for "alert." When printed, this sequence should ring the terminal's bell.

\v for vertical tab (this escape was already supported by many compilers).

\x for hexadecimal constant, much like a blackslash followed by a digit introduces an octal constant.

The number of digits in an octal constant has been formally limited to three; some compilers previously allowed more. This means that \0123 is now always a two-character string: the character with octal value 012 followed by the character 3.

The digits 8 and 9 are no longer allowed in octal constants. This shouldn't be any great surprise. However, some compilers allowed \128 and took it to mean \130.

The Preprocessor

The C preprocessor has always been a source of portability problems, mostly because numerous programmers took advantage of the way a particular processor handled something. A number of preprocessor constructs that are used frequently were never actually specified as part of the language; their use relies on knowledge of how the internals of the preprocessor work.

String Substitution

String substitution in preprocessor macros is one of these areas. Consider the following macro:

```
#define PRINT(value)    printf("value = %d\n", value)
```

Some preprocessors would expand PRINT(x) to:

```
printf("x = %d\n", x)
```

while others would expand it to:

```
printf("value = %d\n", x)
```

This difference depends on how macro parameters are expanded inside character strings. The ANSI standard specifies that the latter behavior is correct, and introduces a new syntax for achieving the former behavior:

```
#define PRINT(value)    printf(#value " = %d\n", value)
```

The #value gets expanded to a quoted version of the parameter (e.g., "x"), and then the string concatenation rules take over to produce the desired result.

Character Constants

The rule that says preprocessor tokens are not replaced inside character strings also applies to character constants. A frequent construct in pre-ANSI C is:

```
#define CTRL(c)    (037 & 'c')
```

This macro produces the control-character version of a regular character. Thus CTRL(L) would produce a CTRL-L. Unfortunately, in ANSI C, this will not work. The simplest way to avoid this problem is to define the macro slightly differently:

```
#define CTRL(c)    (037 & c)
```

This macro is then called as CTRL('L').

Token Pasting

One of the features of some preprocessors is that they allow "token pasting." This has never been a documented behavior, but is used frequently. With a token-pasting preprocessor, there are at least two ways to combine two tokens:

```
#define self(a)      a
#define glue(a,b)    a/**/b

self(x)1
glue(x,1)
```

Both of these are intended to produce a single token, **x1**. In ANSI C however, they both produce two separate tokens, **x** and **1**.

The ANSI C standard defines a new syntax for token pasting:

```
#define glue(a, b)    a ## b
```

Since **##** is now a legitimate operator, programmers have much more freedom in the use of white space in both the definition and invocation of token pasting macros.

The #elif Directive

The ANSI C preprocessor now provides a directive **#elif** that may be used in conjunction with **#ifdef** and **#endif**.

The #error Directive

The ANSI C preprocessor provides **#error**, a directive that prints the error message given as an argument and then exits. This allows code of the form:

```
#if defined(BSD)
... BSD stuff ...
#elif defined(SYSV)
... System V stuff ...
#else
#error "One of BSD or SYSV must be defined."
#endif
```

Predefined Symbols

All preprocessors offer the predefined symbols **__FILE__** (the current source file as a quoted string) and **__LINE__** (the current line number as an integer). The ANSI C standard has added **__DATE__** and **__TIME__**, which give the current date and time (as of when the program was compiled) as quoted strings.

The constant `__STDC__` is defined as 1 in compilers that are compliant with ANSI C. This can be used to test whether or not ANSI C features may be used:

```
#ifdef __STDC__
... ANSI stuff ...
#else
... Non-ANSI stuff ...
#endif
```

NOTE

In the ANSI standard, the only defined value for `__STDC__` is 1. If it is defined to any other value, the meaning is undefined. Unfortunately, the standard is somewhat ambiguous on this point.

This is a problem on SVR4, where AT&T uses `__STDC__` with a value of 0 to enable certain ANSI C features outside of a strictly ANSI C-compliant environment. This means that the test above for an ANSI environment no longer works; it must be rewritten as:

```
#if __STDC__ == 1
... ANSI stuff ...
#else
... Non-ANSI stuff ...
#endif
```

Text After #else and #endif

Most preprocessors have always allowed constructs like:

```
#ifdef FOO
...
#else FOO
...
#endif FOO
```

However, this has never been strictly legal, since `#else` and `#endif` are not supposed to have arguments. In ANSI C this syntax is now expressly forbidden (although most compilers will just print a warning and accept it); it should be rewritten:

```
#ifdef FOO
...
#else /* FOO */
...
#endif /* FOO */
```

Declarations

The ANSI C standard has cleaned up variable declarations, both by formalizing the use of some non-standard types, and defining a few new ones.

The void Type

Most newer non-ANSI compilers accept some form of the void type, but support for all of its features is varied. The void type has three uses in ANSI C:

1. Declaring a function with a return type of void means that the function returns no value. By declaring functions that *do* have a return value appropriately, and indicating functions that do not have a return value with a type of void, the compiler can perform type checking for the programmer.

2. Declaring a function prototype (see below) with a parameter specification of void means that the function has no arguments. The compiler can use this for checking parameter lists in function calls.

3. The type void * is now used as the universal pointer. Prior to the invention of void, the char * type was usually used; this did not work well on systems that used different sized pointers for different objects.

The enum Type

The ANSI C standard has officially codified the enum data type. Use of enum variables as array subscripts is explicitly allowed; some compilers previously disallowed this.

The char Type

Because there is no standard among hardware vendors as to whether a char is signed or unsigned, there is also no standard defined by ANSI. The signedness or unsignedness of a char in ANSI C is explicitly *hardware-dependent*.

If a specific type (signed or unsigned) is needed, the familiar unsigned qualifier and the new-to-ANSI signed qualifier may be used when declaring variables of type char.

Type Qualifiers

ANSI C has defined two new type qualifiers:

const

> This qualifier identifies a constant, indicating that the object will not be modified. This allows the compiler to refuse to modify the object; it also allows the

compiler more freedom in making optimizations. Note that *initializing* an object is not the same as *modifying* the object. For example, the following is perfectly legal:

```
const int True = 1;
```

The use of the `const` qualifier is somewhat tricky, however. For example, the declaration

```
const char *s;
```

means that s will only point at characters that will not be modified through s (although they might be modified through some other means). It does *not* mean that s will not be modified. To declare that, you would instead say

```
char *const s;
```

volatile

This is the opposite of `const`. It tells the compiler that this variable may change in ways the compiler cannot predict. Basically, it tells the compiler not to optimize references to this variable, since the optimizations may not be accurate in all circumstances.

Functions

ANSI C has also made two significant changes to the way functions are declared and called.

Function Prototypes

The most visible change in ANSI C is the introduction of *function prototypes*, borrowed from C++. With function prototypes, the number and type of a function's parameters are specified when the function is declared. This allows the compiler to perform type checking, and also to avoid unnecessary type promotions.

We have used function prototypes throughout this book. For example:

```
FILE *fopen(char *filename, char *mode);
```

This is the most explicit of the prototype syntaxes. It is also possible to leave out the variable names in the prototype, e.g.,

```
FILE *fopen(char *, char *);
```

However, the variable names help in remembering what parameter goes where; the second form provides no clue in this regard. And, of course, the old pre-ANSI syntax is still valid:

```
FILE *fopen();
```

However, in this case, the compiler is not able to perform type checking.

Function definition may follow either the most explicit of the prototype syntaxes,

```
FILE *
fopen(char *filename, char *mode)
{
    ⋮
}
```

or it may follow the old pre-ANSI syntax:

```
FILE *
fopen(filename, mode)
char *filename, *mode;
{
    ⋮
}
```

Note, however, that the type of each parameter must be specified explicitly, even if two consecutive parameters have the same type. In other words,

```
FILE *fopen(char *filename, char *mode);
```

is correct, but

```
FILE *fopen(char *filename, *mode);
```

is not.

Functions with a variable number of arguments are handled with a trailing "...". This means that there may be zero or more parameters after this point. For example, the prototype for the fprintf function looks like:

```
int fprintf(FILE *, const char *, ...);
```

Note that this syntax requires that the "..." be last in the list.

Finally, functions with no parameters are now declared using the void type:

```
int getpid(void);
```

This allows the compiler to make sure that no parameters are passed to the function when it is compiled.

Handling prototypes in non-ANSI environments

Even though you may be using an ANSI C compiler, it is quite likely that the code you are writing will have to be compiled on a system that does not have an ANSI compiler. Rather than avoiding the use of function prototypes altogether, there are a few approaches you can take.

The simplest approach simply has two declarations for every function:

```
#ifdef __STDC__
int fact(int);
#else
int fact();
#endif

#ifdef __STDC__
int fact(int n)
#else
int fact(n)
int n;
#endif
{
    :
}
```

Unfortunately, this is rather ugly. Another possibility is to do the above for the declarations, but use old-style definitions:

```
#ifdef __STDC__
int fact(int);
#else
int fact();
#endif

int fact(n)
int n;
{
    :
}
```

This is less ugly, but still requires declaring the function twice, leaving a potential for error.

A more elegant solution, one that you will see used often, is to define a macro, usually called _P or _proto, that handles the prototypes, and then use old-style definitions:

```
#ifdef __STDC__
#define _P(args)     args
#else
#define _P(args)     ()
#endif
```

```
int fact _P((int));

int fact(n)
int n;
{
    ⋮
}
```

When `__STDC__` is defined, the prototype expands to

```
int fact (int);
```

while when `__STDC__` is not defined, it expands to

```
int fact ();
```

Widened Types

In K&R C, the compiler had no way to type-check function parameters, and would promote all arguments of types smaller than `int` to `int`, and all arguments of type `float` to `double`. Since most compilers at the time performed all floating-point arithmetic in double precision anyway, this wasn't usually a problem.

ANSI C still promotes function parameters to their widened types when a function is called. However, inside the function, the widened types are converted back to their original, narrower sizes. This can cause some serious problems with carelessly-written pre-ANSI code.

One of the most common errors is to assume that `float`s are really `double`s. For example:

```
foo(f)
float f;
{
    bar(&f);
}

bar(d)
double *d;
{
    ⋮
}
```

The problem here is that in pre-ANSI C, f never really was a `float`. It was declared as one, but the compiler treated it as a `double`. So in `bar`, where we assumed a pointer to a `double`, you could get away with it, because that's how things really worked.

In ANSI C, you will not get a warning from the compiler about this, because, being pre-ANSI C, there are no function prototypes (which serves to prove that function prototypes are a good thing). But, when you try to execute your program, `bar` will fail in any one of a number of different ways trying to use `*d` as if it were actually a `double`.

To avoid this problem, when writing code to be used both with and without function prototypes, use only widened types—no `char` or `short` (use `int`), and no `float` (use `double`). Pointers to any of the types (widened or unwidened) are okay.

Expressions

Perhaps the most significant divergence of ANSI C from widely accepted practice is in expression evaluation. In original K&R C, `unsigned` specified exactly one type. There were no `unsigned chars`, `unsigned shorts`, or `unsigned longs`. This is not to say that most compilers did not support these types, just that they were never "official." Naturally, since the rules for how these unofficial types behaved in expressions in which they were mixed with other types did not exist, different compiler implementors used different rules.

In most C compilers, a "sign preserving" rule is used. If an unsigned type needs to be widened, it is widened to a larger unsigned type. When an unsigned type mixes with a signed type, the result is an unsigned type. This makes a certain amount of sense, but can lead to unexpected results in certain situations. For example, subtracting `unsigned short` 5 from `unsigned short` 3 will produce a large unsigned number with the same bit pattern as -2.

ANSI C, on the other hand, specifies that a "value preserving" rule should be used. When an unsigned type smaller than an `int` needs to be widened, it is widened to a *signed* `int` if that is large enough to hold the type, otherwise it is widened to an `unsigned int`. This produces more intuitive behavior in cases like the above (in which the result would be a `signed int` -2), and makes no difference in most other cases. However, programs that rely on the earlier behavior will need to be modified (usually by inserting appropriate typecasts) if they are to work correctly.

Summary

For the most part, the changes made in ANSI C are a good thing. ANSI C is rapidly becoming available on almost all UNIX platforms, and its growing use will result in code that is both more portable and less prone to error, provided that features such as function prototypes are used wherever possible.

B

Accessing Filesystem Data Structures

Many system administration tasks require information about one or more mounted filesystems. Although it is usually possible to obtain this information using existing commands, there are times when it's easier to "roll your own." This appendix describes the functions and procedures necessary for doing just that.

NOTE

The functions and procedures described in this appendix differ from one version of UNIX to another. They even differ among the various vendors' versions of SVR4. The text and examples in this appendix describe the situation as it exists in Solaris 2.*x*. However, the online examples for the book also include working copies of these programs for HP-UX 10.*x* and IRIX 5.*x*; compare those files for information about how those operating systems differ from what is described here.

The Mounted Filesystem Table

The file */etc/mnttab* contains a list of the filesystems that are currently mounted, and some information about them. This file is maintained mostly by the *mount* and *umount* commands, although other processes such as the automounter and the volume management daemon can also make updates to it.

In SVR4, the */etc/mnttab* file is a text file, consisting of one-line entries. In most other versions of UNIX, it is a binary file, with each entry consisting of a structure that contains more or less the same information. The functions provided for reading this file use a structure of type `struct mnttab` to describe each entry. This structure is declared in the include file *sys/mnttab.h*:

```
struct mnttab {
    char    *mnt_special;
    char    *mnt_mountp;
    char    *mnt_fstype;
    char    *mnt_mntopts;
    char    *mnt_time;
};
```

The fields of the structure are:

mnt_special

The name of the block-special device where the filesystem resides.

mnt_mountp

The name of the filesystem mount point, i.e., the directory that it is mounted on.

mnt_fstype

The type of the filesystem (e.g., `ufs`, `nfs`, `hsfs`, or `pcfs`).

mnt_mntopts

A comma-separated list of the options with which the filesystem was mounted. The legal values vary with the filesystem type, but this includes things such as read-only, no set-user-id, and so forth.

mnt_time

The time the filesystem was mounted. This is a character string containing the `time_t` value in ASCII; it must be converted to an integer with `atoi` and then passed to `ctime` or whatever (see Chapter 7, *Time of Day Operations*).

Three functions read the */etc/mnttab* file:

```
#include <stdio.h>
#include <sys/mnttab.h>

int getmntent(FILE *fp, struct mnttab *mnt);

int getmntany(FILE *fp, struct mnttab *mnt, struct mnttab *mntref);

char *hasmntopt(struct mnttab *mnt, char *option);
```

The `getmntent` function reads the next entry from the file referenced by `fp`, and stores the broken-out fields of the entry in the area pointed to by `mnt`. The `getmntany` function searches the file referenced by `fp` for an entry that matches the non-null fields of `mntref`, and stores the broken-out fields of the entry in the area pointed to by `mnt`. Notice that neither of these functions opens, closes, or rewinds the */etc/mnttab* file.

Both `getmntent` and `getmntany` return 0 if an entry is successfully read, and -1 if end-of-file is encountered. If a formatting error occurs in the file, they return one of the following:

`MNT_TOOLONG`
A line in the file exceeded the maximum line length.

`MNT_TOOMANY`
A line in the file contains too many fields.

`MNT_TOOFEW`
A line in the file does not contain enough fields.

The `hasmntopt` function scans the `mnt_mntopts` field of `mnt` for a substring that matches `option`. It returns a pointer to the substring if it is present, and `NULL` if is not.

The Filesystem Defaults File

The file */etc/vfstab* contains "default" information about filesystems. This information includes device names, mount points, mount options, and so forth. The table is used by the system bootstrap procedure to mount the filesystems that should be mounted automatically. It may also be used to record the location of other filesystems that are mounted only on command. A filesystem does not have to be listed in this file to be mounted; listing it here simply makes the *mount* command simpler.

On most other versions of UNIX, including HP-UX 10.*x* and IRIX 5.*x*, this file is called */etc/fstab*, and has a slightly different format.

Each line in the file constitutes an entry, which is described by a structure of type `struct vfstab`, declared in the include file *sys/vfstab.h*:

```
struct vfstab {
    char    *vfs_special;
    char    *vfs_fsckdev;
    char    *vfs_mountp;
    char    *vfs_fstype;
    char    *vfs_fsckpass;
    char    *vfs_automnt;
    char    *vfs_mntopts;
};
```

The fields of the structure are:

`vfs_special`
The name of the block-special device on which the filesystem resides.

vfs_fsckdev

The name of the character-special device on which the filesystem resides. This field is so named because the *fsck* program uses this device to check the filesystem's integrity at boot time.

vfs_mountp

The name of the filesystem mount point; that is, the directory it is to be mounted on.

vfs_fstype

The type of the filesystem (e.g., ufs, nfs, hsfs, or pcfs).

vfs_fsckpass

When *fsck* runs, certain filesystems must be checked before others. This number indicates which pass of *fsck* should check this filesystem.

vfs_automnt

An indication of whether or not the filesystem should be mounted automatically when the system boots.

vfs_mntopts

The options that should be used when mounting this filesystem. These vary with the filesystem type.

Any of these fields that do not apply to the filesystem in question will be null.

Four functions read the */etc/vfstab* file:

```
#include <stdio.h>
#include <sys/vfstab.h>

int getvfsent(FILE *fp, struct vfstab *vfs);

int getvfsfile(FILE *fp, struct vfstab *vfs, char *file);

int getvfsspec(FILE *fp, struct vfstab *vfs, char *spec);

int getvfsany(FILE *fp, struct vfstab *vfs, struct vfstab *vfsref);
```

The getvfsent function reads the next entry from the file referenced by fp, and stores the broken-out fields of the entry in the area pointed to by vfs. The getvfsfile function searches the file for an entry whose vfs_mountp field is the same as file and stores the broken-out fields of the entry in the area pointed to by vfs. The getvfsspec function searches the file for an entry whose vfs_special field is the same as spec and stores the broken-out fields of the entry in the area pointed to by vfs. The getvfsany function searches the file referenced by fp for an entry that matches the non-null fields of vfsref, and stores the broken-out fields of the entry in the area pointed to by vfs. Note that none of these functions opens, closes, or rewinds the */etc/vfstab* file.

All four of these functions return 0 if an entry is successfully read, and -1 if end-of-file is encountered. If a formatting error occurs in the file, they return one of the following:

VFS_TOOLONG

A line in the file exceeded the maximum line length.

VFS_TOOMANY

A line in the file contains too many fields.

VFS_TOOFEW

A line in the file does not contain enough fields.

Obtaining Filesystem Statistics

Several filesystem statistics are of interest to system administration programs, including the amount of space used or available in the filesystem, the number of files in the filesystem, and so forth. The `statvfs` and `fstatvfs` functions can be used to obtain this information:

```
#include <sys/types.h>
#include <sys/statvfs.h>

int statvfs(const char *path, struct statvfs *stats);

int fstatvfs(int fd, struct statvfs *stats);
```

The `statvfs` function obtains statistics about the filesystem in which the file named by `path` resides, and returns them in the area pointed to by `stats`. The `fstatvfs` function does the same thing, but uses a file descriptor instead of a pathname to refer to the file. Both functions return 0 on success; if an error occurs, -1 is returned and `errno` is set to indicate the error.

Both of these functions return statistics in a structure of type `struct statvfs`:

```
typedef struct statvfs {
    u_long    f_bsize;
    u_long    f_frsize;
    u_long    f_blocks;
    u_long    f_bfree;
    u_long    f_bavail;
    u_long    f_files;
    u_long    f_ffree;
    u_long    f_favail;
    u_long    f_fsid;
    char      f_basetype[FSTYPSZ];
    u_long    f_flag;
    u_long    f_namemax;
```

```
    char      f_fstr[32];
    u_long    f_filler[16];
} statvfs_t;
```

The fields of this structure are:

f_bsize

The preferred filesystem block size.

Reads and writes on the filesystem should use this block size for optimum performance.

f_frsize

The fundamental filesystem block size.

This is also called the fragment size. This is the smallest unit of disk space that can be consumed by a file (i.e., even if a file is smaller than this value, it consumes a block of this size on the disk).

f_blocks

The total number of blocks that can be used in the filesystem, in units of **f_frsize**.

f_bfree

The total number of free blocks in the filesystem.

f_bavail

The number of free blocks in the filesystem available to non-privileged processes.

The system reserves a small amount (usually ten percent) of the space for use only by the superuser.

f_files

The total number of files (i-nodes) that can be created in the filesystem.

This value is not available for filesystems mounted via NFS.

f_ffree

The total number of free files (i-nodes) in the filesystem.

This value is not available for filesystems mounted via NFS.

f_avail

The number of free files (i-nodes) in the filesystem available to non-privileged processes.

The system can reserve a small number of these for use only by the superuser, although this is rarely done. This value is not available for filesystems mounted via NFS.

f_fsid

A unique identifier for the filesystem.

f_basetype

The filesystem type name.

f_flag

A bit mask of flags.

Possible values are:

ST_RDONLY

The filesystem is read-only.

ST_NOSUID

The filesystem does not support set-user-id and set-group-id bit semantics.

ST_NOTRUNC

The filesystem does not truncate filenames longer than the maximum length.

f_namemax

The maximum length of a filename on this filesystem.

f_str

A filesystem specific string used only by the kernel.

Example B-1 shows a program that reads the mounted filesystem table and, for each filesystem, prints out the information stored for it in the table. It also looks up the filesystem in the filesystem defaults table and prints any information it finds there. Finally, it uses `statvfs` to obtain statistics about the filesystem, and prints them out.

Example B–1: fsysinfo

```
#include <sys/types.h>
#include <sys/statvfs.h>
#include <sys/time.h>
#include <string.h>
#include <stdio.h>
#include <sys/mnttab.h>
#include <sys/vfstab.h>

char    *mnttabFile = "/etc/mnttab";
char    *vfstabFile = "/etc/vfstab";

struct statvfs  *getfsInfo(char *);
struct mnttab   *getmnttabEntry(FILE *);
struct vfstab   *getvfstabEntry(FILE *, struct mnttab *);

int
main(void)
```

Example B-1: fsysinfo (continued)

```
{
    time_t clock;
    struct mnttab *mnt;
    struct vfstab *vfs;
    struct statvfs *stats;
    FILE *mnttabFP, *vfstabFP;

    /*
     * Open the mounted file system table.
     */
    if ((mnttabFP = fopen(mnttabFile, "r")) == NULL) {
        perror(mnttabFile);
        exit(1);
    }


    /*
     * Open the file system defaults file.
     */
    if ((vfstabFP = fopen(vfstabFile, "r")) == NULL) {
        perror(vfstabFile);
        exit(1);
    }


    /*
     * For each file system...
     */
    while ((mnt = getmnttabEntry(mnttabFP)) != NULL) {
        /*
         * If it's not an "ignore" file system, look it
         * up in the defaults file and get its current
         * stats.
         */
        if (hasmntopt(mnt, "ignore") == 0) {
            vfs = getvfstabEntry(vfstabFP, mnt);
            stats = getfsInfo(mnt->mnt_mountp);
        }
        else {
            stats = NULL;
            vfs = NULL;
        }

        clock = atoi(mnt->mnt_time);

        /*
         * Print the mnttab structure.
         */
        printf("%s:\n", mnt->mnt_mountp);
        printf("  %s information:\n", mnttabFile);
        printf("    file system type:     %s\n", mnt->mnt_fstype);
        printf("    mounted on device:    %s\n", mnt->mnt_special);
        printf("    mounted with options: %s\n", mnt->mnt_mntopts);
        printf("    mounted since:        %s", ctime(&clock));
```

Example B-1: fsysinfo (continued)

```
        /*
         * Print the vfstab structure.
         */
        if (vfs != NULL) {
            printf("  %s information:\n", vfstabFile);
            printf("      file system type:    %s\n",
                    vfs->vfs_fstype ? vfs->vfs_fstype : "");
            printf("      mount device:        %s\n",
                    vfs->vfs_special ? vfs->vfs_special : "");
            printf("      fsck device:         %s\n",
                    vfs->vfs_fsckdev ? vfs->vfs_fsckdev : "");
            printf("      fsck pass number:    %s\n",
                    vfs->vfs_fsckpass ? vfs->vfs_fsckpass : "");
            printf("      mount at boot time:  %s\n",
                    vfs->vfs_automnt ? vfs->vfs_automnt : "");
            printf("      mount with options:  %s\n",
                    vfs->vfs_mntopts ? vfs->vfs_mntopts : "");
        }

        /*
         * Print the statvfs structure.
         */
        if (stats != NULL) {
            printf("   statvfs information:\n");
            printf("      maximum name length: %u\n", stats->f_namemax);
            printf("      preferred block size: %u\n", stats->f_bsize);
            printf("      fundam. block size:  %u\n", stats->f_frsize);
            printf("      total blocks:        %u\n", stats->f_blocks);
            printf("      total blocks free:   %u\n", stats->f_bfree);
            printf("      total blocks avail:  %u\n", stats->f_bavail);
            printf("      total files:         %u\n", stats->f_files);
            printf("      total files free:    %u\n", stats->f_ffree);
            printf("      total files avail:   %u\n", stats->f_favail);
        }

        putchar('\n');
    }

    /*
     * All done.
     */
    fclose(mnttabFP);
    fclose(vfstabFP);
    exit(0);
}

/*
 * getmnttabEntry - read an entry from the mount table.
 */
struct mnttab *
getmnttabEntry(FILE *fp)
{
```

Example B-1: fsysinfo (continued)

```
        int n;
        static int line = 0;
        static struct mnttab mnt;

        /*
         * Until we get a good entry...
         */
        for (;;) {
            /*
             * Read the next entry.
             */
            n = getmntent(fp, &mnt);
            line++;

            switch (n) {
            case 0:                 /* okay                */
                return(&mnt);
            case -1:                /* end of file         */
                return(NULL);
            case MNT_TOOLONG:
                fprintf(stderr, "%s: %d: line too long.\n", mnttabFile, line);
                break;
            case MNT_TOOMANY:
                fprintf(stderr, "%s: %d: too many fields.\n", mnttabFile, line);
                break;
            case MNT_TOOFEW:
                fprintf(stderr, "%s: %d: not enough fields.\n", mnttabFile, line);
                break;
            }
        }
}

/*
 * getvfstabEntry - look up the file system defaults for the file system
 *          described by mnt.
 */
struct vfstab *
getvfstabEntry(FILE *fp, struct mnttab *mnt)
{
    struct vfstab vfsref;
    static struct vfstab vfs;

    /*
     * Have to rewind each time.
     */
    rewind(fp);

    /*
     * Zero out the reference structure.
     */
    memset((char *) &vfsref, 0, sizeof(struct vfstab));
```

Example B–1: fsysinfo (continued)

```
    /*
     * Look for an entry that has the same special device,
     * mount point, and file system type.
     */
    vfsref.vfs_special = mnt->mnt_special;
    vfsref.vfs_mountp = mnt->mnt_mountp;
    vfsref.vfs_fstype = mnt->mnt_fstype;

    /*
     * Look it up.
     */
    if (getvfsany(fp, &vfs, &vfsref) == 0)
        return(&vfs);

    return(NULL);
}


/*
 * getfsInfo - look up information about the file system.
 */
struct statvfs *
getfsInfo(char *filsys)
{
    static struct statvfs stats;

    if (statvfs(filsys, &stats) < 0) {
        perror(filsys);
        return(NULL);
    }

    return(&stats);
}


    % fsysinfo
    /:
      /etc/mnttab information:
        filesystem type:    ufs
        mounted on device:   /dev/dsk/c0t3d0s0
        mounted with options: rw,suid
        mounted since:       Mon Dec  5 09:05:28 1994
      /etc/vfstab information:
        filesystem type:    ufs
        mount device:        /dev/dsk/c0t3d0s0
        fsck device:         /dev/rdsk/c0t3d0s0
        fsck pass number:    1
        mount at boot time:  no
        mount with options:
      statvfs information:
        maximum name length: 255
        preferred block size: 8192
        fundam. block size:  1024
```

```
          total blocks:        23063
          total blocks free:   7696
          total blocks avail:  5396
          total files:         13440
          total files free:    10936
          total files avail:   10936
/usr:
  /etc/mnttab information:
     filesystem type:     ufs
     mounted on device:   /dev/dsk/c0t3d0s5
     mounted with options: rw,suid
     mounted since:       Mon Dec  5 09:05:28 1994
  /etc/vfstab information:
     filesystem type:     ufs
     mount device:        /dev/dsk/c0t3d0s5
     fsck device:         /dev/rdsk/c0t3d0s5
     fsck pass number:    2
     mount at boot time:  no
     mount with options:
  statvfs information:
     maximum name length: 255
     preferred block size: 8192
     fundam. block size:  1024
     total blocks:        129775
     total blocks free:   15669
     total blocks avail:  2699
     total files:         64512
     total files free:    53128
     total files avail:   53128
     .
     .
     .
/vol:
  /etc/mnttab information:
     filesystem type:     nfs
     mounted on device:   msw:vold(pid174)
     mounted with options: ignore
     mounted since:       Mon Dec  5 09:06:33 1994
```

Reading Filesystem Data Structures

There are certain tasks for which it is preferable to access a filesystem by reading the disk directly, rather than going through the operating system kernel. The most common of these is filesystem backups. The principal reason for this type of access is speed; it is much faster to read the disk directly. It is also the only way to read a file that contains "holes" and obtain only the actual disk blocks in use.

Reading the disk directly, however, is complex. The program must understand the layout of the filesystem data structures on the disk, and must be able to interpret a number of "private" bits of information correctly. Because it bypasses all security mechanisms (file ownership and permissions bits), this operation is usually restricted to the superuser (by setting the ownership and permissions of the block and character special devices for the filesystem).

Two common on-disk filesystems have been developed over the years; the original filesystem as invented by Ken Thompson and Dennis Ritchie, and the Berkeley Fast File System, developed by Kirk McKusick, Bill Joy, Sam Leffler, and Robert Fabry. In SVR4, both filesystems are supported: the (slightly modified) original is called the "System V File System," and the Fast File System is called the "UNIX File System." Solaris 2.*x* supports only the Fast File System ("UNIX File System"); support for the "System V File System" has been removed. In this section we will only discuss the Fast File System, since that is by far the more popular of the two. The discussion applies for the most part to the older filesystem as well, although the details are different (generally, the older filesystem is somewhat simpler to implement, but it is also substantially less efficient).

NOTE

Silicon Graphics uses their own filesystem format, the Extended File System (EFS). Although it is fairly similar to the UFS filesystem described in this seciton, there are some differences.

Disk Terminology

In order to understand how the filesystem is laid out on the disk, it is first necessary to understand a little bit about how a disk drive works.

A disk drive contains one or more *platters*, on which data is stored. Each platter is a circular piece of metal with a hole in the middle, much like a phonograph record or compact disc. The platter is coated with a substance that responds to magnetic fields, similar to the coating on a video tape. The platter(s) are mounted on a *spindle*, with gaps between them. Each platter has two surfaces on which data can be recorded, but the outer surfaces of the top and bottom platters are usually not used.

There is one read/write head for each platter surface in the disk drive. Usually, the heads are mounted to a common assembly so that they all move together, although this is not always the case. The heads move in and out from the edge to the center of the platters; there is no side-to-side motion. During a read/write operation, the heads are held stationary over a given section of the platters while the platters rotate at a high speed (several thousand revolutions per minute) underneath them.

The area on one side of a single platter that can be read or written without moving the head is called a *track*. Tracks are concentric circles, and each time a platter completes a full revolution, an entire track has passed under the read/write head. There may be anywhere from a few hundred to a few thousand tracks on each side of each platter. If each track is extended up and down to include the same track on all the other platters, this is called a *cylinder*. Thus, there are the same number of cylinders on the disk drive as there are tracks on a single platter. For a six-platter disk drive, there are ten tracks in each cylinder (remember, the outer surfaces of the top and bottom platters are not used).

Tracks are further subdivided into *sectors*. Each sector is 512 bytes in size, and is the smallest addressable unit on a disk drive. Thus, when a file that is fifteen bytes long is stored on the disk, it actually consumes 512 bytes of space. The term *disk block* (or just *block*) is often used as a synonym for sector, but this term is often ambiguous and should be avoided if possible.

Information is recorded on the tracks of a disk by writing data into one or more sectors. To perform this operation, the disk must be told the head number, track number, and sector number where the data is to be stored. When a write (or read) operation begins, the disk must first position the head assembly over the proper track. It then has to wait for the proper sector to arrive under the read/write head. Once this occurs, the data transfer can take place. There are, thus, three factors affecting the rate at which a disk can transfer data:

- *seek time*—the amount of time it takes to position the head assembly over the proper track

- *latency time*—the amount of time it takes for the right sector to arrive under the heads

- *transfer rate*—the speed at which the drive can transfer the data to or from the disk, given that the heads are in position

(Additional factors affecting the final transfer rate include the speed of the disk controller, the speed of the system's input/output bus, and the speed of the system's memory; but these are outside the control of the disk manufacturer.)

The Super Block

The *super block* is the most important part of a filesystem. It contains all of the information necessary to locate the other filesystem data structures on the disk. Without the super block to indicate where these data structures are located, the filesystem would be a meaningless collection of bits. Because the super block is so critical to the operation of the filesystem, it is replicated in several places on the disk when the filesystem is first created. Since the critical information in the super block does not change, it is not necessary to update these copies.

The super block structure is declared in the include file *sys/fs/ufs_fs.h*:

```
struct  fs {
      struct fs *fs_link;         /* linked list of filesystems     */
      struct fs *fs_rlink;        /* used for incore super blocks    */
      daddr_t      fs_sblkno;     /* addr of super-block in filesys  */
      daddr_t      fs_cblkno;     /* offset of cyl-block in filesys  */
      daddr_t      fs_iblkno;     /* offset of inode-blocks in filesys */
      daddr_t      fs_dblkno;     /* offset of first data after CG   */
      long         fs_cgoffset;   /* cylinder group offset in cylinder */
      long         fs_cgmask;     /* used to calc mod FS_NTRAK       */
      time_t       fs_time;       /* last time written               */
      long         fs_size;       /* number of blocks in FS          */
      long         fs_dsize;      /* number of data blocks in FS     */
      long         fs_ncg;        /* number of cylinder groups       */
      long         fs_bsize;      /* size of basic blocks in FS      */
      long         fs_fsize;      /* size of frag blocks in FS       */
      long         fs_frag;       /* number of frags in a block in FS */
/* these are configuration parameters */
      long         fs_minfree;    /* minimum percentage of free blocks */
      long         fs_rotdelay;   /* num of ms for optimal next block */
      long         fs_rps;        /* disk revolutions per second     */
/* these fields can be computed from the others */
      long         fs_bmask;      /* ``blkoff'' calc of blk offsets  */
      long         fs_fmask;      /* ``fragoff'' calc of frag offsets */
      long         fs_bshift;     /* ``lblkno'' calc of logical blkno */
      long         fs_fshift;     /* ``numfrags'' calc number of frags */
/* these are configuration parameters */
      long         fs_maxcontig;  /* max number of contiguous blks   */
      long         fs_maxbpg;     /* max number of blks per cyl group */
/* these fields can be computed from the others */
      long         fs_fragshift;  /* block to frag shift             */
      long         fs_fsbtodb;    /* fsbtodb and dbtofsb shift constant*/
      long         fs_sbsize;     /* actual size of super block      */
      long         fs_csmask;     /* csum block offset               */
      long         fs_csshift;    /* csum block number               */
      long         fs_nindir;     /* value of NINDIR                 */
      long         fs_inopb;      /* value of INOPB                  */
      long         fs_nspf;       /* value of NSPF                   */
/* yet another configuration parameter */
      long         fs_optim;      /* optimization preference, see below*/
/* these fields are derived from the hardware */
      long         fs_npsect;     /* # sectors/track including spares */
      long         fs_interleave; /* hardware sector interleave      */
      long         fs_trackskew;  /* sector 0 skew, per track        */
/*a unique id for this filesystem (currently unused and unmaintained)*/
/* In 4.3 Tahoe this space is used by fs_headswitch and fs_trkseek  */
/* Neither of those fields is used in the Tahoe code right now but  */
/* there could be problems if they are.                            */
      long         fs_id[2];      /* filesystem id                   */
/* sizes determined by number of cylinder groups and their sizes   */
      daddr_t      fs_csaddr;     /* blk addr of cyl grp summary area */
      long         fs_cssize;     /* size of cyl grp summary area    */
      long         fs_cgsize;     /* cylinder group size             */
```

```
/* these fields are derived from the hardware */
    long        fs_ntrak;        /* tracks per cylinder          */
    long        fs_nsect;        /* sectors per track            */
    long        fs_spc;          /* sectors per cylinder         */
/* this comes from the disk driver partitioning */
    long        fs_ncyl;         /* cylinders in filesystem      */
/* these fields can be computed from the others */
    long        fs_cpg;          /* cylinders per group          */
    long        fs_ipg;          /* inodes per group             */
    long        fs_fpg;          /* blocks per group * fs_frag   */
/* this data must be re-computed after crashes */
    struct      csum fs_cstotal; /* cylinder summary information  */
/* these fields are cleared at mount time */
    char        fs_fmod;         /* super block modified flag    */
    char        fs_clean;        /* filesystem state flag        */
    char        fs_ronly;        /* mounted read-only flag       */
    char        fs_flags;        /* currently unused flag        */
    char        fs_fsmnt[MAXMNTLEN];/* name mounted on           */
/* these fields retain the current block allocation info         */
    long        fs_cgrotor;      /* last cg searched             */
    struct csum *fs_csp[MAXCSBUFS];/* list of fs_cs info buffers */
    long        fs_cpc;          /* cyl per cycle in postbl      */
    short       fs_opostbl[16][8]; /* old rotation block list head */
    long        fs_sparecon[55];/* reserved for future constants */
#define fs_ntime fs_sparecon[54]/* INCORE only; time in nanoseconds */
    long        fs_state;        /* filesystem state time stamp  */
    quad        fs_qbmask;       /* ~fs_bmask - for use with quad size*/
    quad        fs_qfmask;       /* ~fs_fmask - for use with quad size*/
    long        fs_postblformat;/* format of positional layout tables*/
    long        fs_nrpos;        /* number of rotaional positions */
    long        fs_postbloff;    /* (short) rotation block list head */
    long        fs_rotbloff;     /* (u_char) blocks for each rotation */
    long        fs_magic;        /* magic number                 */
    u_char      fs_space[1];     /* list of blocks for each rotation */
/* actually longer */
};
```

Most of these fields are not of interest here; they are used by the kernel for implementing the filesystem, but have little meaning outside of that context. Some of the fields that are of interest are:

fs_bsize

The filesystem block size, in bytes.

The filesystem block size is some multiple of the disk sector size; it is more efficient to access the filesystem in larger units. The usual block size for a Fast File System is 8192 bytes (the old filesystem uses 512 or 1024 bytes). Since the maximum size of any individual file in the Fast File System is 2^{31} bytes, this limits the minimum filesystem block size to 4096 bytes.

`fs_fsize`

> The filesystem fragment block size.

> The larger block sizes introduced in the Fast File System, although they make input and output more efficient, also waste more of the disk. For example, if the smallest available block size were 4096 bytes, a 1027-byte file would waste 3069 bytes on the disk. For this reason, the Fast File System allows a filesystem block to be divided into two, four, or eight *fragments* of equal size. A file will take up some number of full filesystem blocks, and then the last little bit of the file will be written into one or more fragments. The other fragments in the same block may be used by some other file. Thus, with a 4094-byte filesystem block size and a 1024-byte fragment size, a 5120-byte file would consume one filesystem block (4096 bytes) and one fragment (1024 bytes). The other three fragments could be used by other files.

`fs_frag`

> The number of fragments in a filesystem block.

> This is easily computed from the above two parameters, but is precomputed here for speed.

`fs_size`

> The total number of blocks in the filesystem, in units of the fragment size.

> This includes the blocks used to store other bookkeeping information as well as the blocks actually used for data storage.

`fs_dsize`

> The number of filesystem data blocks in the filesystem that may be used for data storage, in units of the fragment size.

`fs_ncg`

> The number of *cylinder groups* in the filesystem.

> See the following sections for a discussion of cylinder groups.

`fs_ipg`

> The number of i-nodes per cylinder group.

> See the following sections for a discussion of cylinder groups. This number, when multiplied by `fs_ncg` (above), gives the maximum number of distinct files that may be stored in the filesystem.

`fs_fsmnt`

> The name of the mount point on which this filesystem is currently mounted. If the filesystem is not currently mounted, this will contain the name of the last mount point on which it was mounted.

I-Nodes

As explained in Chapter 5, *Files and Directories*, the *i-node* structure is used to store all of the important information about a file, such as its type, owner, group, mode, size, number of links, last access time, last modification time. As we shall see below, the i-node also contains the addresses of all the disk blocks used to store the contents of the file.

There is one i-node for each file in the filesystem. The i-nodes are allocated when the filesystem is created, which means that the number of files that can be created in the filesystem is static. If all the i-nodes are used up with very tiny files, it is possible to have a large quantity of free data blocks that simply cannot be used (because no more files can be created). However, it is much more common to run out of data blocks before running out of i-nodes.

There are two i-node structures; the one stored on the disk, and the one used in memory by the kernel. The in-memory one has some extra fields, used for book-keeping purposes. The common part between the two structures is stored in a structure of type `struct icommon`; the on-disk i-node is called a `struct dinode`. These structures are defined in the include file *sys/fs/ufs_inode.h*:

```
struct  icommon {
     o_mode_t ic_smode;     /*  0: mode and type of file              */
     short       ic_nlink; /*  2: number of links to file            */
     o_uid_t     ic_suid;  /*  4: owner's user id                    */
     o_gid_t     ic_sgid;  /*  6: owner's group id                   */
     quad        ic_size;  /*  8: number of bytes in file            */
#ifdef _KERNEL
     struct timeval ic_atime;/* 16: time last accessed               */
     struct timeval ic_mtime;/* 24: time last modified               */
     struct timeval ic_ctime;/* 32: last time inode changed          */
#else
     time_t      ic_atime; /* 16: time last accessed                 */
     long        ic_atspare;
     time_t      ic_mtime; /* 24: time last modified                 */
     long        ic_mtspare;
     time_t      ic_ctime; /* 32: last time inode changed            */
     long        ic_ctspare;
#endif
     daddr_t     ic_db[NDADDR];/* 40: disk block addresses           */
     daddr_t     ic_ib[NIADDR];/* 88: indirect blocks                */
     long        ic_flags;    /* 100: status, currently unused       */
     long        ic_blocks;   /* 104: blocks actually held           */
     long        ic_gen;      /* 108: generation number              */
     long        ic_mode_reserv;/* 112: reserved                     */
     uid_t       ic_uid;      /* 116: long EFT version of uid        */
     gid_t       ic_gid;      /* 120: long EFT version of gid        */
     ulong       ic_oeftflag; /* 124: reserved                       */
};
```

```
struct dinode {
    union {
        struct  icommon di_icom;
        char    di_size[128];
    } di_un;
};
```

```
#define di_ic            di_un.di_icom
#define di_mode          di_ic.ic_smode
#define di_nlink         di_ic.ic_nlink
#define di_uid           di_ic.ic_uid
#define di_gid           di_ic.ic_gid
#define di_smode         di_ic.ic_smode
#define di_suid          di_ic.ic_suid
#define di_sgid          di_ic.ic_sgid
#if defined(vax) || defined(i386)
#define di_size          di_ic.ic_size.val[0]
#endif
#if defined(mc68000) || defined(sparc) || defined(u3b2) || defined(u3b15)
#define di_size          di_ic.ic_size.val[1]
#endif
#define di_db            di_ic.ic_db
#define di_ib            di_ic.ic_ib
#define di_atime         di_ic.ic_atime
#define di_mtime         di_ic.ic_mtime
#define di_ctime         di_ic.ic_ctime
#define di_ordev         di_ic.ic_db[0]
#define di_blocks        di_ic.ic_blocks
#define di_gen           di_ic.ic_gen
```

The di_mode, di_nlink, di_uid, di_gid, di_size, di_atime, di_mtime, and di_ctime elements of this structure have the obvious meanings. These are copied to the `struct stat` structure when the `stat` or `fstat` functions are called.

The di_db array stores the addresses of the first NDADDR data blocks in the file. These are called *direct blocks*, because their addresses are stored directly in the i-node. The value of NDADDR can vary, but is usually 12. The di_ib array stores NIADDR levels of *indirect blocks*. As with NDADDR, the value of NIADDR can vary, but is almost always 3.

The first element of the di_ib array contains the address of a singly-indirect block. This block is used to store the addresses of more direct blocks. Thus, for a filesystem block size of 8192, the first level of indirection allows another 2048 data blocks to be addressed.

The second element of the di_ib array contains the address of a doubly-indirect block. This block is used to store the addresses of more singly-indirect blocks. Thus, for our 8192-byte block size, the second level of indirection allows another 2048 singly-indirect blocks to be addressed, which in turn means that over four million additional data blocks can be addressed.

The third element of the `di_ib` array, of course, contains the address of a triply indirect block. This block is used to store the addresses of more doubly-indirect blocks. A triply-indirect block allows over eight trillion more data blocks to be addressed.

Cylinder Groups

In the original UNIX filesystem, the i-node structures were stored on the disk immediately following the super block, and then the data blocks followed the i-nodes. This is a simple layout, but results in a lot of back-and-forth head motion when accessing files. The Fast File System solves this problem by dividing the disk into several groups of cylinders called, appropriately, *cylinder groups*.

Each cylinder group contains a structure defining bookkeeping information for the group, a redundant copy of the super block, some i-node structures, and data blocks. The cylinder group bookkeeping information includes a list of which i-nodes in the group are in use, and which disk blocks are not in use. The cylinder group concept allows a file's data blocks to be laid out as much as possible in a contiguous fashion, minimizing the rotational latency from one block to the next.

The cylinder group information is stored in a structure of type `struct cg`, defined in the include file *sys/fs/ufs_fs.h*:

```
struct cg {
      struct    cg *cg_link;      /* linked list of cyl groups     */
      long      cg_magic;         /* magic number                  */
      time_t    cg_time;          /* time last written             */
      long      cg_cgx;           /* we are the cgx'th cylinder group*/
      short     cg_ncyl;          /* number of cyl's this cg       */
      short     cg_niblk;         /* number of inode blocks this cg  */
      long      cg_ndblk;         /* number of data blocks this cg   */
      struct    csum cg_cs;       /* cylinder summary information   */
      long      cg_rotor;         /* position of last used block    */
      long      cg_frotor;        /* position of last used frag     */
      long      cg_irotor;        /* position of last used inode    */
      long      cg_frsum[MAXFRAG];/* counts of available frags      */
      long      cg_btotoff;       /* (long) block totals per cylinder*/
      long      cg_boff;          /* (short) free block positions   */
      long      cg_iusedoff;      /* (char) used inode map          */
      long      cg_freeoff;       /* (u_char) free block map        */
      long      cg_nextfreeoff;   /* (u_char) next available space  */
      long      cg_sparecon[16];  /* reserved for future use        */
      u_char    cg_space[1];      /* space for cylinder group maps  */
/* actually longer */
};
```

Putting it All Together

Example B-2 shows a program that reads filesystem data structures directly from the disk to calculate the disk usage for each user. Running this program requires the ability to read the character-special device for the filesystem, which usually means it must be run as the superuser.

This example will not work on IRIX 5.*x*, which uses the EFS filesystem.

Example B-2: diskuse

```
#include <sys/param.h>
#include <sys/time.h>
#include <sys/vnode.h>
#include <sys/fs/ufs_inode.h>
#include <sys/fs/ufs_fs.h>
#include <unistd.h>
#include <limits.h>
#include <fcntl.h>
#include <stdio.h>
#include <sys/vfstab.h>
#include <pwd.h>

#define sblock   sb_un.u_sblock

/*
 * We need a union to hold the super block, because it takes up an
 * entire disk block (the smallest unit in which you can read), but
 * the structure is not actually that big.
 */
union {
    struct fs u_sblock;
    char      u_dummy[SBSIZE];
} sb_un;

/*
 * Keep track of usage with this.  We need to save the uid so that
 * we can sort the array by number of blocks used.
 */
struct usage {
    int    u_uid;
    size_t u_blocks;
} usageByUid[UID_MAX];

/*
 * Name of the file system defaults file.
 */
char    *vfstabFile = "/etc/vfstab";

int diskuse(char *);
int bread(int, daddr_t, char *, int);
int compare(const void *, const void *);
```

Example B-2: diskuse (continued)

```
int
main(int argc, char **argv)
{
    int n;
    FILE *fp;
    char *fsname;
    struct passwd *pwd;
    struct vfstab vfstab;

    /*
     * Open vfstab.
     */
    if ((fp = fopen(vfstabFile, "r")) == NULL) {
        perror(vfstabFile);
        exit(1);
    }

    /*
     * For each file system...
     */
    while (--argc) {
        fsname = *++argv;

        /*
         * Rewind vfstab.
         */
        rewind(fp);

        /*
         * Look up the file system so we can get the
         * character device it's on.
         */
        if (getvfsfile(fp, &vfstab, fsname) != 0) {
            fprintf(stderr, "%s: not found in %s.\n", fsname, vfstabFile);
            continue;
        }

        /*
         * Zero out our counters.
         */
        memset(usageByUid, 0, UID_MAX * sizeof(struct usage));

        /*
         * Put the uids in the counters.  The array is
         * initially in uid order, but later we sort it
         * by blocks.
         */
        for (n = 0; n < UID_MAX; n++)
            usageByUid[n].u_uid = n;

        /*
         * Calculate disk usage.
```

Example B–2: diskuse (continued)

```
         */
        if (diskuse(vfstab.vfs_fsckdev) < 0)
            continue;

        /*
         * Sort the usage array by blocks.
         */
        qsort(usageByUid, UID_MAX, sizeof(struct usage), compare);

        /*
         * Print a header.
         */
        printf("%s (%s):\n", vfstab.vfs_mountp, vfstab.vfs_fsckdev);

        /*
         * Print the usage information.
         */
        for (n = 0; n < UID_MAX; n++) {
            /*
             * Skip users with no usage.
             */
            if (usageByUid[n].u_blocks == 0)
                continue;

            /*
             * Look up the login name.  If not found,
             * use the user-id.
             */
            if ((pwd = getpwuid(usageByUid[n].u_uid)) != NULL)
                printf("\t%-10s", pwd->pw_name);
            else
                printf("\t#%-9d", usageByUid[n].u_uid);

            /*
             * Print the usage.  The number we have is in
             * 512-byte (actually DEV_BSIZE) blocks; we
             * convert this to kbytes.
             */
            printf("\t%8d\n", usageByUid[n].u_blocks / 2);
        }

        putchar('\n');
    }

    fclose(fp);
    exit(0);
}


/*
 * diskuse - tabulate disk usage for the named device.
 */
int
```

Example B-2: diskuse (continued)

```
diskuse(char *device)
{
    ino_t ino;
    daddr_t iblk;
    int i, fd, nfiles;
    struct dinode itab[MAXBSIZE / sizeof(struct dinode)];

    /*
     * Open the device for reading.
     */
    if ((fd = open(device, O_RDONLY)) < 0) {
        perror(device);
        return(-1);
    }

    /*
     * Sync everything out to disk.
     */
    (void) sync();

    /*
     * Read in the superblock.
     */
    if (bread(fd, SBLOCK, (char *) &sblock, SBSIZE) < 0) {
        (void) close(fd);
        return(-1);
    }

    /*
     * The number of files (number of inodes) is equal to
     * the number of inodes per cylinder group times the
     * number of cylinder groups.
     */
    nfiles = sblock.fs_ipg * sblock.fs_ncg;

    for (ino = 0; ino < nfiles; ) {
        /*
         * Read in the inode table for this cylinder group.  The
         * fsbtodb macro converts a file system block number to
         * a disk block number.  The itod macro converts an inode
         * number to its file system block number.
         */
        iblk = fsbtodb(&sblock, itod(&sblock, ino));

        if (bread(fd, iblk, (char *) itab, sblock.fs_bsize) < 0) {
            (void) close(fd);
            return(-1);
        }

        /*
         * For each inode...
         */
```

Example B-2: diskuse (continued)

```
        for (i = 0; i < INOPB(&sblock) && ino < nfiles; i++, ino++) {
            /*
             * Inodes 0 and 1 are not used.
             */
            if (ino < UFSROOTINO)
                continue;

            /*
             * Skip unallocated inodes.
             */
            if ((itab[i].di_mode & IFMT) == 0)
                continue;

            /*
             * Count the blocks as used.
             */
            usageByUid[itab[i].di_uid].u_blocks += itab[i].di_blocks;
        }
    }

    return(0);
}

/*
 * bread - read count bytes into buf, starting at disk block blockno.
 */
int
bread(int fd, daddr_t blockno, char *buf, int count)
{
    /*
     * Seek to the right place.
     */
    if (lseek(fd, (long) blockno * DEV_BSIZE, SEEK_SET) < 0) {
        perror("lseek");
        return(-1);
    }

    /*
     * Read in the data.
     */
    if ((count = read(fd, buf, count)) < 0) {
        perror("read");
        return(-1);
    }

    return(count);
}

/*
 * compare - compare two usage structures for qsort.
 */
int
```

Example B-2: diskuse (continued)

```
compare(const void *a, const void *b)
{
    struct usage *aa, *bb;

    aa = (struct usage *) a;
    bb = (struct usage *) b;

    return(bb->u_blocks - aa->u_blocks);
}



    # diskuse /usr
    /usr (/dev/rdsk/c0t3d0s5):
            root                 58148
            bin                  52888
            lp                    2289
            uucp                   779
            sys                      1
            adm                      1 .
```

The program begins by using the `getvfsfile` function to determine the character-special device for the filesystem. It then opens this device for reading. The first thing read from the disk is the super block. This is used to determine the number of i-node structures in the filesystem, which is computed by multiplying the number of cylinder groups by the number of i-nodes per cylinder group. The program then enters a loop, reading through all the groups of i-nodes. On each pass through the outer loop, a block of i-nodes is read in from the disk. The inner loop iterates over the block of i-nodes, and, for each allocated i-node, records the number of blocks used by that file.

This program does not read the data blocks associated with each file, since the information it needs is recorded in the i-node itself. To read the data blocks, it is necessary to first read the direct blocks, and then the indirect blocks. This can be done in a recursive function, as shown by the code in Example B-3.

This example will not work on IRIX 5.*x*, which uses the EFS filesystem.

Example B-3: readblocks.c

```
#include <sys/param.h>
#include <sys/time.h>
#include <sys/vnode.h>
#include <sys/fs/ufs_inode.h>
#include <sys/fs/ufs_fs.h>
#include <unistd.h>

int bread(int, daddr_t, char *, int);
int readDataBlocks(int, struct fs *, struct dinode *, int (*)(char *, int));
int readIndirect(int, struct fs *, daddr_t, int, int *, int (*)(char *, int));
```

Example B-3: readblocks.c (continued)

```c
int
readDataBlocks(int fd, struct fs *sblock, struct dinode *dp,
               int (*fn)(char *, int))
{
    int i, n, count;
    char block[MAXBSIZE];

    /*
     * Read the direct blocks.   There are NDADDR of them.
     */
    count = dp->di_size;

    for (i = 0; i < NDADDR && count > 0; i++) {
        /*
         * Read in the block from disk.
         */
        n = min(count, sblock->fs_bsize);

        if (bread(fd, fsbtodb(sblock, dp->di_db[i]), block, n) < 0)
            return(-1);

        count -= n;

        /*
         * Call the user's function on the block.
         */
        (*fn)(block, n);
    }

    /*
     * Now read the indirect blocks.   There are NIADDR of them.
     * Recall that the first address is a singly indirect block,
     * the second is a doubly indirect block, and so on.
     */
    for (i = 0; i < NIADDR && count > 0; i++) {
        if (readIndirect(fd, sblock, dp->di_ib[i], i, &count, fn) < 0)
            return(-1);
    }

    return(0);
}

int
readIndirect(int fd, struct fs *sblock, daddr_t blkno, int level, int *count,
             int (*fn)(char *, int))
{
    int i, n;
    char block[MAXBSIZE];
    daddr_t idblk[MAXBSIZE / sizeof(daddr_t)];

    /*
     * Read the block in from disk.
```

Example B–3: readblocks.c (continued)

```
     */
    if (blkno)
        bread(fd, fsbtodb(sblock, blkno), (char *) idblk, sblock->fs_bsize);
    else
        memset(idblk, 0, sizeof(idblk));

    /*
     * If level is zero, then this block contains disk block
     * addresses (i.e., it's singly indirect).  If level is
     * non-zero, then this block contains addresses of more
     * indirect blocks.
     */
    if (level == 0) {
        /*
         * Read the disk blocks.  There are NINDIR
         * of them.
         */
        for (i = 0; i < NINDIR(sblock) && *count > 0; i++) {
            n = min(*count, sblock->fs_bsize);

            if (bread(fd, fsbtodb(sblock, idblk[i]), block, n) < 0)
                return(-1);

            *count -= n;

            /*
             * Call the user's function.
             */
            (*fn)(block, n);
        }
    }
    else {
        /*
         * Decrement the level.
         */
        level--;

        /*
         * Handle the next level of indirection by calling
         * ourselves recursively with each address in this
         * block.
         */
        for (i = 0; i < NINDIR(sblock); i++) {
            n = readIndirect(fd, sblock, idblk[i], level, count, fn);

            if (n < 0)
                return(-1);
        }
    }

    return(0);
}
```

Example B–3: readblocks.c (continued)

```
/*
 * bread - read count bytes into buf, starting at disk block blockno.
 */
int
bread(int fd, daddr_t blockno, char *buf, int count)
{
    /*
     * Seek to the right place.
     */
    if (lseek(fd, (long) blockno * DEV_BSIZE, SEEK_SET) < 0) {
        perror("lseek");
        return(-1);
    }

    /*
     * Read in the data.
     */
    if ((count = read(fd, buf, count)) < 0) {
        perror("read");
        return(-1);
    }

    return(count);
}
```

Summary

Reading a filesystem's data structures directly off the disk is not inherently difficult, but is hindered by the fact that there is very little documentation available on the structures used to implement the filesystem. A number of the fields in these structures are stored in various units (e.g., filesystem blocks), and must be converted to other units (e.g., disk blocks) to be used. The units used, as well as the formulas to convert them, are not generally documented.

There is nothing "wrong" with reading a filesystem in this way; indeed, sometimes it is necessary. However, it is a relatively non-portable approach, and also requires privileged processes. Both of these concerns must be addressed when making any decision about going through the kernel or reading the filesystem directly.

The /proc Filesystem

In older versions of UNIX, access to process data such as that obtained by the *ps* command is obtained by reading kernel memory directly. This process, aside from being very complex, requires superuser permissions and is inherently non-portable. To get around these problems, and to provide a general interface to process' memory images, SVR4 (as well as some other newer versions) offers the */proc* filesystem.

NOTE

Because it does not provide the */proc* filesystem, the information in this appendix does not apply to HP-UX 10.*x*.

The */proc* filesystem contains one file for each process currently running on the system; the name of the file is the same as the process ID for the process. The owner of the file is set to the process' real user ID, and the permission bits are set so the file is readable and writable only by its owner. The superuser, of course, may open, read, and write any file (process). For security reasons, an open of a file in */proc* fails unless both the user ID and group ID of the caller match those of the process, and the process' object file is readable by the caller. Files corresponding to set-user-id and set-group-id processes may be opened only by the super-user.

The interface to the */proc* filesystem is the normal filesystem system calls: `open`, `close`, `read`, `write`, and `ioctl`. An open for reading and writing enables control of the process; this is used by debuggers and the like. An open for reading only allows inspection but not control of the process; this is used by *ps* and so forth. The control of processes as performed by debuggers is beyond the scope of this book; we will discuss only the features for process inspection here.

Information about a process is obtained via the `ioctl` function:

```
#include <sys/types.h>
#include <sys/signal.h>
#include <sys/fault.h>
#include <sys/syscall.h>
#include <sys/procfs.h>

int ioctl(int fd, int code, void *ptr);
```

The `fd` parameter is a file descriptor for the open process, `code` is a code describing the operation to be performed (see below), and `ptr` is a pointer to a structure in which to store results. The structure type varies depending on the value of `code`. The `ioctl` function returns 0 on success; if it fails it returns -1 and stores an error indication in `errno`.

Obtaining Process Status

The `PIOCSTATUS` code returns status information for the open process, and places it into a structure of type `prstatus_t`, which looks like this in Solaris 2.*x* (it's slightly different in IRIX 5.*x*):

```
typedef struct prstatus {
  long        pr_flags;     /* Flags (see below)                            */
  short       pr_why;       /* Reason for process stop (if stopped)         */
  short       pr_what;      /* More detailed reason                         */
  siginfo_t pr_info;        /* Info associated with signal or fault         */
  short       pr_cursig;    /* Current signal                               */
  u_short     pr_nlwp;      /* Number of lwps in the process                */
  sigset_t pr_sigpend;      /* Set of signals pending to the process        */
  sigset_t pr_sighold;      /* Set of signals held (blocked) by the lwp */
  struct      sigaltstack pr_altstack; /* Alternate signal stack info       */
  struct      sigaction pr_action; /* Signal action for current signal      */
  pid_t       pr_pid;       /* Process id                                   */
  pid_t       pr_ppid;      /* Parent process id                            */
  pid_t       pr_pgrp;      /* Process group id                             */
  pid_t       pr_sid;       /* Session id                                   */
  timestruc_t pr_utime;     /* Process user cpu time                        */
  timestruc_t pr_stime;     /* Process system cpu time                      */
  timestruc_t pr_cutime;    /* Sum of children's user times                 */
  timestruc_t pr_cstime;    /* Sum of children's system times               */
  char        pr_clname[PRCLSZ]; /* Scheduling class name                   */
  short       pr_syscall;   /* System call number (if in syscall)           */
  short       pr_nsysarg;   /* Number of arguments to this syscall          */
  long        pr_sysarg[PRSYSARGS]; /* Arguments to this syscall            */
  id_t        pr_who;       /* Specific lwp identifier                      */
  sigset_t pr_lwppend;      /* Set of signals pending to the lwp            */
  struct ucontext *pr_oldcontext; /* Address of previous ucontext          */
  caddr_t     pr_brkbase;   /* Address of the process heap                  */
  u_long      pr_brksize;   /* Size of the process heap, in bytes           */
  caddr_t     pr_stkbase;   /* Address of the process stack                 */
```

```
    u_long      pr_stksize;     /* Size of the process stack, in bytes    */
    short       pr_processor;   /* processor which last ran this LWP      */
    short       pr_bind;        /* processor LWP bound to or PBIND_NONE   */
    long        pr_instr;       /* Current instruction                    */
    prgregset_t pr_reg;         /* General registers                      */
} prstatus_t;
```

Some of the more interesting fields of this structure are:

pr_pid
> The process' process ID.

pr_ppid
> The process' parent process ID.

pr_pgrp
> The process' process-group ID.

pr_sid
> The process' session ID.

pr_utime
> The amount of *user time* the process has accumulated.

> User time is accumulated when the CPU is executing the process' program code. The `timestruc_t` structure is similar to a `struct timeval`, but contains elements for seconds and nanoseconds (as opposed to seconds and microseconds). The elements of the structure are `tv_sec` and `tv_nsec`, respectively.

pr_stime
> The amount of *system time* the process has accumulated.

> System time is accumulated when the CPU is executing operating system kernel code on behalf of the process; in other words, this is the amount of time the process has spent doing system calls.

pr_cutime
> The sum of the user time accumulated by all of the process' children.

> This number includes only those processes that have exited and been waited on.

pr_cstime
> The sum of the system time accumulated by all of the process' children.

> This number includes only those processes that have exited and been waited on.

pr_brksize

The size in bytes of the process' *break* (the amount of memory that has been allocated via the `brk` and `sbrk` system calls).

Generally, this number gives the amount of memory the process has dynamically allocated using `malloc` and its associated routines.

pr_stksize

The size in bytes of the process' stack.

The stack grows automatically as more space is needed.

Obtaining Process Information

The `PIOCPSINFO` code returns miscellaneous information about a process and stores it in a structure of type `prpsinfo_t`, which looks like this in Solaris 2.*x* (it's slightly different in IRIX 5.*x*):

```
typedef struct prpsinfo {
    char        pr_state;       /* numeric process state (see pr_sname)    */
    char        pr_sname;       /* printable character representing pr_state */
    char        pr_zomb;        /* !=0: process terminated but not waited for */
    char        pr_nice;        /* nice for cpu usage                       */
    u_long      pr_flag;        /* process flags                           */
    uid_t       pr_uid;         /* real user id                            */
    gid_t       pr_gid;         /* real group id                           */
    pid_t       pr_pid;         /* unique process id                       */
    pid_t       pr_ppid;        /* process id of parent                    */
    pid_t       pr_pgrp;        /* pid of process group leader             */
    pid_t       pr_sid;         /* session id                              */
    caddr_t     pr_addr;        /* physical address of process             */
    long        pr_size;        /* size of process image in pages          */
    long        pr_rssize;      /* resident set size in pages              */
    caddr_t     pr_wchan;       /* wait addr for sleeping process          */
    timestruc_t pr_start;       /* process start time, sec+nsec since epoch */
    timestruc_t pr_time;        /* usr+sys cpu time for this process       */
    long        pr_pri;         /* priority, high value is high priority   */
    char        pr_oldpri;      /* pre-SVR4, low value is high priority    */
    char        pr_cpu;         /* pre-SVR4, cpu usage for scheduling      */
    o_dev_t     pr_ottydev;     /* short tty device number                 */
    dev_t       pr_lttydev;     /* controlling tty device (PRNODEV if none) */
    char        pr_clname[PRCLSZ];    /* scheduling class name             */
    char        pr_fname[PRFNSZ];     /* last component of execed pathname  */
    char        pr_psargs[PRARGSZ];   /* initial characters of arg list    */
    short       pr_syscall;     /* system call number (if in syscall)      */
    short       pr_fill;
    timestruc_t pr_ctime;       /* usr+sys cpu time for reaped children    */
    u_long      pr_bysize;      /* size of process image in bytes          */
    u_long      pr_byrssize;    /* resident set size in bytes              */
    int         pr_argc;        /* initial argument count                  */
    char        **pr_argv;      /* initial argument vector                 */
    char        **pr_envp;      /* initial environment vector              */
```

```
    int       pr_wstat;     /* if zombie, the wait() status     */
    long      pr_filler[11]; /* for future expansion            */
} prpsinfo_t;
```

Some of the more interesting fields of this structure are:

pr_sname

A character representation of the process' current state.

The possible values are:

I   Idle; the process is being created.

O   The process is currently running on a processor.

R   Runnable; the process is on the run queue.

S   Sleeping; the process is waiting for an event to complete (such as device input/output).

T   Stopped (traced); the process has been stopped by a signal or because another process is tracing it.

X   SXBRK status; the process is waiting for more primary memory.

Z   Zombie; the process has exited, but its parent has not waited for it yet.

pr_nice

The process' *nice* value (see Chapter 11, *Processes*).

pr_uid

The process' user ID.

pr_gid

The process' group ID.

pr_pid

The process' process ID.

pr_ppid

The process' parent process ID.

pr_pgrp

The process' process-group ID.

pr_sid

The process' session ID.

`pr_start`

> The time the process started; this can be printed with the `ctime` function, among others.

`pr_time`

> The sum of the process' user and system times.

`pr_ctime`

> The sum of the process' child process' user and system times.
>
> This value only includes processes that have exited and been waited on.

`pr_pri`

> The process' scheduling priority; higher values are better than lower ones.

`pr_lttydev`

> The major/minor device numbers of the controlling terminal, or `PRNODEV` if there isn't one.

`pr_fname`

> The last component of the `exec`'d path name (i.e., the name of the command).

`pr_psargs`

> The first several bytes of the command and its argument list.

`pr_bysize`

> The size of the process (text segment, data segment, and stack) in bytes.

`pr_byrssize`

> The size of the process' *resident set size*, the amount of memory the process is actually taking up (which, because of demand paging, is usually much smaller than its total size).

Obtaining Process Resource Usage

The `PIOCUSAGE` code obtains the process' resource usage information and stores it in a structure of type `prusage_t`:

```
typedef struct prusage {
    id_t            pr_lwpid;      /* lwp id.  0: process or defunct   */
    u_long          pr_count;      /* number of contributing lwps      */
    timestruc_t     pr_tstamp;     /* current time stamp               */
    timestruc_t     pr_create;     /* process/lwp creation time stamp  */
    timestruc_t     pr_term;       /* process/lwp termination time stamp */
    timestruc_t     pr_rtime;      /* total lwp real (elapsed) time    */
    timestruc_t     pr_utime;      /* user level CPU time              */
    timestruc_t     pr_stime;      /* system call CPU time             */
    timestruc_t     pr_ttime;      /* other system trap CPU time       */
    timestruc_t     pr_tftime;     /* text page fault sleep time       */
    timestruc_t     pr_dftime;     /* data page fault sleep time       */
```

```
    timestruc_t        pr_kftime;     /* kernel page fault sleep time  */
    timestruc_t        pr_ltime;      /* user lock wait sleep time     */
    timestruc_t        pr_slptime;    /* all other sleep time          */
    timestruc_t        pr_wtime;      /* wait-cpu (latency) time       */
    timestruc_t        pr_stoptime;   /* stopped time                  */
    timestruc_t        filltime[6];   /* filler for future expansion   */
    u_long          pr_minf;          /* minor page faults             */
    u_long          pr_majf;          /* major page faults             */
    u_long          pr_nswap;         /* swaps                         */
    u_long          pr_inblk;         /* input blocks                  */
    u_long          pr_oublk;         /* output blocks                 */
    u_long          pr_msnd;          /* messages sent                 */
    u_long          pr_mrcv;          /* messages received             */
    u_long          pr_sigs;          /* signals received              */
    u_long          pr_vctx;          /* voluntary context switches    */
    u_long          pr_ictx;          /* involuntary context switches  */
    u_long          pr_sysc;          /* system calls                  */
    u_long          pr_ioch;          /* chars read and written        */
    u_long          filler[10];       /* filler for future expansion   */
} prusage_t;
```

Some of the more interesting fields of this structure are:

pr_rtime
: The elapsed time since the process was created.

pr_utime
: The amount of user time used by the process.

pr_stime
: The amount of time spent by the process in system calls.

pr_slptime
: The amount of time the process has spent sleeping.

pr_stoptime
: The amount of time the process has spent in the stopped state.

pr_minf
: The number of *minor page faults* incurred by the process.

   A minor page fault is one that can be serviced without any I/O activity by reclaiming the page from the list of pages awaiting reallocation.

pr_majf
: The number of *major page faults* incurred by the process.

   A major page fault is one that requires I/O activity to service.

`pr_nswap`

The number of times the process has been swapped out of main memory.

`pr_inblk`

The number of blocks input for the process by the filesystem.

`pr_oublk`

The number of blocks output for the process by the filesystem.

`pr_sigs`

The number of signals received by the process.

`pr_sysc`

The number of system calls made by the process.

`pr_ioch`

The number of characters input and output by the process to terminal-like devices.

An Example

Example C-1 shows a program that uses the `PIOCPSINFO` and `PIOCUSAGE` codes to obtain information about the processes named on the command line. For each process, it prints out several of the fields in these structures.

Example C-1: procinfo

```c
#include <sys/param.h>
#include <sys/signal.h>
#include <sys/fault.h>
#include <sys/syscall.h>
#include <sys/procfs.h>
#include <sys/stat.h>
#include <dirent.h>
#include <fcntl.h>
#include <stdio.h>

char    *procFileSystem = "/proc";

void    printTime(char *, time_t);
void    printProcInfo(prpsinfo_t *, prusage_t *);

int
main(int argc, char **argv)
{
    int fd;
    prusage_t prusage;
    prpsinfo_t prpsinfo;
    char procname[BUFSIZ], tmp[BUFSIZ];

    /*
     * For each argument...
```

Example C-1: procinfo (continued)

```
     */
    while (--argc) {
        /*
         * Create the file name in the proc file system.
         */
        sprintf(procname, "%s/%s", procFileSystem, *++argv);

        /*
         * Open the file.
         */
        if ((fd = open(procname, O_RDONLY)) < 0) {
            perror(procname);
            continue;
        }

        /*
         * Get the "ps" information.
         */
        if (ioctl(fd, PIOCPSINFO, &prpsinfo) < 0) {
            sprintf(tmp, "%s: PIOCPSINFO", procname);
            perror(tmp);
            close(fd);
            continue;
        }

        /*
         * Get the resource usage information.
         */
        if (ioctl(fd, PIOCUSAGE, &prusage) < 0) {
            sprintf(tmp, "%s: PIOCPRUSAGE", procname);
            perror(tmp);
            close(fd);
            continue;
        }

        /*
         * Print the information.
         */
        printProcInfo(&prpsinfo, &prusage);
        close(fd);
    }

    exit(0);
}

/*
 * printProcInfo - print "interesting" fields of the prpsinfo and prusage
 *           structures.
 */
void
printProcInfo(prpsinfo_t *prpsinfo, prusage_t *prusage)
{
```

Example C-1: procinfo (continued)

```
        printf("Command: %s\n", prpsinfo->pr_psargs);
        printf("Started at: %s", ctime(&prpsinfo->pr_start.tv_sec));
        printf("Process-ID: %d  Parent Process-ID: %d\n", prpsinfo->pr_pid,
               prpsinfo->pr_ppid);
        printf("Process Group Leader: %d   Session-ID: %d\n", prpsinfo->pr_pgrp,
               prpsinfo->pr_sid);
        printf("User-ID: %d  Group-ID: %d  ", prpsinfo->pr_uid,
               prpsinfo->pr_gid);
        printf("Priority: %d Nice: %d\n", prpsinfo->pr_pri, prpsinfo->pr_nice);
        printf("Process Size: %d KB  Resident Set Size: %d KB\n",
               prpsinfo->pr_bysize / 1024, prpsinfo->pr_byrssize / 1024);
        printTime("Process Elapsed Time", prusage->pr_rtime.tv_sec);
        printTime(" Process User CPU Time", prusage->pr_utime.tv_sec);
        putchar('\n');
        printTime("Process System Call Time", prusage->pr_stime.tv_sec);
        printTime(" Process System Trap Time", prusage->pr_ttime.tv_sec);
        putchar('\n');
        printTime("Process Page Fault Time", prusage->pr_tftime.tv_sec +
               prusage->pr_dftime.tv_sec + prusage->pr_kftime.tv_sec);
        printTime(" Process Sleep Time", prusage->pr_ltime.tv_sec +
               prusage->pr_slptime.tv_sec + prusage->pr_wtime.tv_sec);
        putchar('\n');
        printTime("Process Stopped Time", prusage->pr_stoptime.tv_sec);
        putchar('\n');
        printf("Major Page Faults: %d  Minor Page Faults: %d  Swaps: %d\n",
               prusage->pr_majf, prusage->pr_minf, prusage->pr_nswap);
        printf("Input Blocks: %d  Output Blocks: %d  Character I/O: %d\n",
               prusage->pr_inblk, prusage->pr_oublk, prusage->pr_ioch);
        printf("System Calls: %d  Signals Received: %d\n", prusage->pr_sysc,
               prusage->pr_sigs);
        putchar('\n');
}


/*
 * printTime - convert a number of seconds to days, hours, minutes, and
 *            seconds, and print it out.
 */
void
printTime(char *str, time_t secs)
{
        int d, h, m, s;

        s = secs;

        /*
         * Simple conversion to days, hours, minutes, seconds.
         */
        d = s / 86400;
        s = s % 86400;
        h = s / 3600;
        s = s % 3600;
        m = s / 60;
```

Example C-1: procinfo (continued)

```
    s = s % 60;

    /*
     * Print the label.
     */
    printf("%s: ", str);

    /*
     * Print the days.
     */
    if (d)
        printf("%dd", d);

    /*
     * Print the hours, minutes, and seconds.
     */
    printf("%02d:%02d:%02d", h, m, s);
}
```

```
% procinfo 12567
Command: /usr/local/bin/emacs appC.sgml
Started at: Wed Mar 29 14:13:34 1995
Process-ID: 12567  Parent Process-ID: 262
Process Group Leader: 12567  Session-ID: 262
User-ID: 40  Group-ID: 1  Priority: 59  Nice: 20
Process Size: 4028 KB  Resident Set Size: 700 KB
Process Elapsed Time: 01:17:16  Process User CPU Time: 00:01:35
Process System Call Time: 00:00:25  Process System Trap Time: 00:00:00
Process Page Fault Time: 00:00:02  Process Sleep Time: 01:15:11
Process Stopped Time: 00:00:00
Major Page Faults: 154  Minor Page Faults: 0  Swaps: 0
Input Blocks: 17  Output Blocks: 107  Character I/O: 2004141
System Calls: 150222  Signals Received: 4
```

Without superuser privileges, this program can obtain information about any process owned by its caller that is not running with set-user-id or set-group-id permissions.

Summary

This appendix has only touched on the capabilities available with the */proc* filesystem. Debuggers and similar programs can use a number of other features to control the execution of a process, examine its memory, and even change its memory. For a complete set of available commands, see the *proc*(4) manual page.

The */proc* filesystem is a substantial improvement over the old method of obtaining process information, reading kernel memory and the swap area. Not only is it simpler for the programmer to implement, it is also portable between different versions of the operating system that support */proc*.

In this appendix:
- BSD Pseudo-Terminals
- SVR4 Pseudo-Terminals

Pseudo-Terminals

There are times when it's useful to be able to execute a program on a terminal, but to have the input and output of the program connected to a program, rather than to the keyboard and screen. For example, some programs, such as *passwd*, insist on reading from the terminal—it is impossible to talk to programs like this via a pipe. Programs like *rlogin* and *telnet* need to set up a "terminal" on the remote host so that things like text editors will work, but their input and output must be connected, via the network, to the user's keyboard and screen. There are also times when it is convenient to be able to record all the input and output of a session; this is what the *script* utility does.

Most modern versions of UNIX provide a facility called *pseudo-terminals* that can be used for just these purposes. A pseudo-terminal is a software construct that acts like a terminal. A program running on a pseudo-terminal has no way of knowing whether it is attached to a real terminal or a pseudo-terminal (other than looking at the name of the device).

A pseudo-terminal is implemented as two devices, called the *master* and the *slave*. The master is opened by the controlling process (the one that wants to be the "keyboard" and "screen"). The slave is opened by some process as its standard input and output; the process will see the slave as a terminal device. When the controlling process writes to the master device, the data will appear as input on the slave device, where the process there will see it as if it were typed on the keyboard. When the process running on the slave device writes to the "screen," it will appear as input that the controlling process may read from the master device.

BSD Pseudo-Terminals

On BSD systems, where pseudo-terminals were first implemented, master pseudo-terminals have device names like */dev/ptyXX*, and slave pseudo-terminals have names like */dev/ttyXX*. The procedure for opening a pseudo-terminal is to cycle through all the possible masters, trying to open one. If the open fails, the device is already in use. Once the master side is open, the slave side can also be opened. The code looks something like this:

```
char *s, *t;
int master, slave;
char mastername[32], slavename[32];
    :
for (s = "pqrs"; *s != '\0'; s++) {
    for (t = "0123456789abcdef"; *t != '\0'; t++) {
        sprintf(mastername, "/dev/pty%c%c", *s, *t);
        if ((master = open(mastername, O_RDWR)) >= 0)
            goto out;
    }
}

if (*s == '\0' && *t == '\0')
    /* all pseudo-terminals in use */

sprintf(slavename, "/dev/tty%c%c", *s, *t);

slave = open(slavename, O_RDWR);
    :
```

There are problems with this approach. If the number of pseudo-terminals is ever increased, the program will have to be modified to know about the new device names. Further, there is a race condition between opening the master and opening the slave. This race condition presents certain security problems.

SVR4 Pseudo-Terminals

In SVR4, the race condition has been solved by creating a special "clone device" to use when allocating a master pseudo-terminal. The clone device, when opened, returns a file descriptor referring to an unused pseudo-terminal, and locks out the corresponding slave device so that it cannot be opened by another process. The process that has the master side open can then unlock the slave and open it itself.

Example D-1 shows an implementation of the *script* command. This program executes a copy of the user's shell on a pseudo-terminal, and copies all the user's input and output to a file, creating a record of the entire session.

Example D-1: script

```
#include <sys/types.h>
#include <sys/ioctl.h>
#include <sys/time.h>
#include <stropts.h>
#include <termios.h>
#include <stdlib.h>
#include <signal.h>
#include <unistd.h>
#include <string.h>
#include <fcntl.h>
#include <stdio.h>

#define MAXARGS 32                          /* max. cmd. args    */

char        *shell = "/bin/sh";             /* default shell     */
char        *filename = "scriptfile";       /* default file      */
char        *mastername = "/dev/ptmx";      /* pty clone device  */

int     master;                             /* master side of pty */
FILE        *script;                        /* script file       */
struct termios  newtty, origtty;            /* tty modes         */

void    finish(int);
int ptyopen(char *, struct termios *);

int
main(int argc, char **argv)
{
    char *p;
    int n, nfd;
    time_t clock;
    fd_set readmask;
    char buf[BUFSIZ];

    /*
     * If an argument is given, it's a new script file.
     */
    if (argc > 1)
        filename = *++argv;

    /*
     * 1. Use the user's shell, if known.
     */
    if ((p = getenv("SHELL")) != NULL)
        shell = p;

    /*
     * 2. Open the script file.
     */
    if ((script = fopen(filename, "w")) == NULL) {
        perror(filename);
        exit(1);
```

Example D-1: script (continued)

```c
    }

    /*
     * 3. Get the tty modes.  We'll use these both to
     *    set modes on the pseudo-tty, and to restore
     *    modes on the user's tty.
     */
    if (tcgetattr(0, &origtty) < 0) {
        perror("tcgetattr: stdin");
        exit(1);
    }

    /*
     * 4. Grab a pseudo-tty and start a shell on it.
     */
    if ((master = ptyopen(shell, &origtty)) < 0)
        exit(1);

    /*
     * Print a little start message.
     */
    time(&clock);
    fprintf(script, "Script started on %s", ctime(&clock));
    printf("Script started, file is %s\n", filename);

    /*
     * 5. We need to catch signals, now that we're going
     *    to change tty modes.
     */
    sigset(SIGINT, finish);
    sigset(SIGQUIT, finish);

    /*
     * 6. Change the user's tty modes such that pretty
     *    much everything gets passed through to the
     *    pseudo-tty.  Set "raw" mode so that we can pass
     *    characters as they're typed, etc.
     */
    newtty = origtty;
    newtty.c_cc[VMIN] = 1;
    newtty.c_cc[VTIME] = 0;
    newtty.c_oflag &= ~OPOST;
    newtty.c_lflag &= ~(ICANON|ISIG|ECHO);
    newtty.c_iflag &= ~(INLCR|IGNCR|ICRNL|IUCLC|IXON);

    /*
     * 7. Set the new tty modes.
     */
    if (tcsetattr(0, TCSANOW, &newtty) < 0) {
        perror("tcsetattr: stdin");
        exit(1);
    }
```

Example D–1: script (continued)

```
/*
 * 8. Now just sit in a loop reading from the keyboard and
 *    writing to the pseudo-tty, and reading from the
 *    pseudo-tty and writing to the screen and the script file.
 */
for (;;) {
    FD_ZERO(&readmask);
    FD_SET(master, &readmask);
    FD_SET(0, &readmask);
    nfd = master + 1;

    /*
     * 8a. Wait for something to read.
     */
    n = select(nfd, &readmask, (fd_set *) 0, (fd_set *) 0,
               (struct timeval *) 0);

    if (n < 0) {
        perror("select");
        exit(1);
    }

    /*
     * 8b. The user typed something... read it and pass
     *     it on to the pseudo-tty.
     */
    if (FD_ISSET(0, &readmask)) {
        if ((n = read(0, buf, sizeof(buf))) < 0) {
            perror("read: stdin");
            exit(1);
        }

        /*
         * The user typed end-of-file; we're
         * done.
         */
        if (n == 0)
            finish(0);

        if (write(master, buf, n) != n) {
            perror("write: pty");
            exit(1);
        }
    }

    /*
     * 8c. There's output on the pseudo-tty... read it and
     *     pass it on to the screen and the script file.
     */
    if (FD_ISSET(master, &readmask)) {
        /*
         * The process died.
```

Example D-1: script (continued)

```
                    */
                if ((n = read(master, buf, sizeof(buf))) <= 0)
                    finish(0);

                fwrite(buf, sizeof(char), n, script);
                write(1, buf, n);
        }
    }
}

/*
 * ptyopen - start command on a pseudo-tty and return a file descriptor
 *      with which to speak to it.
 */
int
ptyopen(char *command, struct termios *ttymodes)
{
    char *p;
    pid_t pid;
    char *slavename;
    char *args[MAXARGS];
    int nargs, master, slave;

    /*
     * 9. Break the command into arguments.
     */
    nargs = 0;
    p = strtok(command, " \t\n");

    do {
        if (nargs == MAXARGS) {
            fprintf(stderr, "too many arguments.\n");
            return(-1);
        }

        args[nargs++] = p;
        p = strtok(NULL, " \t\n");
    } while (p != NULL);

    args[nargs] = NULL;

    /*
     * 10. Get a master pseudo-tty.
     */
    if ((master = open(mastername, O_RDWR)) < 0) {
        perror(mastername);
        return(-1);
    }

    /*
     * 11. Set the permissions on the slave.
     */
```

Example D-1: script (continued)

```
if (grantpt(master) < 0) {
    perror("granpt");
    close(master);
    return(-1);
}

/*
 * 12. Unlock the slave.
 */
if (unlockpt(master) < 0) {
    perror("unlockpt");
    close(master);
    return(-1);
}

/*
 * 13. Start a child process.
 */
if ((pid = fork()) < 0) {
    perror("fork");
    close(master);
    return(-1);
}

/*
 * 14. The child process will open the slave, which will become
 *     its controlling terminal.
 */
if (pid == 0) {
    /*
     * 14a. Get rid of our current controlling terminal.
     */
    setsid();

    /*
     * 14b. Get the name of the slave pseudo-tty.
     */
    if ((slavename = ptsname(master)) == NULL) {
        perror("ptsname");
        close(master);
        exit(1);
    }

    /*
     * 14c. Open the slave pseudo-tty.
     */
    if ((slave = open(slavename, O_RDWR)) < 0) {
        perror(slavename);
        close(master);
        exit(1);
    }
```

Example D–1: script (continued)

```
/*
 * 14d. Push the hardware emulation module.
 */
if (ioctl(slave, I_PUSH, "ptem") < 0) {
    perror("ioctl: ptem");
    close(master);
    close(slave);
    exit(1);
}


/*
 * 14e. Push the line discipline module.
 */
if (ioctl(slave, I_PUSH, "ldterm") < 0) {
    perror("ioctl: ldterm");
    close(master);
    close(slave);
    exit(1);
}


/*
 * 14f. Copy the user's terminal modes to the slave
 *      pseudo-tty.
 */
if (tcsetattr(slave, TCSANOW, ttymodes) < 0) {
    perror("tcsetattr: pty");
    close(master);
    close(slave);
    exit(1);
}


/*
 * 14g. Close the script file and the master; these
 *      are not needed in the slave.
 */
fclose(script);
close(master);


/*
 * 14h. Set the slave to be our standard input, output,
 *      and error output.  Then get rid of the original
 *      file descriptor.
 */
dup2(slave, 0);
dup2(slave, 1);
dup2(slave, 2);
close(slave);

/*
 * 14i. Execute the command.
 */
execv(args[0], args);
```

Example D-1: script (continued)

```
            perror(args[0]);
            exit(1);
    }

    /*
     * 15. Return the file descriptor for communicating with
     *        the process to our caller.
     */
    return(master);
}

/*
 * finish - called when we're done.
 */
void
finish(int sig)
{
    time_t clock;

    /*
     * 16. Restore our original tty modes.
     */
    if (tcsetattr(0, TCSANOW, &origtty) < 0)
        perror("tcsetattr: stdin");

    /*
     * Print a finishing message.
     */
    time(&clock);
    fprintf(script, "\nScript finished at %s", ctime(&clock));
    printf("\nScript done, file is %s\n", filename);

    /*
     * 17. All done.
     */
    fclose(script);
    close(master);
    exit(0);
}
```

The steps executed in this program are as follows.

1. Use the `getenv` function (Chapter 16, *Miscellaneous Routines*) to obtain the name of the user's shell. If this cannot be determined, use */bin/sh* as the default.

2.   Create the script file, where all input and output will be recorded.

3.   Get the modes of the user's terminal (Chapter 12, *Terminals*). These are needed both to copy them to the pseudo-terminal, and to change them on the user's terminal.

4.   Call the `ptyopen` function to allocate a pseudo-terminal and start the shell on it. This function is described beginning with Step 9, below.

5.   Catch the interrupt and quit signals (the ones that can be generated from the keyboard). We need to do this before we change the user's terminal modes; once they are changed, catching these signals will allow us to restore them if an interrupt is received.

6.   Change the user's terminal modes (Chapter 12). Because the keyboard and screen will now be tied to the pseudo-terminal through our program, most of the terminal input/output processing on the user's real terminal needs to be disabled. In particular, ECHO needs to be turned off (since the operating system will echo all characters "typed" on the pseudo-terminal, the controlling process will see them as "output" on the pseudo-terminal). The terminal is also placed in "raw" mode so that as each character is typed it will be read and delivered to the pseudo-terminal.

7.   Actually change the user's terminal modes.

8.   The controlling program now enters the following loop:

     a.   The `select` function (Chapter 6, *Special-Purpose File Operations*) is used to monitor both the standard input (the keyboard) and the "screen" of the pseudo-terminal. The function will block until something is available to be read.

     b.   If the standard input (file descriptor 0) appears in the bitmask returned by `select`, this means the user has typed something on the keyboard. The program must read this, and then write it to the pseudo-terminal. The process attached to the pseudo-terminal will see this as "keyboard" input. Note that the user's input is *not* written to the script file here; if the pseudo-terminal has ECHO turned on, the operating system will echo the characters and they will be seen as output.

     c.   If the pseudo-terminal file descriptor appears in the bitmask returned by `select`, this means the program attached to the pseudo-terminal has written some output to its "screen." The controlling program must read this data and print it to the user's screen, and also copy it to the script file.

The program continues in this loop until a read from either the user's terminal or the pseudo-terminal returns 0, indicating either that the user has typed an end-of-file character, or the program on the pseudo-terminal has exited.

9. Call the `ptyopen` function to execute the pseudo-terminal allocation code. The function begins by breaking the command it is to execute into individual arguments.

10. Open the clone device, */dev/ptmx*, to begin pseudo-terminal allocation. If the open succeeds, it will return a file descriptor that may be used to read and write to the master side of an unused pseudo-terminal.

11. Call the `grantpt` function to change the modes and ownership of the slave pseudo-terminal device to those of the user calling the functon:

    ```
    #include <stdlib.h>

    int grantpt(int fd);
    ```

    The argument should be the file descriptor attached to the master pseudo-terminal. The `granpt` function works by executing a small set-user-id "root" program to do its work.

12. Use the `unlockpt` function to clear the lock on the slave pseudo-terminal device, so that it can be opened:

    ```
    #include <stdlib.h>

    int unlockpt(int fd);
    ```

    Again, the argument should be the file descriptor attached to the master pseudo-terminal.

13. Now a child process is started, to execute the command given as an argument to `ptyopen` (Chapter 11, *Processes*).

    The child process is responsible for opening the slave side of the pseudo-terminal and executing the command:

    a. The `setsid` function (Chapter 11) is called to begin a new session. This has the side effect of clearing the process' controlling terminal.

    b. The `ptsname` function returns the device name of the slave side of the pseudo-terminal:

    ```
    #include <stdlib.h>

    char *ptsname(int fd);
    ```

    The `fd` parameter should be the file descriptor attached to the master side of the pseudo-terminal.

c. The slave side of the pseudo-terminal is opened. As a side effect of this, because the process has no controlling terminal (it was cleared by `set-sid`), the slave device will become the process' controlling terminal. This means that any signals generated from the slave side's "keyboard" will be sent to the slave process, since it is the session leader.

d. The "`ptem`" module is pushed onto the stream from the pseudo-terminal. This is a module built into the kernel that allows the pseudo-terminal to emulate a real terminal. It intercepts all the terminal mode change requests and adjusts the pseudo-terminal driver to behave accordingly.

e. The "`ldterm`" module is pushed onto the stream from the pseudo-terminal. This is a module built into the kernel that allows the pseudo-terminal to emulate the line discipline functions (Chapter 12) associated with real terminal devices.

f. The user's terminal modes are copied to the pseudo-terminal.

g. The script file and master pseudo-terminal file descriptors, opened in the parent process, are closed. The child process has no use for these.

h. The `dup2` function (Chapter 3, *Low-Level I/O Routines*) is used to attach the child process' standard input, output, and error output to the slave pseudo-terminal. The original file descriptor is then closed, as it is no longer needed.

i. The command is executed. When this succeeds, the command will be running on the slave pseudo-terminal (which it will see as a real terminal), and the command's input and output will be attached to the controlling process through the master side of the pseudo-terminal.

14. The file descriptor attached to the master side of the pseudo-terminal is returned to the controlling process, which can now use it to communicate with the command.

    Once the command on the pseudo-terminal has exited or the user has typed end-of-file, the program restores the user's original terminal modes.

    It then closes the script file, and closes the master pseudo-terminal. If the process on the pseudo-terminal has not yet exited, this close will generate an end-of-file on its input, causing it to exit now.

The clone-device method of allocating pseudo-terminals is generally easier to use than the old Berkeley method. It is not the only solution though; other vendors have developed other methods for opening pseudo-terminals. However, most of them are similar to one of the two methods described here, and differ only in some minor details.

Accessing the Network at the Link Level

In Chapter 14, *Networking with Sockets*, and Chapter 15, *Networking with TLI*, we described the operating system interfaces provided to allow programs to communicate via a network. This appendix describes those tasks that cannot be accomplished via these interfaces.

Low-Level Protocol Interfaces

The socket and TLI functions provide the programmer with an interface to protocols designed for end-to-end communication. The underlying network, however, is hidden from the programmer by these interfaces. There is no way for the programmer to tell (and no need for her to know) whether the underlying network hardware is Ethernet, Fiber Distributed Data Interface (FDDI), Asynchronous Transfer Mode (ATM), or something else altogether.

This has advantages, in that the programmer need not worry about esoterica such as packet formats and other details that really have nothing to do with the task at hand—getting data from here to there. However, there are disadvantages too. Because the interfaces hide the underlying network from the programmer, there is no way to use those interfaces to send or receive data at the underlying network level.

There are valid reasons for doing this, however. One of them is shown in the *in.rarpd* command. When a diskless workstation is first turned on, it has no notion of what its network address is. Because it has an Ethernet chip, it has an Ethernet address, but this is not the same as an Internet Protocol address. And it needs to know its Internet Protocol address to talk to its server and begin the boot process.

So, it sends out a special Ethernet broadcast packet using the Reverse Address Resolution Protocol (RARP), asking "Hey, does anybody know what my Internet Protocol address is?" The *in.rarpd* program, running on a server, receives this packet, looks up the workstation's address in a database (usually the */etc/ethers* file), and sends a RARP reply packet back to the workstation saying, "Yes, your address is AAA.BBB.CCC.DDD."

The RARP protocol is *not* an Internet protocol like TCP and UDP are. The RARP protocol has its very own packet format that is defined differently for each network medium on which it is used. Thus, *in.rarpd* cannot use the socket or TLI interfaces to send or receive RARP packets. Instead, it must monitor the Ethernet directly waiting for these packets to arrive, and it must then format its own Ethernet packets in which to send its responses.

Network Monitoring

The other task that cannot be performed through the socket and TLI interfaces is network monitoring. A network monitoring program, such as the *snoop* program included with SVR4, must be able to receive all packets on a network, regardless of who they are addressed to. But the socket and TLI interfaces require a program to specify an address at which it wishes to receive data. There is no way to specify "give me everything on the network, including all the stuff addressed to other machines."

In order to monitor the network, a network monitoring program has to be able to place the system's network interface(s) into *promiscuous mode*. In this mode, the network interface copies all packets from the network rather than just those that are destined for the local host. The operating system must then arrange for the monitoring program to be given a copy of all of these packets. While it's doing that, though, it also has to continue processing all the packets addressed to it in the normal fashion, or else turning on a network monitor would turn off everything else.

The Data Link Provider Interface

SVR4 provides the *Data Link Provider Interface* (DLPI) as a solution to both of the problems described above. The DLPI is a STREAMS-based interface to the low-level network device drivers. It is similar in functionality to the Network Interface Tap (NIT) provided in SunOS 4.*x*, and the Berkeley Packet Filter (BPF) provided by recent versions of BSD UNIX. Most other vendors provide similar functionality.

NOTE

In order to preserve backward compatibility with earlier releases, Silicon Graphics does not supply the DLPI interface. Instead, they provide the *snoop* interface with IRIX 5.*x*.

A program accesses the DLPI through a file descriptor. When the program reads from the file descriptor, it receives raw network packets with all of their headers still attached. The program is responsible for extracting necessary information from these headers, stripping them off to get at the data, and so forth. Depending on the type of packet and what is to be learned from it, this can be a complex task. When the program writes to the file descriptor, the data is transmitted on the network. The program is responsible for formatting its data into a legal packet format including headers, checksums, and so forth. If anything, this can be even more complex than reading packets.

Sample Program

Because accessing the network at the link layer is so complex, we can't include an example in the text of this appendix. Aside from the code to set up the DLPI, which is straight-forward but non-trivial, it is necessary to show how to process the data once it is received, or how to format it in order to be sent. However, the topic is of sufficient interest to systems programmers that a sample program has been included in the electronic distribution of the example programs for this book. The preface to this book provides instructions on how to obtain this distribution.

The sample program is a complete packet monitoring tool. It monitors a network and captures all packets transmitting it. These packets are broken down into numerous classifications (local or foreign traffic, network protocol, application protocol, etc.) and recorded in a series of counters. The counters are saved periodically to a file, from which they can later be added together and printed out. The tool can thus be used to perform long-term traffic analysis of a network. The program is well-commented, and should be sufficient for understanding not only the DLPI, but also how to process the various packet formats transmitted on an Ethernet network.

NOTE

This sample program makes use of extensions to the DLPI interface that are available only in Solaris 2.*x*.

Additional Documentation

In addition to the example program, the electronic distribution includes a copy of a white paper written by Neal Nuckolls of Sun Microsystems' Internet Engineering group. This paper, which comes complete with a set of working example programs, describes each feature of the DLPI in detail, and shows how to use it both to receive packets as well as send them.

Index

About the Author

David A. Curry is employed as a Senior Internet Security Analyst for the IBM Internet Emergency Response Service (IBM-ERS), where he is a member of the IBM-ERS Level 3 technical team. IBM-ERS provides Internet security services, incident management and response functions, and firewall testing services to IBM-ERS customers. Dave is responsible for the IBM-ERS Security Vulnerability Alert function of the the service, and for developing the service's quality management program. He received a Bachelor of Science Degree in Computer Science from Purdue University in 1993.

Dave began his UNIX systems programming career at the Purdue University Engineering Computer Network in 1985, where he worked through 1988. He then moved to California where he worked as a Research Associate for the Research Institute for Advanced Computer Science at NASA Ames Research Center, and as a Senior Systems Programmer for the Information, Telecommunications, and Automation Division at SRI International in Menlo Park, CA. Following his marriage in 1991, Dave decided he really hated living in California, and returned to the Midwest and Purdue University, where he served as the Manager of the UNIX Systems Programming Group for the Purdue University Engineering Computer Network until December, 1995.

Dave is a member of the USENIX Association and the National Computer Security Association. He also serves as the IBM-ERS representative to the Forum of Incident Response and Security Teams (FIRST). Dave has written several popular programs distributed widely on the Internet, and authored the document "Improving the Security of Your UNIX System," distributed by SRI International in 1990. He is also the author of two other books: *Using C on the UNIX System*, published by O'Reilly & Associates, and *UNIX System Security: A Guide for Users and System Administrators*, published by Addison-Wesley.

Colophon

Our look is the result of reader comments, our own experimentation, and distribution channels. Distinctive covers complement our distinctive approach to technical topics, breathing personality and life into potentially dry subjects. UNIX and its attendant programs can be unruly beasts. Nutshell Handbooks help you tame them.

The animal featured on the cover of *UNIX Systems Programming for SVR4* is a lion, a large, carnivorous cat inhabiting western India and Africa south of the

Sahara. The most sociable of cats, lions live in prides consisting of one to four males and a collection of up to thirty females and cubs. However, the members of a pride are seldom all together at one time, instead moving about their territory as individuals or small groups. A pride's territory may be anywhere from 15 to 150 square miles, depending on the abundance of food, and is marked by scent and roaring.

Lions eat both fresh kill and carrion—dead animals or the kill of other animals. When they do kill, they show a preference for large prey such as zebra or wildebeest which will feed the entire pride. Females do the majority of the hunting, frequently working cooperatively to encircle or bring down large game. During the hunt, lions are careful to move under cover of darkness or foliage, but tend to disregard the wind direction and thus frequently give themselves away.

Edie Freedman designed this cover and the entire UNIX bestiary that appears on Nutshell Handbooks, using a 19th-century engraving from the Dover Pictorial Archive. The cover layout was produced with Quark XPress 3.3 using the ITC Garamond font.

The inside layout was designed by Jennifer Niederst and Nancy Priest. Text was prepared by Erik Ray in SGML DocBook 2.4 DTD. The print version of this book was created by translating the SGML source into a set of gtroff macros using a filter developed at ORA by Norman Walsh. Steve Talbott designed and wrote the underlying macro set on the basis of the GNU troff -gs macros; Lenny Muellner adapted them to SGML and implemented the book design. The GNU groff text formatter version 1.09 was used to generate PostScript output. The text and heading fonts are ITC Garamond Light and Garamond Book. The illustrations that appear in the book were created in Macromedia Freehand 5.0 by Chris Reilley.

UNIX Programming

Programming Python

By Mark Lutz
1st Edition October 1996
906 pages, ISBN 1-56592-197-6

This O'Reilly Nutshell Handbook describes how to use Python, an increasingly popular oject-oriented scripting language freely available over the Net. Python is an interpreted language, useful for quick prototyping and simple programs for which C++ is too complex and unwieldy. The Python interpreter is available on most popular UNIX platforms, including Linux, as well as Windows, NT, and the Mac.

Programming Python, the only source of user material available for this scripting language, complements online reference material provided with Python releases. It has been both reviewed and endorsed by Python creator Guido van Rossum, who also provides the foreward. You'll find many useful running examples, which become more complex as new topics are introduced. Examples that describe Graphical User Interface (GUI) use TK as well as Python. The appendix contains a short language tutorial. Includes a CD-ROM containing Python software for all major UNIX platforms, as well as Windows, NT, and the Mac.

Pthreads Programming

By Bradford Nichols, Dick Buttlar & Jacqueline Proulx Farrell
1st Edition September 1996
284 pages, ISBN 1-56592-115-1

The idea behind threads programming is to have multiple tasks running concurrently within the same program. They can share a single CPU as processes do, or take advantage of multiple CPUs when available. In either case, they provide a clean way to divide the tasks of a program while sharing data. The POSIX threads standard, which is the subject of this book, is supported by the Distributed Computer Environment (DCE), as well as Solaris, OSF/1, AIX, and several other UNIX-based operating systems.

In this book you will learn not only what the pthread calls are, but when it is a good idea to use threads and how to make them efficient (which is the whole reason for using threads in the first place). The author delves into performance issues, comparing threads to processes, contrasting kernel threads to user threads, and showing how to measure speed. He also describes in a simple, clear manner what all the advanced features are for, and how threads interact with the rest of the UNIX system.

UNIX Systems Programming for SVR4

By David A. Curry
1st Edition July 1996
620 pages, ISBN 1-56592-163-1

Any program worth its salt uses operating system services. Even a simple program, if practical, reads input and produces output. And, most applications have more complex needs. They need to find out the time, use the network, or start and communicate with other processes. Systems programming really means nothing more than writing software that uses these operating system services.

UNIX Systems Programming for SVR4 gives you the nitty gritty details on how UNIX interacts with applications. If you're writing an application from scratch, or if you're porting an application to any System V.4 platform, you need this book.

The first part of the book presents simple functions and concepts supported by numerous code fragment examples and short demonstration programs. These examples become building blocks for the application program examples that appear later in the book to illustrate more advanced, complex functions.

UNIX Systems Programming for SVR4 is thorough and complete and offers advice on:
*   Working with low-level I/O routines and the standard I/O library
*   Creating and deleting files and directories, changing file attributes, processing multiple input streams, file and record locking, and memory-mapped files
*   Reading, printing, and setting the system time and date
*   Determining who is logged in, times users log in and out, how to change a program's effective user ID or group ID, and writing set user ID programs
*   Changing system configuration parameters for resource limits
*   Creating processes, job control, and signal handling
*   Using pipes, FIFOs, UNIX-domain sockets, message queues, semaphores, and shared memory for interprocess communication
*   Reading and setting serial line characteristics including baud rate, echoing, and flow control
*   Network programming with Berkeley sockets, Transport Layer Interface (TLI), a less popular but more flexible interface to network programming, and the data link provider interface

UNIX Programming (continued)

Power Programming with RPC

By John Bloomer
1st Edition February 1992
522 pages, ISBN 0-937175-77-3

A distributed application is designed to access resources across a network. In a broad sense, these resources could be user input, a central database, configuration files, etc., that are distributed on various computers across the network, rather than found on a single computer. RPC, or remote procedure calling, is the ability to distribute the execution of functions on remote computers outside of the application's current address space. This allows you to break large or complex programming problems into routines that can be executed independently of one another to take advantage of multiple computers. Thus, RPC makes it possible to attack a problem using a form of parallel processing or multiprocessing.

Written from a programmer's perspective, this book shows what you can do with Sun RPC, the de facto standard on UNIX systems. It covers related programming topics for Sun and other UNIX systems and teaches through examples.

POSIX Programmer's Guide

By Donald Lewine
1st Edition April 1991
640 pages, ISBN 0-937175-73-0

Most UNIX systems today are POSIX compliant because the federal government requires it for its purchases. Even OSF and UI agree on support for POSIX. Given the manufacturer's documentation, however, it can be difficult to distinguish system-specific features from those features defined by POSIX.

The *POSIX Programmer's Guide*, intended as an explanation of the POSIX standard and as a reference for the POSIX.1 programming library, helps you write more portable programs. This guide is especially helpful if you are writing programs that must run on multiple UNIX platforms. This guide also helps you convert existing UNIX programs for POSIX compliance.

"*POSIX Programmer's Guide* belongs on the shelf of every Unix system programmer. Posix texts will be written, and Posix reference manuals will be produced, but it is rare to find such an interesting compromise between the two."
—Ed Gordon, BDataSystems, *IEEE Software Magazine*

POSIX.4

By Bill O. Gallmeister
1st Edition January 1995
568 pages, ISBN 1-56592-074-0

Real-world programming (typically called real-time programming) is programming that interacts in some way with the "real world" of daily life. Real-world programmers develop the unseen software that operates most of the world that surrounds you, software typically characterized by deadlines—and harsh penalties if the deadlines aren't met.

When you've just rear-ended another car, it's no consolation that a sudden flurry of input slowed down your brake processor, so it couldn't react quickly enough when you hit the pedal.

This book covers the POSIX.4 standard for portable real-time programming. The POSIX.4 standard itself is a massive document that defines system interfaces for asynchronous I/O, scheduling, communications, and other facilities. However, this book does more than explain the standard. It provides a general introduction to real-time programming and real-time issues: the problems software faces when it needs to interact with the real world and how to solve them. If you're at all interested in real-time applications—which include just about everything from telemetry to transaction processing—this book will be an essential reference.

POSIX.4 includes problem sets, answers, and reference manual pages for all functions and header files.

Programming with curses

By John Strang
1st Edition 1986
78 pages, ISBN 0-937175-02-1

Curses is a UNIX library of functions for controlling a terminal's display screen from a C program. It can be used to provide a screen driver for a program (such as a visual editor) or to improve a program's user interface.

This handbook will help you make use of the curses library in your C programs. We have presented ample material on curses and its implementation in UNIX so that you understand the whole, as well as its parts.

Tools

Programming with GNU Software

By Mike Loukides & Andy Oram
1st Edition Fall 1996
264 pages (est.), ISBN 1-56592-112-7

This book and CD combination is a complete package for programmers who are new to UNIX or who would like to make better use of the system. The tools come from Cygnus Support, Inc., a well-known company that provides support for free software. Contents include GNU Emacs, *gcc*, C and C++ libraries, *gdb*, RCS, and *make*. The book provides an introduction to all these tools for a C programmer.

Applying RCS and SCCS

By Don Bolinger & Tan Bronson
1st Edition September 1995
528 pages, ISBN 1-56592-117-8

Applying RCS and SCCS is a thorough introduction to these two systems, viewed as tools for project management. This book takes the reader from basic source control of a single file, through working with multiple releases of a software project, to coordinating multiple developers. It also presents TCCS, a representative "front-end" that addresses problems RCS and SCCS can't handle alone, such as managing groups of files, developing for multiple platforms, and linking public and private development areas.

lex & yacc

By John Levine, Tony Mason & Doug Brown
2nd Edition October 1992
366 pages, ISBN 1-56592-000-7

This book shows programmers how to use two UNIX utilities, *lex* and *yacc*, in program development. The second edition contains completely revised tutorial sections for novice users and reference sections for advanced users. This edition is twice the size of the first, has an expanded index, and covers Bison and Flex.

Managing Projects with make

By Andrew Oram & Steve Talbott
2nd Edition October 1991
152 pages, ISBN 0-937175-90-0

make is one of UNIX's greatest contributions to software development, and this book offers the clearest description of *make* ever written. Even the smallest software project typically involves a number of files that depend upon each other in various ways. If you modify one or more source files, you must relink the program after recompiling some, but not necessarily all, of the sources. *make* greatly simplifies this process. By recording the relationships between sets of files, *make* can automatically perform all the necessary updating. This book describes all the basic features of *make* and provides guidelines on meeting the needs of large, modern projects.

Software Portability with imake, 2nd Edition

By Paul DuBois
2nd Edition September 1996
410 pages, ISBN 1-56592-226-3

imake is a utility that works with *make* to enable code to be compiled and installed on different UNIX machines. *imake* makes possible the wide portability of the X Window System code and is widely considered an X tool, but it's also useful for any software project that needs to be ported to many UNIX systems.

This Nutshell Handbook—the only book available on *imake*—is ideal for X and UNIX programmers who want their software to be portable. The book is divided into two sections. The first section is a general explanation of *imake*, X configuration files, and how to write and debug an *Imakefile*. The second section describes how to write configuration files and presents a configuration file architecture that allows development of coexisting sets of configuration files. Several sample sets of configuration files are described and are available free over the Net.

The second edition covers X Window System X11 R6.1. New material includes a discussion of using *imake* for Windows NT and covers some quirks that occur when imake is used under OpenWindows/Solaris.

Tools (continued)

Porting UNIX Software

By Greg Lehey
1st Edition November 1995
538 pages, ISBN 1-56592-126-7

If you work on a UNIX system, a good deal of your most useful software comes from other people—your vendor is not the source. This means, all too often, that the software you want was written for a slightly different system and that it has to be ported. Despite the best efforts of standards committees and the admirable people who write the software (often giving it away for free), something is likely to go wrong when you try to compile their source code.

This book deals with the whole life cycle of porting, from setting up a source tree on your system to correcting platform differences and even testing the executable after it's built. The book exhaustively discusses the differences between versions of UNIX and the areas where porters tend to have problems. The assumption made in this book is that you just want to get a package working on your system; you don't want to become an expert in the details of your hardware or operating system (much less an expert in the system used by the person who wrote the package!). Many problems can be solved without a knowledge of C or UNIX, while the ones that force you to deal directly with source code are explained as simply and concretely as possible.

Exploring Expect

By Don Libes
1st Edition December 1994
602 pages, ISBN 1-56592-090-2

Written by the author of Expect, this is the first book to explain how this new part of the UNIX toolbox can be used to automate Telnet, FTP, passwd, rlogin, and hundreds of other interactive applications. Based on Tcl (Tool Command Language), Expect lets you automate interactive applications that have previously been extremely difficult to handle with any scripting language.

The book briefly describes Tcl and how Expect relates to it. It then describes the Expect language, using a combination of reference material and specific, useful examples of its features. It shows how to use Expect in background, in multiple processes, and with standard languages and tools like C, C++, and Tk, the X-based extension to Tcl. The strength in the book is in its scripts, conveniently listed in a separate index.

X User Tools

By Linda Mui & Valerie Quercia
1st Edition November 1994
856 pages, Includes CD-ROM, ISBN 1-56592-019-8

X User Tools provides for X users what UNIX Power Tools provides for UNIX users: hundreds of tips, tricks, scripts, techniques, and programs—plus a CD-ROM—to make the X Window System more enjoyable, more powerful, and easier to use. This browser's book emphasizes useful programs culled from the network, offers tips for configuring individual and systemwide environments, and includes a CD-ROM of source files for all—and binary files for some—of the programs.

UNIX Power Tools

By Jerry Peek, Mike Loukides, Tim O'Reilly, et al.
1st Edition March 1993
1162 pages, Includes CD-ROM
Random House ISBN 0-679-79073-X

Ideal for UNIX users who hunger for technical—yet accessible—information, UNIX Power Tools consists of tips, tricks, concepts, and freeware (CD-ROM included). It also covers add-on utilities and how to take advantage of clever features in the most popular UNIX utilities.

This is a browser's book...like a magazine that you don't read from start to finish, but leaf through repeatedly until you realize that you've read it all. You'll find articles abstracted from O'Reilly Nutshell Handbooks®, new information that highlights program "tricks" and "gotchas,"tips posted to the Net over the years, and other accumulated wisdom.

The goal of UNIX Power Tools is to help you think creatively about UNIX and get you to the point where you can analyze your own problems. Your own solutions won't be far behind.

"Let me congratulate you all for writing the best and the most complete book written for UNIX. After glancing and skimming through the book, I found [it] to be a very powerful reference/learning tool. The best part...is the humor.... Thanks for providing a good/solid/funny UNIX book."
—Shawn Gargya, scgargya@vnet.ibm.com

Stay in touch with O'REILLY™

Visit Our Award-Winning World Wide Web Site

http://www.ora.com/

VOTED

"Top 100 Sites on the Web" —*PC Magazine*
"Top 5% Websites" —*Point Communications*
"3-Star site" —*The McKinley Group*

Our Web site contains a library of comprehensive product information (including book excerpts and tables of contents), downloadable software, background articles, interviews with technology leaders, links to relevant sites, book cover art, and more. File us in your Bookmarks or Hotlist!

Join Our Two Email Mailing Lists

LIST #1 **NEW PRODUCT RELEASES:** To receive automatic email with brief descriptions of all new O'Reilly products as they are released, send email to: listproc@online.ora.com and put the following information in the first line of your message (NOT in the Subject: field, which is ignored): **subscribe ora-news "Your Name" of "Your Organization"** (for example: **subscribe ora-news Kris Webber of Fine Enterprises)**

List #2 **O'REILLY EVENTS:** If you'd also like us to send information about trade show events, special promotions, and other O'Reilly events, send email to: **listproc@online.ora.com** and put the following information in the first line of your message (NOT in the Subject: field, which is ignored): **subscribe ora-events "Your Name" of "Your Organization"**

Visit Our Gopher Site

- Connect your Gopher to **gopher.ora.com**, or
- Point your Web browser to **gopher://gopher.ora.com/**, or
- telnet to **gopher.ora.com** (login: **gopher**)

Get Example Files from Our Books Via FTP

There are two ways to access an archive of example files from our books:

REGULAR FTP — ftp to: **ftp.ora.com** (login: **anonymous**—use your email address as the password) or point your Web browser to: **ftp://ftp.ora.com/**

FTPMAIL — Send an email message to: **ftpmail@online.ora.com** (write "help" in the message body)

Contact Us Via Email

order@ora.com — To place a book or software order online. Good for North American and international customers.

subscriptions@ora.com — To place an order for any of our newsletters or periodicals.

software@ora.com — For general questions and product information about our software.
  • Check out O'Reilly Software Online at **http://software.ora.com/** for software and technical support information.
  • Registered O'Reilly software users send your questions to **website-support@ora.com**

books@ora.com — General questions about any of our books.

cs@ora.com — For answers to problems regarding your order or our products.

booktech@ora.com — For book content technical questions or corrections.

proposals@ora.com — To submit new book or software proposals to our editors and product managers.

international@ora.com — For information about our international distributors or translation queries.
  • For a list of our distributors outside of North America check out:
  http://www.ora.com/www/order/country.html

O'REILLY™

101 Morris Street, Sebastopol, CA 95472 USA
TEL 707-829-0515 or 800-998-9938 (6 A.M. to 5 P.M. PST)
FAX 707-829-0104

Titles from O'REILLY™

INTERNET PROGRAMMING

CGI Programming on the
    World Wide Web
Designing for the Web
Exploring Java
HTML: The Definitive Guide
Web Client Programming with Perl
Learning Perl
Programming Perl, 2nd. Edition
    (Fall '96)
JavaScript: The Definitive Guide,
    Beta Edition
WebMaster in a Nutshell
The World Wide Web Journal

USING THE INTERNET

Smileys
The Whole Internet User's Guide
    and Catalog
The Whole Internet for Windows 95
What You Need to Know:
    Using Email Effectively
Marketing on the Internet (Fall '96)
What You Need to Know: Bandits on the
    Information Superhighway

JAVA SERIES

Exploring Java
Java in a Nutshell
Java Language Reference
    (Fall '96 est.)
Java Virtual Machine

WINDOWS

Inside the Windows 95 Registry

SOFTWARE

WebSite™ 1.1
WebSite Professional™
WebBoard™
PolyForm™
Statisphere™

SONGLINE GUIDES

NetLearning
NetSuccess for Realtors
NetActivism
Gif Animation (Fall '96)
Shockwave Studio (Winter '97 est.)

SYSTEM ADMINISTRATION

Building Internet Firewalls
Computer Crime:
    A Crimefighter's Handbook
Computer Security Basics
DNS and BIND
Essential System Administration,
    2nd Edition
Getting Connected:
    The Internet at 56K and Up
Linux Network Administrator's Guide
Managing Internet Information Services
Managing Usenet (Fall '96)
Managing NFS and NIS
Networking Personal Computers
    with TCP/IP
Practical UNIX & Internet Security
PGP: Pretty Good Privacy
sendmail
System Performance Tuning
TCP/IP Network Administration
termcap & terminfo
Using & Managing UUCP
Volume 8: X Window System
    Administrator's Guide

UNIX

Exploring Expect
Learning GNU Emacs, 2nd Edition
    (Fall '96)
Learning the bash Shell
Learning the Korn Shell
Learning the UNIX Operating System
Learning the vi Editor
Linux in a Nutshell (Fall '96 est.)
Making TeX Work
Linux Multimedia Guide (Fall '96)
Running Linux, 2nd Edition
Running Linux Companion
    CD-ROM, 2nd Edition
SCO UNIX in a Nutshell
sed & awk
UNIX in a Nutshell: System V Edition
UNIX Power Tools
UNIX Systems Programming
Using csh and tsch
What You Need to Know:
    When You Can't Find Your
    UNIX System Administrator

PROGRAMMING

Applying RCS and SCCS
C++: The Core Language
Checking C Programs with lint
DCE Security Programming
Distributing Applications Across
    DCE and Windows NT
Encyclopedia of Graphics File
    Formats, 2nd Edition
Guide to Writing DCE Applications
lex & yacc
Managing Projects with make
ORACLE Performance Tuning
ORACLE PL/SQL Programming
Porting UNIX Software
POSIX Programmer's Guide
POSIX.4: Programming for
    the Real World
Power Programming with RPC
Practical C Programming
Practical C++ Programming
Programming Python (Fall '96)
Programming with curses
Programming with GNU Software
    (Fall '96 est.)
Pthreads Programming
Software Portability with imake
Understanding DCE
Understanding Japanese Information
    Processing
UNIX Systems Programming for SVR4

BERKELEY 4.4 SOFTWARE DISTRIBUTION

4.4BSD System Manager's Manual
4.4BSD User's Reference Manual
4.4BSD User's Supplementary
    Documents
4.4BSD Programmer's Reference
    Manual
4.4BSD Programmer's Supplementary
    Documents

X PROGRAMMING
THE X WINDOW SYSTEM

Volume 0: X Protocol Reference Manual
Volume 1: Xlib Programming Manual
Volume 2: Xlib Reference Manual
Volume. 3M: X Window System
    User's Guide, Motif Edition
Volume. 4: X Toolkit Intrinsics
    Programming Manual
Volume 4M: X Toolkit Intrinsics
    Programming Manual,
    Motif Edition
Volume 5: X Toolkit Intrinsics
    Reference Manual
Volume 6A: Motif Programming
    Manual
Volume 6B: Motif Reference Manual
Volume 6C: Motif Tools
Volume 8 : X Window System
    Administrator's Guide
Programmer's Supplement for Release 6
X User Tools (with CD-ROM)
The X Window System in a Nutshell

HEALTH, CAREER, & BUSINESS

Building a Successful Software Business
The Computer User's Survival Guide
Dictionary of Computer Terms
The Future Does Not Compute
Love Your Job!
Publishing with CD-ROM

TRAVEL

Travelers' Tales: Brazil (Fall '96)
Travelers' Tales: Food (Fall '96)
Travelers' Tales: France
Travelers' Tales: Hong Kong
Travelers' Tales: India
Travelers' Tales: Mexico
Travelers' Tales: San Francisco
Travelers' Tales: Spain
Travelers' Tales: Thailand
Travelers' Tales: A Woman's World

TO ORDER: **800-889-8969** (CREDIT CARD ORDERS ONLY); **order@ora.com; http://www.ora.com/**
OUR PRODUCTS ARE AVAILABLE AT A BOOKSTORE OR SOFTWARE STORE NEAR YOU.

International Distributors

Customers outside North America can now order O'Reilly & Associates books through the following distributors. They offer our international customers faster order processing, more bookstores, increased representation at tradeshows worldwide, and the high-quality, responsive service our customers have come to expect.

EUROPE, MIDDLE EAST AND NORTHERN AFRICA (except Germany, Switzerland, and Austria)
INQUIRIES
International Thomson Publishing Europe
Berkshire House
168-173 High Holborn
London WC1V 7AA, United Kingdom
Telephone: 44-171-497-1422
Fax: 44-171-497-1426
Email: **itpint@itps.co.uk**

ORDERS
International Thomson Publishing Services, Ltd.
Cheriton House, North Way
Andover, Hampshire SP10 5BE,
United Kingdom
Telephone: 44-264-342-832 (UK orders)
Telephone: 44-264-342-806 (outside UK)
Fax: 44-264-364418 (UK orders)
Fax: 44-264-342761 (outside UK)
UK & Eire orders: **itpuk@itps.co.uk**
International orders: **itpint@itps.co.uk**

GERMANY, SWITZERLAND, AND AUSTRIA
International Thomson Publishing GmbH
O'Reilly International Thomson Verlag
Königswinterer Straße 418
53227 Bonn, Germany
Telephone: 49-228-97024 0
Fax: 49-228-441342
Email: **anfragen@oreilly.de**

AUSTRALIA
WoodsLane Pty. Ltd.
7/5 Vuko Place, Warriewood NSW 2102
P.O. Box 935, Mona Vale NSW 2103
Australia
Telephone: 61-2-9970-5111
Fax: 61-2-9970-5002
Email: **info@woodslane.com.au**

NEW ZEALAND
WoodsLane New Zealand Ltd.
21 Cooks Street (P.O. Box 575)
Wanganui, New Zealand
Telephone: 64-6-347-6543
Fax: 64-6-345-4840
Email: **info@woodslane.com.au**

ASIA (except Japan & India)
INQUIRIES
International Thomson Publishing Asia
60 Albert Street #15-01
Albert Complex
Singapore 189969
Telephone: 65-336-6411
Fax: 65-336-7411

ORDERS
Telephone: 65-336-6411
Fax: 65-334-1617

JAPAN
O'Reilly Japan, Inc.
Kiyoshige Building 2F
12-Banchi, Sanei-cho
Shinjuku-ku
Tokyo 160 Japan
Telephone: 81-3-3356-5227
Fax: 81-3-3356-5261
Email: **kenji@ora.com**

INDIA
Computer Bookshop (India) PVT. LTD.
190 Dr. D.N. Road, Fort
Bombay 400 001
India
Telephone: 91-22-207-0989
Fax: 91-22-262-3551
Email: **cbsbom@giasbm01.vsnl.net.in**

THE AMERICAS
O'Reilly & Associates, Inc.
101 Morris Street
Sebastopol, CA 95472 U.S.A.
Telephone: 707-829-0515
Telephone: 800-998-9938 (U.S. & Canada)
Fax: 707-829-0104
Email: **order@ora.com**

SOUTHERN AFRICA
International Thomson Publishing Southern Africa
Building 18, Constantia Park
240 Old Pretoria Road
P.O. Box 2459
Halfway House, 1685 South Africa
Telephone: 27-11-805-4819
Fax: 27-11-805-3648

O'REILLY™